GW00361044

A Crack

of the Whip

Antony Johnson

First published in Great Britain in 2019 by Killer Hill Press

Copyright © Antony Johnson

Edited, designed and produced by Tandem Publishing Limited http:// tandempublishing.yolasite.com/

ISBN: 978-1-5272-4568-6

10 9 8 7 6 5 4 3 2 1

A CIP catalogue record for this book is available from the British Library.

Printed and bound in Great Britain by CPI Group (UK) Ltd, Croydon CR0 4YY.

For Richard, Simon and Sam and in
loving memory of Jemima.

Contents

Foreword

Gaul, according to Caesar, 'was divided into three parts'. You could say the same of Antony Johnson's adventurous and convivial life. First there was his time as an accomplished amateur rider and then racehorse trainer. Then there came the Barbados years based in Maddox, the beautiful house he bought from Oliver Messel's family. Finally came a third-stage career as an enthusiastic world traveller escorting small select groups of fortunate friends to exotic destinations around the world from Ukraine to Botswana, from Cambodia to Guatemala.

Before those periods there had been too a financial apprenticeship with Lazards the bankers, two years of National Service (a fair portion of that spent *hors de combat* after breaking his leg while skiing for an Army team) and a spell working for the former family firm of wire manufacturers Richard Johnson & Nephew.

Although we have corresponded for some time I don't know Antony well but what is clear from this autobiography is that he is a man who has had a great capacity for making friends on his way through a zestful life. Those friends included my *Spectator* predecessor as a writer about racing, Jeffrey Bernard. Antony Johnson, 'Screamer' Lewis and the late, irrepressible Doug Marks were among those who over bibulous lunches used to help Jeffrey with scurrilous gossip for his columns and it was the *Spectator* scribe who awarded his elegant Lambourn host and provider of vodka and cigars the spurious decoration of the *Croix de Gucci* in his Colonel Mad column in *Private Eye*.

Those reading this book will surely include anybody who has ever been anybody in Cheshire, Barbados or Lambourn society or who shares Antony's memories of the old Four Hundred nightclub, bargain dinners at the Café de Paris, the Curzon Club or the Allegro Room at Quaglino's, not to mention popping over to Le Touquet with the likes of Billy and Bobby McAlpine for a weekend at the fashionable Westminster Hotel to attack the local casinos. Around such haunts he seems to have known just about everybody worth an anecdote.

The *Crack of the Whip* title, however, gives me the firm belief that the happiest stage of Antony Johnson's life was the part of it he spent with horses, including his eight years as a licensed trainer. Sir Winston Churchill once wrote that no hour of life is wasted that is spent in the saddle and added 'There is something about the outside of a horse that is good for the inside of a man.' Antony's relatives and family friends included the Derby-winning trainer Arthur Budgett (later to behave shabbily towards him) and great uncle Atty Persse, trainer of The Tetrarch, the spotted wonder who, as the author says, was 'the Frankel of his time'. His grandfather and father hunted before him and Antony's father had horses in training with George Owen. The Mayo Clinic diet which enabled him to pare down a 11st. 7lb frame to a riding weight of 10st. 2lb was acquired from Scobie Breasley, another family friend. One has to note too that it took true courage for him to become an accomplished rider over jumps himself because when Antony was only a schoolboy his father was shockingly paralysed by a jumping fall which gave him thirty years of suffering bravely endured.

At Wellington Antony's tutor tore up the order form he had to authorise for the chosen daily newspaper because Antony's selection was *The Sporting Life*. The ingenuity he showed at my old school, joining the fire brigade squad because even juniors in it were allowed a bicycle which facilitated visits to the village bookie, obviously came in handy later when he was part of an amateur team participating in the London to Sydney motor rally in the year 2000.

As a permit trainer in Cheshire he enjoyed use of the gallops owned by Eric Cousins, the handicap genius who was the first racehorse trainer I ever interviewed when I was on the *Liverpool Daily Post* and he learned race riding at George Owen's alongside such as Tim Brookshaw, Dick Francis and Stan Mellor. He has classic tales to tell about a coup engineered by Captain Sir Cecil Boyd-Rochfort, about Lester Piggott's carefulness with the pennies and about the out-of-saddle exploits of the serial womaniser Gay Kindersley, who asked a girl's name after a dance having had a vigorous affair with her a year or two previously. I cherish too the mental picture of Antony complimenting John Magnier on the quality of the staff cottages at Coolmore to be told that they were actually looking at the stallion boxes!

Watch out too for the story in his Lambourn days of how Champion Jockey Pat Eddery's amorous exploits set off the fire alarm at a party of Peter Walwyn's. Antony turns out to be a believer in marriage, having four times embarked upon that particular adventure! But while he acknowledges that the horsey set 'worked hard and played hard' it was too much for one Johnson marriage when he discovered that one vital cog in the machine wasn't just looking after his horses: 'I couldn't have my wife having an affair with my vet.'

These are memoirs without rancour, enlivened by some splendid anecdotes. Read and enjoy.

—Robin Oakley

In the Beginning...

'This is the BBC Home Service. Here is the News, read by Frank Phillips.' These were the first words that I was conscious of hearing on the wireless. Conscious because I heard them early every morning coming from my father's dressing room, always followed by the progress of the war: advances and retreats, casualties and prisoners of war. Informative and authoritative, with a 'Come on chaps, this is the News so do sit up and listen' attitude. Certainly not a pussyfooting, overpaid Welshman reading the news in a plaintive manner, before turning to a well-primed colleague who wouldn't know the difference between a Bren gun and a blunderbuss, asking for his 'reaction'. Alvar Liddell was another newsreader, also John Snagge, probably better known for his stentorian annual commentaries on the Oxford and Cambridge Boat Race. What it was all about meant nothing to me; I was not yet four years old, having been born in December 1936.

The beginning was in a lovely medium-sized Cheshire house set in a small arable farm. My parents had bought it for £3,200 soon after they were married in 1933. Approached through a light metal gate set into crescent-shaped iron railings, flanked by four magnificent horse chestnut trees, then down a bumpy drive to a second gate, by the side of which stood a wonderful copper beech tree. Then, on one side of the drive a lawn led up to the house; on the other side was a walled kitchen garden and an oval-shaped pond. A cobbled yard led to the main entrance towards the rear of the house. It had been built as a small farm and hunting lodge at the turn of the 19th century, and was a very comfortable family house with six bedrooms plus staff accommodation, stabling for six horses in caged boxes, groom's flat and ample brick barn space.

Hens, geese and turkeys roamed freely, although I was frightened by some cockerels and particularly by the geese; ducks nested beside the pond next to the kitchen garden where vegetables – peas, broad beans, cabbage, spinach, runner beans and potatoes – were grown. A high south-facing wall supported plum, peach, apricot and nectarine trees; there was a prolific fig tree and gooseberry, raspberry, black and redcurrant bushes and strawberry beds. Tomatoes grew in the greenhouse and lettuces were brought on in the cold frames outside. In the orchard bloomed apple, pear and cherry trees. Next to the stable yard stood the pigsties, and I loved watching the inmates, particularly at feed times. The stables themselves were empty: before the war, I was told, they had been occupied by horses that my father owned and trained privately. He was an amateur jockey, in addition to being Chairman and Managing Director of a large firm of steel and non-ferrous-metal wire manufacturers based in Manchester, which bore the family name and had been in existence since 1773, the same year as the Boston Tea Party.

In pre-war times my father had laid down a gallop round the perimeter of the farm and employed a groom who lived in a flat above the stables, but all that changed on the outbreak of war. Two, sometimes three, farm workers were employed full time and the senior one, George, was my hero. I would spend hour after hour with him sitting on the toolbox of the old Fordson tractor when he was ploughing, sowing, harrowing or rolling, and at feed times for all the poultry. Most exciting of all, however, was harvest time: cutting the corn with an ancient 'binder', making the stooks, carting the corn into the Dutch barns and stacking, plus the magic of the visiting threshing machine complete with steam-driven traction engine. There was a POW camp not very far away and some of the prisoners were allocated to work on farms within a certain area. There must have been some sort of screening but one, sometimes two, were dropped off by lorry with an armed guard at the end of the drive at eight in the morning and collected again at five in the afternoon. Frequently we had the same prisoners on a daily basis. Why a guard was necessary for transport but not for work remains unexplained but none of them showed any inclination or indeed desire to escape.

Perhaps one of my earliest recollections was being pushed in my pram by my nanny, whose name was Tibbins, for an outing on a hot summer's day, along the drive to the house which passed by the front lawn and where my mother and some guests were frolicking on the lawn. Quite at what I remained unaware, because I remember Tibbins saying extremely strictly 'Don't look.' When Tibbins departed at some later date she was replaced by a Belgian refugee and her daughter, Janine, who was about the same age as myself. It was only at bath time that I first learnt that we were made a little differently. One of the consequences of my Belgian nanny was that at the age of five or six I could probably speak French better than English, which was to stand me in good stead when I went to school.

My mother and her two sisters had been made wards of their cousin Hugh Budgett and his wife Hazel when they were in their mid-teens, owing to the early death of both their parents, and they went to live with the Budgetts in their very large house, Kirtlington, near Oxford. While my father was at Oxford he hunted with the Bicester, of which Hugh Budgett was Master, so not surprisingly my father made the acquaintance of the three Worthington girls at the round of parties and Hunt Balls attended by undergraduates, as well as at Oxford College Balls. Subsequently, during the late 20s, my father was based at the firm's London office during the week. At about this time Hugh Budgett had decided that it was high time that

Joan Worthington started to earn a living, slightly unusual for young ladies at that time. She was enlisted as a trainee nurse at Charing Cross Hospital and had a room in the Nurses' Home, but judging from her letters to Hazel Budgett and indeed from the Matron of Charing Cross Hospital to Hazel Budgett, it was a situation totally abominated by my mother both as regards occupation and accommodation. She did, however, seem to be having a pretty good time when she was not nursing, as long as she could escape from the Nurses' Home; she attracted the attention of several young men of suitable social standing, Billie Astor, who had lodgings at Micklem Hall, Oxford, being one of them. My father was another, but when he started to press his suit my mother had already got secretly engaged to a charming and romantic young novelist called Ralph Arnold. Fortunately for all concerned the engagement was terminated and a little while later my father got another chance, which he didn't let slip again. Happily Ralph Arnold and the lady he sub-sequently married, called Constantia, became good friends of both of them. The engagement was announced in October 1932 but not before my father had secured the permission of Hugh Budgett to marry his ward. The wedding took place at St Mary's Church, Kirtlington on Wednesday 15th February 1933 with the reception at Kirtlington afterwards. The bride's wedding dress from Marte Robes of 78 Grosvenor Street W1 was white Parme velvet trimmed with orange blossom, costing 21 guineas, plus a white Alencon net bridal veil, edged with orange blossom at four guineas. There were six bridesmaids including the two sisters, Mary and Betty, and my father's sister, Bryony. Stephen Tempest was the only page and Eric was his brother's best man.

The happy couple left almost immediately from Southampton on the Union Castle Line's *Windsor Castle*, bound for Cape Town but spending a few days at Reid's Hotel in Madeira – evidently very fashionable in those days – and catching the next Union Castle ship, the *Warwick Castle*, on to Cape Town. They were not scheduled to return until the following November, so a near nine-month honeymoon. To be fair, my father was due to spend a lot of time with the company's agents in the Cape and Johannesburg as well as visiting customers, South Africa being still a major market for fencing wire, but nevertheless not bad! Letters from the Cape were ecstatic; my mother writes on 23rd March: 'We have got a car which we are frightfully pleased with, it is a Ford eight ... and cost £250' and 'we are starting on our travels next week ... by stages to Johannesburg.' And so they did – via Port Elizabeth, East London and Durban before turning inland and northwards through Basutoland (now Lesotho) and Natal before tragedy struck. Near Louis Trichardt in northern Transvaal a large out-of-control lorry crashed head-on into the Ford. My father, driving, miraculously escaped with broken ribs, cuts and bruises but my mother suffered major facial injuries: her jaw and cheek bones were badly broken, her nose was smashed to bits, her skull cracked and she lost most of her teeth. Having seen photographs of what was left of the car, it is a miracle they were not both killed. My mother spent weeks in hospital in Johannesburg, after which both of them convalesced first with a friend of my father's, Erroll Hay, in Johannesburg and then with Cora Lyons (née Persse), my father's cousin, near Durban. Mother writes to Hazel Budgett that she looks like an old hag with no hair and hardly any teeth, and how glad she is that the accident happened after and not before her marriage! They eventually arrived home on the *Arundel Castle* in mid-October to coincide with the announcement that Germany would withdraw from the League of Nations owing to the refusal of France, the United States and Britain to agree to Germany's request to re-arm. Across the Atlantic the American gangster John Dillinger was freed from jail by members of his own gang, killing a sheriff in the process. Dillinger celebrated his release by robbing a bank of $75,000 a few days later but was shot and killed by police a year later.

Towards the end of the war, 1944–45, I learnt to ride at a nearby riding school. I can't say at that stage I was enamoured; in fact a trifle bored walking round in a circle on a very docile pony, becoming a little irritated by a young lady who placed a penny between both knees and the saddle and made me get off and pick them up each time either fell to the ground. However, I must have made some progress because my parents gave me a pony called Gypsy Boy on whom and with I had a lot of fun as the war ended and things started to get back to normal, whatever that was. I rode with my father, he on a racehorse and me following on behind on Boy; we went hunting with the Cheshire Forest Hounds and I was taken to local gymkhanas, which I didn't much like except for the bending races which we usually won as Boy was fast and loved it as much as I did. Otherwise there were always a lot of large ladies giving orders and shouting at their children. My mother was not in that category.

That carefree and idyllic life ended because school beckoned and I was dispatched to a simply ghastly institution called Lambrook, near Bracknell in Berkshire, owned and run by a Dickensian character called Mr Forbes and his equally terrifying wife, who would have made a second row forward in any women's rugger team. Archibald and Flora were their Christian names although they were, of course, 'Sir' and 'Mrs Forbes' to us little innocents. My mother had taught me to read at an early age and the aforementioned Belgian lady had taught me to speak French, but that was about all I knew.

I hated all the four years I spent at Lambrook and, looking back, I have no reason to change my mind; the teaching was appalling, not that surprising after five years of war with the Masters having been too old for military service or just plain useless and intimidating. The food was so disgusting but we were not allowed to leave the table until we had eaten it; I remember sitting for what seemed hours watching pieces of unknown animals growing cold under a mass of dark congealed sauce and secreting bits and pieces in my handkerchief to be flushed down the loo later.

Games-wise I didn't excel but played cricket, football and rugger to the best of my very limited ability. Beatings were plentiful and severe at the hand of Mr Forbes and his cane. Once for an answer given in a Geography exam: asked to describe a volcano I wrote, 'A volcano is a mountain being sick.' Another time I was overheard by the matron telling a rather fat boy that the hole in his underpants must have been caused by a fart.

In November 1948, about halfway through my time at Lambrook, my home life and that of my parents changed suddenly and dramatically. My father was riding a horse called Kloof in a steeplechase at Manchester, quite an important racecourse in those days. In the Easter holidays that same year I had seen him win on the horse at the now defunct Woore racecourse. Some three fences from home Kloof fell and my father was totally paralysed, having broken his neck. He was taken to Salford Hospital but my mother, who was with him, was told that he was unlikely to survive the night and that even if he did would probably only live a matter of days. That he did not only survive but would live for a further thirty years, albeit with many dysfunctional parts of his body, was nothing short of a miracle. I was, naturally, unaware of all this being at school but Mr Forbes summoned me to his study a couple of days later and told me that my father had had a bad accident and would never ride again. The rest of that term remains a bit of a blur, but when I arrived home for the Christmas holidays I began to realise that things would never be the same again.

My father was not there, being in hospital where he would remain for most of the next three years. My parents were devoted to each other and my mother spent much of the time at his bedside in hospital and, thinking that it would be better for me not to be at home at this very difficult time, it was arranged that a crusty old schoolmaster from Lambrook would be engaged to take me and my cousin John Asprey skiing at Engelberg in Switzerland. My parents knew Engelberg very well and were friends of the Odermatt family who owned and ran the Bellevue Hotel. I had been to Engelberg once before, in the summer of 1946 when the ravages of war were scarcely over. Petrol rationing had still been in force and my father's 'large' car was up on chocks in the garage where it had been since the outbreak of war, but there was also a Morris 10 and in this my father, mother and I set off from home, across the Channel and through France. We stayed in a bombed hotel in Laon where the staircase was on the outside of the building, the rest having been flattened, and saw the magnificent Rheims cathedral rising above a mainly devastated area, and many shelled tanks and military vehicles wrecked by the roadside, particularly around Belfort and Mulhouse. I remember picking up an abandoned German helmet for which the unfortunate owner had no further use, owing to a round hole in the centre…

As 1948 drifted into 1949 and beyond, everything at home was very different. My father was moved to various hospitals for changes in treatment. At one stage he was flat on his back for nine weeks, lying on a plaster cast made to fit his body exactly in University College Hospital in London. He had regained some movement in his left side and my mother had the bright idea of having a television set built on a bracket above his head in his room in the hospital. He could reach the controls with his left hand and it was not unusual to walk into his room to see other visitors lying on the floor watching television. But for him it was all terrible and anybody without his immense strength of character and determination would have succumbed. Gone from his life was any prospect of not only riding but shooting, skiing and tennis, at all of which he competed with enthusiasm and not a little skill. It wasn't just the paralysis that was the problem; he also suffered a great deal of pain and lack of control internally. His mind, however, remained spot on and he continued to run the business from his hospital bed, as far as possible, and with the help of very loyal senior directors and executives. He had a very sharp wit, a wonderful sense of humour, was a very good mimic and composer of highly amusing and frequently extremely vulgar ditties and limericks. For me it was the end of normal fun father-and-son activities, but never for the remaining thirty years of his life the end of love, respect, advice and companionship.

I knew only one of my four grandparents. Both of mother's parents died before she was fifteen. The middle of the three sisters, as described she completed her upbringing in the care and financial security of the Budgetts in the palatial Kirtlington. The house was about ten miles from Oxford, built by Sir James Dashwood in 1740–45, designed by the architect James Gibbs with interior work by the famous plasterer Roberts and by Grinling Gibbons. All the bedrooms were named after Oxford Colleges and the park designed by Capability Brown. The Budgetts were pretty well-off and the family owned a profitable sugar broking business in London, but it must have been quite a shock to the family to be landed with three teenage girls, they already having two sons of their own of roughly similar ages, Alan and Arthur. Hugh (known as Sming by the family) Budgett was Master of the Bicester Hounds for many years in the 1920s and 30s but he was also quite an eccentric. In 1931 he sold the entire dining room – contents, furniture, ornamental plaster and stucco work, doors, painted ceiling of the Four Seasons, floorboards and portraits – to the Metropolitan Museum in New York, where it remains to this day. During the course of the negotiations for the sale Budgett had meticulously arranged for every single item to be copied and the dining room was rein-stated as new after the original had been numbered, packed and dispatched to New York. At another time he developed a passion for breeding bloodhounds, frequently sending my mother or one of her sisters out into the park to lay a trail to test their scenting abilities. Hazel Budgett was my mother's 'second' mother and was her greatest friend and supporter for the rest of her life, becoming my godmother after I was born in 1936.

My paternal grandfather was Ernest. While up at Oxford he had formed a great friendship with a very talented and dashing Irish horseman and fellow undergraduate called Henry Seymour Persse, always known throughout his life as Atty because he couldn't pronounce Henry as a child. Atty lived with his family in great style at Glenarde, near Galway, and Ernest was frequently asked to stay and to hunt with the Galway Blazers, as the hunt was known. Various Persses were Masters of the Blazers over many generations, probably the most famous of which was Robert Burton Persse, my great, great grandfather, who was Master from 1852 until he died in 1885. The 'Blazers' got their name in a typically Irish fashion: for several years they used to be invited to hunt the Ormond country at a specified time each season and in 1840 the ensuing festivities at Dooley's Hotel in Birr resulted the hotel being burnt down – hence the 'Blazers'.

The Persse family lived for hunting and in their spare time made whiskey. Atty became a very well-known amateur jockey on both sides of the Irish Sea and finished third in the 1906 Grand National. Subsequently he came to England and trained horses at Chattis Hill, near Stockbridge, including one of the most famous of all time: the unbeaten The Tetrarch who was the Frankel of his time.

During Ernest's visits to Glenarde he fell in love with Atty's younger sister Violet, a high-spirited Irish beauty who swept Ernest off his feet. I have a portrait of her aged about six by Stanhope Forbes, a then itinerant artist in search of commissions at Irish country houses and who subsequently achieved fame as one of the founders of the Newlyn School of Art in Cornwall. Ernest and Violet became engaged not long after Ernest's father Thewlis's death, and the wedding, a splendid affair reported in the *Galway Express* on 14th November 1896 under the heading 'Fashionable Wedding', took place in Galway with eight bridesmaids and two pages. Atty and Violet's quite distant cousin on their mother's side, Dermot McCalmont, was described in the newspaper as 'a charming little page attired in a mauve satin costume, period Louis XV, son of General and the Hon. Mrs McCalmont'. For their honeymoon they went to Southern Spain and Tangier.

Violet and Ernest, my grandparents, had three children, my father being the youngest; his elder brother Eric was born in 1897, his sister, Bryony, in 1900 and my father in 1904. They lived at Ashton Hayes, a large Queen Anne house about eight miles from Chester, set in parkland with a Home Farm plus three tenanted farms. Although my grandfather hunted and was interested in racing, he devoted his working life to the business, and in order to raise more capital and to retain its position as a leader in the wire manufacturing trade he floated the company on the Stock Exchange in 1929. The following year, in March of 1930, he died of pneumonia just a few hours before the horse that he had tipped, Shaun Goilin, won the Grand National.

***

1949 was thankfully my last year at Lambrook and in 1950 I passed the Common Entrance exam for Wellington, where I was to spend the next four years in the same house my father had been 1918–22. As far as I can establish our scholastic and school sporting careers were similarly undistinguished. My housemaster, or Tutor as they were called, was a fierce, very tall Classics master so we had nothing in common, but actually he had a good sense of humour and a human touch. This did not extend that far, however: all boys were allowed to order their own newspapers which, along with goods from the school shop, known as Grubbies, were charged on the school bill. Any item thus billed had to be written on an Order Form and countersigned by one's Tutor. Therefore I completed my newspaper Order Form and presented it to my Tutor thus:

'This is for a newspaper, Sir.'

'Oh yes, Johnson, which newspaper do you want?'

'*The Sporting Life*, Sir.'

I thought he was going to have a heart attack as he tore up my Order Form in a complete rage. In my book, not having the *Sporting Life* (the equivalent of the *Racing Post* in those days), was similar to a Clergyman not having a Bible. He had the impression that racing was an elite sport that harboured toffs and villains in equal quantities and was not to be encouraged. By contrast, the well-known racing journalist and thoroughbred breeding expert Peter Willett, who died recently aged ninety-six, and his great friend and brother officer Jack (later Major General Sir Jack) Harman, who were both at Wellington in the early 1930s, were both allowed *The Sporting Life* and had distinguished careers at the school, Willett having been Head of School and Harman Head of his House.

Although Wellington was a considerable step up from Lambrook, in common with many other public schools it was still suffering a post-war hangover and was nothing like the superb establishment it is today. The academic curriculum was stereotyped and limited, extracurricular activities even more so and the games field centred on cricket, rugger, athletics and hockey. An exception was racquets with an excellent professional but only one court so teaching and availability was very limited. I loathed hockey, was not good enough for serious rugger and was a pitifully slow runner at anything less than a mile. I did enjoy playing cricket but was not good enough to make any of the major teams. The only sport that I was good enough to represent the school at was boxing, considered very much a minor sport but I was in the team pretty well all the time I was at Wellington.

Being originally an army school – the school mottos being *Virtutis Fortuna Comes* (Fortune Favours the Brave) and *Heroum Filii* (Sons of Heroes) – there was a strong CCF which was compulsory, my only contribution being playing the cymbals in the band. One thing I did twig fairly early on was how much more convenient it would be if I had a bicycle as the College grounds covered a very large area. The problem was that only very senior boys were allowed one but there was one loophole: members of the school fire brigade were allowed a bicycle, the theory being the 'fire boys' could get to any blaze quicker on a bike than on foot. I became a member of the fire brigade. The 'fire engine' consisted of little more than a small water tank on wheels with a mechanical pump and various lengths of hoses. Unless there was a convenient vehicle at hand plus someone able to drive it, the 'fire engine' was manually propelled. Once or twice per term we had a fire exercise which involved little more than pulling the contraption out of its shed, starting up the pump and standing around looking at it for about half an hour and then pushing it back again; a small price to pay for having one's own transport. Thereafter, at break or lunchtime I could mount my bike and pedal furiously along a path which was a shortcut to the village of Crowthorne and the village shop, which doubled up as the (illegal and out-of-bounds) College bookmaker. It follows that the highlight of being taken out by my parents on a Saturday or Sunday were the occasions when we could drive to Lambourn to see my great uncle and go round the horses.

Atty had moved to Kingsdown, Lambourn from Chattis Hill after the war. His only son, John, was killed on active service in Italy during the war and Atty and his wife Emily were devastated. Emily, a former actress, was the daughter of Sir George Brooke and a sister of Geoffrey Brooke who became Atty's assistant and later was a successful trainer in Newmarket. Atty only decided to resume training after the war having been persuaded to do so by one his best owners, Jack Olding. He had some more good horses, too, including Thames Trader and Durante, the latter winning consecutive Great Jubilee Handicaps, then one of the principal handicaps of the season and a great betting medium.

The great Irish jockey Michael Beary, who rode for Atty, was frequently at Kingsdown when we came. Brilliant as he was, Beary had a somewhat chequered career, his temperament getting him into trouble with the Stewards at times, but on his day he was superb and Atty, to whom he had been apprenticed, thought the world of him. Atty finally retired in 1954 and died in 1960 aged ninety-one. He was buried at Stockbridge just a few miles from Chattis Hill.

At home my father continued to regain some movement and could now take faltering steps with the aid of callipers on his right leg. His left leg and arm became fully mobile and he learnt to write left-handed; however, he had no feeling whatsoever in his left side. For instance you could prick him with a pin and he would feel nothing. His right arm was useless. He had been a very strong swimmer and the doctors thought that if he could go for an extended period to a warm country where he could swim he might benefit considerably. It's an ill wind that blows nobody any good, and this resulted in my being taken to Kyrenia in Cyprus in the early 50s during the school holidays and also to Majorca where we stayed in a tiny (the only) hotel with about ten rooms, at Cala Fornells, for 10 shillings (50p) per day. Kyrenia, too, was marvellous in those days long before all the troubles engulfed the island: a sleepy little village with a beautiful harbour under the walls of a huge 16th-century castle built by the Venetians on the site of an even older crusader fortification. The sea and swimming were fantastic with virtually nobody around. My parents became great friends of an ex-army officer who lived there and ran a Country Club. His name was Brigadier Jack Anstice who had a brilliant war record in Burma in the Second World War under General (later Field Marshal Viscount) Slim. Anstice was Commander of the 7th Armoured Brigade in 1941 and Slim paid great tribute to him in his book *Defeat into Victory* for the part played by Anstice in the rear-guard action round Mandalay and the defence of the crossing of the River

Irrawaddy. He also had a ravishingly beautiful daughter called Sally who was most enamoured with and subsequently married a Turk called Fikret Jemal. The marriage, predictably, didn't last and later she married the 9th and last Duke of Newcastle as his third wife and lived for many years in Kenya. She died, aged eighty-seven, in July 2015. Kyrenia is now a large and sprawling town but on a recent visit I was glad to see that the harbour with the castle walls towering above had hardly changed at all and is traffic-free.

In the spring of 1954 I was seventeen and it was time to look to the future. It was father and son time, but probably for the first time we embarked on a different form of relationship and it was a pretty smooth transition. Although still at school I felt I was treading water: I was not going to make any of the top games teams and, academically, my interests were spreading outside the current school curriculum. Without wishing to be snobbish, it has to be remembered that in those days one only considered one out of two universities and we were an Oxford family. But that meant staying on at Wellington for a further year in order to take and, with any luck, pass the necessary exams. Then three years up at Oxford at the end of which I would be twenty-one/ two. But there was two years' National Service to be done either before or after university. So, in my eyes, I would be twenty-four/ twenty-five before I had done a 'tap', in racing parlance. And, did I need a degree? The answer was 'no'. I had a potential job to go to at Richard Johnson & Nephew Ltd, once a family firm but a public company since 1929, as previously referred to. Probably today it would have been different but my father and I agreed, after due, serious and most congenial discussions, that I should leave Wellington at the end of the summer term 1954, wait for my call-up papers but make a bit of hay in the meantime.

Father always had two or three horses trained by George Owen whose stables were in the magnificent yard of Cholmondeley Castle, owned by the Earl of Rocksavage, subsequently the

Marquess of Cholmondeley (pronounced 'Chumley') about twenty miles away. George, a terrific man, was Cheshire born and a former professional National Hunt jockey who won, among many other top races, the Cheltenham Gold Cup in 1939 on Brendan's Cottage, trained by George Beeby, the father of my subsequent great friend Harry Beeby. As a trainer George Owen won lots of high-class races including the 1963 Champion Two Mile Steeplechase at Cheltenham with Sandy Abbot; however, he was probably better known as the trainer of the 1947 Grand National winner Russian Hero, a 66/1 chance owned by a local Cheshire farmer. George, a softly spoken mild man, was not just a very good trainer of horses, he also taught and brought on jockeys who went right to the top and became Champion Jockeys. The first was the legendary Dick Francis who went to George having been discharged from the RAF at the end of the war and who achieved even greater fame as a novelist after he had retired as a jockey.

It was Dick who rode the ill-fated Devon Loch, owned by Queen Elizabeth, the Queen Mother who was about to win the Grand National of 1956 by a comfortable margin when he mysteriously jumped in the air, maybe mistaking a shadow for a fence, about 40 yards from the winning post and landed spread-eagled on his stomach allowing ESB, ridden by Dave Dick, to overtake him and win. Then there was Tim Brookshaw, Shropshire born and completely fearless, who started and made his name with George Owen and went on to be Champion Jockey in 1958/59. Tim would have won the Grand National of 1959 on Wyndburgh but for a stirrup leather breaking: he rode the last eight fences without irons and even then was beaten by only half a length. Tim's career as a jockey ended in 1963 as a result of a very bad fall, which left him semi-paralysed. Defying the doctors who told him he would never walk again let alone ride, he recovered enough to do both but with only very limited power and movement. He had another fall in 1981 while out exercising from which he did not recover and died six days later. I knew Dick and Tim pretty well but not as well as the third 'Owen' jockey to become Champion – Stan Mellor. George had a cartoon by the great cartoonist, Giles, hanging in his house of himself standing on the take-off side of a fence brandishing a whip urging a very reluctant horse with all three jockeys, Dick, Tim and Stan on board, to jump it.

Having passed my driving test, I made a beeline for George's stables early most mornings for the rest of the summer and early autumn 1954 to ride out, first of all mainly road work and cantering, but as I progressed under George's tutorage, then faster work and ultimately schooling horses over hurdles and fences. There was a young full-time lad about the same age as myself called Stanley. Small and light, he hadn't been at George's very long but showed considerable promise, having ridden since he was a child and competed in pony club events. We became quite friendly, particularly when we started to ride work together. I remember very well my first schooling session, the two other jockeys taking part being Tim Brookshaw and Stan(ley) Mellor; on the run-up to the first fence, it seemed to me impossible to jump a fence going so fast. Luckily George had put me on a pretty experienced horse so it was more me being schooled than the horse. It was a thrilling and exciting experience and I was totally hooked. Looking back it is extraordinary that, in those days, we wore no protective clothing or helmets of any kind for riding out or even schooling. For racing the headgear was a cork (for lightness rather than safety) helmet with no chin strap over which the appropriate colour cap was fitted and tied by a bow in front.

Later in the autumn I made my first visit to Ireland, on the night ferry from Liverpool to Dun Laoghaire, to take a riding and stable management course at Col. Joe Hume Dudgeon's famous academy at Burton Hall, Stillorgan, then a village in its own right but now swallowed up and a suburb of Dublin.

Joe Dudgeon won an MC in the first war and subsequently was captain of the British Show Jumping team. He was a magnificent rider and teacher and any illusions that I might have had about being able to ride were swiftly dispelled on my first morning by the Scottish RSM-type chief riding master when I rode into the collecting ring: 'Who the hell do you think you are, Gordon Bloody Richards?' he yelled. I was minded to say that any such accolade would be a great honour but held my peace and dropped my leathers by six holes. The course was hard work but intensely rewarding; we were taught so much, not just on the riding side but about the practical side of stable management: mucking out, grooming, feeding, the anatomy of the horse, all of which was to stand me in good stead in the future. I lived in digs about five miles away under the strict eye of a Miss FitzGerald who stood no nonsense. Transport was by a very unreliable bus service or by bicycle but after a week or two I managed to hire a Ford Prefect car for £6 per week – not easy in Ireland then when the official minimum age for car hire was twenty-five.

Living at that time in Co. Limerick was a middle-aged spinster cousin called Venice Price. Her brother, Jack Price, a cousin of my father's, was my godfather and lived in a lovely house called Rhiwlas, near Bala, north Wales. Venice was great fun, very social, mad on hunting and with a wonderful and sometimes extremely vulgar sense of humour. It was arranged that, at the end of my course with Joe Dudgeon, I should go and stay with Venice where she lived just outside a hamlet called Kildimo, near Adare, Co. Limerick. I had arranged to go by train from Dublin but on handing in my car a big, burly Irishman was in the process of hiring one to go Limerick for an important hurling match and offered to give me a lift. Eager to save the train fare I accepted. What I had not anticipated was that my new friend was intent on not missing any pub on the road from Dublin to Limerick, with the result that it was well after midnight by the time we hit Limerick and I had to call my poor cousin Venice to drive fifteen miles to come and pick me up. I felt dreadful about it but she was as sympathetic and understanding as possible.

The whole Co. Limerick scene was just great: hunting two, sometimes three days per week with the Limerick, whose Master was Lord Toby Daresbury of the Greenall brewing family. Venice knew everybody in the hunting and racing fraternity and was so kind arranging hirelings for me to ride, sometimes letting me ride one of her horses, taking me to fun dinner parties and introducing me to all her friends. I fell madly in love with the two Wyndham-Quin sisters Melissa and Caroline, both much older than me, daughters of the Earl of Dunraven and his American wife Nancy, feelings of which they were totally unaware and which were certainly not reciprocated. Their brother Thady, who succeeded his father in 1965, I got to know quite well much later; he was a wonderful man, spending his life in a wheelchair after having contracted polio at the age of eighteen and devoting so much of his life afterwards in support of the disabled in Ireland. He also owned and ran the Fort Union Stud, which produced many top-class horses.

2

O.H.M.S.

Back home in Cheshire a few days before Christmas just in time to receive my National Service call-up papers and instructions to report to the 7th Royal Tank Regiment at Waitwith Camp, Catterick. Catterick, in north Yorkshire, is the largest British Army garrison in the world, with the camp itself covering some 2,400 acres with another 20,000 acres of training ground. A winter in Catterick is probably not one's first choice at the best of times but for a naïve eighteen-year-old accommodated, along with about twenty-four others from all walks of life, in a 35-yard-long Nissen hut it was quite a culture shock. The hut had a polished stone floor and a blackened cast-iron stove with a circular metal chimney in the centre. There was a row of beds on either side of the hut, each with a wooden cupboard. That was all. Bedding consisted of two very rough sheets, a pillow and three blankets. There were several other similar huts and a central washing and lavatorial hut about 50 yards distant. The signing-on interview and registration was uncompromising: walking smartly into a room in an admin building and uttering the previously instructed 'Good morning Sir'; the officer seated behind a table said 'Name?' I told him. 'Age?' Again I told him. He looked up for the first time and said 'Hmm, you don't look it.' Interview over. The rest of the day was taken up with the issue of army kit – uniforms, boots (two pairs), shirts, underclothes, sports clothes, mess tins and all sorts of other paraphernalia plus the inevitable army haircut. I had taken the precaution of having

20

a haircut a couple of days before but should not have bothered. In vain did I place a shilling into the outstretched hand of the barber before he got busy with the shears and I emerged, a few minutes later, a virtual skinhead.

We were to undertake a five-week initial training course with the NCO in charge of our barrack room, as it was known, being a Cpl Perryman. Above him was Sgt Gubbins who had charge of three barracks rooms with, above him, an officer whose name I can't remember, being in charge of the whole 'intake'. Cpl Perryman I considered a typical example of the army NCO seen on the movies. Sgt Gubbins (his real name) on the other hand was a rough, tough, no-nonsense Somerset man with whom one took liberties at one's own risk but was honest and straight-forward. After a few days and during a five-minute break from intense square bash drilling, I happened to notice Sgt Gubbins running his finger down the racing page of the *Daily Mirror* and it came to rest against the name of a particular horse. In the same race was a horse I mildly fancied:

'That'll win that one Sergeant,' I said, pointing at my selection.

'Fuck off, arsehole, it's got no chance with the favourite.'

'All right, Sergeant,' I replied. 'There's a pound of mine that says the one I fancy beats yours.'

'You can kiss the snotty end of my cock,' said Sgt Gubbins without looking up. For the record neither horse won the race but mine did beat his.

We had a 'hard case' in our barrack room. Reveille was sounded at six a.m. swiftly followed by the appalling Cpl Perryman bursting in and banging his cane against the stove, but one man, fortunately at the far end of the hut from me, refused to budge and just lay in bed smoking a cigarette. His attitude was that he didn't want to come into the army and for all Cpl Perryman's yelling and screaming at him, he wasn't going to budge and cer-tainly not go on parade. In the evening he was still there, in bed. Next morning exactly the same but by the evening he was gone with a dishonourable discharge and never seen again.

The five-week Basic Training was pretty tough with masses of drill by Perryman and Gubbins, a great deal of PE and obstacle training under the control of a PTI (physical training instructor), long route marches, some in the late evening and night. And, of course, Bull: there was never a moment when one wasn't cleaning, blancoing, shining brasses, buckles, and cap badges, polishing boots and mess tins, and ironing uniforms and shirts. And that's not all: the barrack room itself had to be absolutely spotlessly clean and tidy with the floor polished and the stove blackened and shiny. So much so that there was no point in lighting it even though it was the only form of heating and Catterick in the winter was freezing cold. The run to the wash house was often made barefoot across snow-covered ground for fear of dirtying one's boots before an early morning kit inspection. The method of bed-making was strange: blankets and sheets had to be folded in a particular way and placed at the head of the bed with one blanket wrapped around the other bedclothes with precise 90-degree corners. We cut out small pieces of strong cardboard to insert into the corners to make them stand proud. Because this had to be so accurate it took some time to assemble the complete package so again for early morning kit inspections we slept on the floor beside the bed. We were so tired the floor was almost comfortable.

The original shyness of a group of totally differing young men being thrown together gradually wore off, natural barriers started to break down and degrees of friendship were formed. We all had to pull together not just for ourselves but for the common good of our hut; there was also a strong element of competition. None of us wanted to have our bedding or kit strewn about the place by Cpl Perryman or Sgt Gubbins during the daily inspections and we wanted our hut to be better than the others when the serious kit inspections took place. At the end of the five-week period we were a very different group of people, much fitter and sharper than when we first joined the army. We also had seventy-two hours of leave – the first time any of us had left the camp.

On returning after the weekend's leave, most of which was spent catching up on sleep, I must have done OK during the Basic Training course because I was ordered to report to the Potential Officers Wing and started immediately on a tough six-week course, the culmination of which was a five-day Unit Selection Board examination to determine if one was, or was not, considered of a high enough standard to go before the War Office Selection Board (WOSB) to become an officer. The course was hard, very hard at times, but I found it challenging and really interesting: we were taught a range of subjects from dismantling and re-assembling an assortment of guns – rifles, Sten and Bren guns – rudimentary mechanical knowledge of tanks, armoured cars and lorries, detailed map reading, initiative tests and instruction on day and night exercises plus masses of drill with and without rifles during which we all had periods of taking command. However, on the down side, the 'bull' was much more extreme than in the Basic Training course. Everything had to be absolutely perfect: clothes folded in precisely the regulation way, spotlessly clean, and laid out in the correct order on the bed, kit blancoed and brasses shined, boots and mess tins polished so brightly that they could be used as mirrors, bedding folded to a higher quality than before, so much that not only did we use cardboard for the corners but we actually stitched the cardboard into the sheets, blankets and clothes without it being seen to ensure they stood totally straight. All this had to be done in the evening after the day's ordinary course work; the consequence was that it was usually around one a.m. before we were finished, frequently sleeping on the floor.

The officer in charge of the course was Major Ian Manning of the 5th Royal Inniskilling Dragoon Guards (the Skins). I remember his name well because I was to meet him on many occasions in very different circumstances in the years to come.

Short and wiry with jet black hair, the Major always looked immaculate whether it be in the middle of the night on the moors or at six o'clock in the morning doing a kit inspection. He had a deep and very penetrating stare which, although not actually hostile, wasn't friendly either. I dreaded his arrival each time but the difference between him and the dreadful Cpl Perryman was that if the Major said something was wrong, it *was* wrong – well perhaps not wrong but not *perfect*. He had an amazing eye for detail and was icy in his criticism. Another major difference in this course to the Basic Training was the company; we were about fifteen to twenty all told with more common ground to share and talk about.

The dreaded day of the start of the Selection Board test dawned and we were moved to a completely different part of the camp and so were entirely isolated from anybody who might have been able to help or advise. The culmination of the five days was an all-night exercise on the moors in which each candidate took it in turns to be in charge of the platoon and to carry out a mock attack on a target. Each member of the platoon was only briefed on what he had to do immediately before his turn came. The 'enemy' were regular soldiers. My task, when it came, was to attack and capture an enemy machine-gun post in a derelict building which, I was told, was about 200 yards away. As it was pitch dark I thought the best thing to do would be to make a recce and then form a plan. I appointed one member of the platoon to remain in charge while I went forward taking one man with me. I selected someone with whom I had become very friendly during the course called Tony Turl who owned a red MG 'TD' sports car of which I was very envious. We crept forward very stealthily in the direction I understood the building to be and managed to locate it without being seen. Then I had a stroke of luck: the moon suddenly appeared in the gap in the clouds, only for a few seconds but long enough for me to spot a small hillock on the other side of the building, which, by making a wide left

24

flanking movement, would give us enough dead ground to make a short and sudden attack. Back with the platoon I explained the strategy emphasising the need for stealth and silence and ordered them to follow me in single file with Tony Turl in the rear. The plan worked; we regrouped just below the top of the little hill out of sight from the target to the rear of the building and then burst forward in a charge of the last twenty yards taking them completely by surprise and catching one poor chap a pretty sharp blow with the butt end of my rifle.

Later that night, under someone else's command, I had a nasty mishap. Taking a step forward in the extreme darkness my leading leg found no ground on which to stand. It was like walking off a roof. As I fell I hurled my rifle to one side; I hit water and went on down for what seemed an age and well out of my depth until I touched the bottom and got tangled up in reeds. I was wearing boots and full combat kit but struggled to the surface and soon found a very steep bank. Very frightened and exhausted I managed to haul myself up and retrieved my rifle. I was very cold, drenched and totally lost, other members of the platoon being unaware of my predicament having gone on. Eventually I saw some lights and found my way back to the centre of operations. Apparently I had fallen down a disused lead mine.

At the end of the five days I didn't think that I had passed so was overjoyed to find that I was one of five or six who had got through and therefore qualified to go to the WOSB examination held at the army garrison at Warminster, Wiltshire. There was, however, a caveat or slight sting in the tail. I was sent for by my CO, who was very pleasant but said that the result was a quite a close call but what had swung it in my favour was the success of the night exercise. He went on to say that I had earned the right to go to WOSB but, in his opinion, my youthful appearance and lack of maturity might count against me and he advised me to wait another couple of months to gain more experience and become more streetwise. I thanked him but was having none of it and elected to go as soon as possible. Then I went home for a weekend's leave.

I returned to Catterick in my own transport: my parents had given me a Morris Minor for my 18th birthday. What a fabulous present, like a passport to freedom and I thought it was wonderful. I can even remember the number plate: SND 286. It was pretty basic, no such things as a heater or radio and with indicators that flipped out of the bodywork on the side of the car between the doors, green in colour with an 800 cc engine, top speed around 65 mph. The cost was £400, new. Nowadays a 1955 Morris Minor, if you can find one, costs a minimum of £4,500.

It was a party of four of us, the survivors of those who passed the Unit Selection Board, who set off a fortnight later to WOSB. I took them all in my new car to Warminster for the three-day Test. There were candidates from several other training camps in different parts of the country but on the whole it seemed to go quite well; again my exercise scheme, this time in daylight, was, I thought, quite good and I was quietly confident when the results were handed round, so was very disappointed to receive what was called a Deferred Watch. This meant that the examiners were satisfied that I could make the grade but thought I needed more time. So, my Commanding Officer at Catterick had been right and I should have listened to him and taken his advice. Of my three companions, two passed and one failed outright so it was with mixed feelings that we drove northwards to Catterick.

The question was, what to do next in the intervening period. Since I was scheduled to go into a Cavalry Regiment (aka the RAC, Royal Armoured Corps) it seemed a good idea to learn more about the chief weapon of the corps, the tank. The Centurion Tank was originally designed in 1943 and commissioned in 1945. In 1955 we had the Mark III updated version with a crew of four: commander, driver in a separate compartment at a low level in front, gunner and loader/wireless operator. The tank weighed 55 tons, had a 105mm (just over four inches) gun, was powered by a Rolls-Royce Meteor engine giving a top speed of 22 mph with a range of 280 miles. I took a wireless operator's course which included, in addition to the fairly complicated methods and technique of wireless communication, quite a lot of time spent on tank manoeuvres which was really quite exciting and good fun. Life in general was easier with less bull. Most of the course work was done in daytime which meant more free time in the evenings. The problem was that one had to sign out of the camp perimeter at the guard house on departure but there was a 10 p.m. curfew by which time one had to be back in camp. This problem was solved: going out on tank exercises I got to know quite a few of the tank trails, rough concrete roads which led onto the moors. Occasionally these trails crossed minor by-roads and lanes so it was not too difficult to leave the camp on one of the trails and turn off on a by-road. Hence no signing out or in. One had to be careful, it was better after dark using only side lights and preferably, if there was any moonlight, no lights at all.

There was a well-known racehorse trainer at that time called Harry Peacock, a member of one of the most famous racing families in England, let alone Yorkshire. Harry trained at Hurgill Lodge, Richmond very near Catterick and numbered Lord Zetland among his owners. My father knew him, having bought a backward two-year-old from him in 1939 that he thought might make a jumper. The horse, named Kloof, was turned out all during the war but when it was over my father sent him to George Owen who trained him to win a number of races. It was on Kloof that my father had his near-fatal fall at Manchester in 1948 but the horse went on to win more races ridden by father's great friend Mickey Moseley. Father got me an invitation from Harry Peacock, who was quite old by now, to visit him and go round the horses at evening stables. It was a great thrill to meet the old man. When he retired a few years later, his son-in-law

'Buster' Fenningworth took over. Harry Peacock died in 1961 but 'Buster' was very successful, until he tragically died as a result of a car accident while driving to Ayr races in 1967.

Army life is not all fun and games: I was driving inside the camp perimeter one day when a big, strapping PTI Lance Corporal, who I knew slightly, was walking in the opposite direction; the Lance Corporal mistakenly saluted smartly as he passed. I wound down my window, grinned at him and waved back. Why he should have thought that an officer would be driving around in a Morris Minor I don't know, but later that evening I received a message that he wanted to see me. He told me that he was reporting me and that I would be charged for pretending to be an officer and returning his salute. He went on to say that if I gave him £50 he would forget all about it. Apart from the blackmail, £50 was a lot of money in those days when I could fill up my car with petrol for less than £1. He said that if I said anything about it, the injuries I would suffer would be incalculable. I told him what he could do with his £50 and related the incident to my CO. The PTI was charged with attempted blackmail and intimidation, found guilty and sentenced to a severe reprimand and a warning as to his future conduct. I was pretty careful not to go down any dark alleys for the next week or two.

Another weekend leave marked the end of the wireless operator's course but this one didn't go very well. It was winter, the roads were icy and I ended up at the bottom of a deep ditch head on to the opposite bank. Not in my Morris Minor but in my father's top of the range Rover, quite a smart car in those days. Apart from a few scratches I thought I was all right until I realised that the steel dashboard of the car had two deep holes where it had been penetrated by my knees, which very soon blew up like footballs. Subsequent X-rays showed up considerable damage (to the knees!) and I was horizontal from the waist down and bored to tears for three months.

Back at Catterick there were decisions to be made. I had now been in the army for six months; waiting for another WOSB would take a further month. Again assuming success – by no means a certainty – this would be followed by a four-month OCTU (Officer Cadet Training Unit) course so nearly a year, i.e. half of the whole National Service, would be over. It seemed a bit of a no-brainer and I elected for an immediate posting to the 17th/21st Lancers in Munster, Germany as Tpr Johnson. By troop ship and train to Harwich – Hook of Holland – Munster and to former Luftwaffe barracks that were Claridge's compared to Catterick. I was assigned to 'C' Squadron under the command of Major (Tony) Dacres-Dixon, my troop leader being Lt (Simon) Walford. Dacres-Dixon was just about the most laid-back man I have ever met with a very pretty wife, but I did not get on with Walford, an Anglo-Irishman who I was to see from time to time in future life as he had a thoroughbred stud farm in Ireland. Life on the whole was quite congenial; I got on fine with my co-squaddies, was assigned as wireless operator to the R.E.M.E. detachment going on manoeuvres in tanks, armoured cars and half-tracks to attend to tanks that had broken down, played a bit of cricket, made the mistake of entering the regimental boxing competition at light welterweight (10st. 2lbs) without too much damage but didn't make the final and a bigger mistake by entering the regimental cross-country race – really as a part of getting fit for boxing. My mistake was finishing far too near the front – 6th or 7th I think, but was then selected for the regimental team and subsequently the brigade team to compete against army teams from different areas over cross-country courses of around eight miles. Didn't enjoy it much.

The most exciting time during this period came during the build-up of two major world events, either or both of which could have resulted in armed conflict. First was the Hungarian Uprising: Stalin had died in 1953 and the Hungarians had hoped for a relaxation in the tyrannical regime under Khrushchev. By October 1956 not enough progress had been made and massive street demonstrations started. On 31ˢᵗ October Hungary threatened to withdraw from the Warsaw Pact, whereupon Russia sent in the tanks to Budapest: 30,000 people were killed and 200,000 fled and were left homeless. The Uprising failed and order under Soviet rule was re-established by mid-November. The second was the Seven-Day Suez War. Here President Nasser nationalised the Anglo-French Suez Canal in July 1956 to the fury and outrage of both countries. At the end of October and after secret negotiations by us with the Israelis, the latter country attacked Egypt and advanced to within ten miles of the Canal. We landed some troops a few days later. However, in view of a UN resolution condemning the use of force, a UN Peacekeeping Force was put in place and we withdrew. The Prime Minister, Anthony Eden, who was unwell, resigned a few weeks later in January 1957 citing the failure of the Suez offensive as the main reason. For both of the above crises the regiment was on full alert with tanks loaded on trains and fully armed. For three nights during the height of the crisis and in my capacity as the R.E.M.E. wireless operator, I slept in a special room with a coded telephone awaiting instructions as to whether we were going to Budapest or Suez. It was the nearest I got to military action!

My big break came soon afterwards. Quite by chance I happened to come across a notice that the regiment had been invited to produce a team for the Army Ski Championships. I had skied quite a lot by this stage, was reasonably proficient and had competed in a few minor races with a couple of downhill victories. I think there may have been a bit of a stir when I put my name down. This was, after all, only the mid-50s and squaddies weren't expected to be able to ski at that time. However the team was published as Captain (Christopher) Bashford, Lieutenants (Michael) Molloy and (Peter) Hornby and Trooper Johnson. Furthermore it was decided that the team either separately or together should have a month's special training leave before meeting up at Bad Gastein in Austria the following February.

I was due for some leave anyway which meant that I could go home for Christmas before setting off by train to Austria. My parents had started a year or so back to take an extended break in Barbados during the winter and would be leaving early in the New Year so it was lovely to get home to see them. It had been agreed that I would do my ski training separately from the others, which was probably sensible, and that I should arrive in Bad Gastein a week before the Championship races, consisting of downhill, slalom and giant slalom. I selected Zurs, then a small resort, quite high and with very good all-round skiing, as my training centre but I also went to Lech, St Christophe and St Anton. I really loved skiing so took it very seriously, skied hard all day but had a jolly good time too. For a brief period the principal and mainly English girls from a finishing school in Lausanne stayed in the same hotel as me as part of their term's activities. It was all good fun but was not approved of by the principal, particularly on one night when four of the girls tied their bed sheets together and slid down from their first-floor balcony and we were caught in the local nightclub.

Arriving in Bad Gastein, I stayed in a different hotel to the others, the married ones having brought their wives. The strict army discipline had all but disappeared but we kept our distance and I was, in any case, the junior member by reason of age if nothing else. But it is also true to say that I was a considerably better skier than any of them. The regiment had booked a private trainer for us and we had daily morning and afternoon sessions with him. A very pleasant young man, a super and experienced racing skier; it was exhilarating and exciting. It so happened that the downhill course for the army race was the one being prepared for the following year's World Championships and a trial race down the course was due to take place a couple of days before the army race for nominated entrants from all countries, provided that they were sponsored by their National Ski Federations or other recognised bodies. I was informed that the army organisers of our Championships had nominated me for this race, presumably at the suggestion of Chris Bashford, our team captain; I was the only one from the army to be nominated, I might say.

The day before the race we had a final flat-out run down the course led by our trainer with me immediately behind him. I had never been so fast. Three quarters of the way down it all went pear-shaped: I completely misjudged a right turn leading to a control by leaving it too late, left the pisted course into crust and that was that. I broke my right leg very badly below the knee, tibia and fibula in six places. It makes me quite sick to think of it even now – all my hopes of success having gone up in smoke, not that I had any chance of winning the Austrian race but I did think I had a squeak in the army races, particularly the downhill and giant slalom.

The situation wasn't helped when, after I had been strapped into the blood wagon and was on the way down, some lunatic, out of control, cannoned into it and knocked it over. In very considerable pain I was taken to a clinic operated by an elderly Austrian doctor who, after a brief examination, proclaimed that I had 'your leg gebrochen', at which point I complimented him on his powers of observation. At about that time there was, back in Eastbourne, a doctor called John Bodkin Adams who was supplementing his income by hoodwinking elderly ladies into parting with serious sums of money in his favour before helping them on their way to join the Almighty. My man, whose name was Dr Heinzel, approached me, holding aloft a large syringe and, as he was thrusting it into my arm, said 'My name is John Bodkin Adams.'

When I woke up I was in a small room with my right leg in plaster from hip to toe and a large cradle over my lower half to keep the weight of the blankets off my legs. There was another bed in the room which to my immense surprise and considerable delight was occupied by a friend from Cheshire called James

Clegg. I knew him but not terribly well at that time because he was a few years older than me and, at the age of eighteen, a few years make a big difference. James was a most delightful character, maddeningly a natural sportsman and games player; he was in the Eton Cricket XI aged fifteen, an excellent skier, tennis player and golfer without ever seeming to make any effort. He had a wicked sense of humour with a quiet softly spoken voice. Several years later skiing with him in Klosters we were making our way in an unhurried fashion to the cable car at around 10 o'clock in the morning when a rather breathless Englishman rushed up and said: 'Is this the way to the slopes?'

James languidly removed his skis from his shoulders, thought for a moment and said:

'The Slopes, I'm not quite sure but the Evans have taken that chalet up there on the left and may be able to help you.'

James had broken his leg on the same day as me but it was only quite a mild break and he wasn't in too much discomfort, unlike me I'm afraid. He also had a constant stream of visitors, mainly very pretty young ladies, but also a young man who subsequently became a lifelong friend of mine. His name was David Penny, now David Marchwood having inherited the viscountcy on the death of his father in 1979.

David spent most of his working life with Schweppes undertaking overseas stints for them in Canada and in Paris. When he married his wife Tessa, he invited me to be an usher. The day of his wedding coincided with the day a horse which he strongly fancied, and on which he had invested enough money to pay for the honeymoon, was running, the race taking place at the same time as the wedding service. Seated at the back of the church with Harry Beeby, also an usher, we were able to leave by the rear door, sprint across the village green and into the pub to watch the race on television, getting back to the church just in time to greet the bride and groom with the news that the horse had won.

In Dr Heinzel's clinic, in contrast to James, I didn't have many visitors. Actually for the first few days I didn't want any because I was so drugged up with painkillers and pretty drowsy. The others in the team came and were most supportive; they worked wonders by dealing with the regiment back in Munster, with the army authorities and with making arrangements to get me to hospital in England as soon as possible rather than to a British Army hospital in Germany. But I did have a couple of other visitors: staying in the same hotel as me in Bad Gastein were two English girls, both members of the English ski team who were there on the ski racing circuit and competing in the female version of the race I was supposed to take part in. I had skied a bit with them while not on sessions with my team; we had dinner together in the evenings and got on well. Their names were Elspeth Nicoll and Zandra Nowell; Zandra had been a member of the Great Britain Olympic Team in Cortina the previous year and had finished best of the British Ladies in all three events, downhill, giant slalom and slalom. Among her teammates was Noel Harrison, son of Rex Harrison, the well-known actor and film star who played Henry Higgins in *My Fair Lady*. Zandra told me that she lived in Cheshire, not all that far from my own home so we agreed to get in touch in the future.

She and Elspeth very sweetly came to see me, as did another guest in my hotel by the name of Wing Commander Tim Vigors and his first wife, Jan. Tim, a decorated Battle of Britain Spitfire pilot and all round larger-than-life character, was better known in racing circles as a prominent Irish bloodstock agent and racing manager. The story goes that his grandfather, when caught in bed with a maid by his wife, said 'If you are going to appreciate Chateau Lafite, my dear, one must occasionally have a glass of vin ordinaire.' His father had bought a farm in Co. Tipperary called Coolmore which Tim inherited, started to build it up into a stud farm before selling much of it to his friend Vincent O'Brien, Vincent's son-in-law John Magnier and Robert Sangster. Now the whole operation is owned by the Magnier family, being probably the most famous stud farm in the world. I first went to Coolmore in the mid-70s having been invited to lunch by John and Sue Magnier. Driving up the tree-lined drive and approaching the imposing Georgian house, I noticed, partially concealed on the right, what seemed to be a row of very nice cottages. Inside I complimented John on what I took for staff accommodation. 'They're not for staff,' he corrected me, 'Those are the stallion boxes!'

After about a week it was considered that I was fit enough to be flown back to England and here my godmother, Hazel Budgett, came into play. In consultation with my parents in Barbados she got me booked into the London Clinic (where, incidentally, I was born) and under the care of one of the top orthopaedic surgeons, Sir Reginald Watson Jones. Chris Bashford and the team arranged an ambulance to the train station, enough room for me to lie horizontally on the train to Salzburg, another ambulance to the airport, three seats on the British European Airways flight to Heathrow and an ambulance to the London Clinic. It so happened that Tim and Jan Vigors were also travelling to England on the same day so most kindly said that they would look after me. All went well until arriving at Heathrow where no forklift truck was available to lift me down from the plane (there'd been one in Salzburg!). The problem was solved by Tim lifting me bodily down the steps of the plane and into the waiting ambulance. He must have been immensely strong; although I was probably not more than 10½st, the plaster on my leg weighed another stone. Tim and Jan came with me in the ambulance all the way to the Clinic before saying goodbye. I shall never forget how grateful I was to them both.

I spent a month in the Clinic. The Austrian 'John Bodkin Adams' hadn't done a great job setting the leg and it had to be re-broken twice under general anaesthetic to get it straight. Eventually I was allowed to go home but not in great shape; I had lost a lot of weight, was still in plaster from hip to toe and felt very wobbly on my crutches for a while. As I was still in the army, I wrote to my CO in Munster telling him of my situation and received a sympathetic reply virtually saying 'keep us informed,' which I did but I would not be fit for any active duties for the remainder of my period of National Service; I never did go back and eventually received my discharge papers plus, I might add, a 'War Disability Pension'! It wasn't much and after a year or so I received an offer of £150 final payment which I accepted. It was three years, though, before I was fully sound again, part of the problem being that my right knee and ankle had seized up after having been encased in plaster for such a long time.

3

South Africa and
Utopian Southern Rhodesia

But life goes on. My girlfriend, Zandra, came back from her skiing season and immediately embarked on her English activity, playing tennis which she did up to county standard. I started to see quite a bit of her but I had to get round the transport problem, i.e. driving. Me and my Morris Minor solved this in an ingenious but perhaps unorthodox manner: the gearbox housing emerged from the engine compartment and into the body of the car by means of a raised section, at the end of which was the gear lever. I found that I could get into the car, tuck up my good leg and lift manually the useless and plaster-encased right leg, resting my right heel in its plaster on top of the gear housing 'bank'; then I could manoeuvre my left leg under the right in order to operate the clutch and brake pedals. In emergencies if I needed to operate both pedals simultaneously I depressed the clutch to engage neutral and then switched to the brake pedal, using the handbrake in the meantime. This left the matter of the accelerator. In addition to my crutches I carried in the car a thick walking stick with a curved handle and a big rubber stopper on the end. I held it in my right hand to operate the accelerator. After a little practice I grew quite adept at this method and succeeded in driving to London, although it was a bit tricky negotiating Hyde Park Corner. This was well before the days of motorways and the journey from Cheshire to

London took about 4½ hours.

By the time my leg came out of plaster for the last time the summer was nearly over. The leg was matchstick thin with the knee and ankle requiring several weeks' physiotherapy to get them moving again. Any thoughts of riding or any other forms of strenuous exercise were out of the question. Long term the plan was that I should take the family route into the firm of Richard Johnson & Nephew so, looking to the future, my father put forward a splendid idea: that I should travel by ship to Cape Town, visit and spend time with the company's agents in the Cape and then do likewise in the Johannesburg area before going on to Southern Rhodesia (now Zimbabwe) to stay with cousins who had very large farming interests in that country.

The sea voyage to Cape Town, with a brief stop in the Canary Islands was just amazing; I travelled on an old ship of the Holland Africa Line, the *Bloemfontein*, on one of her last voyages as she was so slow and reaching the end of her commercial life. It took three weeks with life on board being pretty carefree and, to me, luxurious. Champagne was six shillings a bottle and gin, whisky etc threepence a tot (23p nowadays, so still cheap), a waterproof canvas swimming pool was rigged up on the deck, two racehorses were being shipped out to Cape Town in loose boxes also constructed on the deck and I won the mixed doubles at padder tennis with a girl called Justine who, unfortunately, was sharing a cabin with her mother or possibly grandmother who kept an eagle eye on her all the time. That I do remember but not a lot more, except that coming into Cape Town harbour at six a.m. with Table Mountain rising behind like a guarding colossus was an awesome and never-to-be-forgotten sight. I had a terrific time in the Cape, staying the first night at the Mount Nelson Hotel and then moving on to stay with the agents of Richard Johnson & Nephew, a charming man called Ray North and his wife, Babs, who lived at Somerset West. I stayed the best part of a week and Ray and I spent much of each day riding in the fabulous countryside. It was the first time I had ridden since my leg came out of plaster so I took it very carefully to start with as it was still pencil thin and very weak. From Cape Town I flew up to Johannesburg but really only for a short stop-over on the way to Salisbury (now Harare), where I was met by Anthony and Alice Browne and driven out to the farm in a large American Buick.

Alice's mother, named Cora, was born in 1870, being the daughter of Charles Graham Persse whose brother Henry Seymour Persse was the father of my grandmother Violet and her brother, also Henry, but known since childhood as Atty. So Cora and my grandmother were first cousins. Both Cora's parents died before she was four years old and for some reason she was largely educated in a convent in Belgium where she learnt to be fluent in French, German and Italian. In 1896 she married a doctor, Charles John Lyons from Ledeston, Co. Westmeath. At the start of the Boer War Charles joined the Royal Army Medical Corps and sailed to South Africa. At the end of the Boer War his wife joined him and they lived the rest of their lives in South Africa but it so happened that when the Great War broke out in 1914 Cora and Alice were in England in order for Alice to be settled in a suitable school. Cora hastened back to South Africa but my grandmother, Violet, her first cousin, was appointed Alice's guardian for the period of the war. Hence Alice spent the next four years at Ashton Hayes in company with Eric (until he left for the war), Bryony and my father, Michael.

Anthony Browne's family came from Northumberland. Anthony had an elder brother, Alexander, the fifth consecutive eldest son of the family to be so named, the family seat being the pre-12th-century Callaly Castle. Hunting was the family passion and Alexander IV (Simon and Anthony's father) was Master of the Percy for a number of years. He was also a keen and competitive cricketer, with teams from private houses competing with one another. In order to win Alexander IV secured the services of George Hirst and Wilfred Rhodes, both of whom played for

Yorkshire and England, enlisting them as 'gardeners' on the estate. Simon and Anthony's mother was born Edith Mary Cookson; she and Alexander IV were married in 1894 but were later divorced with Alexander going off to live and hunt near Pau in south western France. Callaly was handed over to Simon (Alexander V), his father remarried Lady Enid Stanhope with whom he had another son, left France and went to live in Southern Rhodesia where his own mother had married Sir Raleigh Grey following the death of her first husband, Alexander III.

Raleigh Grey was the great grandson of the first Earl Grey, a very distinguished soldier at the time of the Seven Years War, the War of American Independence and the French Revolutionary Wars. His son, Charles, the second Earl, became Prime Minister but he had an illegitimate daughter with Georgiana, Duchess of Devonshire. Raleigh Grey KBE, CMG, CVO, also had a distinguished career in the army first with the 6th Dragoons (Inniskillings), saw service in the Anglo-Zulu War, took part in the Jameson Raid of 1895, after which he was imprisoned for five months, and served in the Boer War. On retiring from the army he remained in Southern Rhodesia developing political, mining and farming interests until returning to England in the late 1920s, where he remained until he died in 1936.

It was a combination of all these South African and Southern Rhodesian interests that drew Anthony Browne, a second son, to Southern Rhodesia and where he met his future wife, Alice. Her father, Charles Lyons, became a specialist in NTE (Non Trauma Emergency) surgery in Johannesburg and Alice, his only child, was born in Jeppestown, in those days an attractive suburb of Johannesburg, in 1903. To me life in Southern Rhodesia at that time was as close to Utopia as I imagined possible. The main farm was at Glendale, about sixty miles north of Salisbury (Harare) along a road tarmacked in the middle but with wide gravel strips on both sides passing through country with soft rolling hills stretching for 360 degrees and to the horizon. Scattered clumps of trees provided shade, cattle grazed and vegetation, either cultivated or natural jungle, was fed by occasional small rivers and streams. Turning off the main road close to Glendale, a gravel road led through the farm and to Anthony and Alice's house, called Ewart House. Single storey with a red roof, not large in the number of rooms but very spacious, the drawing room leading onto a beautiful and well-manicured garden with lawns and beds with all manner of tropical flowers and plants – a profusion of kaleidoscopic colours. I had my own separate accommodation about 50 yards away from the main house consisting of a large and airy bedroom with huge windows and a bathroom. The days started quite early; I was awoken by an African dressed in a white shirt, reddish trousers, wearing a red fez type hat and bringing a large glass of fresh orange juice at five a.m. Breakfast was at 5.30 and by six o'clock it was off to the farm office a few hundred yards away. I was provided with a Peugeot pick-up truck but for the first few days went around with Anthony to get my bearings and some idea of the locations of the different areas of the farm and the crops growing on them. The longer I remained the more I was struck by the complete harmony that existed at all levels. Happy smiling black faces everywhere, I forget how many workers on the farm but several hundred all going about their business in the open and mainly unfenced cultivation areas or in the machine sheds and feeding units for the livestock. It wasn't long before I was entrusted to drive in my Peugeot to different areas bringing machine parts, fertilisers, tools or whatever was needed. Sometimes just to give messages or instructions to foremen passed to me by Anthony or his farm manager. I loved every moment of it. Then there were the visits to Salisbury for Alice to buy food and supplies for the house and Anthony to attend farming meetings and discuss farm machinery requirements with the distributors. In those days Salisbury bore a resemblance to old-fashioned towns in wild west movies. Meikles Hotel was famous even then as THE place where ladies used to meet for morning coffee or tea, either in the garden or in a large conservatory type room suitably furnished with comfortable armchairs or sofas, in front of which elegant tables supported silver trays of coffee or teapots and Spode china cups and saucers brought by uniformed waiters. Behind the sofas and armchairs boys gently waved palm fronds to disturb the air just enough. In another room the menfolk gathered to discuss farming matters and other affairs of state over a cold beer. I was struck, too, by the very feudal nature of the life. Owners of the farms and plantations provided accommodation for their workers by way of houses, meeting halls and games fields; they built schools and arranged for the children to be taught and have lessons; they built churches for the communities and arranged for spiritual education. They looked after them all and, in return the Africans worked happily knowing that as long as they did so, their future was secure. Little did any section of the community know what was to come all too soon.

I remained on the farm for about three months visiting both of Anthony and Alice's two children on their own farms and staying for a few days on each. Well actually the son Nicholas and wife Marguerite farmed a separate section of the main farm but the daughter, Olga, and her husband Alec Kerr had their own farm at Concession about fifteen miles away from Glendale. Here I stayed in their small 'rondavel', a little apart from their house; before going to bed on my first night Alec had warned me to make sure the door was properly shut and locked because where they lived was rather more isolated and jungly than at Glendale and occasionally animals did wander in. I had hardly put my light out when there was a loud knocking on the door. I thought it must have been Alec having forgotten to tell me something so I opened the door to be faced with an enormous animal; it was pitch dark so, terrified, I slammed the door closed and made sure there was no other way this wild beast could gain entry. In the morning I recounted my story and thanked Alec for the animal warning. Both he and Olga fell about laughing: the 'wild animal' was one of their Alsatian dogs allowed to roam around at night and who had come to visit me in the hope of being given something to eat.

In December we set off from Glendale in the Buick to drive to Isipingo near Durban, where Anthony and Alice were to spend Christmas with Alice's mother Cora Lyons, her husband having died some years previously in 1951.

The journey took us south, through Salisbury, on to Fort Victoria (now Masvingo) close to the Great Zimbabwe Ruins which I would visit again with Nicholas Browne some thirty years later and across the Limpopo River which formed a natural border with South Africa at Beitbridge. The whole journey took three days, staying at small 'rondavel' type hotels, the first being not far from Louis Trichardt and close to the scene of my parents' terrible car accident twenty-four years previously. Passing though the eastern Transvaal we continued into Natal and down to Ladysmith, the scene of the famous siege in the Boer War in 1899 which lasted for 118 days until relief came on 28th February 1900, with Winston Churchill being a member of the relief party. From there it was Pietermaritzburg and Durban before arriving in the (then) small seaside town of Isipingo. I stayed about a week at my venerable cousin Cora's house during which Anthony and Alice took me to Durban which had a delightful and old colonial feel to it. We went to the races where I backed a 20 to 1 winner and met Fred Rickaby who was a trainer based in Durban and brother to one of the top jockeys in England then, Bill Rickaby, who won the 1,000 Guineas and Oaks in 1961 on Sweet Solera and the 2,000 Guineas on Privy Councillor in the following year, plus many other big race successes, including landing a huge gamble when winning the Lincolnshire Handicap on Commissar for Arthur Budgett in 1948.

My time was up. I had to go home and get on with life but never will I forget the wonders of Southern Africa – the unbelievable vastness of the scenery, the happy people, the climate and, I suppose, the way of life. But I was still naïve and if there were undercurrents I failed to notice them. It was inspirational.

4

Richard Johnson
& Nephew Ltd

Back for Christmas, it was my father's hope and expectation that I would join the former family-owned company of Richard Johnson & Nephew, wire manufacturers whose head office and main works were in Manchester. However, it was considered that some business experience should be gained elsewhere first and where better to go than the City of London. The company's financial advisors were the merchant banking firm of Lazard Brothers and this firm was persuaded to take me on for a two-year business training and work experience period – but first a little about the family and history of the business.

The original firm of Richard Johnson & Nephew was founded in 1773, the same year as the Boston Tea Party, by one James Howard, a pin maker in Market Street, Manchester. This was before the American War of Independence, while New York was still in the British Empire, and six years before New Zealand was discovered. In those days a journey from Manchester to London in the new 'Flying Coach' took 4½ days, Manchester being described by a visitor as 'the most modest town in respect of expense and pleasure. No playhouse or public gardens, and in their way of living, very moderate.' However, in 1760 a procession of the most affluent traders in the city marched through the streets to celebrate the Coronation of King George III. Manchester was to change with the burgeoning Lancashire cotton and other industries, of which wire drawing was one. James Howard prospered and established a pin and wire drawing factory in the basement of School Mills in Long Millgate. However, education was poor and working conditions appalling.

Abroad, the Fall of the Bastille in 1789 and the French Revolution put much fear into rising capitalist society in Manchester, but gradually, the improvements in the manufacture of iron, greatly helped by James Watt's steam engine, led to an increase in the need for wire, which had been manufactured commercially only in Pittsburgh, Massachusetts since 1775. The business attracted the attention of an ambitious young man called John Johnson, who turned twenty-one at the same time as Nelson's victory at the Battle of Copenhagen in 1801. Soon afterwards James Howard was seeking retirement and John Johnson bought the business. In 1817 he was thirty-seven years old, living in Piccadilly, Manchester with his wife and two sons, Richard and William. His father, also Richard, was a silk and cotton manufacturer and his mother, Elizabeth Heywood, came from York. Under his auspices the business continued to prosper amid substantially increased demand, but also faced considerable competition.

John Johnson was a keen sportsman and racing addict; he was a friend of 'Gentleman Cooper' who, for thirty successive years, walked from Manchester to Doncaster to see the St Leger (first run at Cantley Common, then moved to Town Moor, Doncaster in 1778 for the third running). John Johnson lived into his nineties, dying in 1873, very exceptional for that time, but handed over the running of the business to his sons Richard and William in the 1840s when the firm traded as Richard Johnson & Brother. Clearly staunch royalists, they gave all their workers time off to attend the celebrations of the marriage of Queen Victoria to Prince Albert. John Johnson may have retired, but most mornings he would ride in his carriage to the factory (now in Dale Street), arriving at 12 o'clock, spend 1½ hours castigating any of the eighty workers whom he considered was not working hard enough, before riding home again.

In the late 1830s to early 1840s electric communication advanced from a dream to a reality and the Johnson brothers were not slow to get off the mark, manufacturing copper as well as steel wire, copper being second only to silver as an electrical conductor. In 1850 a communication cable was laid between England and France with most of the steel armouring wire and copper communication wire supplied by Richard Johnson & Brother. The export trade expanded in keeping with home trade and Johnsons supplied the wire for the Niagara Suspension Bridge and later, in 1857, 950 tons for the first transatlantic cable, the first messages being sent by Queen Victoria to President James Buchanan of the USA. An interesting little side story on this: a New York jeweller named Mr Tiffany bought the surplus stock left over from the cable and turned it into souvenir paperweights, umbrella and whip handles, bracelets and the like which the Americans bought in huge quantities.

Both brothers lived well and comfortably in large houses fully staffed with cooks, maids, governesses for the children and gardeners. Richard, however, was quite parsimonious, walking to work each day, saying that he would not ride until he was worth £10,000. William, though a quiet scholarly type, shy and rather inarticulate in public, rode to work on his horse Tarragon. All was going well; they owned two factories not too far from each other plus several houses occupied by their workers. Another factory was constructed in a small village then well separated from Manchester called Bradford (not to be confused with Bradford, Yorkshire). Railway lines were springing up everywhere, many totally impractical, which prompted *Punch* magazine to suggest 'A Great North Pole Railway forming a Junction with the Equinoctial Line with a branch to the Horizon'. Matters changed in 1859 when Richard Johnson suffered a severe mental breakdown, leaving the business in the hands of his brother William and the brilliant Works Manager, George Bedson. However, William died suddenly the following year aged only forty-nine and Bedson – who, brilliant as he was, nevertheless had had an up-and-down relationship with the two brothers – decided to leave, not wishing to shoulder the financial responsibility of the partnership offered to him by Richard Johnson. Rescue, however, was at hand in the shape of old John Johnson's grandson, John Thewlis Johnson, the son of John's youngest son Thomas and his wife Hannah Thewlis. He was my great-grandfather, born in 1836 exactly a hundred years before me.

Thewlis started working for the family firm in 1860 but was not formally made a partner until 1865, from whence the firm was renamed Richard Johnson & Nephew, with George Bedson having been brought back into his old position as Works Manager. He married his wife Amelia on 14th June the same year, his diary entry for the day reads 'Married. To Carlisle 4.45. Staying at Station Hotel.' Very romantic. Climbing Ben Nevis is the most noteworthy diary entry during his honeymoon, but as part of the wedding celebrations he hired a private train to Blackpool for all the firm's employees (now numbering 1,000) to enjoy a day's excursion.

The business continued to prosper both at home and abroad, with Thewlis making several European trips with the times of ships and trains meticulously recorded in his diary. On 1st October 1867 he attended a dinner given by the Liverpool Chamber of Commerce to those involved in the supply and laying of the Atlantic cable. The President of the Board of Trade, Sir Stafford Northcote, presided and among the two hundred guests were the Foreign Secretary, Lord Stanley (the future 5th Earl of Derby) and the American Consul General. Glancing at the menu, it is no surprise that although dinner commenced at 6.30, it did not finish until after midnight. There were fourteen speeches. On 13th June 1869 Thewlis and Amelia embarked on the S.S. *China* for New York, arriving on 22nd June and staying 'at 5th Avenue Hotel. First impressions not favourable owing to gloomy weather.' The trip included inspecting the site of the Hudson suspension bridge, for which Johnson's were supplying the wire, having previously done the same for the 2,252-foot-long Cincinnati bridge. Then up to Niagara Falls via Albany, Syracuse and Rochester. Across Lake Ontario and up the St Lawrence River to Montreal and Quebec; then Boston, back to New York, a side trip south to Philadelphia with business calls at all the above, before spending a few days R & R at Newport, Rhode Island, finally boarding the S.S. *Russia* and arriving in Liverpool on 20th August. Diary entry: 'passage was a quick one but should have done better. Landed & took 11 p.m. train from Lime Street. Arrived Manchester 12.30. Slept at Palatine Hotel. Office and home two p.m.'

Continuing apace, wire was supplied for cables as far afield as the West Indies, Panama and China – Singapore – Carpentaria. On July 20th 1870 my grandfather, Ernest, was born. Diary entry: 'London, returning five p.m. Ernest born 5.20 p.m.' He was Thewlis and Amelia's second son, with Herbert, always known as Bertie, having been born in July 1866. A month later John Thewlis was off to America again, this time to Chicago where he met Abraham Lincoln's son. The following year he was in Moscow which he found 'hot, dusty and full of disagreeable smells'. At a British Association meeting in Brighton he met and spent considerable time with H. M. Stanley, recently returned from having found Dr Livingstone. He seems to have been obsessed with travel and was magnetised by Livingstone's stories and adventures in Africa.

In December 1871 Thewlis writes in his diary: 'Since last Friday the illness of the Prince of Wales has been the absorbing object of interest throughout the country. Today, the 10th anniversary of Prince Albert's death, bulletins give the first indication of hope.' On 27th February 1872 he writes, 'Went to St Paul's for a Thanksgiving Service in commemoration of the recovery of the Prince of Wales. Had a capital position under the Dome … later seeing the illuminations got in a crush on Ludgate Hill.'

Later that year he and Bedson realised that they were fast running out of production space if they wanted to keep pace with the competition, so started to look for further premises. With an eye to the future he considered that it might be advantageous to have a new factory in a different area in order draw labour from a new source, so he and Bedson went to see an old forge with a considerable area of uncultivated and wooded land, including a large house, in the little village of Ambergate, near Belper in Derbyshire. They decided to buy it and build a brand new factory. John Thewlis, his wife and children moved into the house, called Oakhurst, which became home for the rest of his life.

At this time Johnson's had an interest in another local company called The Manchester Screw Company, of which Bedson was General Manager and Thewlis was elected as Chairman. Subsequently the company was sold to Nettlefolds in 1880. Nettlefolds were an old established business manufacturing screws, iron turning, locks and even lawn mowers, but Thewlis continued as a director. In 1900 Nettlefolds 'reluctantly' sold the business to Guest, Keen & Co. for £630,000 and the conglomerate of Guest, Keen, Nettlefold (GKN) was formed. Much later another GKN company, Tinsley Wire, became serious competitors of Richard Johnson & Nephew.

The firm was receiving a very large quantity of business from America and this necessitated Thewlis making another trip in the spring of the following year, when he travelled 16,000 miles in two months visiting existing customers and attracting new ones in New York, Washington (where he saw the White House), Baltimore, Philadelphia, Charleston, New Orleans, St Louis (where he met an inhabitant of that city whom he described as a 'blasphemous infidel'), and San Francisco, returning via

Montreal and Boston to New York and thence home. Quite some feat when one considers that the only mechanised land transport available was the railway.

John Thewlis Johnson led a very hectic and full life. Not only did he travel extensively on business in Europe and America but also enjoyed walking trips to the Alps, covering long distances and usually ending up with a bit of culture and more light-hearted entertainment in places like Florence and Paris. At home he shot grouse in Scotland and pheasant and partridge in England. Not much mention of hunting but he was a keen racing fan and always recorded the results of the Derby, including the time of the winner in his diary, even if he did not go to Epsom. For instance, in 1870 the race was won by Kingcraft in a time of 2.45, owned by Lord Falmouth, trained by Matt Dawson and ridden by Tom French. By way of comparison, a hundred years later in 1970, Nijinsky was the winner in a time of 2.34, owned by Charles Englehard, trained by Vincent O'Brien and ridden by Lester Piggott.

Thewlis took particular note of an article in *The Times* headed: 'The Telegraph at Ascot' which stressed the amount of wire used to transmit information directly from the course to London and Manchester during the four days of the Royal Meeting. He was a member of the Reform Club, lunched with Lord Salisbury, then Secretary of State to the India Office, and showed Henry Bessemer round the Bradford Works during a conference of the Iron and Steel Institute in Manchester. At Oakhurst he employed a butler, footman, a host of other indoor servants and gardeners, his head gardener being one George Holmes who was trained at Chatsworth where his family had worked for generations for the Dukes of Devonshire. Yet it is remarkable, and a tribute to the man himself, the huge number of days where the only comment in his diary is 'Office all day.'

The Ambergate Works was officially opened by Richard Johnson on 22nd May 1876, when he drew the first coil of wire.

Although he was still a partner and took an active interest in the firm, he was now sixty-seven and never fully recovered from his breakdown, so was less heavily involved, spending much time in Italy. He paid his final visit to the Bradford Works on 22nd December 1880 to lay a Memorial Stone for a gigantic chimney of 493,804 bricks to take the place of six smaller chimneys, plus to open a new Public Hall. It was a bitterly cold day with rain turning to sleet and snow; as a result he contracted a severe cold and fever from which he did not recover and died on 16th February 1881. On the day of the funeral the whole firm closed for the day, three hundred wire drawers walked at the head of the cortège, followed by twenty-five carriages, then the hearse, five mourning carriages and five more private carriages. Eight men from the Bradford Works carried the coffin to the family vault. He had worked for the company for fifty years, been President of the Manchester Chamber of Commerce, Justice of the Peace and a Governor of Manchester Grammar School.

His wife, son and daughters had all pre-deceased him and, at the time of his death, we were having a bad time of it abroad: Parnell was stirring up Irish Nationalism, the battle of Isandlwana and the siege of Rorke's Drift happened a few months previously and the army had suffered a defeat at the hands of the Boers at Majuba Hill. In Manchester the American Circus was playing to packed houses and in Cheshire the Empress of Austria went hunting with Sir Watkin Wynn's hounds (now the Wynnstay). This noble lady was the wife of Emperor Franz Josef of Austria who had led his army into battle at Solferino in 1859 against the combined armies of France under Napoleon III and Victor Emmanuel, the first King of Italy, the last time when all the armies were under the command of their respective sovereigns. Keen to escape the formalities of Court in Vienna and inspired by the Prince of Wales during a visit to that city, the Empress embarked on the first of many seasons hunting in England, much of it with the Cheshire. She was out one day when a member of the field overran the hounds, jumped a fence and landed on one of the best bitch hounds, killing her. He was rounded upon by the Master, Captain E. W. Park Yates, and told in the hearing of the Empress that he deserved to be publicly buggered in Tarporley by six Irish navvies. Her companion, for want of a better word, was the celebrated huntsman and Gentleman Rider, Captain 'Bay' Middleton and, when in Cheshire, they used to stay with the Rocksavages at Cholmondeley. Later in her life she suffered the death of her son Rudolf and his mistress in a mysterious murder/suicide in their hunting lodge in Germany and she herself was assassinated by a fanatic while travelling in Geneva in 1898, and it is said that her husband Franz Josef never fully recovered. He died in 1916.

Thewlis had for some time talked to his younger brother, Clarkson, about joining the firm, and after their uncle Richard's death it was agreed between the two of them that Clarkson should join as a partner. Clarkson had been a cotton spinner, was bright, full of ideas and Thewlis wanted him to bring new and innovative incentives to the operations side of the business. Industry was changing, international competition growing and a feeling of complacency was present in the air. Clarkson was just the man – a no-nonsense disciplinarian with zero tolerance of slipshod and lazy tactics. He was needed because, although the firm was continuing to keep its head well above water, there was a general depression in Europe as a whole. Far worse, Thewlis and his two sons suffered a great tragedy when his wife and their mother, Amelia, died suddenly in January 1882. Thewlis was distraught and subsequently furious when he discovered that his solicitor had lost her Will. Several entries in his 1882 diary bear witness to his deep devotion, such as 'today is the 17th anniversary of my wedding day' (14th June), 'Church – no Amelia' (9th July) and 'Church in afternoon. A miserable damp day – a fitting end to the saddest year of my life' (31st December).

Thewlis was back at work immediately in the New Year of

1883 at both works, Bradford (Manchester) and Ambergate and also took part in discussions in London with telegraph engineers at the Board of Trade, but there were signs quite early on that widowhood did not entirely suit him and name of 'Anne Higgins' began to appear quite frequently.

The Manchester family of Higgins were old friends. James Higgins, a machine engineer who in 1851 was employing 622 workers, had a son, Frederick, five years younger than Thewlis and a daughter, Anne, who was born in 1854. Fred was a great friend of Thewlis: he was a cotton spinner in Manchester before becoming Conservative MP for Salford North in 1895. Thewlis records in his diary on 23rd February 1883: 'Anne Higgins promises to be my wife.' They were married on 22nd September and after a couple of days shooting partridges in the early part of the following week, left on a Grand Tour honeymoon starting in Brussels, then on to Cologne and all points east including Munich, Salzburg, Vienna, Bucharest, Buda and Pest (in those days two cities separated by the Danube), thence by the *Orient Express* to Constantinople where they took a caique round the Golden Horn, went up the Galata Tower, went into the Hagia Sophia (then a mosque) and saw the Whirling Dervishes. From there by ship to Athens, spending considerable hours at the Acropolis, Piraeus, Corinth, Corfu and Naples where they went up Mount Vesuvius on the now defunct Thomas Cook cable railway, then to Rome and eventually home via Genoa and Paris. Thewlis was very cross that the 24-hour train journey from Genoa to Paris arrived one hour late. Not a bad little trip, lasting fifty-nine days. Thewlis seems to have kept a side glance on business, attending an Electrical Exhibition in Vienna, meeting the Director of Telegraphs in Athens and a rather strange diary entry on 20th November: 'business at Vatican.'

Thewlis was soon back at work but the next year or so saw not only a regression in trade but also the deaths of family members, including his mother and sister, and also those of senior colleagues in the business, so he was deeply involved in maintaining the position of the firm at the forefront of the industry, to the exclusion of much leisure time. Very much a family man and deeply religious – he went to church every Sunday, sometimes twice – he had decided to send his two sons to different schools, Bertie to Harrow and Ernest to Winchester but now, with his new wife, it didn't take long before a new offspring was on the way and a son, James Gerald, was born on 29th July 1886.

In the previous year the major event in Manchester was the decision to construct the 35½-mile-long and 28-foot-deep Manchester Ship Canal, costing £17,000,000 over the next ten years. One of the main reasons for its construction was that Manchester was losing trade to Liverpool due to heavy railway charges both on imports and exports through Liverpool. Needless to say Liverpool strongly resisted the plan, which was finally sanctioned by Parliament in 1885 at the third attempt. The canal was completed ahead of time in 1894 and Manchester became Britain's third-largest port, handling 18 million tons of goods at its peak in 1958. However, with the advent of much larger ocean-going vessels, the tonnage dwindled to seven million in 2011, but with reorganisation and planning to concentrate on container ships the estimate is that from a present level of 8,000 containers p.a. this will increase to 100,000 by 2030.

By 1887 business had improved, Johnsons had recovered from a ten-week strike when wire drawers had refused a wage reduction when trade was slack, only terminated when strike funds ran out. Thewlis could now spread his wings a bit more. He found the Reform Club an excellent sanctuary to air his views and listen to others in Trade and Industry; he watched the Queen's Diamond Jubilee procession from the Club and arranged for senior Government officials and overseas guests such as the Chinese Ambassador to come to the Manchester Works. On the sporting front he had many days shooting and fishing in Scotland, Yorkshire and Derbyshire. On the golf course it seems he was no expert, recording that he defeated his son Bertie by three shots – 139 to 142 but after only playing thirteen holes. Fishing with Ernest during a trip to Norway, which included crossing into the Arctic Circle, was more successful. In 1889 he attended a Royal Levée at St James's Palace, went to Ascot, saw Lily Langtry in *Cleopatra*, was elected Vice-President of the Manchester Chamber of Commerce and, in May, made another business trip to New York, Pittsburgh and Chicago. In New York Thewlis was photographed by the famous fashionable photographer of the time, Napoleon Sarony, joining the likes of General William T. Sherman, Mark Twain and Oscar Wilde.

Back in England, Clarkson Johnson died aged only forty-eight in March 1890. This was a big loss: Clarkson had achieved all and more of the improvements in efficiency and discipline that Thewlis had engaged him for, all in the comparatively short number of years he had been a partner. Bertie, Thewlis's eldest son, now aged twenty-four, had been with the firm for a year or two and was now made a partner. After Harrow and Oxford Bertie had been gazetted as a Lieutenant into the 3rd/4th Battalion of the Manchester Regiment and had completed his military training in Yorkshire. Around midnight on 2nd December 1890 Thewlis was knocked down by a hansom cab on the corner of St James's Street and Bennet Street in London, resulting in cracked ribs and him feeling 'shaken and stiff'. This did not prevent him from travelling back to Manchester the following afternoon. Whether he had been celebrating or not he does not say, but a few days before the contretemps with the hansom cab, he records 'Anne's second son born 2.45 a.m. with considerable promptitude and very little inconvenience to anyone but herself. Some snow this morning.'

In February 1892 Thewlis followed in the footsteps of his uncle Richard and was elected President of the Manchester Chamber of Commerce, succeeding Mr Henry Lee, the head of the cotton firm Tootal, Broadhurst and Lee and Member of Parliament for Southampton from 1880 to 1885. Thewlis became a JP in Manchester and in the same year saw the consecration of the church at Ambergate that he had built and paid for, the Bishop of Southwell presiding. The church was named St Anne's as a dedication to his wife and contained a memorial window in remembrance of his first wife, Amelia. His attitude to family and workers was the same: stern but fair and always with a human touch. As the wording of his diaries confirms, there was a wicked sense of humour lurking behind the script. Moments such as when Thewlis went to Ascot and bumped into Ernest, who had absconded from Oxford for the day were met with a disapproving raising of eyebrows – implying a reprimand but nothing else. Coincidentally this situation was repeated at Hurst Park racecourse many years later when my father, who was supposed to be at school, spotted his father, Ernest, but knocked his umbrella to the ground and escaped while his father was bending down to pick it up.

In May 1894 Queen Victoria opened the Manchester Ship Canal, but Thewlis did not attend the opening because he and Anne had set off on a five-week tour, first by rail to Naples and thence by ship, with a view of Stromboli on the right, passing through the Straits of Messina and on to Port Said and Cairo, staying at Shepheard's Hotel from where they made a trip to the Pyramids, which surprisingly attracted no diary comment. Next by ship to Jaffa (Tel Aviv) and by train to Jerusalem where they saw the Church of the Holy Sepulchre, the Wailing Wall, Tomb of David, the room of the Last Supper, the Mount of Olives and the Garden of Gethsemane and 'much more in some heat'. As a result the following entry reads: 'Annie in bed all day – fatigued' and so Thewlis went to the Pools of Solomon alone.

The journey home was all by sea on the Orient Line ship *Orova*. This tour, or indeed pilgrimage, must have made a big impression because the next year Thewlis and Anne repeated the general theme, this time taking nine weeks and going down the Nile to Luxor and Aswan with the Pyramids and temples receiving more favourable comment than in the previous year. The return Mediterranean crossing from Cairo to Naples was on the P & O ship *Caledonia* in very fast time, comments Thewlis. He and Anne called at the Pirelli Works in Milan during their rail journey home – in later years RJ&N supplied huge tonnages of wire for the manufacture of motor car tyres. Not long after his return Thewlis enters in his diary: 'When I was a child I was taught that King George III reigned for fifty-nine years, three months and four days. It dawned on me this evening that this is my exact age today.' It was 26th June 1895. Little did he suspect that he had only six months and fifteen days left to live.

Since the death of Clarkson Johnson, Thewlis had been the sole owner of the firm but on 9th February 1895 he writes in his diary: '… signed new Partnership articles with Bertie and Ernest. Had our last grouse for dinner – killed December 8th.' Shortly afterwards he and Anne left on what turned out to be his last major trip abroad, for increasingly, after their return in April, there are many entries concerning his state of health, particularly with breathing, although he continued with an active business life both in Manchester and London. While in London in mid-June on other matters he went to a sale at Christie's, where Gainsborough's portrait of Lady Mulgrave was sold for 10,000 guineas. He does not relate any interest that he might have had. By this time Thewlis's eldest son, Bertie, was taking more of his father's workload, including the American market, and on one of his business trips there he met and fell in love with an American girl called Ethel Alexandra Barnard, to whom he became engaged. In mid-October Thewlis records that 'Mrs & Miss Barnard arrive on the RMS *Lucania*' and came to stay at Broughton House. He does not confide to his diary any opinion of his future daughter-in-law either as to looks or character. He is, however, by this time distinctly unwell and was unable to join other family members who set sail from Liverpool to New York on 30th November. Bertie and Ethel Alexandra were married in Brooklyn on 11th December, the wedding invitations having gone out in the name of the bride's grandparents, Mr and Mrs George W. Alexander.

The newly-weds arrived back in England just before the New Year but Thewlis was sinking fast. His last diary entry was on 9th January 1896 and he died a week later on the 16th. He was only fifty-nine years old but what a life he had packed in. Very much respected in his business and personal life, he was stern but scrupulously fair in all his dealings, did not suffer fools gladly but had a great sense of right and wrong, was generous to a degree with an inbuilt sense of humour, worked, played and travelled hard. He saw a great many changes in his comparatively short life, including much of the Industrial Revolution and the rise of socialism – he abhorred that dogma but understood and sympathised with the causes.

Their father's death at an early age left Bertie and Ernest the owners and managers of a large industrial company, at the ages of twenty-nine and twenty-six respectively. Quite a formidable task, you might think, but Thewlis had not only left the company in good shape with good secondary management but he had done a pretty good job in training up his sons. Clarkson Johnson's son Harold joined the firm, the 20th century dawned, the Boer War was ravaging South Africa and Queen Victoria died but the firm continued to prosper, with Bertie concentrating on the Ambergate Works and Ernest looking after Manchester. The growth of industrial products increased the demand for wire and the company took advantage of the expansion of the electricity market by substantially increasing the manufacture of copper and aluminium wire.

Ernest's eldest son, Eric, was born in 1897 and he, after Winchester and Sandhurst, was commissioned into the 16th Lancers. A daughter, Bryony, was born in 1900 and my father, Michael, in 1904 at Swettenham Hall, near Congleton in

Cheshire. The family remained at Swettenham until 1909 when Ernest first leased and then bought a large Queen Anne house with a substantial amount of land and tenanted farms called Ashton Hayes, about nine miles from Chester. Although he was mildly interested in racing he was never a great enthusiast, hunting and shooting being his main outside interests. He once rode in a point-to-point but was disqualified for missing out several of the obstacles.

His great friend and brother-in-law Atty Persse had moved from Ireland and came to train horses at Chattis Hill, near Stockbridge and hit the headlines big time in 1913 with a grey colt that he had bought for 1,300 guineas at Doncaster yearling sales. Atty's cousin Dermot McCalmont, at that stage a subaltern in the 7th Hussars, returned with his regiment from Afghanistan soon afterwards and enquired from Atty if he had a yearling that might suit him! Named The Tetrarch he was unbeaten in all his starts as a two-year-old including the Woodcote Stakes at Epsom, the Coventry at Ascot, the National Breeders at Sandown and the Champagne at Doncaster. Known as The Spotted Wonder due to many dark splodges on his grey coat, he was by far the greatest racehorse of his era if not of all time. Atty used to say that he would have won anything from five furlongs to five miles and it was a tremendous tragedy when he injured himself at the back end of his two-year-old career. Atty hoped he had recovered after a winter's rest but it was not to be and he went wrong again shortly before the 2,000 Guineas of the following year and never ran again. Dermot himself was no mean performer as a horseman, excelling not only on the hunting field and polo grounds but also as an amateur steeplechase rider winning, among many other good class races, the Grand Military Gold Cup at Sandown in 1909 on Vinegar Hill.

The catalyst to the outbreak of the First World War in 1914, during which 17 million people died, was the assassination of

Archduke Franz Ferdinand, but tensions had been rising between Europe's ruling powers for some time who, for simplicity's sake, can be divided into two main cliques: Great Britain, Russia and France on one side with Germany, Austria/Hungary and Italy on the other. Nevertheless, when war was declared, we, Great Britain, were very underprepared. But perhaps this cannot be said about Bertie and Ernest Johnson for both had taken on military roles in addition to their duties at Richard Johnson & Nephew. Bertie, or to give him his military rank and name Colonel Herbert Johnson, had commanded the 4th Battalion of the Manchester Regiment since 1905 and Ernest was a Major commanding a squadron of the Duke of Lancaster's Yeomanry. Bertie went to France on the outbreak of war, commanding the 17th Manchester Regiment only a year shy of his 50th birthday. He was badly wounded on the Somme and eventually repatriated to England. Ernest went with General Braithwaite's Division of the Yeomanry, leaving Harold Johnson in charge of the firm. Young Eric Johnson, Ernest's eldest son and my uncle, who had lied about his age when joining up, found himself stationed on The Curragh in Ireland in 1916 aged eighteen at the height of the Irish Uprising. In 1917 he went to France and actually rode into battle on his charger. He was wounded twice, the second time, unbeknown to him, at almost the same moment as the armistice was signed. His Record of Service states 'Awarded Military Cross 1918. Lt Eric Seymour Thewlis Johnson, 16th Lancers. For conspicuous gallantry and initiative on 11th November 1918, at Ville Ghislain. When reconnoitring a hostile gun position, he suddenly came on the machine guns covering the battery, he immediately attempted to gallop them, he and all his men being hit.'

When Eric recovered from his wounds he was posted to the Middle East in 1919 where he spent a year in Egypt, Syria and Palestine. Following demobilisation and back in England he joined the business but this was not a success. At least he had a job to go to, but like a lot of young men coming back from the horrors of war he found it impossible to settle down to a business life. Thousands of men suffered a rude awakening on returning to civilian life, finding no jobs, low wages and the dumping of foreign goods at way below domestic prices. Industrial strikes were rife, culminating in the General Strike of 1926 started by the miners who struck over the mine owners' demands for more work for less pay. Other trades came out in sympathy, including workers from rail, bus, electricity, gas, building, printing and steel. *The Flying Scotsman* was derailed in Northumberland. However, volunteers appeared from all over: my father became a train guard. After nine days the TUC called off the strike, but it took many months for normality to be restored, the miners being the last to return to work. Eric Johnson was one of those who sought a better and more energetic life abroad, emigrating to British Columbia, Canada, where he certainly found that in cattle ranching as well as organising local race meetings, where he frequently owned and trained the winners. In 1925 he won the grandly named Quesnel Derby with a horse called Hasten On, the 6/4 favourite; a few days later he won another race with Sleepy Sam, ridden by his younger brother Michael, my father.

Michael had not been sent to Winchester but to Wellington; he was asthmatic and his parents thought that the pine forests round Wellington would be better for his health. He did, however, follow the family tradition by going up to Brasenose, Oxford where he took an honours degree and joined the family business at a salary of £100 p.a., after coming down from the university in 1925. While at Oxford he found time to enjoy the good things in life by going racing, hunting with the Bicester and Old Berks hounds, riding in point-to-points and National Hunt races. In 1925 he won the Oxford University Point-to-Point on his own horse, Prince Consort.

During the war Ashton Hayes was transformed into an Auxiliary Hospital to care for wounded servicemen and women, very capably run and managed by my grandmother, and in 1919 she was awarded an MBE in recognition of her services to the community during the war. Also, in 1919, the directors of Richard Johnson & Nephew took over the pleasure gardens of Belle Vue, Manchester for a Peace and Victory Celebration for the successful conclusion of the war for 2,000 of their workforce. There were speeches of welcome from the Colonel and the Major, in which the workforce was praised for their hard work and contribution to the war effort, followed by athletic races over distances from 60 yards to one mile, high and long jump competitions, tugs of war between the various departments and other events with the prizes presented by my grandmother. A huge tea followed and in the evening a series of Music Hall entertainments took place. The company had been, currently was and continued to be for another fifty years the largest independent manufacturer of ferrous and non-ferrous wire in the United Kingdom. In 1927 Ernest, who had been mulling this over for some time, decided that in order to maintain and increase the firm's share of the market, the time had come to float the company on the stock market. The issue was made, which was heavily oversubscribed and two new outside directors were appointed to the Board, Lt-Gen Sir Walter Campbell KCB, KCMG, DSO and a Mr Trask representing shareholders. General Campbell was gazetted to the Gordon Highlanders and had served with distinction in India and the Boer War; he had taken part in the evacuation of Gallipoli and became Quartermaster General for the Armed Forces before retiring from the army shortly before joining the Board of RJ&N.

After the first Annual General Meeting of the new limited company, Ernest, Violet and their daughter Bryony took an extended trip to South Africa and Southern Rhodesia, spending time in the Cape as well as visiting customers and agents and staying with Violet's cousin Alice Browne and her husband,

Anthony, in the Glendale area north of Salisbury in Southern Rhodesia, where I was to visit some twenty-five years later. Alice's mother, Cora Persse, and my grandmother were first cousins. Ernest had been under a lot of pressure: his brother Bertie (the Colonel) had died suddenly of a heart attack at his home, Allestree Hall in Derbyshire, which naturally had caused him great distress as well as increasing his workload. The floating of the company and the industrial unrest during and after the General Strike had taken its toll of his health and he was badly in need of a complete break and change of air. He returned in October full of vigour, fit and well after a fabulous trip. My father, Michael, was at this time based in the London office for most of the week, frequently coming home to Ashton Hayes on a Thursday evening, spending Friday in Manchester, home for the weekend, hunting or racing on Saturday, Manchester on Monday and back to London in the evening. This suited him well; he could enjoy London life during the week and the country at the weekend. The following February, during a bitterly cold period, Ernest took the chair at a meeting at the local school to be addressed by his friend Col. Roddy Fenwick Palmer, the (subsequently defeated by 1,200 votes) Unionist candidate for the Eddisbury by-election in 1929. Roddy Fenwick Palmer owned Cefn Park, near Wrexham where he trained many successful National Hunt racehorses. A very hard frost that night prevented hunting the next day and Ernest, who had a slight chill anyway, developed a fever which turned to pneumonia. After a worrying few days he appeared to be on the mend and even managed to play golf with my father, who felt it was now safe to return to London. No sooner had he done so than an urgent message called him back to Ashton Hayes where his father had collapsed and died on the evening before the Grand National – as mentioned he had tipped the winner, Shaun Goilin. He was fifty-nine, the same age as his own father John Thewlis had been when he died and two years older than his brother Bertie had been.

Soon after my grandfather died my uncle Eric came back from Canada and Sir Walter Campbell became Chairman of Richard Johnson & Nephew Ltd, the first non-family member to hold that position. The choice of Walter Campbell was a very good one: of the other possible contenders, Harold, Clarkson Johnson's son, who had been left in charge during the war, did not want the job and was not in the best of health, and my father was too young and, as yet, relatively inexperienced. Harold's son Robert – always known as Bobby – had joined the firm some years previously but was primarily involved throughout his long career on the works management side of the business. My father returned to Manchester full time, and he liked and got on with Walter Campbell extremely well.

Eric's return was different. He had been away abroad and living a completely alternative form of life for seven years, and now had to find his feet living at Ashton Hayes, where his mother assumed the matriarchal role and ran the show. It cannot have been easy. Some of his friends suggested that he took up training horses in England as he had been successful in Canada, including his uncle Atty Persse, who we were all brought up to refer to as Uncle Harry. There were plenty of stables and enough parkland at Ashton Hayes to train National Hunt horses to a certain degree of fitness, and the long sandy beaches at Hoylake were within reach to take horses for some fast work on the sands at low tide. He had his own schooling fences and hurdles constructed in the park and so went ahead with the plan. Soon he was sending out a few winners; they were mostly moderate horses and competed in races to suit their ability. My father rode some of them but otherwise it was the likes of George Owen, Gerry Wilson or Edgeley. The horse names that ring bells are Big Black Patch, Fancy Dress and Russian Sentry – particularly the latter who, having won a race at longish odds, was commented on by Clive Graham in the

Daily Express that he couldn't understand why the horse started at such long odds when 'everybody knows how fast a Russian Sentry can run.' But there was a little 'trouble at t'mill'. My grandparents had brought very considerable benefit to the local village of Ashton Hayes; they totally refurbished the church and built on a large side chapel, they bought a one-acre plot of land next to the church on which they had constructed a Village Hall for the use of the community and had provided the land for a cricket ground and built a pavilion in the park among other things. My grandfather had been Patron of the Living at Ashton and, following his death, my grandmother had taken on the role. Church for the family on Sundays and Holy Days was de rigueur. It so happened that one Boxing Day Eric had a couple of fancied horses due to run at Wolverhampton and naturally he wanted to breeze them up a couple of furlongs the previous day – Christmas Day. Feigning a cold he managed to escape church but due to one of the horses being somewhat fractious, and having misjudged the length of the sermon, the returning church cortège, with my grandmother in the leading car, was seen making its steady way up the drive just as the horses were pulling up and in plain view. Eric was in his mid-thirties and with an MC to his name, but it wasn't a happy Christmas lunch.

Back in Manchester, after 150 years of mainly excellent industrial relations between management and the workforce, problems broke out in 1934 due to redundancies caused by improvements in machine efficiencies, resulting in over-manning. A long strike of some 300 to 400 men occurred in some sections of the Manchester Works but General Campbell was just the man for the job, advised and assisted by my father with the help of the Lord Mayor of Manchester as an intermediary; he, as a very young man, had worked for Richard Johnson & Nephew. The strike was well documented by the Communist newspaper the *Daily Worker,* including minutes of a meeting agreed by all participants as confidential but leaked by one of them, Mr Seed, the local union secretary. The strike was eventually called off after the union lost a High Court case against the company, with costs awarded against the union – which were never paid.

While my parents were away in South Africa on their honeymoon my grandmother had been scouting around for a possible house for them and had come across an old Cheshire farmhouse and buildings called Sculshaw Lodge, with just over 50 acres of land, deep in the country, midway between Northwich and Knutsford and about twenty miles away from Ashton Hayes. My parents went to see it as soon as they could, loved it and bought it. It needed a lot of attention but this is where I started this story – it would become my home for the first twenty-two years of my life. But I'm jumping the gun – I wasn't even born yet!

My mother needed a lot more surgical treatment on her facial injuries on her return from South Africa and became an early patient of two doctors, Archibald McIndoe and Harold Gillies, both later knighted for their brilliant facial reconstruction of badly wounded soldiers, sailors and airmen in the Second World War. Having fully recovered she and my father were off on their travels again in August 1935, this time the main destination being New Zealand where, at that time, huge tonnages of Johnson's fencing wire was exported. They sailed from Liverpool, seen off by my grandmother Violet and Eric. Violet insisted on coming to my parents' cabin on the RMS *Laconia* to say prayers for their safe journey, thrusting religious pamphlets into my mother's hands while 'Eric stood by and smoked his cigar.' During the war the *Laconia* was torpedoed and sunk by a German U-boat in September 1942 with the loss of 1,649 lives. They disembarked in Boston and travelled by train to New York. It was my mother's first visit so they did the round of sites for a couple of days including going to a revue on Broadway which, according to my mother, would not have got past the Lord Chamberlain in London. In New York it was very hot but my mother reported that 'the restaurants and theatres are air cooled in some sort of way.' From New York to Niagara Falls and on to Chicago where, to my mother's disappointment, they failed to see a gangster, only 'policemen bristling with bullets, revolvers and truncheons and a few smashed windows'. Then two days in a train to the Grand Canyon, magnificent and probably not much changed today. Another train to San Francisco and by ship to Los Angeles, including Hollywood but no film stars, Honolulu apparently lovely and unspoilt, Pago Pago (American Samoa) where the sanitary arrangements were 'privys' on piers jutting out into the sea, to Fiji where there was a bit of wire business to be done and their final destination, the Grand Hotel, Auckland – 'cold, wet, windy and horrid'.

Actually they subsequently had a very good and profitable journey throughout the whole of New Zealand, travelling mostly by car. At one place they visited they went swimming in a river; my mother had red painted toenails and, sitting on an overhanging rock, she dipped her foot in the water to test the temperature; her whole foot was taken by a huge conga eel. Screaming, she waved her leg frantically in the air; gradually the eel was forced to let go, taking much of her foot's surface skin with it. My poor mother was very frightened but luckily no serious damage was done.

The company's New Zealand agents were a firm called Joseph Nathan & Co, owned and run by two brothers, Charles and Phil Nathan, both tremendous Anglophiles, great salesmen and fiercely loyal. Like a lot of Jews they had an excellent sense of humour: Charles Nathan happened to be with my parents in Dunedin when the news came through of the death of King George V on January 20th 1936. Memorial services were held throughout New Zealand but there was no synagogue anywhere near for Charles; as he explained later in the day, 'I came to your church but it was standing room only so I went and joined the Roman Catholics instead.' From New Zealand they went on to tour round much of Australia including Sydney, Melbourne and

Brisbane, but here business was drying up owing to the rise in the ability of Australia to produce its own steel and low carbon wire, such as for fencing, by Broken Hill Pty. The return journey was the completion of a circumnavigation of the world via Java, Bali, the Red Sea, Suez Canal, Port Said and the Mediterranean. I've sometimes wondered if my being conceived at sea, which seems the most likely probability, is the reason for my lifelong love of travel and adventure.

Sir Walter Campbell died in August 1936. He had been Chairman of RJ&N for six years and had given great service to the company in terms of leadership and very sound experienced advice. He had also provided another service of great value in that, without being in any way condescending, he had filled a very necessary gap after the early death of my grandfather and before my father was ready enough to take over as Chairman, which he now was and did at a time of considerable problems in the steel industry due to demand for steel products overtaking supply capabilities. My father became Chairman of a committee of British wire manufacturers to structure a quota of steel from European suppliers to satisfy the temporary shortfall in home production. Having missed a whole winter racing season while he was in New Zealand and Australia, he made up for lost time in as much spare time as was possible. At Sculshaw Lodge he laid out a grass gallop round the perimeter of his land and installed a row of schooling fences in order to train as well as ride a few horses of his own. In this hobby he received a great deal of supporting feedback from the workforce at both the Manchester and Ambergate Works who admired the bravery and sporting nature of their boss, regarding him as a bit of a hero even though very few of them saw much of him personally. I was born in December 1936 and a few days later my father rode a winner at Chepstow for the Epsom trainer Jack Pendarves. Congratulated with Pendarves by Clive Graham after the race on the 'double' of riding a winner and having a son, he was asked if he thought the boy might make a jockey one day. 'No,' he replied, 'he makes such a noise, we're going to set him up as a bookmaker.' In the spring of 1938 the brilliant Irish steeplechaser Royal Danielli was sent over from Ireland for the Grand National and completed his final training on the gallops at Ashton Hayes only to be beaten a short head by the tiny horse Battleship at 40/1 ridden by the seventeen-year-old Bruce Hobbs, who went on to be a most successful flat race trainer in Newmarket.

Following the depression of the early 30s and the subsequent industrial unrest, business and trade had picked up considerably during 1936 and 1937 so that at the AGM in 1938 the company was able to record a profit of £76,356, which could have been a lot more had the steel been available on the home market. Nevertheless this figure is the equivalent of £3,593,277 today. But the war clouds were looming and once again we were caught napping. The Munich Agreement came and went and it was noticeable how aloof and offhand the German representatives had become at international meetings. Leading up to the outbreak of war in 1939 my father had many meetings with the War Office because it was clear that much of the production at both Manchester and Ambergate would need to be switched to wire needed for the Armed Forces and away from such things as mattress and furnishing springs, countless household items and even clothing – ladies how do you think your bras remain so firm? Rationing was introduced for food, petrol and clothing and here's a funny little story: exemptions for clothes rationing were made for workers involved with the manufacture of goods needed for the war effort, and these included wire drawers in Manchester and Ambergate. The operator of a wire drawing machine is known as a 'wire drawer', but the application for exemption of clothes rationing for such people was refused by the War Office on the grounds that machine operators were unlikely to wear 'wire drawers'.

Petrol rationing was very strict and exemptions difficult to obtain. My father's big car, a large and powerful Ford, was put up on chocks for the duration of the war and instead of using the lawn mower he bought a flock of geese to keep the grass down; they made a terrible mess, a hideous noise and scared the living daylights out of me. Only car side lights or heavily hooded dipped headlights were allowed at night, all road sign posts were removed to confuse the enemy and blinds or curtains had to be drawn over windows at night. At Old Trafford the cricket ground was grazed by a flock of sheep. My parents bought a tandem which they used to visit friends which created a source of some discontent for both of them but great amusement for others. Both Manchester and Ambergate Works raised their own Home Guard detachments, in which my father and Bobby Johnson, who had been made a director on the retirement of his father Harold, served. The Johnson Home Guard provided the Battalion HQ where arms drill was carried out and a rifle range constructed in one of the warehouses, although some of the weaponry might not have been much use against the Panzer Divisions. At weekends the two detachments met up for training exercises alongside regular soldiers on the Lancashire Moors and Derbyshire Hills. The company also had its own fire brigade and ambulance service.

The importance of the wire industry in support of the war effort cannot be stressed too highly. The list is endless but it stretched from all kinds of steel hawsers for ships, barrage balloons, mine moorings and boom defences to flail chains for tanks and heavy duty recovery vehicles, springs for all manner of weapons, mines and grenades, wire for anti-submarine netting, track laying and temporary airstrips and so many more. For instance a Sten gun needed welding wire for the fabrication of the various parts, and most of the mechanism including the return was made from wire. And that's only for steel wire; for non-ferrous, i.e. copper, anything electrical needed wire in its fabrication, on land or sea and in the air. A major project in which the company was heavily involved was operation P.L.U.T.O., which stood for Pipeline Under The Ocean. This was a pipeline, actually a series of pipelines, laid on the bottom of the English Channel to pump petrol to our troops in Normandy after the D-Day landings. In all about 5,000 tons of wire was used to armour these flexible pipes. It should be noted that prices for all steel products manufactured for the Armed Forces during the war years were controlled by the Iron and Steel Control and quite rightly so. There was, therefore, no possibility of profiteering from the war. Indeed the reverse was the case as far as Johnson's was concerned.

At the post-war General Election in 1945, Labour, led by Clement Attlee, swept to power with a landslide victory, with Winston Churchill being unceremoniously dumped out of office. Labour, pushed by their left wing, demanded nationalisation of the core of British industries – coal mines, railways, electricity, shipbuilding and steel. Johnson's were not steelmakers but without going into too many technicalities they were on the list of firms to be nationalised in that the products the firm bought from the steelmakers were known as billets – 28–30 feet lengths, 2.5 inches square. The first operation was to hot roll the billets in a rolling mill to produce what were known as rods – large coils of circular steel. As can be imagined the rod mill was an enormous piece of kit with a gigantic furnace holding several hundred tons of billets at a time operating twenty-four hours a day, seven days a week. Suppliers of rods were to be nationalised as set out by George Strauss, the Minister of Supply, in his Iron and Steel Bill. My father, who was on the Executive Committee of the Iron and Steel Federation, got to work with the aid of Sir Andrew Duncan, a man with a wealth of experience in industry and who had been President of the Board of Trade during the war and also with Sir Robert Shone, a senior member of the Federation. Our view was that, first, 90 per cent of the rods that we produced were for our own consumption for the onward production of wire of all kinds and second, that our financial turnover in steel was less than our turnover in non-ferrous products i.e. copper and aluminium. This was because the basic cost of copper was much higher than steel. Our actual ferrous (steel) tonnage produced was far higher than copper and aluminium. For quite a while it didn't look at all promising, however strong our case looked on paper, but on the 15th November 1948 my father was in the House of Commons listening to the debate. We were excluded from the Nationalisation Bill. A week later my father was in hospital, paralysed with a broken neck after his fall. During all the long periods that he was in hospital he was most ably assisted by his right-hand man on commercial and administrative matters, Reginald Hardie, who had been Company Secretary for many years before coming on the main board in 1955. Hardie, a Lancastrian, was a softly spoken, quite private man but with a twinkling sense of humour and the ability to grasp important matters extremely quickly. Not a leader of men but a brilliant quartermaster.

On the outbreak of war my uncle Eric packed up his stables at Ashton Hayes and rejoined the army, serving with the 51st Training Regiment, Royal Armoured Corps and at the RAC depot. At the end of the war he went into politics and stood, unsuccessfully, as a Liberal candidate for the Lancashire constituency of Droylesdon in the 1945 Election. By the time of the 1951 General Election he had joined the ranks of the Conservatives and won the Manchester constituency of Blackley from the incumbent Labour member, Jack Diamond, with a majority of 2,272. He proved to be a very good and well-respected backbench MP, very popular in his mainly urban and working class constituency, always well dressed and smoking a large cigar. He could talk to his constituents from whatever party in language they could understand and took great care to deal with their problems. In the House he paid particular attention to the war wounded and limbless ex-service men and women and played an active role with the Charity BLESMA (British Limbless Ex-Servicemen's Association). He eventually lost his seat in the 1964 Election to Paul Rose (Labour) by 1,222 votes. Eric never married; he had a number of lady friends but the ones he produced at Ashton Hayes were pronounced unsuitable by my grandmother. My father told me there was one quite longstanding lady called June, an actress, whom I believe he met but she was never shown to the rest of the family.

In London Eric lived in his own rooms in the Cavalry (now the Cavalry and Guards) Club at the top end of Piccadilly, close to Apsley House, the London home of the first Duke of Wellington from where the Duke used to ride his horse to the Houses of Parliament when he was Prime Minister. He developed a keen interest in greyhound racing, owning a number of dogs that raced at White City. In his later years he suffered badly from arthritis and became very lame; he, often accompanied by a retired and eccentric Brigadier cousin, John Bourke, used to set off from London during the late summer in his very large and powerful Mercedes Benz 600 and drive to an Austrian mountain resort to bask in the healing thermal waters. John Bourke lived a bachelor life in a hotel in Fleet, Hampshire rather like the Major in *Fawlty Towers*. Eric died on 22nd July 1978 quite suddenly in his rooms at the Cavalry Club on a day when one of his greyhounds won an important race at the White City at long odds. In the words of his obituary in the 16th Lancers Regimental Magazine, 'he would have been there to see had not death intervened.'

In my mid-teens I started to go to more formal and grown-up lunches and dinners with my parents to Ashton Hayes. It was another world. I learnt some time later that it was my father who had to handle the family finances. Eric, being the eldest son, should have done but didn't; having been scolded over his Christmas Day crime and various other misdemeanours he took the easy way out, burying himself in politics, his old regiment and the Cavalry Club. Bryony was useless and expected everything to be done for her, and so it was left to the youngest son, my father, who was also Chairman and Managing Director of a large public company with many very serious responsibilities to try to control over-expenditure and all matters related. Sure, I knew my grandmother but was always in awe of her. She used to write to me at school occasionally; one such letter she wrote clearly in the wake of some financial disagreement with my father: 'Your father,' she wrote, 'had a horse running last week. I don't know what its name is but I looked in the paper and it was last.'

The approach to Ashton Hayes was via a half-mile drive, at the entrance to which was a very elegant carved wooden gate and a lodge. The gate was always closed: the sole job of the retired occupant of the lodge was to open the gate for all visitors and close it behind them. In order to alert the occupant that he was required to perform his duties, the instructions were to blow one's horn. On no account was one to dismount from one's car and open the gate. The same procedure in reverse was to be followed on departure. On arrival at the main door of the house, a footman emerged to open the car doors and escort the arriving party into the large stone-floored hall. A butler in white tie and tails served drinks in the drawing room, approached up an immensely wide mahogany staircase and along a wide circular corridor. During either lunch or dinner, he and two footmen served the various courses and remained standing throughout just in case a napkin were dropped or anything else required their attention. There was a seventeen-acre garden and my grandmother had probably the best herd of Ayrshire cattle in the north of England which won all the prizes but failed to pay the bills.

Towards the end of her life my grandmother fell and broke her hip, following which she drove herself at alarming speeds round the steep gradients of the garden in an electrically pro-pelled three-wheeled conveyance. Following her death in 1968 two in-hand farms were sold, leaving one tenanted farm and the Home Farm consisting entirely of two park areas, known as the Top and Bottom, each with separate drives to the centrally placed house. Later, with Bryony as the only full-time occupant, and with Eric there for some weekends only, the decision was taken to pull down Ashton Hayes owing to the enormous cost of maintaining such a property. It was very large with, for instance, 80 yards of stone passages on the ground floor. Nowadays it wouldn't be allowed but then there were no such restrictions and a number of uneconomical country houses suffered the same fate. In its place was built a quite small house using as much as possible of the original building materials and some of its features but, to my mind, it was of an unimaginative design and disappointing.

I've not written much about my aunt Bryony, born in 1900 and the middle of three children born to my grandparents. I've also seen the word 'bryony' described in a horticultural magazine as 'a climbing Irish weed'. That's being a little unfair to my aunt who, if for no other reasons than her distinctly plain looks and short-sightedness, deserved a more attractive name. She had a very highly cultivated sense of humour and could, when on her best form, be most entertaining and good company. But she had an unattractive and haughty manner that she inherited and developed by having spent almost all her life in company with her mother, but without the latter's charm to get away with it.

Once, while still at school, I was browsing through a second-hand bookshop and came across a publication called *A Glossary of Cheshire Slang*. I bought it for 10 shillings and gave it to my father for his birthday. He was delighted with it and, thumbing through the pages, came upon the word 'mulligrubs'. Evidently, if you have 'the mulligrubs', you are 'of perpetual ill humour'. My aunt Bryony was known as Mulligrubs for the rest of her life. The poor thing never married; the one chance she had ended sadly: in the 30s she had become engaged to an officer in the Indian Army who, shortly after the engagement was announced, chose to dive into a swimming pool which, sadly, was devoid of water at the time. The 'new' Ashton Hayes became known as Mulligrubs Hall.

5

A Proper Job

Right, I am back from South Africa and am about to start work at Lazard Brothers in early 1958. My leg was 85 per cent OK but such sporting activities as serious riding and skiing were still out; the bones had knitted well but there were problems in getting flexibility in the knee and ankle joints, having spent six months in plaster. I had a number of contacts in London but no special friends but managed to find 'digs' consisting of a small bedroom with a cupboard and washbasin on the top floor of No. 21 Lowndes Street. There were two other bedrooms on the floor and a shared bathroom and loo. I paid £5 per week. Parking meters had not been invented so I could park my car – still the same Morris Minor – outside and walk to either Knightsbridge or Sloane Square tube station taking the sixpenny fare to Bank station. To fill up my car with petrol cost £1. Lazards paid me £400 p.a. Dress was formal – dark suit, black shoes, sober shirt, socks and tie. One wore a bowler hat and carried a furled umbrella. The staff entrance was down an alleyway off No. 11 Old Broad Street. Lunch was provided in the form of Luncheon Vouchers with a value of 3/6 (three shillings and sixpence or 17 new pennies to the nearest penny) which could be exchanged at some of the local restaurants. Most other firms gave luncheon vouchers only to the value of three shillings.

Lazards, I have to admit, did not fill me with intense excitement. The people at all levels were extremely considerate, helpful and kind. The working hours, too, were not over taxing: arrive

9.30 in the morning and leave at five o'clock in the afternoon plus one in three Saturday mornings. I was shifted around from department to department spending a few months in each, but it dawned on me before very long, as I am sure it did on my superiors, that I was not cut out to be a banker; unlike a young man with whom I founded an as-yet unbroken lifetime friendship called Michael Kelton. He was everything I wasn't, spending his entire working life in the City, first rising to be head of the Private Clients department at Lazards before moving on to be a senior partner in a stockbroking firm. An excellent shot and fisherman and an enthusiastic golfer but not a horseman, whereas I have never fished, am an appalling golfer and never shot until I gave up the horse. It took me, I suppose, about a week and among my perambulations in the immediate locality to discover, that midway down Throgmorton Street and on the right-hand side, there was a covered walkway called Warnford Court with offices on either side. On the entrance door to one of these offices was written, rather inconspicuously, Ladbroke & Co. I pushed it open and entered a world a touch more familiar: there were two rooms, one contained a desk behind which sat a most congenial man called Driscoll; this room led into another larger room in which there were several armchairs, even a sofa or two, a ticker tape machine, a couple of small tables on which the *Sporting Life*, *Sporting Chronicle*, racing form books plus *The Times* and *Telegraph* lay. A television was mounted in one corner and there was an audio-enhanced 'blower' telephone which fed all betting information and race commentaries from all the main meetings of the day. If you wanted to have a bet, you simply wrote it on one of the pads of paper dotted around and gave it to Driscoll (Dris as he was known) for him to relay to Head Office. The official Gaming Act legalising off-course betting did not come into force in England, Wales and Scotland until 1960, although there were betting shops in Ireland some years before that. How Ladbrokes got round this law I have no idea but it had very much a club atmosphere. I was by far the youngest regular so nobody took any notice of me and I hardly spoke, but people like Stephen Raphael and Philip Kindersley, the father of Gay who features strongly later in this narrative, were regular attendees. Philip Kindersley's cousin, Lord Kindersley, was Chairman of Lazards at the time and his son Hugo, to whom I was introduced, later succeeded his father and became a director and Vice Chairman. If I ran fast I could cover the distance between Lazards' office and Ladbrokes, in about 50 seconds or about as long as a horse takes to cover the straight five furlongs at Epsom.

Socially, London can be a lonely city if one doesn't have many already established friends, which I didn't, so it took a little while to find my feet until I met up with the likes of David Penny (Marchwood) and his equally delightful but totally different younger brother Ricky, Harry Beeby, son of the successful National Hunt trainer George Beeby for whom my mentor George Owen rode a Cheltenham Gold Cup winner and my new work friend at Lazards, Michael Kelton. David Penny had a long and successful career with Schweppes until, on the death of his father and having inherited the title, he moved to Moët & Chandon as Managing Director, subsequently Chairman of their UK company. He most kindly invited me many years later for a weekend at the Moët Chateau in Epernay where we drank copious amounts of superb Champagne including the last of the vintage specially made for the Queen's Silver Jubilee in 1977. The weekend culminated in spending the afternoon in the Moët box at Longchamps for the Prix de l'Arc de Triomphe. Ricky, on the other hand, did not take kindly to employment: never without a carnation in his buttonhole, he was a Deb's delight, went to all the parties, and enjoyed life. His enjoyment was infectious to all who knew him. Going into the old Four Hundred night-club off Leicester Square with either of the Penny bros, the band would break off from whatever they were playing and strike up *Pennies from Heaven*. Ricky married Vanessa, a lovely lady who was a highly successful businesswoman, made enormous sums of money and was therefore able to keep Ricky in the style to which he had always been accustomed. It was a great tragedy when he died of cancer far too young.

Some of the top restaurants and cabaret spots in London, keen to attract younger clientele, gave special rates to those under twenty-five. The Café de Paris was one; if you were a member of their Guinea Pig Club – at no cost – you and your lady friend could have a wonderful dinner including a fabulous cabaret for a guinea (£1.05). I saw Marlene Dietrich, introduced by Noël Coward and a marvellous comedy cabaret by Robert Morley. Another was the Allegro Room at Quaglino's, off Jermyn Street. Here, a regular cabaret artist was the legendary Hutch, a black singer/pianist who sang romantic and frequently risqué songs. Noel Harrison, son of Rex who was in the same Olympic ski team as Zandra at Cortina in 1956, also used to perform at the Allegro. Evenings often used to start by meeting up with friends at the old Berkeley Hotel in Piccadilly where Bobby Harvey was the resident pianist in the cocktail bar.

I used to go home to Cheshire quite a lot at weekends. Zandra's parents had a holiday house in a rather bleak and unattractive seaside village in Anglesey called Rhosneigr to which they decamped during the summer months; sometimes I used to go up there by train from Euston to Holyhead on Friday evening, returning on the night sleeper on Sundays. The weather was usually pretty awful but we had a lot of fun messing about in boats among a congenial group of young and trying the new craze of water skiing at which both Zandra and I became quite good.

Zandra and I were married in Cheshire on a lovely summer's day in early July 1959. It was quite a big wedding; by that time I had made a number of good new friends in London and we both had a lot of friends in Cheshire. Charles Weatherby was my best man; he and I had been friends for a long time and his father and mother, Bill and Rose Weatherby, were great friends of my parents, always coming to stay at Sculshaw for the Grand National. Charles was soon to become engaged to and later married a second cousin of mine, Susie Lee.

The firm of Weatherbys descended from a Northumbrian lawyer, James Weatherby, being appointed by the Jockey Club as secretary and stake holder in 1770 – roughly the same time as the founding of Richard Johnson & Nephew. Since that time the business has been continued by the family as the administrators of racing under the auspices of the Jockey Club, although in recent times the Jockey Club adopts a more monarchist role with the many-sided business sections being run by separate bodies. But still Weatherbys handle such as racing entries, the collection of entry fees, the distribution of prize money, licences to trainers, jockeys, stable staff, registration of racing colours and all manner of other aspects of the sport. For instance, an owner coming into racing opens an account with Weatherbys' banking section from which entry and jockeys fees are debited and prize money (if any!) credited. Weatherbys remain an integral part of racing.

We spent our honeymoon in Tenerife, Canary Islands, at that time only just becoming known as a holiday destination; in fact our hotel was barely finished. The weather was awful with a lot of rain while England was in the midst of a heatwave, there wasn't a lot to do so it wasn't much fun and we were quite happy to come home. A couple of months earlier I had moved out of my digs in Lowndes Street into a one-bedroom flat on the ground floor of 33 Tedworth Square SW3. A step up the ladder you might think; well in a way, it was: it cost me £8 per week. There were the odd disadvantages: for instance the drawing room was separated from the rest of the accommodation by what was known as 'the common parts', being a hall immediately on the inside of the front door from the square leading to a staircase to upstairs flats and a corridor to another one on the ground floor; the bathroom was a semi-partitioned area off the kitchen with a basin, bath and loo. Otherwise it was fine and this was where us honeymooners returned.

My two-year stint at Lazards ended at the close of 1959 with the most surprising and generous gift of a silver cigarette case, so it was goodbye to London and back up to life in Cheshire and the advent of work in Manchester with the firm of Richard Johnson & Nephew. Before that, however, we took an extended skiing holiday, the leg being perfectly mended and functioning properly again. Starting off in Megève to stay for a few days with French friends of Zandra's then on to Verbier followed by St Moritz; I always enjoyed skiing in St Moritz for two reasons: first the skiing is very good and, second, it is not overcrowded, with so many hotel beds occupied by non-skiers. Finally to Klosters, one of my very top Alpine skiing resorts.

Now it was back to Cheshire and to work in Manchester. It was, as my father used to say, a 'Proper Job'. Training racehorses, for instance, would not qualify as such. Although I had a lot of childhood friends in Cheshire, I had not really lived there since leaving school, getting on for five years previously after going to Ireland, then the army, then the South African trip and straight to London, so there was a fair amount of catching up to be done. I rented a cottage with the grand-sounding name of Glen Royal, for which I paid £150 per year, belonging to a very good friend called Gordon Fergusson who lived near Tarporley in a house with a lot of land but not much money.

The story is that Gordon's father, Jock Fergusson, who my father knew well, was a perfectly competent racehorse trainer but Mrs Fergusson, Violet, was rather more socially ambitious and formed an attachment with, among others, Col. William Hall Walker, subsequently the first (and last) Baron Wavertree, from a wealthy Scottish brewing family. Hall Walker was a keen polo player but his main passion was breeding and owning race-horses. His horse The Soarer won the 1896 Grand National and he bred Minoru, the Derby winner in 1906 and Prince Palatine who won the St Leger in 1912. Perhaps more importantly, he bought land and built up a very successful stud farm near Tully, Co. Kildare with the idea of establishing a British National Stud. In 1943 the Irish Government bought the whole property and it is now the Irish National Stud, at just under a thousand acres. When my great uncle, Atty Persse, first came over to England it was in the capacity of private trainer to Hall Walker at Russley, near Lambourn. Hall Walker also owned land and stables near Liverpool and became Conservative MP for Widnes in 1900. He was elevated to the peerage in 1919, taking the name of Wavertree which has Liverpool connections. He was known colloquially as 'Daft Old Waveybugs', not without reason as we shall see. Jock Fergusson trained National Hunt horses for him at Sandy Brow, near Tarporley which was owned by Wavertree. When he died in 1933 he left Sandy Brow house, stables, buildings and land in Trust to Violet Fergusson's male heir and his first male descendant in perpetuity, having no legitimate children of his own. Gordon himself, the product of his mother's affair with Wavertree, after coming down from Oxford joined the army and became ADC to the Governor of Gibraltar, where he met and subsequently married Marie-Lou Gaggero of the well-known Gibraltarian family who owned the Rock Hotel and much more besides.

I joined the firm of Richard Johnson & Nephew Ltd in March 1960 as a management trainee and spent several months working in the various commercial departments learning how they functioned, getting to know my colleagues, learning about the company's customers and the huge spread of industries in which they operated, from agricultural fencing to electrical fuse wire. I spent time on the factory floor with the managers, charge hands and machine operators learning as much as possible about the physical side and chemical make-up of wire production. As time went by I started to visit customers with the manager of the relevant department and to look after customers who came to visit the works to see how their wire was produced and to outline their requirements. Competition was intense; we held a large share of the market in all fields but others were always knocking on the doors of customers to increase their own share. Generally speaking there were two levels of competition: first, those companies which took regular tonnages of wire for, say, bed springs, fencing, cables, bicycle spokes, railway sleepers and many more and, second, for construction companies competing themselves for a major contract such as a power station, major building project or suspension bridge. For these jobs they needed a specific, and usually very large, tonnage of wire which they put out to tender to the major producers such as Rylands (subsidiary of Lancashire Steel), British Ropes, Tinsley Wire Industries (subsidiary of Guest Keen & Nettlefolds) and ourselves. Here, reliability, quality and service were at least as important as price. It was exciting work, plenty of variety, never dull and I met many very interesting people among customers and competitors. I have mentioned earlier that we had another large factory at Ambergate, near Belper in Derbyshire, where I used to go quite often for meetings with customers and with the splendid Works Manager, a man called Frank Wood who spent his entire working life at Ambergate, from when he was fourteen until he retired.

Now, the local MP for Belper was George Brown, who served as Deputy Leader of the Labour Party and held various Cabinet posts including Foreign Secretary in the 1960s and who, at various times such as those leading up to General Elections, used to request coming to the works to make a speech. It was part of my job to go to Ambergate to meet George Brown, introduce him to the workforce and entertain him to lunch afterwards in the managers' dining room. At that time, there was a strong wish by the Labour Government to renationalise the steel industry again and we were on the list of companies that could be taken into public ownership, so any visit by Mr Brown was an opportunity not to be missed. I have to say that I found him absolutely charming, reasonable and understanding. He was a good old-fashioned socialist, the son of an immigrant Polish Jew with a great sense of humour. We could talk the same language, but coming from different sides of an argument. I honestly believed that he was against steel nationalisation, having seen that it didn't work first time around, and I was certain that coming to talk to the workers at Ambergate, most of whom probably voted for him, did nothing to change his views. The trouble with George was that he was too outspoken for his own good among his own party, particularly with Harold Wilson who knocked spots off him diplomatically, and also George was very fond of a drink or three. I saw him several times at Ambergate, a few times in London and had a very soft spot for him.

Being back in Cheshire brought another huge bonus: I could start riding seriously again after a gap of some four years. George Owen had moved from Cholmondeley to a farm near Tarporley owned by Lord Leverhulme. This was only a few miles from where I lived so I started to ride out for him as often as possible. Socially Zandra and I soon got into the swing of things and reconnected with old friends who had grown up and also married, with many of them living in reasonably close proximity. Central and south Cheshire was quite social with plenty of like-minded people around and something going on pretty well every weekend. The days of Cheshire being superb hunting country were probably over but it was still very good and the then Master, Richard Tomkinson and his wife, Antoinette, known as Tink, were very good friends. Richard lived at his old family home Willington Hall in great style and which was the scene of many good parties. It was rumoured that he had undergone a vasectomy performed by the local vet, Ted Greenway, a former top-class amateur jockey and point-to-point rider. Nowadays Willington Hall is a popular country house hotel. Our nearest neighbours, apart from Gordon and Lou Fergusson, were a lively young couple called Ross and Ginny Pigot. Ross was a director of Greenall Whitley, the brewing company formed in 1772 in St Helens by the Greenall family, long associated with National Hunt racing and hunting. Sir Gilbert Greenall was created Lord Daresbury in 1927 and his son 'Toby' who lived in Ireland was Master of the Limerick when I was hunting there in 1954. Everybody was in love with Ross's wife Ginny who had the uncanny knack, when dancing with her, of making you feel that you were the only man in her life.

Zandra had a socially mobile older sister who was married to a very pleasant well-off Liverpool cotton broker called David Stern, and we saw quite a lot of them but the couple who I had known for a while but who became very close friends were Bobby McAlpine and his wife, Jane. Bobby was a member of the northern section of the McAlpine family building and construction dynasty started by his great grandfather, Robert, in 1869. In the mid-1930s it was decided to split the business into two separate companies, with the northern one under Bobby's grandfather Sir Alfred McAlpine. When I first got to know him, his father Jimmy was Chairman of the company but Bobby eventually succeeded him. He has chronicled his life in and around his business in his excellent book *One Shot At Life*. Our friendship was not business based – McAlpines having very little call for wire – but with both of us having a passion for racing and all that goes with it. He played a large part in my life for many years to come. Bobby had a really smashing younger brother called Billy who also worked in the business and lived in a cottage close to Bobby and Jane that he rented from a large, impecunious, rascally and incurably womanising landowner, John Leche. Billy was tremendous fun, enjoyed all the good things in life and still a bachelor had delightful girlfriends, loved racing, fast cars and lived life to the full until tragedy struck on an early Monday morning in May 1961 when a milk lorry pulled out of a farm entrance without the driver seeing Billy's E-Type Jaguar coming. Billy was rushed to hospital in Chester suffering from multiple injuries including a compound fracture of the skull.

For some time the prognosis was encouraging, with a fair chance of him making a full recovery, but in the end a blood clot went from his leg to his brain and he died a couple of days later. The funeral at the family estate at Llanarmon, north Wales was the saddest and most harrowing occasion I had ever experienced. Billy was immensely popular with young and old, with friends coming from far and wide to attend. The overwhelming out-pouring of grief on losing such a dear friend and contributor to life swept over the entire congregation. There is an indescribable feeling over the sudden death of someone so young and special – as I was to experience again myself many years later.

Life was good; I was learning more about the business as time went by and was beginning to take on more responsibilities. Glen Royal was good too. Gordon and Lou Fergusson had three small children, two girls and then luckily the badly needed boy, and allowed us full use of a 50-acre lake which practically bordered the end of our small garden and, with his encouragement, David Stern and I bought an Albatross speedboat, quite small, with seating for four people which Gordon allowed us to keep on the lake. It had a Coventry Climax inboard engine and went like the clappers; ideal for water skiing on which we were all very keen. We designed and laid down a water skiing slalom course on the lake which was very popular with all our friends and resulted in lots of terrific parties and barbecues most weekends and bank holidays during the summer. The Cheshire Polo Club ground was very close by; all the players were friends and they plus visiting teams with their Argentinian 'hired assassins' used to come and somehow one of us seemed to know a star playing a summer season in either Manchester or Liverpool who was dead keen to escape on their Sunday off. The comedian, 'Professor' Jimmy Edwards, was a regular, sometimes bringing his tuba on which he played what he called 'emergency music'. Many years later Gordon and Lou's younger daughter, Didi, married my great friend James Clegg who, it will be recalled, broke his leg skiing on the same day that I did several years previously. James had become a stockbroker in Liverpool along with two brothers Keith and Colin Rae, both somewhat older than me but, with their wives, very much in our circle of friends; Colin's wife Pam, reddish hair and quite feisty, I liked enormously but made sure I kept on the right side of her. Keith seemed to be rather dour and sometimes uncommunicative but I discovered a long time later that he had a brilliant war record, having undertaken acts of extreme bravery which I wonder may have had an effect on his character in later life. In any event his wife Naomi preferred the attentions of Sebastian de Ferranti, the debonair, generous and successful head of the electronic and engineering company in Manchester of that name founded by his Italian grandfather. Sebastian and his then wife Mona divorced and he and Naomi married. Sebastian played polo most enthusiastically and was mad keen on hunting with the Cheshire, Wynnstay and Meynell hounds. He had a habit of turning up at meets on the late side, leaving his office in Manchester at the last moment and flying his own helicopter (in which I was sometimes a passenger) and arriving close to where hounds were meeting. This upset one of the great Masters of the Meynell, Dermot Kelly, who told him one day, when Sebastian had arrived late: 'Sebastian, if you arrive late again in that confounded machine and upset my hounds, I shall send you home.' Sebastian did – and so did Dermot. Sebastian was sent packing. Later that evening a contrite Sebastian telephoned Dermot to apologise. Having said sorry he asked Dermot if he might make a gesture to the local farmers on whose land he had landed the helicopter by giving a small dinner for them in the local pub. Dermot agreed and said he would make the arrangements. Nearer the agreed date Sebastian rang Dermot to ask about how many would be turning up for the dinner. 'About three hundred', said Dermot. Practical jokes were rife: one that I recall was on the occasion of the 40th birthday of a friend of us all, David Miller, who kindly invited a large number of his best friends to a summer lunch party on the lawn outside his very lovely house. The house was approached by either of two longish drives. Unknown to David, Sebastian de Ferranti had engaged two colliery brass bands to entertain the guests and gave each of them separate strict instruction as to the time they were to assemble at the end of one of the two drives and then to march up to the house playing rousing military music. What he had not told them was that there was another band starting at the end of the other drive at precisely the same time. Neither could hear the other because of the loud but totally different music they were playing and neither could they see each other until they both rounded corners of the house from opposite directions and in front of the assembled guests. Total chaos and huge hilarity but they all took it in good heart and I'm sure were amply rewarded.

In the early to mid-60s a few of us including Bobby McAlpine and his brother Billy used to go over to Le Touquet, stay at the Westminster Hotel, quite fashionable in those days, for a weekend and attack the local casino. At that stage casinos were illegal in Britain. The problem was that we still had exchange control but pound notes were attractive to French hoteliers. Credit in the casinos was a different matter. When I was at Lazards I was provided with a Lazards bank account into which my tiny salary was paid. On leaving Lazards my account was closed but I still had my cheque book. Lazards was very much an Anglo-French company, the French section being called Lazard Freres. On my first visit to Le Touquet casino I marched up to the head cashier's desk clutching my cheque book and without disclosing that the account was a long time closed, asked for £1,000 in chips.

'Certainly Monsieur, how you like to pay?'

Producing my Lazards cheque book, I wrote out a cheque for £1,000. The cashier took it away, returning a few moments later and smilingly handed me a thousand pounds' worth of chips. Entering the gambling hall I made a quick £200, immediately returned to the cashier with the original £1,000 worth of chips, which I exchanged for my cheque, promptly torn up. This little coup established my credit with all French casinos. On all future occasions, not just in Le Touquet but all over France including Monaco, all I had to do was produce my passport and there appeared to be no limit to my requests for credit. I was never a big gambler but on the occasions when I lost, I had a polite visit a week or so later from a discreet man in England to whom I would give a cheque drawn on my normal English bank.

Daytime in Le Touquet did not start early, most of the morning being spent getting ready for lunch, usually at one of the local bistros, outside, weather permitting. Quite jolly affairs they were sometimes: I remember Michael Stoddart, subsequently to become a prominent merchant banker and venture capital pioneer, getting involved in an argument as to whether it would be quicker to eat two hard boiled eggs or drink a bottle of champagne. He backed the eggs but lost the bet; however, there was a Stewards Enquiry because the drinker of the champagne was unable to keep the substance inside his body for more than the stipulated one minute. It was Michael who told me about the ingenious game, tickle-belly-slap-cock. This was a game played by gentlemen to while away a hot summer's afternoon. The ingredients were a pot of honey, the attention of an attractive young lady and a large fly. I don't think I need go any further.

6

Family, Friends and Bumps
on the Turf

Life changed somewhat late in 1961, for at 6.30 a.m. on Sunday December 20th our daughter, Jemima, was born exactly a quarter of a century after me at the same time and on the same day of the week. If that wasn't an event exciting enough it was made even better as a result of the book I had made on the impending birth: most punters thought she would be a boy and nobody bet that she would be born on my birthday. The profits from the book paid for the christening party, two of the Godparents being David Penny (now Marchwood) and my first teenage girlfriend Patricia Moseley, both of whom have remained lifelong friends. Actually, I wasn't allowed to christen Jemima thus due to opposition from both sets of grandparents. 'Oh, poor thing, she'll always be called Puddleduck' was the cry, but Jemima she remained and was never called anything else ever and I still think it a lovely, happy name.

At around the same time that Zandra and I moved into Glen Royal Gordon, Fergusson leased his stables and gallops to Eric Cousins (the previous incumbent, Joe Hartigan, who had preceded me at Glen Royal, having moved to Yorkshire). Eric, born in 1921, had served in the RAF as a pilot during the war. From farming stock in Lancashire he rode fifty odd winners as an amateur National Hunt jockey before starting to train from a base in Staffordshire, first hitting the headlines with a horse called Bonhomie in the Ascot Stakes in 1957. He had bought a yearling by Tin Whistle very cheaply for 400 guineas for a friend of mine from London days, Nick Robinson, whose grandfather Sir Foster Robinson, of the then well-known printing, paper and packaging firm E S & A Robinson, had horses in training with my mother's cousin, Arthur Budgett. The Tin Whistle colt, named Kwela Boy, went on to win a couple of small races trained by Cousins, which kindled Nick's interest in racing. His grandfather had a quite useful horse called Chalk Stream with Budgett that he had decided to sell at the Horses In Training sale at Tattersalls, Newmarket. Nick, never one to miss a trick, had met a young man called Robert Sangster, the son of Vernon Sangster the owner of Vernon's Pools. Robert and his young wife Christine lived on the Wirral, Cheshire from where Robert worked at Vernon's. Nick suggested to Robert that he buy the horse Chalk Stream and send it to Eric Cousins. Robert agreed and bought Chalk Stream for 1,000 guineas.

So started Robert Sangster's meteoric career in racing to become a mega-million-pound international business. Chalk Stream landed a massive betting coup for him by winning the Great Jubilee Handicap at Kempton in 1961. In those days the 'Jubilee' was always a great betting medium favoured by those who were looking for a big gamble. Atty Persse won it six times. 1961 was before the days of starting stalls and Chalk Stream had a reputation of being a bit dodgy at the starting gate. The apprentice jockey Brian Lee had been engaged to ride while Sangster took up a position next to the rails bookmakers, Cousins went to the top of the stands to obtain a bird's eye view of the start where Sangster could see him clearly: if Cousins took his hat off when the tapes went up it meant that Chalk Stream had got away well. If, however, Cousins kept his hat on, there should be no bet. Cousins waved his hat in the air and Sangster waded in immediately with a huge bet on his horse which won by a head at 8 to 1. It was the start of an extraordinary and brilliant run of successes in big handicaps for Cousins during the 60s, winning the Jubilee again with Water Skier, twice, and Commander in Chief, the Lincolnshire Handicap in successive years with John's Court and Hill Royal, the Victoria Cup at Ascot with Tudor Treasure, the Portland Handicap at Doncaster with Audrey Joan, the Ayr Gold Cup three times with Dawn Watch, Kamundu and Brief Star and the Cambridgeshire with Commander in Chief.

Most of the above horses were bought as castoffs from other trainers, as in the case of Chalk Stream, but a filly bred by Nick Robinson and owned equally by him and Sangster, Shell Shock, finished third to Mysterious in the 1973 1,000 Guineas. Before one of Water Skier's victories in the Jubilee I had taken a photograph of Eric skiing behind our Albatross on Oakmere lake and gave it to the *Daily Mail,* who was printed it on their racing page the next day with the headline OUR COLD TIP FOR THE DAY. Eric and his wife Pat became very good friends and I used to ride out there often and sometimes was put on a horse doing fast work. Usually managed to have a bit on them when they won, too!

By the spring of 1963 Zandra and I had been living at Glen Royal for three years and, with the coming of Jemima, now into her second year, it was time to look for rather more spacious accommodation. There was a house very nearby called Sandymere that came on the market and I tried hard to buy it but was outbid, which as it turned out was probably a blessing in disguise. However, another rather large house, also very near and owned by Lord Delamere who lived in Kenya, became available for rent, having been occupied by the same, elderly, couple for very many years. Approached by a longish drive, the house had big and airy downstairs rooms with large windows looking out over 90 acres of parkland surrounded by trees, a large pond and garden, several good-sized bedrooms on the first floor and lots of small unused ones on the top floor. It was much bigger than we needed but there was a stable yard in bad condition, stable flat and a lodge at the end of the drive. We took it on a seven-year lease with an option to renew and moved in during the summer. Abbots Moss, the name of the house, was only a mile from Glen Royal so moving was no big deal even to the extent that Gordon allowed us to continue to use Oakmere lake and to keep our boat there. Space wise it was like moving from Mr Badger's house to Toad Hall; I counted about thirty bats in our bedroom the first night we slept in it. It was high time we moved in any case because Zandra was pregnant again and a lot needed to be done to the inside of the house since the old couple had been there for decades and it very badly needed a bit of modernisation. In common with a lot of old and large houses it was distinctly light on bathrooms and the electrics were old-fashioned to say the least. The stable yard and flat hadn't been touched for a very long time. After Christmas Zandra went for a gentle skiing holiday with her parents and our son Richard was born in April 1964 just under 2½ years after Jemima, who had remained at home with me and the nanny while her mother was away.

On the business front, things were going quite well. I had been appointed Group Commercial Manager in 1963. I travelled extensively on behalf of the company, visiting customers on a regular basis within the UK and Europe but also on trade meetings within the industry. Further afield I went to South Africa and several times to the USA. One particular trip I remember was behind the Iron Curtain to Leipzig in East Germany to a Trade Exhibition where we had a stand. There was a team of about five of us but I decided to go by car and took a colleague with me. At that stage I had an Austin Healey 3000 which caused quite a stir not only at the crossing from West to East Germany, at which the car was systematically searched, but also in the city of Leipzig where it attracted crowds of onlookers. Our team was allocated to stay in various apartments with the occupying families who, no doubt, were instructed to report on our every move. Spotlessly clean, and we were provided with an excellent breakfast each day including eggs cooked in whichever way we required. My German was about on a par with the family's English but we learned that the food they provided was completely subsidised by the state and eggs, for example, were only available because we were there. In the huge exhibition hall we were allocated an 'interpreter'. For interpreter, read 'spy'. There were contracts up for grabs open to wire manufacturers from various countries for which we were competing. I gave strict instructions to our team that no prices were to be mentioned in the hearing of our spy or, if they were they had no bearing on what we intended quoting. After one of our team meetings I carefully followed our spy and, as I thought likely, he headed straight for the central admin office where I could see him speaking vociferously to his bosses and gesticulating in the direction of our stand. Happily we came away with a very satisfactory share of the main contract we were after. On leaving our apartment at the end of the exhibition the very nice head of the family handed me a parcel and asked if I would kindly post it on arrival back in England. I had no idea what was in the parcel but I told him that I had to decline, trying to explain as best I could that this was as much for his own safety as mine.

***

I had been riding work and schooling horses over fences and hurdles for George Owen and, more recently, for Eric Cousins ever since I had come back from London. For a while I had been on the lookout for a suitable horse at a price that I could afford to ride in races. Enter two people: one who provided the first element, the horse, and the second who helped with the wherewithal to pay for it. Doug Francis, a trainer who lived very close to Bobby McAlpine, knew what I was looking for, said to me one day that he had a horse, no world-beater but had been around a bit and had won a race. His owner was getting old and wanted out. Doug was a great character as well as an astute trainer who placed his quite small string cleverly. He also had a younger brother, Dick who, as has been related earlier, went to George Owen after coming out of the services at the end of the war and subsequently to Peter Cazalet who trained for the Queen Mother, was Champion Jockey in the 1953/4 season and Devon Loch's jockey when the horse either slipped or tried to jump an imaginary fence close to the winning post in the Grand National of 1956. Dick and my father were friends from his riding days and I got to know him and his wife Mary quite well later when he had become a famous bestselling novelist.

Doug was different. If you didn't know him he looked like a villain with slightly sardonic features and a deep, gruff voice but what a mischievous and wicked sense of humour he had and was the best friend anybody could want. He hated being known as Dick Francis' brother and happily used to repeat the story of an enthusiastic man who, on being introduced to Doug said 'Are you really Dick Francis' brother?' 'No,' growled Doug, 'but Dick Francis is my brother.' I bought the horse, called Wilmslow Boy, with the help of the other person in the triumvirate, my mother. She knew how desperately I wanted this and even though she shared with my father the fear of having to go through all which they had both endured with his accident, realised that as I was determined to do it anyway, she might as well jump on the wagon, to my eternal gratitude. She took a half share in Wilmslow Boy but I paid the expenses.

So, now I had a horse and obtained a Licence to Ride from the Jockey Club, not too difficult; all I had to do was complete a form and send on a letter from George Owen and Eric Cousins saying that I was a fit and proper person to be granted a licence to ride. Registering my racing colours was slightly more tricky: I went along to Weatherbys' office, then at 15 Cavendish Square, London and told a charming old chap that I would like to register colours of Primrose, Chocolate Sleeves and Cap. After a short while he came back and said that he was very sorry but these colours were already taken. 'Oh dear,' I said, 'that is most disappointing. I had hoped to take on my great uncle's colours who had died a couple of years ago.'

'Who was your great uncle?' he asked.

'Atty Persse,' I replied.

'Ah, well, in that case leave it to me for a minute.'

He was back very soon. 'All fixed,' he said. 'I shall tell this other person to change the colour of the cap so you can have Mr Persse's colours and I will register them for you for life.' A good old-fashioned way of doing things.

With Doug's agreement I transferred Wilmslow Boy to George as it was half the distance for me drive to George's to ride out in the early morning before going off to work in Manchester. The big day finally came on 14th November 1963 in a hurdle race at Worcester over two miles with eight runners, but look at the other jockeys: the great Fred Winter on the hot favourite, two Champion Jockeys, Terry Biddlecombe and Josh Gifford, and Grand National winning riders Bobby Beasley (Nicolaus Silver 1961) and Tim Norman (Anglo 1966). A little incident as I was weighing out provided a welcome distraction: sitting on the scales I glanced up at the Clerk of the Scales and thought 'I know that face; surely it can't be?' Back in the changing room I hurriedly looked at my race card and, sure enough, there it was, Clerk of the Scales: Major Ian Manning. The same Major Manning of the 5th Royal Inniskilling Dragoon Guards of whom I was terrified when he was the Officer i/c of my Officer Training Course at Catterick during my National Service days. The butterflies in my tummy were churning round like a swarm of wasps disturbed in their nest as we lined up at the start but as the tapes went up they disappeared into thin air and we settled into the job in hand. I don't remember much talking but suppose I was concentrating so hard that nothing else could come into my mind. What I do remember, and very vividly, was sitting just behind Fred Winter's horse at the end of the back straight with two to jump and seeing the great man pick up his stick on the favourite with nil result. My new best friend ran on like a Trojan and finished second, well beaten by the winner ridden by Ron Vibert but 10 lengths ahead of Bobby Beasley on the third horse. The feeling of exhilaration on dismounting was so way out of consideration of what was a very minor achievement, to be completely laughable, but it was there nevertheless.

Racing is a great leveller; after a couple more races over hurdles in which Wilmslow Boy had run prominently but unplaced, it was decided that we should tackle fences, i.e. run in a steeplechase. A handicap over two miles at Haydock Park was selected. I remember everything about it until the first fence but nothing afterwards until I woke up in the ambulance with a nasty headache and had a hot cup of sweet tea put into my hands by my valet in the weighing room. However, we were back at Haydock a couple of weeks later with a bit better result, finishing fourth, beaten a short head by the legendary Fred Winter for third place. More races and a few more placed horses followed but still the elusive first winner never came and I had to wait until the following season before the luck changed and it was on dear old Wilmslow – actually the result was declared a dead heat; photo-finish cameras were still not operating on every racecourse in those days but I and the other jockey thought I had won. Anyway this was swiftly followed up by an easy win next time. More success followed during the remainder of the season on other horses which prompted me, no doubt stupidly, to enter Wilmslow for the Grand National of 1965 to be run at Aintree on 27th March. Just over two weeks before the 'National' there was a race, unofficially labelled as a Grand National Trial, called The White Rabbit Steeplechase at Haydock on 12th March. Wilmslow Boy and I won it quite easily by 10 lengths, beating some pretty good horses. Could we possibly have a chance in the 'National' itself ? I had already won a couple of races at Aintree but not over the 'National' fences. I could hardly sleep at night with excitement. Was this a dream or was it real?

The weekend before the 'National' my very dear friend Harry Beeby, who was working for Ken Oliver on the Bloodstock Sales side of his business but also helping Ken and his wife, Rhona, with their very successful training operation, rang me up and asked if I could ride a horse of theirs at Ayr on the Tuesday. I had ridden the horse for them once previously and was going well with a good chance of winning when it rather surprisingly fell three fences from home, so I was very pleased to be asked again and accepted with alacrity. Disaster struck: the horse fell again and I broke a collarbone. End of Grand National dream. Probably just as well; in all reality and fairness I don't think Wilmslow Boy would have had much of a hope in coping with the National fences of those days when they were much more formidable than they are today, but it would have been wonderful to have had a go and I have to confess that it was through slightly gritted teeth that I watched another amateur jockey, the American Tommy Smith, ride his own horse, Jay Trump, to victory in Saturday's Grand National while I stood in the stands with my arm in a sling.

7

Moonlighting

On the business front the mid-60s was an exciting time; the takeover age was in full swing brought about, at least in part, by high personal taxation, increased Government interference placing enormous burdens on business administration and therefore costs with such Acts as the Restrictive Trade Practices Bill. RJ&N had always been strong supporters of Trade Associations and had played a prominent part in maintaining a high level of their administration and integrity. My father and other leaders felt that the new restriction placed upon them cut against the principles of being innocent of any wrong-doing unless and until proven otherwise. During this period Johnsons bought a small succession of privately owned companies whose previous owners were finding it difficult to survive in an expanding world with administrative problems as outlined above. Peerless Fence and Products was one such company, being manufactures of chain-link fencing and all wire related products to do with fencing, having previously bought their wire from Johnson's. The main addition to the group was the purchase of the Spencer Wire Company, an old established Yorkshire-based company who were not only competitors but also large manufacturers of reinforced concrete wire mesh for the building trade. A small Manchester based transport company was also bought to help streamline Johnson's transport and deliveries throughout the UK and abroad. My cousin Peter – Robert Johnson's son – and I became directors of Spencers and I was appointed Chairman of

Peerless. Since Great Britain's entry into the Common Market, as it was called then, there had been increased communication – cooperation is too strong a word – between the wire manufacturers both ferrous and non-ferrous in the Common Market countries. I went to such a conference in Holland during which an awful lot was said, nothing given away, promises of further meetings, lots of hand shaking, a jolly drink at the end and that's about all. It reminded me about the popular song at the time about digging a hole – I wouldn't dig it here, I'd dig it elsewhere – and drinking cups of tea before going home.

By the mid-60s we had a Labour Government with Harold Wilson as Prime Minister, very high taxation and a trade union bonanza. It is relevant to record here, as I write now with the country having voted by Referendum to leave the European Union, the words of my father in a speech at the company's AGM on 28th June 1968,

It must be accepted that owing to the incidence of personal taxation the reward of the Manager has not kept pace with inflation, while his duties have increased. In the last decade we have had a spate of industrial legislation dating from the Restrictive Trade Practices Act 1956 – surely a monumental piece of muddled thinking – and it falls to the lot of the Manager to see that these consequent additional obligations upon industry are carried out. It may not be generally realised that there are many people today who are performing functions which call for no particular training or skill, but who are, nevertheless, being paid amounts which would have been considered a reasonable reward for a factory or commercial manager twenty years ago. It is true that the manager of today also receives basically higher pay, but at the present level of taxation he keeps very little of it. Nor is there a 40-hour week for him. His tasks do not cease when he leaves his place of work. Naturally people, so placed, wonder whether the extra responsibilities and worry are worthwhile, or alternatively whether it would not be better to go abroad where they will receive better value for their services. At all levels the effect of over full employment on the one hand and excessive personal taxation on the other, are a discouragement to enterprise and hard work. I think it is not so much a question of whether the nation can afford a reduction in personal taxation but whether it can afford to suffer the consequences of maintaining it. At the same time I would like to express the view that the time spent in seeking to understand and to interpret correctly all these new laws – some of which bear every sign of over-hasty drafting – and in obtaining legal advice thereon, would, in the national interest, be better spent in straightforward management. Management is, in fact, being choked by too many laws.

Much of the above extract could be applied now, nearly sixty years later, to the mess that has resulted in a perfectly sensible commercial Free Trade area inside Europe being taken over by political and bureaucratic greediness.

In 1965, because of the expansion of the group and because of the resulting increase of the after-tax group profit – there was a record after-tax profit of £1,654,000 for the year ending 31st March 1966 – the decision was taken to make Richard Johnson & Nephew into a holding company, with the Steel and Non Ferrous divisions being made into separate companies along with all the other subsidiaries. Robert Johnson's son, Peter, and I were made directors of both companies along with other senior managers of their respective divisions. This coincided with the retirement of a proportion of senior people with very long service to the company as a whole.

From a tonnage point of view steel wire of very many different qualities and markets took up the vast majority of the production capabilities. The company bought from all the UK steelmakers who made billets. Copper, however, was a very different ball game; the company used approximately 50,000 tons p.a., all of it imported from the mines of the world's major copper producers. Contracts were arranged normally with an annual fixed amount but with a variable amount to be 'priced' i.e. paid for each month on the day to day price on the London Metal Exchange (LME). This was all well and good when the price remained stable but, as in all commodities, when supply and demand or such elements as political, social or climatic changes occurred, huge volatility in the price was the result, making the buyers' job in judging the market a very skilled one. I well remember receiving a call quite early one morning from my father, who was in New York having a meeting with Kennecott Copper, with some advance information that would make the copper price jump substantially when it hit the market and as a result of which we were able to obtain a very beneficial position. It must have been around midnight when he made the call to me. A nice piece of insider information. In those days the price of copper wirebars was around £240 per ton. 50,000 x £240 = £12,000,000. Not a sum to be trifled with.

In October 1967 Johnsons took a stand at an International Exhibition and Conference in Montreal for the promotion of high tensile pre-stressed concrete. This is a very high quality wire used for special contracts such as nuclear reactors, bridges and high rise buildings. The principle is that using this specification of wire enables the concrete to be stronger, and to some degree flexible, so that buildings, for instance, can have less mass and therefore less weight. A further example is that virtually all railway sleepers are made of pre-stressed concrete in order to withstand the variation in weight and vibration caused by very heavy railway engines and rolling stock. Johnsons helped to pioneer this product and were major suppliers to the trade. Montreal is a very beautiful city and the Exhibition was well laid out and attended in a lovely park on the outskirts of the city. We took a powerful team including the sales manager of that division, a delightful man called Fred Carroll with whom I worked closely in my early days with the firm, the group export sales manager, Eric Ogden, a gruff no-nonsense Lancastrian with a keen sense of humour and a passion for traditional jazz. Being a bachelor, travelling frequently to many destinations worldwide was just up his street. Also with us were our top two metallurgists, Frank Brereton and Gordon Sleigh. While at the Exhibition we got wind of a contract that was up for grabs for a pre-stressed concrete pressure vessel for a nuclear power station at Fort St Vrain, Colorado, the first of its type to be built in the USA. Eric Ogden, Gordon Sleigh and I decided to fly on to Los Angeles to meet the representatives of Western Concrete Structures who had the contract to build the reactor. After a couple of days of tough negotiations we flew home with the order for approximately 650 tons in our pocket. Even larger contracts obtained by Johnsons at around this time were for 1,500 tons for the Lausanne to Simplon Highway viaducts, each of 1¼ miles in length carrying the roadway 330 feet above part of the shore of Lake Geneva and 8-foot diameter pipes for a vast irrigation scheme in Israel which needed one ton of wire every 15 feet of pipe.

Back home and about this time it was decided that it would be good PR, and also very beneficial for our senior sales and works personnel, to have our own company aeroplane, with the bonus that we could bring important customers to the works in Manchester. I was given the task of finding a suitable plane. I chose a de Havilland Dove, not very fast but with a comfortable layout to seat six passengers plus two pilots and with a loo. The 'flying unit' was set up and before long the plane was in very full use all over the UK and for short-haul European trips. I have to say that at least on one occasion the plane came in pretty useful for me on a non-business basis. I had been asked to ride a horse at Exeter; now a trip from Cheshire to Exeter and back in the day is quite a flog but, as luck would have it, I saw from the flying unit schedule that the plane had been booked to take a couple of our people on a tour of some West Country customers on the same day so I managed to put in a couple of hours' work in my office in Manchester before hitching a lift on the plane to Exeter and the same on the return journey. The icing on the cake was that the horse won and I hope that my colleagues helped themselves to a bit of the 100/7 that was on offer.

Back on the home front, we had the Cheshire Hunt Ball, one of the highlights of the Cheshire social season, at home at Abbots Moss. For the previous two or three years it had been held at Peckforton Castle, a medieval-style castle built on the summit of a wooded hill for John, 1st Baron Tollemache in the mid-19th century. It had hardly ever been used or lived in and had stood empty without electricity or water for many years. For the years that the Hunt Ball was held there a team of volunteers, of which Zandra and I were included, trooped up the long drive up to the castle armed with buckets, mops, brushes and all forms of cleaning gear for several weeks before the ball. A water tank was installed and temporary electricity connected. We rigged up decorative lighting and made it look as good as possible but it was all pretty Heath Robinson stuff and a hell of a sweat. It was quite expensive as well because we had to employ some professional contractors in order to obtain the necessary licences to hold an event for which people were paying to attend and it never really made much money for the Hunt so in 1967 the Hunt Committee asked us if we would have it at Abbotts Moss. We had a marquee as well as using the house and it turned out to be a very good party. We had Confrey Philipps and his band; Confrey at that time was one of the top social bandleaders in the country and great fun. Of Indian extraction – his father was born in Goa – he spent most of his life in England and the east coast of America. There was also a racing connection: at the time I knew him first he was married to the blonde and beautiful daughter of the jockey Rufus Beasley, of the great Irish racing family.

Rufus used to ride a fair bit for Atty Persse and, one time I was in Lambourn visiting Atty, he told me an amusing story, not about Atty but another doyen of the Turf, Cecil Boyd-Rochfort, the Captain as he was always known, racehorse trainer to HM The Queen and other selected owners. Of formidable appearance and with stature to match, the fact was that he was not that well-off and needed to supplement his income with a few well planned 'investments' during each season. In the year in question, the Captain had taken on a new owner who was a keen gambler and had a two-year-old in the yard with no special pedigree that the Captain had selected for one of his 'investments', in that he thought he could win a modest maiden race without attracting much pre-race attention. He chose a race at Salisbury and Rufus was engaged to ride instead of the retained stable jockey, Harry Carr. As he collected the saddle from Rufus, having weighed out, he told him that he strongly fancied the horse but to take no notice of his instructions in the paddock in front of the owner. In the paddock he duly said 'Beasley, this is a nice sort of horse. Haven't done much with him so he'll definitely need the race and will probably run a bit "green" so look after him and he'll be better for the race.' Those who know Salisbury racecourse will be aware that it is quite a long walk from where the horses pull up after a race to the winner's enclosure. The Captain was not normally known for over exerting himself but there he was as Rufus, having won the race quite comfortably, rode the horse off the track. 'Remember, Beasley, we are surprised' was all he said.

My mother met the Captain once but only by accident; my father having asked her to go to Newmarket Sales to try to buy a particular horse. Geoffrey Brooke, to whom my father was related by marriage – Geoffrey having been Atty Persse's long-time assistant trainer and also his brother-in-law – was now a successful trainer in his own right in Newmarket and bore some resemblance to the Captain. My mother had only met him on a very few occasions but, seeing whom she believed was Geoffrey at the Sales, went up to him and reintroduced herself. Receiving rather a blank stare, she said 'You are Geoffrey Brooke aren't you?' The man drew himself up to his full height and, looking down at my mother said: 'The name is Boyd-Rochfort.'

In the autumn of 1964 the same mother decided that she would like to have a horse of her own so she and George Owen took themselves off to Ireland and came back with a five-year-old mare by the highly regarded National Hunt stallion, Bowsprit, that had won a novices steeplechase at Limerick for Mary Annesley and was trained by Aubrey Brabazon. The mare was called Bonnie Boat and my mother paid 1,200 guineas for her; she very kindly said that as long as I could do the weight, I could ride her in her races.

My father, who never paid much money for his horses, always had two, sometimes three, in training with George Owen. Considering the comparably little money that he paid for them, he had a reasonable amount of success with them and, at that time he probably had the two best horses that he ever had with the possible exception of Kloof, the horse on which he had his terrible fall in 1948 when he broke his neck. The goodish horses that he had in the early 60s were called Conundrum and Dinner Jacket; the former won on the flat and several races over hurdles and fences. Dinner Jacket who cost 500 guineas at Ascot Sales as a four-year-old – and about more later – went on to win 14 races. Anyway, in 1964 for his 60th birthday, I commissioned Lionel Hamilton-Renwick, one of the better known equestrian artists of the day, to come up to Cheshire and paint a portrait of the two horses in a field at Sculshaw Lodge with the house in the background. My father was absolutely delighted with the result. He never wanted me to be a jockey for obvious reasons, seeing what happened to him, although having ignored his advice he supported me wholeheartedly, but this did not extend to letting me ride any of his. However, eventually after I became a little more experienced, he started to put me up just occasionally and I had the odd ride on the above two horses, but by that time they were probably a little past their best.

A word here about weight. In 1963 my natural weight was around 11st. 7lbs. Jockeys are allowed a weight allowance of 7lbs until they have ridden a certain amount of winners, reducing in stages to 5lbs and then 3lbs until they have ridden a total of twenty-five winners. I realised very early on in the piece that I would not have any chance of riding in the vast majority of races at my weight of 11st. 7lbs, the weight range in National Hunt racing being from 10st. to 12st. 7lbs so a pretty severe weight losing campaign was necessary. During a holiday with my parents, who for many years spent much of the winter in Barbados, I met the great Australian jockey 'Scobie' Breasley, a good friend of theirs. I explained my predicament to Scobie and he gave me a copy of a time-limited diet that had been designed for him by the Mayo Clinic in the USA. Without going into boring details, it was calorie controlled over a two-week period. I tried it: the first two days were dreadful, feeling terribly hungry and with no loss of weight. After that, however, the hunger feeling becomes progressively less and the weight just falls off; I lost 20 pounds in the two-week period. Each year at about the end of August I went on the Mayo Clinic diet, my weight having ballooned up during the summer months. The jump season used to start in earnest in early September and go through to the following Whitsun, usually towards the end of May. Nowadays there is little or no break but statistically the season ends after the last meeting at Sandown in April and the new season starts the next day. I liked to maintain a steady weight of 10st. 5lbs and if I needed to be less for a particular race Turkish baths, saunas and/ or runs wearing a multitude of clothing provided the answer. I reckoned that a three-mile run followed by a very hot bath with a whole packet of Radox and half an hour smothered in two large bath towels in a steamy bathroom could get off 3 to 4lbs. The lowest weight that I ever 'did' was 9st. 11lbs which nearly killed me and I never tried to do anything below 10st. 2lbs again. The weight a horse is set to carry includes the saddle as well as the body weight, boots and colours worn by the jockey. My boots were paper thin and my smallest saddle weighed 1½ pounds.

My mother's Irish import, Bonnie Boat, started quite inconspicuously with a couple of slightly disappointing runs, taking her time to adjust to crossing the Irish Sea, so when George Owen suggested we take her to Aintree on January 1st 1965 it was with hope rather than anything else, particularly as the race, over only two miles, was we thought on the sharp side. Normally she jumped pretty well but as I came to find out she usually managed to not jump high enough at least once in a race and today was no exception, clouting one very hard at about halfway. However, that mistake and a slap on the backside by me really woke her up and we came to the last with a chance; she pinged it and we got up close to the line and won by a length. It was the start of even better things to come. She won two more races that season including a valuable race at Towcester and was second once.

After a summer's rest she was back in training and ready for her first race towards the end of October. On 19th November there was a meeting at Ascot largely sponsored by Black & White whisky and Bonnie Boat was entered in the Woolavington Memorial Steeplechase, named after Black & White's founder James Buchanan who became the first Lord Woolavington. It was the highest profile race in which I had ridden and the feature of the BBC's televised races that day. Her Majesty the Queen Mother's horse Oedipe, trained by Peter Cazalet and ridden by Nick Gaselee, was odds-on favourite but things were going well for Bonnie Boat and me until the last open ditch going up the hill before turning in to the straight; here she made her once-per-race nearly catastrophic blunder and very nearly got rid of me. I thought all chance was gone but showing a typical gutsy mare's bloody mindedness she picked up and we went second between the last two fences and I could see that Oedipe's stride in front of me was shortening. It was all or nothing at the last and with sheer bravery and determination she stuck to her task and we won narrowly. I must say that it was an extra special feeling to ride into the winner's enclosure at Ascot where so many giants of the Turf had trodden before.

On the back of the Ascot success the next race, in early December and in desperately heavy going, was an equally important race at Chepstow sponsored by Rhymney Breweries. Two Grand National winners, Toby Balding's Highland Wedding (1969) and Anglo, trained by Fred Winter in 1966, were in the field. After the Ascot race Bonnie Boat was third favourite in the ante post betting and in a field of eleven on the course on the day. I really thought she stood an excellent chance of winning but it was not to be; as I have mentioned before, racing is a great leveller. Going to only the 6th fence a horse called Cotswold fell directly in front of us and brought us and another horse, Witty Tom, down. No damage done but an immense disappointment. The race was won by a good horse called Kilburn who went on to win the Welsh Grand National over the same course and several other good class races. Incidentally the horse that finished second to Kilburn in the Welsh National was Cotswold, the horse that brought us down in the Rhymney Breweries.

1965 was quite an exciting year; many of us had arranged to go skiing in Klosters at about the same time, not actually in a party but there was a small group who linked up most days. The leaders were the two older Palmer-Tomkinson boys, Charlie and Christopher, both absolutely superb skiers and both British ski champions, as was also their younger brother Jeremy who doubled as James Bond for the skiing sequences in the movies. The Palmer-Tomkinsons, whose mother Doris was Swiss, had a lovely flat in Klosters and both knew every run and off-piste track through woods like the back of their hands. We were all of a certain standard but nowhere near the level of the P-T boys who were such huge fun to ski with and immensely patient. Among the little group was HRH Prince William of Gloucester, a hugely likeable young man of about twenty-three. He had no fear and would get down anything, often ending up in a heap at the bottom but with a broad grin on his face. We all had a great time with some of us staying at the Wynegg Hotel run by the indefatigable Ruth Guler, a great Anglophile and matriarch who put up with all sorts of bad behaviour by us young Brits but who could also be very firm if one overstepped the mark; if Ruth didn't like you the Wynegg wasn't the place for you. When Ruth Guler died in 2015 the *Daily Telegraph* published a half-page obituary.

Although I thought I got on quite well with Prince William, it came as something of a surprise when I received a telephone call from him a few months later to say that he had joined the Foreign Office and had been posted as Third Secretary to the British High Commission in Lagos, Nigeria. He said he was leaving by ship from Liverpool quite soon and would it be OK if he could come and stay a night and could I possibly take him to join his ship in Liverpool the next day. Zandra was away but of course the answer was yes and I arranged a small dinner party for him the night he stayed. All went very well except that the paparazzi had been tipped off and there was a gang of them waiting at the dockside with the resultant show of photographs and text in the gossip columns the next day. We corresponded a fair bit after his arrival in Lagos and subsequently so it came as a terrible shock when he was killed piloting his own plane in an air race near Wolverhampton a few years later in August 1972. He was thirty years old.

I had met, casually to begin with, in racecourse weighing rooms, Gay Kindersley who was a few years older than me and very much in the senior rank of amateur jockeys. He, Bob McCreery and John Lawrence (subsequently Lord Oaksey) were known as the Three Musketeers. Gay was Chairman of the Amateur Riders Association of which I was a member but, as far as I can recollect, its main purpose was to have a quite serious lunch in London from time to time. The story goes that after one such lunch Gay and Bob McCreery said goodbye to each other, saying that they had to get home to domesticity, and so got in separate taxis and went on their way. However, approaching from different directions, the same two taxis with the same occupants drew up at the same time outside the block of flats of a certain young lady of my acquaintance, where they were looking forward to spending the rest of the afternoon. It was at one of these lunches that Gay mentioned to me that he was trying to increase the number of flat races limited to amateur jockeys and would it be possible for me to interest Chester racecourse in putting on such a race, preferably attracting a local sponsor. I should say here that the some rules of flat racing are different from jump, or National Hunt racing. One of these differences is that in NH racing amateur jockeys, as long as they hold a Jockey Club licence to ride, can compete on level terms with professional jockeys; on the flat this is not allowed and amateurs cannot ride in the same race as professionals. In those days there were relatively few flat races confined to amateurs, hence Gay's desire to increase the number. Happily now there are many more but still amateurs cannot compete with professionals. I told Gay I would give it a try.

Gay was a splendid man – yes born with a silver spoon, his mother Oonagh being one of the three fabulously beautiful Guinness Girls. Her first husband was Philip Kindersley and they had Gay and his sister Tessa. Brought up largely in Ireland Gay became a fearless rider, being champion amateur jockey in the 1959/60 season, a devotee of Irish folk music, with a charming manner and good looks, friend of actors and entertainers like Peter O'Toole, Oliver Reed and the Dubliners, an incurable romantic in or out of wedlock – lovers included Ann Queensberry and the zither player Shirley Abicair – and giver and attendee of wild and riotous parties. At one such party I remember him having a long and more than cosy dance with a lady friend of mine, at the end of which she told me that he had told her how wonderful she was and asked her name, completely forgetting that they had embarked on a wild three-week romance together in Ireland some years previously.

The directors of Chester racecourse agreed to stage a race for amateur jockeys at their September meeting, which was very good news so I set about securing a ride in the race. A very good friend, Bryan Jenks, who lived near Bridgnorth in Shropshire, had some top-class National Hunt horses trained by Fred Rimell and also flat horses trained by Pat Rohan at Malton in Yorkshire. One of these, a three-year-old called Super Gay, was highly rated as a two-year-old and was even considered a possible Derby horse but subsequently disappointed, so Bryan very kindly said that he would enter him in the Chester race and that I could ride him. A week before the race I drove up to Malton after work one evening, stayed the night with the Rohans, rode a bit of work on the horse first lot in the morning and was back in my office in Manchester by 9.30. The horse went well and I was pleased with him. The evening before the race Gay and his attractive wife Magsie came to stay the night at Abbots Moss and we had a dinner party for them. The race itself was over one mile six furlongs and there were seven runners. Chester racecourse is the sharpest course in the country, left handed circular, about one mile round with a straight run in of just over a furlong. Many high quality races take place at Chester, particularly at their May meeting. The race was a great experience, completing nearly two circuits of the course and seemingly on the turn most of the time. I thought we were going pretty well, hitting the front before the last bend into the straight but were comfortably run out of it by a goodish horse called Sagely trained in Newmarket by Ryan Jarvis and ridden by Nick Gaselee who had been on Oedipe when Bonnie Boat had beaten him at Ascot. But still we did finish second. Chester is not an easy course to ride and, in hindsight, we should have finished closer had I ridden there before. Some time later Bryan transferred Super Gay from Pat Rohan to his friend and near neighbour in Shropshire Jack

Bissill, to be trained for jumping. I rode him a couple of times and on the second occasion we did manage to win the only race he ever did win, which was very disappointing for a horse with so much apparent ability.

It was at about this time that Bobby McAlpine and I decided to have a horse in partnership together and that Doug Francis would train it. Accordingly Doug went off to the sales and bought a horse that had some fair form on the flat without actually winning and Doug thought had good National Hunt potential. Named Marieson, in his first season for us, as a four-year-old and after a couple of 'quiet' runs, he showed useful form being second in a quite good race at Cheltenham before getting his head in front and winning at Wetherby. He had about seven races that season, winning one and being placed in three others and being ridden by top jockeys such as Bobby Beasley, Stan Mellor and Terry Biddlecombe who was on him when he won, so we were well satisfied. The following season started rather disappointingly; Marieson made jumping errors, fell once, was brought down another time and even refused once. He had lost confidence in himself so Doug sensibly gave him time to recover and waited until the New Year and some better weather. I went over to Doug's on several occasions to ride work on him and suggested to Bobby that perhaps I might ride him in a race, give him a quiet run and try to get his confidence back. Bobby wasn't terribly enamoured with the idea but I was supported by Doug who said that I seemed to get on well with him at home so why not give it a go. This is exactly what we did; had a lovely run round at Hereford, the horse ran on nicely towards the end of the race and seemed to be enjoying himself again. This was followed by an even better run at Bangor and he finished up winning three races on the trot, two of them ridden by me as well as being placed second on his final race of the season. Bobby and I had a huge amount of fun with Marieson; Doug suggested that we ran him over fences but although he was normally a sound but not spectacular jumper, he hated the larger obstacles, so we reverted to hurdles and I won another race or two on him. However, the Marieson story ended, if not in tears in a degree of sorrow. Bobby liked to have a decent bet when conditions were right; he thought, quite correctly, that he had a better chance of collecting his money when his horse was ridden by a top jockey rather than an amateur like me. One day, at Doncaster, Marieson was due to run in the last race of the day in which he was well fancied and Bobby's money was down. Stan Mellor, the Champion Jockey of the time, was engaged to ride him. Bobby couldn't get to Doncaster but I was there anyway having a ride in another race. In the penultimate race of the day Stan had a crashing fall on a horse of Tom Jones' and was carted off to hospital. Tom was the famous Newmarket trainer of hugely successful horses under both sets of Rules, including the champion two-mile chaser Tingle Creek (who has an annual steeplechase named after him at Sandown) and the St Leger winner Athens Wood in 1971. Doug was faced with the problem of finding another jockey but, as it was the last race, all jockeys not engaged to ride in it had packed up and gone home. So Doug turned to me; there was, as he put it, no alternative. In the race we were going OK but approaching the last and going flat out with two other horses going a shade better than us, I could see that the only way to possibly win was to meet the hurdle on a long stride and hope for the best. Unfortunately this didn't happen: I asked him for a long one but he didn't pick up, put in an extra stride, hit the hurdle halfway up and turned a somersault. Luckily the horse was perfectly all right and, apart from considerable battering and bruising, so was I. Back at home and in a bath heavily laced with Radox, the telephone rang, Bobby on the line: 'What happened?' he asked.

'He fell at the last but probably would not have won anyway,' was my reply.

'Oh that's terrible. What did Stan say?'

'Stan's in hospital having got laid out in the previous race.'

'Oh, my God. Who the hell rode him then?'

'I did. There was no one else.'

The telephone exploded and I could almost feel the line shaking with rage. Not a word about whether there were any injuries to horse or jockey. Doug received the same treatment but completely substantiated what I had told Bobby. We were due to meet the next day and of course Bobby had calmed down but we both decided that to preserve our friendship we had better end the partnership in Marieson. Most happily in years to come I trained several horses for Bobby and all won except one homebred that couldn't run as fast as his owner but which I did manage to sell on to Jane Kidd who transformed it into a top-class dressage horse. However, I can't leave the Marieson story without relating an extraordinary incident that occurred at Cartmel races on 27th May 1967. Cartmel, a delightful small course set in beautiful countryside in the Lake District, had, in those days, very few race meetings. In fact the whole course was normally used for grazing sheep but on Whitsun weekend each year crowds flocked to the races on the Saturday and the following Monday. It was very much a holiday atmosphere and a bit of an end-of-the-season jaunt for many of us. Marieson was entered for races on both days. I couldn't ride even if I had been selected as I had another broken collarbone and Roy Edwards, a top jockey of the time, rode him. Marieson was second favourite and Bobby and I watched it together standing on the finishing line as Marieson finished second, the result confirmed by the judge and announced over the tannoy. 'Bad luck but well done anyway,' we said to Roy as he rode into the unsaddling enclosure.

'What do you mean, "bad luck"?' said Roy, 'I won by a good neck!'

'Well' we said laughingly, 'if you thought you won, you'd better go and tell the judge.' There was no photo-finish camera at Cartmel in those days and Roy stormed off into the weighing room and put down a formal objection to the winner on the grounds that the judge had made a mistake. It was the last race of the day, Cartmel hospitality towards the racecourse officials, including the Stewards, was liberal and, after holding an enquiry – and indeed after many bookmakers had paid out on the winner – they announced a correction to the result of the race, naming Marieson as the winner. Of course Bobby and I were delighted, having had a good bet on our horse, but in our joint opinion, plus those who were also on the finishing, the original decision had been the correct one. Nevertheless we retired to the bar to celebrate. Marieson was due to run again on the Monday and Doug had engaged a promising young jockey to ride him. In the bar this young man turned to me and asked the best way to ride him:

'Oh, don't worry' I said, 'Just have a good ride round, finish second and then go and tell the judge that you have won!' I turned round to pick up my glass from the bar counter and there, standing next to me, was the judge. It was reminiscent of the racing rhyming couplet:

The Stewards had lunch till half past three
And then went in to have their tea

In the event the heavens opened on Sunday, the course became waterlogged and racing on Monday was abandoned. Many years later, this story has a sequel: I was at Newbury races when Ken Oliver, my great friend Harry Beeby's boss and very successful National Hunt trainer from Hawick, for whom I had the occasional ride, had brought a horse called Fighting Fit down from Scotland to win the Hennessy Gold Cup. Ken, who never wasted an opportunity to have a drink, and I were chatting in the bar with the owner of the winner; somehow the conversation got round to talking about north country racecourses and the name Cartmel cropped up. 'Don't talk to me about that effing place' said the owner of Fighting Fit, 'I once won a race with a horse of mine and the bloody judge, who was three parts to the wind drunk, changed the result.' I remained very silent.

At Abbots Moss, of which I had a seven-year tenancy with about still two to run, I had a stable yard with six loose boxes and a stable cottage. I decided that I would apply for what was known then as a permit to train my own horses, the actual Jockey Club wording being that the permit entitles the permit holder to train horses belonging to himself, his wife and his unmarried daughter. I had relinquished my share of Marieson but still had Wilmslow Boy, by now pretty old and not very sound. My mother transferred Bonnie Boat to me and I bought two more young horses. Eric Cousins, whose land and gallops bordered on mine, very kindly agreed that I could use his gallops and so I was granted my permit. Dear George Owen, to whom I was and am eternally grateful for all that he taught me, was most understanding and supportive so Wilmslow Boy and Bonnie Boat came to Abbots Moss plus my two new boys and I employed a lad and his wife to live in the stable cottage and to work with the horses.

At work things were changing as well. My father had been wanting to retire for some time. He had been Chairman and Managing Director for thirty-three years despite having suffered his appalling racing accident and being more than partially paralysed since 1948, had worked for the firm for forty-four years. He and my mother had for several years been spending about two and a half months of the winter in their house in Barbados, but keeping in close touch with the business all the time. During his time in office the value of the Ordinary Shares had appreciated twelve times and the dividend had been increased thirty times. These figures speak for themselves, and for my father and his most loyal and most excellent Board of Directors. But, with the exception of Peter and myself, they were all on or near to retiring age and for a while my father had been looking to recruit someone who could join the Board with a view to becoming

Chairman while the younger team gained experience. His selection for this role was not universally popular within the industry, as the person concerned had already been appointed Secretary of one of the main Trade Associations and therefore was privy to much information regarding each member company. I have to admit that I did not care for him but others in the company did and so I determined to put any doubts behind me and get on with him when he joined the company in 1968. I was very busy in my own roles as the commercial main board director for both the ferrous and non-ferrous sections of the business and in that year, 1968, we got wind of a large order for pre-stressed concrete wire for a project in Colombia being constructed by an American company. Eric Ogden, the export director of RJ&N (Steel) Ltd and I flew out to Bogota, Colombia and after five days of pretty heavy negotiation managed to secure the order. I was certain that one of the main factors in success in bids like this is to be on the spot: face-to-face with those responsible for placing orders. Much better than telephone (emails didn't exist in 1968) or anything else. Of course you have to have the back-up, quality and reputation to support your argument but of that we were entirely confident. Having obtained the order I realised that, most conveniently, Barbados, where my parents were in residence, was on the plane route home so managed to stop off for a couple of days with them. What was not so convenient was that I suffered a very bad dose of food poisoning on my last night in Bogota and only just succeeded in getting on the plane for a six a.m. take-off.

On the home front all was not rosy and hadn't been for some time. I suppose that both of us had grown up a lot since we married at the age of twenty-two, and should have listened to our respective parents instead of doing precisely the opposite. We were young and foolhardy. Speaking personally and with a lack of self-confidence, I thought I would never get another chance. Social life in Cheshire was active, we had many friends in common and it's difficult to put a finger on anything in particular. In the summer of 1966 we agreed that Zandra would spend a period of time at her parents' holiday house in Anglesey but things were no better on her return. I was extremely busy workwise, spending a considerable amount of time travelling round the country and abroad visiting customers and attending trade association meetings. In the London office we had a couple of brothers, Jimmy and Ron James, as sales reps; real likely lads, very good and loyal at their jobs and keen on racing as well. They persuaded me to take a share in a greyhound with them called Earl's Jungle, which was trained and ran at Catford. We had a lot of fun with it although on both occasions when I went with the James Bros to Catford to see it run, it finished nearer last than first; however, it did win twenty-three races but not of the highest class. Come mid-August, the horses, getting fit for the coming NH season and losing weight occupied all my spare time, riding out very early in the morning before going off to the office in Manchester – a journey of approx. 1½ hours each way. Probably I was burning the candle too much but I did start to notice that a married friend, who lived about a couple of miles away, was frequently at Abbots Moss attacking my whisky bottle on my return home in the evenings. I was told much later by a young girl, the daughter of friends of my parents who I employed as a nanny for Jemima and Richard, that the same friend used to put in a morning visit about 15 minutes after I had left for the office.

On 27th March 1967 I had the worst fall of my riding career. I had bought a young young horse locally a year previously for not much money, and I really liked the look of it. It was by Sir d'Orient out of Delaware and I named it Chinaware. A year later Chinaware was starting to show real signs of ability both in work with my very small string of horses but also when Eric Cousins kindly allowed me to work him with some proven horses of his. I gave him a couple of runs at the end of the 1965/66 season when he was still weak and backward – I fell off him on one of these outings but by the end of 1966 he was feeling much stronger and finished a close third in a big field. So at Wetherby on 27th March I thought we had a possible chance of winning. I had three rides that day, the first one finished third and then came Chinaware's race, about which I can remember nothing until waking up in the medical room at the racecourse, where, I'm told, the racecourse doctor reported me to the Stewards for using foul language. I was taken by ambulance to Leeds Infirmary where it was discovered that I had concussion (I could have told them that), three broken ribs, a collarbone and a dislocated vertebra in my neck which was the chief area of concern. I was in the hospital for six days before being allowed home still very stiff and sore, Bryan Jenks having been kind enough to send his car and driver to collect me. In the hospital I had plenty of time on my own to consider the future and came to the inevitable conclusion. It is best to draw a veil over matters best left unsaid, but Zandra and I were finally divorced about a year later. I moved out of Abbots Moss and set about converting three cottages into one at the Home Farm at Ashton Hayes, lodging with my parents in the meantime. I bought Zandra a house not very far away, into which she moved before the expiry of my lease of Abbots Moss. There were long years of non-speaks but she remarried and now I'm happy to say that we have a friendly if distant relationship. The Chinaware story also had a sad ending: in his next race, when I was still out of action, he came to win his race which, in the words of his jockey, Stephen Davenport, he definitely would have but clouted the second last hurdle so badly that he broke his knee joint and had to be put down.

In the firm, following my father's retirement we had a new Chairman, Philip Rambaut, as described. The main Board consisted of him; Reginald Hardie, a very good and sound man who had been Company Secretary for very many years before coming on the Board; Ian Fairholme, who had worked for a long time on works and works personnel matters under Peter's father, Robert Johnson; Arthur Gill, who had joined the RJ&N Board following our acquisition of the Spencer Wire Company, of which he had been joint Managing Director; Lord (Geordie) Ward, as Non-Executive Director, who was supposed to help and advise on political and all outside matters of industrial and national importance that might affect us; Peter, very good and clued-up on all matters of works management; and me as head of ferrous and non-ferrous commercial matters. It came to our attention that there was a buying run on our shares on the Stock Exchange in the shape of Jessel Securities, headed by Oliver Jessel, a company with a reputation as an asset stripper, something which in my view was the last thing that RJ&N, a company approaching its bicentenary and with a very good and solid reputation worldwide for reliability, quality and service, needed. I received no help or support from the new Chairman, who was himself bent on splitting up and restructuring the company into smaller groups, acquiring a company Ferrari and substantially increasing his pension plan, all within six months of having become Chairman. Geordie Ward, too, was no help in a battle to resist the antics of Mr Jessel. He had been Secretary of State for Air in Harold Macmillan's Government, but was plumb useless as a Non-Executive Director of Richard Johnson & Nephew. Of the other directors, Reg Hardie, superb as he had been as a devotee of my father, was not a decision-maker, was old and approaching retirement himself, Gill had already received his pound of flesh on the sale of Spencer Wire Company, in which he and his brother Charles had been the major shareholders, Ian Fairholme was soon to retire after thirty-seven years' service and Peter was brilliant on technical and factory matters but not on commerce. It was common knowledge that I did not get on with the Chairman and that I mistrusted him. The options for me were:

1. Do I want to spend the rest of my life in industry?

2. If the answer to 1 is 'yes' do I want it to the extent of fighting what amounts to a lone boardroom battle?

3. As I have an alternative career which at present is just a hobby, should I turn it into my main occupation?

I plumped for no. 3 above and resigned from Johnson's. I had had long discussions with my father before doing so. He was massively disappointed with the flawed mechanicalist policies of his successor and fully supported my decision. While all the turmoil was going on and with the company bicentenary coming up in a very few years in 1973, one of my last very pleasing tasks was to find a suitable author to write the history of the company, to be published on the bicentenary. It was an easy task: Michael Seth-Smith, a very good friend of many years standing, was an excellent author of many biographical and historical books, admittedly mainly about racing, including as co-author of *The History of Steeplechasing*. I broached the subject to him and he agreed to come to Manchester where the other directors willingly agreed that he should write the book. He was given a completely free hand and spent many months of painstaking research, and my only suggestion was that he should make comparisons whenever appropriate to national and world events taking place contemporary to the period of company history about which he was writing. The result, which he completed in good time before the bicentenary deadline, *200 Years of Richard Johnson & Nephew*, published in 1973. The book is an important library book and plays a significant part in the history of the wire industry.

Michael, in addition to his writing career, was also the senior racecourse commentator of his time; he had an amazing photographic memory and could read a page of a book and then repeat it verbally word by word. This stood him in very good stead on the racecourse; many was the time when he would invite me up to the commentary box where we would chat about all manner of things before he broke off saying that he had better look at the horses, memorising the colours worn by the jockeys as they went down to the start, even a large field of over fifteen unknown two-year-olds at the beginning of the flat racing season. He would then give a perfect commentary on the race, naming each horse and where it was placed throughout the race. He frequently came to stay at Abbots Moss and later at Ashton Hayes for such as the Grand National meeting at Aintree, the May meeting at Chester and various meetings at Haydock when he was commentating, and indeed subsequently at Berkeley House in Lambourn.

He had yet another string to his bow: a somewhat unofficial association with one of the oldest and most respected wine merchants in London, Christopher & Co. just off Jermyn Street. One of the owners of Christopher's during the 1920s and up to the mid-50s was an old university friend of my grandfather's with the strange Christian name of 'Annie', surname Irish. I remember being taken by my parents, as a going back to school treat, into Christopher's for a glass of sherry with the old man. Later I got to know the MD of the company, Peter Noble, quite well. He rang me one morning saying that he had what he called a 'parcel' of nine cases of Krug 1945, '47 and '49 and would I like any at 30 shillings per bottle. I bought the lot for a total outlay of £162. Some of the '45 was a bit over but the rest was nectar.

It was a very sad day at the Royal Meeting at Ascot in 1986 when Michael Seth-Smith was commentating as usual, but in a comparatively small field he made a series of uncharacteristic errors and collapsed in the commentary box after the race. He was diagnosed with a brain tumour and died less than a year later. Known affectionately and with good humour by his fellow commentators as 'Gus the guesser', he was a one-off and a very dear friend.

8

Career/Life Change

The building and conversion work at the Home Farm at Ashton Hayes having been completed in the spring of 1969, I had moved in. I had six horses at various stages of fitness and a married lad and his wife, both of whom rode out, who occupied an adjoining cottage. Now, not having what my father called a 'Proper Job', I set about, with the help of a childhood friend, Land Agent Oliver Beck, acquiring beef cattle to fatten up and sell on. I had the space and premises and it seemed a sensible thing to do. At around this time my mother's younger sister's daughter, Jane Bromley-Davenport, announced her engagement to a young barrister called Charles Shelton-Agar who was in the same Chambers in Manchester as Jane's elder brother John, both of them being my first cousins. My parents had played an important part in John's early life; his father, Togo, was a senior member of the textile company J & P Coates and was appointed by the company to manage their business in Singapore. He and my aunt Betty lived there for fourteen years, which included the time John was at his prep school so he spent his winter and Easter holidays at Sculshaw Lodge with my parents, going out to Singapore for the summer holidays. I was invited to a celebration engagement dinner party at Capesthorne Hall, the Bromley-Davenport family home near Chelford, Cheshire. Walter Bromley-Davenport and his American wife, Lenette, were very special friends of my parents and Walter's younger brother Togo was married to my aunt Betty, whom the Bromley-Davenport family insisted on calling Elizabeth. Anyway Betty (or Elizabeth) rang me up and asked if I would collect a good friend of Jane's on the way to the dinner party. Her name was Anthea Marshall and she lived not very far from Capesthorne, so it fitted in well, although I did not know her. I turned up at her house, was greeted by her parents and introduced to this attractive young lady dressed from top to toe in black; it was immediately clear that the last thing she wanted to do was to get into the car with me and go to this party for which her invitation had been accepted on her behalf by her mother, whereas she had made her own plans to have dinner with her boyfriend. So it was a journey accomplished without much conversation. The party, however, was a very jolly affair in the main dining room at Capesthorne, a huge red-brick Victorian edifice with an entrance courtyard, towers rising above blue-grey slate roofs and a wing with its own private theatre. I used to go there a lot as a child and thought it resembled a forbidding fairy-tale giant's castle. When the party was over I took Miss Marshall home again and by this time she had thawed out a bit and we seemed to get on better so I asked her for her telephone number before I dropped her off and went home.

Of the six horses at Ashton Hayes, two were relative newcomers. I had been to Ascot Sales to try and buy a horse I had my eye on. This was successful and I was preparing to go home when a Welsh farmer, who I knew slightly, asked me to have a look at a horse that he was selling; he showed me this raw-boned, Roman-nosed deep chestnut gelding. Very immature but a good walker and there was something about his bold and possibly bloody minded outlook that appealed to me. He told me that he had put a reserve of 750 guineas on the horse and asked if I would help in the bidding up to that amount. I agreed and made a few bids but was most surprised when the horse was knocked down to me at 680 guineas. Not pleased, I sought out my 'friend' who, without telling me, had dropped the reserve price. However, I did like the horse and so after a bit of dealing I agreed to pay him £500 and that he would have to reimburse me with the difference that I had to pay the auctioneers.

The horse, with the rather unfortunate name of New Brighton, turned out to be the better of the pair that I bought that day but was a very difficult horse to train. He was, as I suspected, bloody minded but I think this stemmed from the fact that he had been very badly and probably very roughly broken in. He was immensely strong and we really had to start from the beginning and exercise extreme patience and TLC to get him over his not infrequent tantrums. If he had been a human being he would have been a real yobbo, would undoubtedly have been in trouble with the law and would have been sent to a young offenders' institution. The world, in his mind, was against him. He never was what you might call normal, but the good news was that he never lost the bold outlook that I had seen originally. After re-breaking him on long reins we started to ride him again and I rode him out most days, and often on his own, hacking quietly along country lanes, across fields and amongst my beef cattle. Many months later and towards the middle of the 1968 winter we started to do a bit more with him, cantering and trying to make him more supple by trotting in and out of a row of upright poles close together. Then schooling sessions over hurdles behind a lead horse; not easy because he was so strong, took a terrific hold and would just as soon try to barge the hurdles out of the way than actually jump them. However, he got better if not perfect and the time came to increase the workload. I had reasonable grass and sand gallops, good enough to get a horse half or three quarter fit, but nothing suitable for genuine fast work. Eric Cousins at Sandy Brow kindly let me use his gallops on occasion but I also used to take a box-load of horses to the sands at Hoylake, about a 50-minute drive away in a horsebox, so one day I took three horses there including New Brighton. Both the other horses had good winning form so I rode New Brighton with my lad and his wife riding the other two. I told them that I would set off in front at a sensible pace and they were to follow. This was New Brighton's first serious gallop so I said to the other two that after half a mile or so they were to close on me and go on in front for a nice piece of work because both their horses were nearly racing fit. It didn't work out that way: at the end of a good mile, I still had a double handful and a look round showed me the other two toiling away some way behind. 'Couldn't get to you,' they said on pulling up. I realised we had got a racehorse.

I had begun to think during that year that my race-riding career was drawing to a close. The trials and tribulations of the previous year, moving out of Abbots Moss, the divorce, me in one place for a while and the horses in another had taken its toll; I was not as racing fit as I had been and my weight had gone up by around a stone, so I couldn't ride at less than 11st. I did continue at a reduced rate for another season or so but when it came time to start entering New Brighton in races I decided that someone else should ride him. He was a difficult and very headstrong ride and I wouldn't have done him justice. I entered him in a race at Haydock in early March 1969 and asked Pat Buckley to ride him. Pat was first jockey to Neville Crump and had won the Grand National on Ayala, owned by the hairdresser 'Teazy Weazy' Raymond, beating Carrickbeg ridden by John Lawrence (later Lord Oaksey), who jointly owned him with Gay Kindersley. I knew Pat pretty well, a splendid Irishman and good strong jockey. In the paddock before the race I told Pat all that I knew about the horse and that he had ability but was very green and I was sure would need the race and so not to be hard on him when he got tired. Pat did exactly what he was told, except that the horse did not get tired and came to the last hurdle in second place and with every chance of winning. Sadly the last hurdle was the one he tried to barge out of the way instead of jumping it and he fell. Pat was sure he would have won.

Three weeks later he made amends by winning a race at Nottingham, again in the hands of Pat Buckley, by a couple of lengths in a huge field of thirty-four runners at the rewarding odds of 10 to 1; I had managed to secure a handsome bet at 100/7, which brings me to a short word on bookmakers: generally referred to as 'the enemy', which was only true in the sense that they and the punters were legally trying to take money from each other. But they were also friends; my attitude was that we could help each other. I was never a big gambler but liked a bet if conditions – and odds – were good and I found it best to take a bookmaker into my confidence. Take New Brighton's race at Nottingham, for instance: he had only raced once but had shown some ability so nothing was really known about him to the public. There was a northern bookie called John Joyce; he wasn't usually on the 'rails' but in Tattersalls and I liked him so, well before the race, I went up to him and said that I wanted to back my horse and asked the best price he could give me. Right then he knew that I really fancied the horse so he made me a favourable offer which he, in turn, could not only lay off but back the horse himself and make a profit on the race. Everyone happy. Another splendid Tattersalls bookmaker was Ted Sturman who traded under the name of Fred Binns; he was a great character and serious player who loved big gambles and got rather grumpy when there were no big punters around. There were also the professional punters, a few of whom I knew; one of them being Greville Baylis, a husband of the much-married Italian-born singer, actress, model, television announcer and panellist of shows like *What's My Line,* Katie Boyle. She kept the name Boyle after another husband but could also have called herself Lady Saunders following her marriage to the theatrical impresario Sir Peter Saunders. Anyway, she was most attractive and charming. Lower down the scale was a little Lancastrian called Joe Lee who used to skirmish around northern racecourses in search of information and commissions from professional jockeys, who are not allowed to bet, to put bets on for them. Once I was being led round the paddock on a horse and about to go out onto the course when Joe, a small, rotund little man, appeared at my side and hissed 'Hey, do you fancy this one?'

'Oh, I think he'll go OK, Joe, but the ground's a bit too firm for him.'

' I've been out and had a piss on it so it will be all right,' came his reply.

There was another character quite similar to Joe but with a better brain known as The Dodger, so called because he was supposed to be on the run from prison. If that were the case, the police didn't do much of a job because The Dodger was around for years.

One of the most enduring characteristics about the inside of National Hunt racing was, and I've no reason to doubt that it is the same now, the immense sense of camaraderie in the weighing room, or jockeys' changing room to give it its proper title. For one thing, it was out of bounds to all except jockeys and valets. The chit-chat, jargon, general teasing and good-natured practical jokes were hilarious. If you rode a winner the back-patting and congratulations in the weighing room afterwards were genuine and heartfelt. I remember once during a race my horse made a terrible blunder and I was hanging on for grim death but was a virtual gonner when a top jockey – it was Stan Mellor – put out a hand and hoisted me back into the saddle. I went on to win the race, and who was the first to say 'Well done'? – Stan Mellor. I gave him a big hug and thanked him. Jockeys were your friends as well as competitors; we all understood the risks and dangers of what we were choosing to do. Once, quite early on, I had a fall and a bang on the head, coming into the weighing room not having much idea where I was; a hot cup of sweet tea was put into my hands by another jockey, who led me to my peg and sat me down. Ten minutes later I was OK again. In those days there were no ambulances or Stewards in cars following the races round the course. If you fell, as long as you could get up and walk, you were OK. Sometimes it was a long trudge back to the stands unless you were lucky enough to get a lift with the starter in his car. When I was riding I used to make a habit of walking round the course to test the going and maybe get off another half pound. Once, at one of the Midland racecourses, Warwick or Worcester, I forget which, I had got as far as the second-last flight of hurdles when the first race of the day, a big field of about 17 novice hurdlers, came by. There was one other person standing near me, a rather dishevelled oldish man wearing a scruffy mackintosh and flat hat. David Nicolson, a very good jockey and son of the legendry 'Frenchie' Nicolson, was on the favourite and as the runners approached the hurdle he was in the leading group and going flat out, giving it everything. His horse never took off at the hurdle and David, or the Duke as he was always known in the weighing room, was buried with the rest of the field galloping over him and giving him the odd nudge as they did so. The Duke struggled to his feet, battered and bruised and started to limp off only to be greeted by my neighbour, he with the scruffy mac and flat hat thus:

'Fuckin' Nicolson, you couldn't fuckin' ride a fuckin' clothes 'orse.'

The Duke, pencil thin and quite tall for a jockey, started a trend that was not always popular with other jockeys. He used to telephone trainers and ask if he could ride a particular horse of theirs in a particular race. This wasn't the done thing to do in those days. Jockeys waited to be asked to ride by trainers with their wives or family members keeping his 'book'. Jockeys got upset when they found that a horse that they expected to ride for whatever reason was now to be ridden by D. Nicolson. It's all different nowadays of course; jockeys have their agents whose job it is to contact trainers and secure rides for their jockey clients, for which they receive a percentage of the riding fee. When he retired from riding David became a very successful trainer for many years until he died in 2006, having been Champion Trainer twice.

Terry Biddlecombe was another tremendous character, brilliant jockey and serious player. A farmer's son from Herefordshire, he was good-looking with curly fair hair and a big frame, really too big to be a jockey and weight was always a problem for him; this he conquered by severe dieting, constant Turkish baths, saunas plus pretty unmentionable methods, but what a fun guy and party animal. He was known as the Blond Bomber. I saw him once at Chepstow on a Saturday, thin as a rail. I saw him again the following Monday; in the intervening period he had put on and taken off again 9lbs. His main retainer was with Fred Rimell, a super trainer and former jockey himself. Fred, most ably supported by his wife, perhaps slightly inappropriately named Mercy, was a pretty hard taskmaster and got through jockeys like leaves falling off a tree, but he and Terry formed a good if sometimes volatile relationship which lasted several years and during which Terry was Champion Jockey three times. He won the Cheltenham Gold Cup in 1967 on Woodland Venture, beating another great horse of the time in Stalbridge Colonist, ridden by Stan Mellor, and finished second to Well To Do in the Grand National in 1972 on Gay Trip, whose name in those days did not have the same connotations as it would do today. Gay Trip, incidentally, had won the race two years previously when ridden by Pat Taaffe.

I suppose the same could be said about the name of the horse I used to ride, Super Gay, owned by my very good friend Bryan Jenks who had many good horses with Fred Rimell at the time and ridden by Terry. Terry married first time around the sister of another friend of mine, Bill Tyrwhitt-Drake, but that didn't work out and, when he eventually retired as a jockey, the bottle got the better of him and he disappeared to Australia for a while only to return and get himself dried out at Farm Place. He subsequently met and married Henrietta Knight whose sister is married to Lord Sam Vestey. This most unlikely couple lived very happily ever after until Terry died aged seventy-two in 2014. During their marriage Henrietta, with Terry at her side, trained many good horses, the best of which was the very well named Best Mate, who won the Cheltenham Gold Cup three times in 2002, 2003 and 2004.

***

After his victory at Nottingham, New Brighton's next race was in mid-April 1969 at Wetherby where in a big field, and after another howling blunder at the last, he finished second to a horse I had tried to buy a couple of years before but was outbid. The horse's name? Red Rum, who started his racing life by winning a five-furlong two-year-old 'seller' at Liverpool but, as everybody knows, went on to win three Grand Nationals. New Brighton had one more run that season and had taken up the running going to the penultimate hurdle like a winner, but crashed through it and tipped up. It was a characteristic of one huge bloomer per race that was to follow him throughout his career.

***

After my blind date with Miss Marshall I followed it up a little while later and took her out to dinner, during which she opened up rather more and it seemed to go rather well. It turned out that she was an extremely competent event rider and was spending much of her time at a local equestrian eventing establishment run by an autocratic elderly German, who ran the yard, consisting of mainly lady pupils, under a strict code of discipline and with no humour. One wasn't supposed to have 'fun'. Even the jackboots were in evidence and the hat with a clump of feathers sticking out of it. He was, however, according to Anthea, an exceptionally good instructor. Of course anything to do with racing was taboo. I discovered that Anthea had other talents as well – no, not yet – she was a very talented artist and had been accepted for the Slade School of Fine Art at University College, London. The Slade is renowned throughout the world and is recognised as the top art school in England. Anthea, however, turned their offer down in favour of the German horse gruppenführer. We met again and I asked her to come racing when I was riding. She also came to Nottingham when New Brighton won his first race and we started to become quite close, much to the annoyance of her, now, former boyfriend who started to pay nocturnal visits to Ashton Hayes, peppering my bedroom window with gravel and asking to have his girlfriend back.

Traditionally, the National Hunt season used to virtually finish at the Whitsun weekend. Nowadays it's all different, with both jumping and flat racing continuing throughout the year with the advent of all-weather courses for flat racing and racing on Sundays. It must be a trainer's nightmare. Because of long periods of firm or even hard ground expected during the summer months, jump racing is of a lower standard to that of the main season from September/October through to April/early May but, of course, this gives the chance of winning races with more moderate horses, which trainers cannot afford to miss if they are to please their owners who pay the bills. If there were no owners, there would be no racing. Simple as that, but having said so it has never ceased to amaze me how many people can afford the huge expense of having horses in training. I well remember my father having a fit when George Owen increased his training fees from £5 to £6 per week per horse. When I took out my first professional trainer's licence in 1972 I was summoned for an interview before the Licensing Stewards of the Jockey Club and asked by the Senior Steward acting at the meeting, Edward Courage, how much I was going to charge:

'£25 per week, Sir' I said.

'Well done, young man.' (I was in my mid-thirties.) 'We see too many applicants not charging enough.'

Now the basic fees are in the region of £350–£400 per week

plus all extras such as vets' fees, farriers, transport to and from racecourses, let alone entry and jockeys' fees.

But let's have a look at what else was going on in the world in 1969: Richard Nixon was inaugurated President of the USA, Harold Wilson was Prime Minister and there were terrible riots in Northern Ireland. The Beatles broke up and gave their final concert and Concorde made its maiden flight. On 20th July spacecraft Apollo 11 made the first manned landing on the moon and shortly afterwards astronauts Neil Armstrong and Buzz Aldrin stepped out of the craft and walked on the moon. Seems like yesterday. Back on earth, Blakeney won the Derby and, in August, Anthea and I were married.

Quite a small family affair; first a Registry Office in Chester followed by a lunchtime reception with a small number of family and friends at her parents' house, Anthea looking lovely in a sheer darkish blue silk dress, and then back to Ashton Hayes for quite a riotous and great fun evening party with a excellent local band that went on for most of the night. We didn't go for a honeymoon straight away, but a little while later went for a holiday at the Marbella Club in Spain. In those days the Marbella Club was rather smart and no one was allowed to stay there without an invitation and introduction from an existing member. Fortunately this was possible for us via a very good Cheshire friend, Tim Maxwell, whose parents had a house near Marbella and were members.

The Club had been formed in the mid-50s by Prince Alfonso Hohenlohe at his own private residence, which he bought at about the end of the Second World War. A flamboyant playboy, he hit the headlines when, aged thirty-one, he married the fifteen-year-old Princess Ira von Furstenberg in Venice in 1955. From then on for many years the Club became a mecca for film stars, international playboys, diplomats and mega industrialists. Brigitte Bardot and Gunter Sachs were regulars, along with a host of other top stars, a clutch of Kennedys, Adnan Khashoggi and all forms of Eurotrash. For Anthea and I it was a glimpse into another world and actually we very much enjoyed it. We had a most comfortable small chalet-type bungalow to ourselves, the weather was marvellous, food fantastic as long as you didn't mind having dinner at midnight and we made friends with another couple, John Mackinnon and his lovely Argentinian wife, Susanna. John, delightfully pompous in a very amusing way, took it all in his stride and Susanna with her Spanish–Argentinian background and glamorous good looks dressed and played the part. Anthea took under her wing a rather sad but obviously very rich American alcoholic who, in his relatively few sober moments, was good fun. Called Warren Smith, he had a car and showed me with great delight a special compartment built under the back seat in which he could store a dozen bottles of vodka. He gave his address as a chalet in Gstaad and came to stay with us once in England. The Mackinnons became good friends in England for many years until John died far too young.

9

Whatcombe

Back home at Ashton Hayes, Anthea and I set about our new and happy lives together. We had a lovely home, lots of friends, no real worries, plenty to do on the farm and with the horses preparing for the new season. And yet something was beginning to nag at me. I worked it out: I was no longer an industrialist, my hobby had become my business, my riding career was almost over and training a few horses on limited facilities was just not good enough. There was no way that I could transform Ashton Hayes into a professional training establishment. Fun as a hobby but not as a business. I had my last ride at Worcester – where I had had my first – on 1st October 1970 struggling to ride at 11st. on a horse that had no chance of winning, which was how it turned out. I ploughed on with the training during the winter, having three winners and some placed horses, but with itchy feet. It was time to move on. The exciting news was that Anthea was pregnant and the baby was expected early the following June.

During the past ten years I had learnt and gained considerable knowledge and experience of National Hunt racing but knew very little about the mechanics of flat racing which is where, I decided, I wanted to go next. I had always avidly followed flat racing having had two family members who were very success-ful flat racing trainers: Atty Persse, my father's uncle therefore my great uncle, and Arthur Budgett, my mother's cousin. Atty Persse had long since retired and had died in 1960 but Arthur who had bred, owned and trained the previous year's Derby winner, Blakeney, trained at a well-known and famous racing establishment, Whatcombe, about five miles east of Lambourn. He was the son of Hugh and Hazel Budgett, Hugh having been guardian to my mother and her two sisters after their parents died very young, leaving three teenage daughters. Hazel was my mother's godmother and Arthur and his wife, Bay, asked me to be godfather to their eldest son, James, when I was about seventeen. I decided to learn and wrote to Arthur Budgett asking him if there would be any possibility of my coming to work for him as a pupil for a period of time, since I knew that he had taken on various others on the same basis over the years. I explained that I had ten years' experience both in riding and training under NH rules but wanted to learn more about flat racing. I didn't receive a reply for a while but when it did come it was in the form of a telephone call with a most surprising twist. He said that he was intending to retire in the not too distant future and that, if I came to him, would I consider buying his whole establishment and taking over from him? I thanked him and said that I would talk to my family and get back to him.

A family conference was held soon afterwards. It was a momentous and life-changing decision that was to be made. I needed the best possible advice and to be sure that it was supported by my immediate family. Arthur had said on the telephone that he would be asking for £150,000 for Whatcombe, but no further details were discussed. This sum may not seem very much nowadays but in 1970 it was a lot of money and would necessitate the sale of my home, the Home Farm at Ashton Hayes plus another tenanted farm on the estate, leaving just Mulligrubs Hall and what we called the Bottom Park. All the above was in the name of Trustees, these being my father, my uncle Eric and myself. After a meeting of the above plus Anthea it was decided that I should have a meeting with Arthur to take matters forward and find out more.

Accordingly I rang him and he kindly asked Anthea and me to come down to Whatcombe for lunch. This we did and he outlined what he had in mind: Whatcombe consisted of the main house and outbuildings such as secretary's office, garages etc, two stable yards accommodating up to seventy horses, hay and straw barns feedhouse with access to 20 tons of corn, stable lads' hostel with catering and leisure facilities, Head Lad's house, another bungalow and surrounding land – in total 60 acres. In addition were 250–270 acres of gallops which were rented under lease with all rights of way to them. His proposal was that I should come and work/learn for a period of three years unpaid. Halfway through this period contracts would be exchanged and completed; he, then, would officially become my tenant and pay a rent but would remain in control of the property and business for the remaining 18 months, at the end of which he would vacate the property, retire from his business and hand over to me. I would have to find somewhere to live but the underlying tone of the meeting was that he would gradually bring me into the management of the business, introduce me to the owners and make everything as smooth as possible. I would work with him and also ride out, work with his staff and spend a lot of time in the yard with the horses. It sounded wonderful, I thanked him profusely and said we would talk it over ourselves and with the Trustees and get back to him as soon as possible. We drove back to Cheshire tremendously excited.

Both my father and uncle were most supportive, as they had been during the last frustrating year at RJ&N; the news there being that a merger with another competitor, John Rigby and Sons – negotiations having started when I was still with the firm – was completed. However, in 1972 Oliver Jessel became Chairman, my nemesis Rambaut having either resigned or been dismissed. Quite soon afterwards virtually all the old guard departed, including Peter, and Jessel set about his asset stripping techniques, stating that Richard Johnson & Nephew was 'typical of a large old fashioned group' and 'that much of our national wealth is vested in such companies'.

This 'old fashioned group' hadn't done too badly for its shareholders: in my father's tenure as Chairman, as previously related, the value of the ordinary shares appreciated twelve times and the dividends increased thirty times. Mr Jessel proceeded to amalgamate RJ&N with a company called Leeds Assets, no longer in existence, of which he himself was also Chairman, with the 'carrot' that this would bring into the group £6,000,000 worth of quoted securities. All sorts of other hiving off and amalgamations followed, notably, in 1973, with the steelmakers Firth Brown to form a new company Johnson Firth Brown. This company in turn amalgamated with a branch of British Steel Corporation which failed, resulting in the shareholders sacking the Board and setting up a rescue package with sections of the steel wire business being sold to a South African company. Eventually, in 1998, whatever was left was sold to two separate American buyers, one of which was Atchison Castings which failed, the company going into liquidation in 2003. Hence a company which had prospered through sound management and skilful, loyal workers for 200 years and still going strong, completely disappeared.

It was decided that we would go ahead with the Whatcombe plan so I wrote formally to Arthur saying that if his offer was still open, we would be delighted to accept. There was a minor blip in that he said that having examined all his figures he would want £170,000 and not £150,000. We agreed and set about plans to raise the money. There was a great deal to do but the plan was that Anthea and I would look for a temporary place to live as near as possible to Whatcombe and I expected to be able to start in early 1971. On June 6th 1970 and to the delight of everyone concerned our son, Simon, was born. A bonny little chap, he seemed to enjoy being alive and gave the minimum amount of trouble, at least to his father.

On the legal side of the Whatcombe transaction there was not much to be done at that stage because the actual contracts were not scheduled to be exchanged and completed for 18 months after I had started work at Whatcombe, but there was much to be done at Ashton Hayes, the most difficult and unpleasant part being having to give as much notice as possible to my two farm workers who had both been employed at Ashton Hayes for a very long time. For my head man, a wonderful old stager called Arthur Steele, it was not so bad because he was well past retiring age and a widower, his wife having died some several years previously; he was quite happy to take things more easily and continued to do odd jobs for my aunt. John Lloyd was younger, lived locally and, in the event, had no trouble in finding similar farm work when the time came.

I sold all my cattle and horses with the exception of New Brighton, who had won two more races during the latter part of 1969 but had a bit of tendon trouble after his last win and would need a year off to recover. I gave three months' notice to my stable lad and his wife, which gave them ample time to find another position. I also had a young local girl called Maureen working with the horses who easily found another job locally and I told her that if, in the future, she wanted a job in a racing stable in the south, I would find a place for her. With the help of my land agent friend, Oliver Beck, we decided on how the land that I was farming should be split to the minimum of inconvenience to my aunt who was continuing to live in her own house on the property. Oliver also put in hand the sale of the farm including the house in which I lived, adjoining cottage, farm buildings and garden plus negotiating with the long-standing tenant farmer to buy his farm to raise the money that we needed to buy Whatcombe.

By the end of the autumn of 1970 most things had been finalised. Anthea and I, in need of a house for the three-year period agreed with Arthur Budgett, had made several visits to the Lambourn area in search of somewhere to live, but without any success. We couldn't find anything suitable so decided to rent a cottage to start with. There was a small country pub called The Pheasant about five miles from both Lambourn and Whatcombe; the owners of the pub, a very nice quiet sleepy couple, owned a cottage next door to the pub and I gave them a small deposit to secure renting it for £8 per week from 1st February 1971, my parents having invited Anthea and I to come out to Barbados for a holiday with them in their holiday house there in January before I started my new career. Simon, now seven months old, was left with Kay, his nanny, and my parents' devoted couple David and Lottie Reed at Sculshaw.

Christmas and holiday over, Anthea and I set off at the end of January from our comfortable, warm farmhouse in rural Cheshire to Pheasant Cottage, half a mile from Junction 14 of the M4 ... and pretty basic it was. The front door started a couple of inches higher than the red tiled floor and ended a similar distance below the architrave. A circa-1930 Rayburn solid-fuel stove in the kitchen provided the only means of cooking and heating water. Two single-bar electric fires were the only other means of heating. There was a tiny sitting room on the ground floor with two bedrooms and an antiquated bathroom upstairs. Most of the windows had similar types of draft exclusion as the front door. I had sent down enough furniture for the cottage from Cheshire in my horsebox with my two farmhands; any doubts that they may have had about my sanity were immediately confirmed on their arrival at Pheasant Cottage. The pub car park, 50 yards away, was our parking space.

My normal routine in the morning was to arrive at Whatcombe just after seven a.m., have a look on the board in the tack room to see which horse I was allocated to ride, collect my grooming tools, saddle and bridle, do the horse over and tack it up. However, on that first morning I went to the back door of the main house and waited for Arthur Budgett, the Guv'nor, to appear. We walked together the short distance to the entrance to the main yard where the Head Lad, Tom Dowdeswell, and two gallop men were waiting. I was introduced, the gallop men reported on what they had been doing the day before and any problems that had arisen. Then Tom and Arthur had a short discussion about the plans for the morning. Arthur then handed me over to Tom who led me into the yard, introduced me to a few of the lads and showed me the horse I was to ride, already tacked up on this occasion. Being only the beginning of February we were just walking and trotting along the lanes and tracks with the odd gentle canter. Back in the yard I took my tack off, brushed the horse over, rugged him up, checked his water and dashed back the six miles 'home' to the cottage to breakfast prepared by Anthea. Very hurried and time for only a cursory glance at the *Sporting Life* before haring back to Whatcombe to prepare for second lot, which followed the same pattern as the first. Both journeys and breakfast had to be completed inside of 45 minutes. Luckily I had an E-Type Jaguar.

In the afternoon, the lads came back into the yard at four p.m. Each lad had three horses allocated to him on a permanent basis to 'do', in other words to look after even though that did not necessarily mean that he rode the same horses each day. Tom was in sole charge of who rode what. The looking-after meant grooming and mucking out every morning and afternoon, giving them their feed as prepared on an individual basis for each horse by the head feeder morning and night and generally getting to know and deal with all habits, likes, dislikes, idiosyncrasies and peculiarities of each horse. It was very important, I always thought, to talk to them about all things in general rather than to work in silence. At 5.30 the Guv'nor made his round of Evening Stables. Each lad would present each of his horses in turn for inspection and answer any questions as to his or her wellbeing. The Guv'nor would be welcomed at the yard gateway by Tom who would go round with Arthur making whatever comments necessary.

My job in those early days was to return to Whatcombe at 4 p.m. and go to Arthur's office in the house and learn the office procedure. In the main it was what I had been used to myself, only much more so and as part of a business rather than a hobby. *The Racing Calendar*, racing's Bible and weekly publication, had to be gone through each week with great care and attention. It published the entries in each race and the weights to be carried in handicaps; these, particularly, had to be checked each week to see what alterations the handicapper had made to each horse. There were Jockey Club notices and instructions and all manner of details to be absorbed. Tom Dowdeswell's daughter was the secretary and she did all the clerical work, accounts, bills, copying the scribbled entries in races onto the official entry forms and making sure they got in the post in good time each week. There were no such things as the internet or emails in those days and even telex was a rarity. Although it did not apply when I first started at Whatcombe because the flat racing season did not begin until nearly the end of March, when the time did come, there were the form books *Raceform* and *Timeform* to be closely examined every day to try to work out where each horse had the best chance of winning. Form, however, was by no means the only consideration: race distances, going reports, course variations, and locations, weights and availability of jockeys were just some of the other ones. I found plenty and more to occupy myself between the hours of 4 p.m. and 5.30 when I accompanied the Guv'nor on his round of Evening Stables. Spending all morning with the horses and lads I got to know them and, helped by going round in the evenings, the horses as well.

Working in the yard at the time was a young man, James Bethell, fresh out of school, the second son of Lord Westbury. Although James was a lot younger than me, he was great to work with, anxious to learn and eventually became a trainer in his own right with a small but successful stable in Middleham, Yorkshire, the county his family came from.

These were happy and exciting times. Arthur had a stable of sixty to sixty-five horses, a large number for those days when the likes of Cecil Boyd-Rochfort, Jack Jarvis and Gordon Richards had around fifty or fewer. Those with more were John Dunlop, Noel Murless, Dick Hern, Sam Armstrong and Peter Walwyn but not many others and nobody had strings of 100 plus like the big yards of today. Arthur also had a very good, loyal and, in the main, well-off bunch of owners. It was not a betting stable; it didn't need to be. During all the time I was there I never heard the mention of any gamble having been landed. That's not to say that the lads didn't bet; they certainly did and some quite successfully on the horses trained in the yard. With the start of the season drawing near the programme began to change with more cantering and the increase of faster work. I rode most of the older horses in the yard, four-year-olds and over, and one of my favourites was a strapping big four y.o. called Petty Officer, a lovely gelding by Romulus out of Petty France and owned by one of Arthur's longest standing owners, Col. Percy Wright, who owned a share in Blakeney, who had won the Derby for the stable in 1969.

Blakeney was actually bred by Arthur Budgett, being by Hethersett out of his wonderful race mare Windmill Girl, who had won the fillies' St Leger, the Park Hill Stakes at Doncaster. It came as a big surprise to me one morning when, my having ridden Petty Officer, Arthur came to me as I was unsaddling and said that he didn't want me to ride out any more as I was too heavy. I weighed at the time just under 11st. I was most disappointed as was Tom Dowdeswell, as he had lost a riding out jockey. I did not expect to ride serious fast work but for ordinary cantering exercise on the older horses I was by no means too heavy. It is ironic that later in the season Petty Officer won two races for amateur riders, one at Chantilly and the other at

Deauville, carrying 11st. 2lbs in one and 11st. 4lbs in the other. Philip Mitchell, the selected jockey, was a perfectly capable and competent rider, but he only rode in flat races of which there were very few in those days for amateur riders. As I have said before, amateurs were prohibited from riding against professionals on the flat, whereas under National Hunt rules in hurdle races and steeplechases amateurs and professionals competed with each other on level terms. I had, therefore, considerably more race riding experience than Philip having competed in hundreds, as well as a few flat races. How dearly I would have loved to have been chosen to ride Petty Officer!

We had some pretty good horses in the yard and had a good season as far as winners went. The best horse from a quality point of view with Classic potential was Alderney, half-brother to Blakeney by Alcide. He was just below top class but won the March Stakes at Goodwood and was a little unlucky when running in the St Leger, won by Athens Wood, trained by 'Tom' Jones and ridden by Lester Piggott. Falkland, who finished a very close third, had finished behind Alderney at Goodwood. The most successful horse during the season was another four-year-old gelding called Prominent, by High Hat and also owned by Percy Wright who won five races on the trot, starting with a couple of handicaps at Salisbury and Brighton but followed by the John Smith's Magnet Cup at York (a race he won again the next year), a valuable sponsored race at Goodwood and finally the Prix Foy at Longchamps, now a Group Two race. Not an easy horse to train, he stood very high on his pasterns and needed firm ground.

Another quite good horse was Carmine City, a filly by Charlottesville, owned by John (Loopy) Lambton. Poor John was very odd and only what you might call 18 bob in the pound. A member of the well-known Lambton family, he lived alone, looked after by a minder, couldn't drive but loved racing. After I had been at Whatcombe for about six months I started to be sent racing if there were runners at two meetings but, in any event if Carmine City was running it was me who was sent to the races to look after the owner! She won a few good handicaps and was fourth in the Bessborough Stakes at Ascot.

There was a good middle- to long-distance stayer in the yard called Random Shot, by Pirate King, who won the Chester Cup and Aston Park Stakes at Newbury, on the strength of which he was allowed to take his chance in the Ascot Gold Cup. Random Shot was owned by a very rich widow called Gladys Benskin, who had a number of reasonably good horses with Arthur for many years and was a friend of my aunt, Mary Asprey. His problem was that even though he seemed placid enough at home, he was an extraordinarily bad traveller. Usually Arthur used Lambourn Racehorse Transport (LRT) to transport horses to racecourses, but he also had his own private horsebox. I had an HGV driving licence going back to Cheshire days when I had my own box, so Arthur asked me to take Random Shot and his lad very carefully and slowly to Ascot on Gold Cup day. This I did, probably being cursed by hundreds of car drivers on the way, but the horse never turned a hair and his very good lad said that he had never travelled so well to a racecourse. In the race itself Random Shot ran a blinder but was outclassed by the winner, Rock Roi, trained by Peter Walwyn, finishing six lengths behind him but still in second place.

There was a twist to this tale: Rock Roi was routinely drug tested and a 'forbidden' substance was found; he was therefore disqualified and the Ascot Gold Cup awarded to Random Shot. Peter Walwyn was cleared of any wrongdoing and the mystery was never solved. Poor Rock Roi must be about the unluckiest horse ever; not only was he disqualified after the 1971 Ascot Gold Cup but he won the race again a year later, only to be disqualified again, this time for causing interference to the second horse, Erimo Hawk, and was placed second with the race awarded to Erimo Hawk.

Another very useful horse on his day was Royal Echo, a four-year-old colt by Relko, another of Mrs Benskin's. A somewhat moody character, he needed humouring and very careful attention; he started by winning a minor event at Lingfield but then won the valuable *Daily Mirror* Handicap, the race immediately before Mill Reef's Derby at Epsom. However, his best performance in my view was when he was given a superb ride waiting in front by Bruce Raymond when winning the Peter Hastings Stakes at Newbury in September.

Arthur Budgett had a stable jockey in Geoff Baxter, a good all-round jockey who spent all his riding career at Whatcombe starting as an apprentice. He could ride at a handy weight – 7st. 12lbs – rode out every day at Whatcombe unless he was away racing and was an invaluable asset to the yard. As a character he didn't set the world on fire and probably realised his limitations. He did ride most of the horses but had to accept that it did not necessarily follow that any ride was automatically his. For instance he did not ride either of Budgett's Derby winners; Ernie Johnson rode Blakeney and Eddie Hide rode Morston. Similarly Arthur called upon a top 'name' jockey whenever he felt minded to do so.

When I went to the races it was in the capacity of the Trainer's Representative. The Travelling Head Lad went in the horsebox accompanied by the lad or lads who 'did' the horse or horses racing at the meeting on that day. My job was to check on arrival at the racecourse that our runners for the day had arrived safely and their final declarations to run had been made by the Travelling Head Lad. If the owners were present I should make myself known to them and report on the wellbeing of their horses. I would make sure that the booked jockeys had arrived and collect the saddle from the jockey after he had weighed out for the race, take it to the saddling boxes and prepare and saddle the horse for the race, assisted by the Travelling Head Lad. I would then go into the paddock, or parade ring, as some call it, with the owner. When the jockeys came into the paddock I would introduce our jockey to the owner if this was necessary and give him any pre-determined instructions or advice about any peculiarities of the horse that he may encounter. That was it really until after the race. Some owners liked to watch the race with their trainer, others preferred not to. After the race, if one has been lucky, the horse is led into the winners' enclosure, the jockey gives a debrief and there is much celebration; otherwise the debrief takes place in the general unsaddling enclosure without the celebration. Back at home my first job was to report to Budgett on the telephone (remember there were no mobiles then) on how the race had panned out, on what the jockey had said and ditto re the owner if he or she had been present.

Anthea and I had been keeping a watchful eye open all this time for a house we could either buy or rent and about June time we heard that a house about a mile away from Pheasant Cottage was coming on the market. Called Inholmes Lodge it had enough rooms down and up, a short drive off the road, a garden, a one-acre field with a couple of loose boxes and feed/tack room and a separate three-bedroom cottage. The area was called Woodlands St Mary, about three miles from Lambourn. Just the job and I bought it for £22,000. We moved in sometime in August and I let the cottage to Duncan Sasse, one of Barry Hills' learner assistants. It was a mile further away from Whatcombe but that was the least of my worries. Anthea was pregnant with our second child due the following February but at least we were now a united family, joined by Simon, just over a year old, and his nanny, Kay, a good sensible girl, and my two whippets.

Socially we were getting to know the Lambourn area and make a few friends. I had felt a bit sorry for Anthea sometimes when I was out most of the day and away racing a fair bit but at least she could always come racing with me and often did so. Quite a few of the younger Lambourn trainers and assistants used to come to the Pheasant at lunchtime. Paul Cole was one of them, Ben Leigh another. Both were comparatively new on the scene, but on the other end of the scale was Henry Candy, then assistant to his father Derrick who had been an undergraduate friend of my father's at Oxford. He was very good and friendly to Anthea and me in those early days.

In the second half of 1971 in the real world the terrible IRA riots in Northern Ireland were causing untold distress, the EEC agreed terms for UK membership – pretty topical – and the House of Commons voted to join by 356 votes to 244. On the sporting front, the Prime Minister, in the unlikely shape of Edward Heath, competed in the Admiral's Cup sailing races which resulted in a British win and Harvey Smith was stripped of his victory in the Show Jumping Derby for giving the V sign.

At Whatcombe, although I didn't know it at the time, storm clouds were gathering. I had been working there for nine months, one quarter of the three-year period agreed, but more significantly half the time before which we were required to pay for the whole property. I did think that Arthur Budgett and also his wife, Bay, were being perhaps less friendly; however, initially I put that down to my imagination. However, one day he said to me that he was thinking of building a small yard of fifteen to twenty boxes on the property from where he would continue to train a few horses. I could see huge problems with this plan. Our agreement was that at the end of the three-year period he was to leave Whatcombe and retire from training. If he chose to continue – and particularly on the property – I would not be in a strong position regarding taking on the staff and hoping that a significant number of the existing owners would stay. I felt that he would have the pick of both, which would inevitably lead to clashes regarding management of the property, staffing, managing and maintaining the gallops and problems generally.

The other main matter to be tackled was that as it was getting quite near to payment time, the legal side came into play regarding contracts to be drawn up, so enter the lawyers. We had done everything on our side to raise and have prepared the money by having sold the house in which I lived and the Home Farm, plus another tenanted farm, but it was still necessary for the contracts for the sale and purchase of the property to be agreed. Our family solicitors were an old established traditional small firm called William Easton and Sons, their office being in the heart of London's Fleet Street. The senior partner Aubrey Easton was well-known to my father and Eric, my father's brother and co-Trustee, and indeed to me, also a Trustee having already been dealing with the firm for several years. Arthur Budgett's solicitors were a firm in Reading which had also, apparently, been the Budgett solicitors for some time.

One has heard so many times that once lawyers become involved, the problems start and so it turned out to be in this case. What had started as, on the face of it, an agreement between two families, descended into a nightmare. Apart from the threat of the new yard, which would have been on property by then owned by us, other, new obstacles were raised; first, a clause was inserted in the draft contract that there would be a pre-emption right under a complicated and flawed mathematical formula for the Budgett family to buy back the property for a period of twenty-one years in the event of something happening to me which rendered me incapable of continuing to train horses at Whatcombe or indeed if I decided not to continue doing so; second, the price was to rise by £30,000 to £200,000. None of these new game changing demands were of our making but we considered, and indeed were advised by Eastons, that they were unacceptable. In an effort to restore the equilibrium and keep the whole matter afloat, a meeting excluding lawyers between both sets of Trustees was arranged to take place at my parents' flat in Arlington House, London on 21st March 1972, attended by Arthur and Bay Budgett, their Trustee,

Richard Watt, my father Michael Johnson, his brother Eric and myself. The atmosphere was cordial but tense. Agreement was reached on the following basis:

- We agreed to the price increase to £200,000.
- There would be no new yard built on the property.
- Contracts would be exchanged and completed by 1st June 1972.
- Arthur Budgett would finally vacate Whatcombe by two weeks after the December Sales at Newmarket 1973.
- Arthur Budgett would pay rent at 3 per cent of the purchase price of £200,000 on completion up until the time he vacated the property.
- There would be no pre-emption clause but Arthur Budgett would have the right to re-purchase the property at any time after the completion date and before the end of 1973 should circumstances exist whereby I was not able to take over the house and yard.

That should have been 'that'. All that was left to be done was the formal contract to be drawn up. We reported the final agreement terms to Geoffrey Heggs, the partner at Eastons' dealing with the matter. Geoffrey was a very sound, highly capable man who I had known and trusted implicitly for several years. He contacted the Budgett solicitors accordingly seeking clarification over the re-purchasing clause (No. 6 above) so that it could be translated into legal language for the purposes of the contract. In reply he received a letter saying, inter alia, that the 'first refusal' should be for a period of not just until the end of 1973 but for 'the full per-petuity period' which in legal language could last 'for the period of a life or lives and 21 years thereafter'. This prompted Geoffrey Heggs to write to my father on 20th April 1972 expressing, 'Every time you meet Arthur Budgett and reach an agreement with him his Solicitor improves upon the terms.' So we were back not perhaps to square one but not where we thought we were at the end of the meeting on 21st March.

While all this was going on, Anthea produced our second son on Valentine 's Day, 14th February at around six o'clock in the morning. I arrived at the John Radcliffe hospital in Oxford just in time and, before I knew what was going on, had a white gown wrapped round me and was ushered into the delivery room. All went well and I was back at Whatcombe in time for second lot. In the lead-up to the birth various names for the unborn child were shunted around and, not knowing the sex, I plumped for 'Sam'. If she had been a girl she would have been called Samantha and if a boy, just plain Sam. This selection did not have universal approval but, nevertheless, Sam it has always been to family and friends even though he was eventually christened Patrick, by which name he is known in his business circles but, as far as I am aware, nowhere else.

I carried on as normal at Whatcombe, with the new season having started in the last week of March. In mid-April I was sent racing, representing Arthur Budgett on a Saturday. As it was a northern meeting Anthea and I stayed with my parents on the Saturday night, returning to Inholmes Lodge on the Sunday. On Monday morning I arrived at Whatcombe as normal at seven a.m. to prepare for first lot and chatted as usual with Tom Dowdeswell about the stable's runners over the weekend and probable plans for the week ahead, greeting Arthur Budgett when he came into the yard just before 7.30. Everything normal. After first lot I returned home for breakfast soon after nine o'clock and almost immediately received a telephone call from Geoffrey Heggs at Eastons saying that he had had a letter from Budgett's solicitors calling the whole deal off. The bottom dropped out of my world. We, as Trustees, had done everything that we had been requested to do but had been let down and deceived. I had lost my home, farm and future livelihood at the hands of a man trusted by me and my immediate family. I rang Arthur Budgett telling him exactly what I thought of him, pointing out that he had broken his word and hadn't even got the guts to tell me himself when I saw him that very morning. I never saw him again.

I am convinced that Budgett, strongly aided and abetted by his wife, had changed his mind some months previously and that the change in the attitude of both of them referred to earlier had not just been my imagination. Bay, perhaps even more than Arthur, was distinctly unfriendly. She had a maddening habit of coming into the office when I was working out form and weight comparisons, flicking through the form book, making disparaging remarks and going out again. She had a most negative attitude about most things – jockeys in particular. All jockeys were crooks in her opinion and any jockey based north of the Trent was incompetent as well as being a crook. I remember at the infamous 21st March meeting seeing the expression on her face throughout, and also their very nice Trustee, Richard Watt, saying to me as an aside 'Arthur should post a notice on his office door saying BAY KEEP OUT.'

The inevitable family fallout happened. My father, having spoken to Budgett on the telephone, wrote to him on 28th April saying, 'Neither Eric nor Antony nor I have asked for anything more than what was agreed when I came down to meet you in London' and that Heggs only asked for legal language clarification on what we had reported to him and agreed upon as above. He went on 'In no way does this justify the unilateral breaking of the arrangement which we came to on March 21st.'

We were, of course, heavily out of pocket over the whole exercise. Not only did we face large legal expenses from Eastons but I had commissioned and indeed received a comprehensive ten-page survey on the entire property from Dreweatt, Watson & Barton of Newbury and another four-page electrical and drainage survey from Lloyd Enterprises, also of Newbury. Curiously, after the initial time when Anthea and I came down from Cheshire in 1970 to have lunch with Arthur and Bay, I never, in all the fifteen months that I worked at Whatcombe, set foot in any other room in the house except for the office. I never, for instance, ever went upstairs in the house that was to have become ours. I was never invited to come in to meet owners who came to Whatcombe on occasion to see their horses even though the understanding was that the Budgetts would do their best to encourage owners to keep their horses in training at Whatcombe after they had retired. Similarly I was never given an official position in the yard such as Assistant Trainer, a common position in a racing stable for someone doing the same job as me. What I do understand and never disclosed or mentioned at all to any member of the staff while I was working there was the fact that agreement in principle had been made for me to buy the property and take over the training at the end of 1973. A few days after I left on that fateful Monday morning and when the immediate shock and horror had subsided a little I wrote to Tom Dowdeswell and one of the other senior married lads, Joe Vowles, explaining the situation and why I was suddenly no longer working with them. Their replies showed, I think, the respect in which we held each other. Tom told me on more than one occasion that I was the best 'assistant' that he had ever had in a long career as Head Lad, rather contrary to the views spread around by Mr Budgett of my abilities after the separation. Quite early on he told me that he had never mucked out a horse in his life; he relied totally on Tom for all matters to do with running the yard. He took no cognisance that I had a good fifteen years' experience of riding out, riding work and stable management with successful trainers like George Owen, Doug Francis and Eric Cousins, in addition to my race riding experience and all aspects of running my own small stable before coming to him.

A word about Tom Dowdeswell – a pillar of a man in the racing world. He was the younger brother of Jack Dowdeswell who was champion National Hunt jockey in the 1946/47 season having fought with the 8th Army in North Africa and Italy in the Second World War. Jack was a fearless jockey who would ride anything and frequently paid the price for so doing, breaking about fifty bones in his body but winning just about every important race in the NH Calendar except the Grand National. Tom started as an apprentice to Captain Richard Gooch at West Ilsley at stables and land leased from the Lockinge Estate. Marcus Marsh was pupil assistant to Gooch and when he left to set up on his own in 1930, Tom went with him. One of the first horses he 'did' was Windsor Lad and Tom led him up when he won the Derby in 1934. In Tulyar's Derby winning year, 1952, Tom was Marsh's Travelling Head Lad. I remember backing Tulyar, sprinting on my bicycle to the village hairdresser in Crowthorne from Wellington during a break. When Marcus Marsh retired in 1964, Tom came to Arthur Budgett as Head Lad. Tom was everything necessary in a Head Lad: a great stableman, a firm but scrupulously fair minded disciplinarian with an uncanny knowledge of what goes on in a horse's mind and was extremely patient. He was also a brilliant work jockey, never asking a horse to do too much but was very able to report that there was or was not much more left in the tank. He believed firmly that races are won on the racecourse and not on the home gallops. He had a deep kindly voice and never stopped speaking reassuringly to his horses. Everybody liked Tom, he was a tremendous pleasure to work with; I felt honoured to have done so and learned everything that I did learn about training flat racehorses at Whatcombe from Tom. He was awarded the British Empire Medal in the Queen's Birthday Honours in 1978 for services to racing.

During the previous autumn, while I was still at Whatcombe, we started to receive the new batch of yearlings that would become two-year-olds on the following 1st January (the official 'birthday' for all thoroughbred racehorses). Among these was a darkish chestnut colt from Kirtlington Stud by Ragusa out of Windmill Girl. He was, therefore, a half-brother to both

Blakeney and Alderney. He was called Morston, named, as was Blakeney, after a village in Norfolk. Tom Dowdeswell broke in all the yearlings and I remember watching him with Morston, a backward and somewhat delicate colt but potentially a real athlete and beautiful mover. He was never going to be a two-year-old but my last recollection of him in the spring of 1972, when he was going out daily with the string ridden by the very sympathetic lad who 'did' him, was that he would make a lovely horse one day if given time to mature without being hurried. The rest is history: Morston did not run as a two-year-old. In fact he only ran twice in his life: he won a good maiden race over 1¼ miles at Lingfield on 11th May 1973 ridden by Frankie Durr and then just over three weeks later, on 6th June, he won the Derby at 25/1 in a field of twenty-five, ridden by Eddie Hide, Durr having elected to ride Mon Fils on whom he had won the 2,000 Guineas. The selection of Hide as the jockey is difficult to fathom in view of the Budgetts' normal scorn for northern-based jockeys, but in the Derby and with such a big field, all the top named jockeys already had rides on fancied horses. The press story was that the instruction to Hide was to not give Morston a hard race if he was not going well enough to be concerned in the finish, which prompted Hide to say to other jockeys at the start that he had turned down five fancied rides at Ripon to come down to Epsom to ride a non-trier. Morston never ran again, reportedly having suffered an injury in training. He was retired to stud where he was a near complete failure and sired very few winners.

Arthur Budgett behaved disgracefully as far as I and my family were concerned, but it would be wrong to say that he was a poor trainer. Bad trainers do not train two Derby winners; Budgett had not only patience of his own but also of the majority of his owners. I question, however, if he would have had anything like the success he enjoyed were it not for the support, loyalty and utmost skill and knowledge of Tom Dowdeswell.

10

Starting Again

It was time to regroup and, to use a modern expression, 'move on', and the search began for a yard, access to gallops and training grounds together with a house in which to live. While I was at Whatcombe I leased my old National Hunt horse, New Brighton, to my father but he had suffered a tendon injury from which he was recovering so I brought him down to Inholmes Lodge where he was parked in the stable in our field so that I or Anthea could ride him out each day on the local roads and lanes. The news of the Whatcombe/Budgett disaster spread round Lambourn like wildfire. The Budgetts were not popular with the Lambourn racing community, being regarded as aloof and unfriendly. It transpired that Whatcombe had been hawked around to several people before I came along but that all parties had fallen foul of Mr or Mrs Budgett or both. At first, nothing suitable having come up in Lambourn, we went and had a look at possibilities in Newmarket but much as I loved going to Newmarket for the sales and races, as well as having tremendous respect for the history and set-up, I didn't want to live there. Anthea and I went to have a close examination of the Stockbridge area, including Chattis Hill where my uncle Atty used to train but much of the lovely downland had been ploughed up, Chattis Hill itself having been turned into flats and a small housing estate and it was all rather sad. The magnificent arched entrance to the stable yard now leads onto a rectangular block of two-storey houses where once the likes of The Tetrarch and his son Tetratema looked out onto a finely gravelled and spotlessly clean pathway, surrounding a manicured lawn onto which any stable lad trod in fear of his life.

The area around Stockbridge was a famous racing centre in the 19th centrury, the centre of which was the privately owned racecourse, described as one of the prettiest courses in the country and one of the most fashionable, with Royal patronage from George IV to the Prince of Wales who later became Edward VII. Such famous races as The Champagne Stakes, Bibury Cup and Hurstbourne Stakes were held at Stockbridge; these names live on, the former is run at Doncaster and the latter two at Salisbury to this day and, I hope, will be forever more.

The racecourse was closed in 1898 because a section of the course was on land owned by the Barker-Mill family for centuries. The owner in the mid-19th century was a very jolly hunting parson, the Rev. Sir John Barker-Mill, who desported himself in loud check trousers and flamboyant ties. Enter, however, Mrs Marianne Vaudrey Barker-Mill, a strong-minded lady who violently disapproved of all forms of drinking and gambling and cancelled the lease of the land let to the racecourse, forcing its closure because at time the Jockey Club stipulated that all racecourses had to have a straight mile. She also withdrew the licence on several pubs owned by the family in that locality as well as selling land near Southampton to developers who constructed Southampton Docks. Walking amongst the creeper-and-foliage-covered ruins of the old racecourse stands and weighing room in the middle of beautiful rolling farmland it is difficult not to allow one's mind to imagine the conversation among jockeys such as George Fordham, who rode six winners and a dead heat in the afternoon of a June day in 1867, and to listen to the machinations of the Druid's Lodge Confederacy hatching their next plot to enrich themselves at the hands of the bookmakers. Next door to the racecourse was Danebury stables owned by the famous racing family of John Day, father and son... The latter's daughter, Catherine, married a top jockey of the time, Tom Cannon. On John Junior's death Tom Cannon took over the training at Danebury. Tom and Catherine became the great grandparents of Lester Piggott, their daughter having married another jockey, Ernest Piggott...

The Druid's Lodge Confederacy was a curious collection of five people who determined a method of making themselves fistfuls of cash based on secrecy and dishonesty. They were: an Irish vet named Holmer Peard, highly regarded as an excellent judge of a yearling; Percy Cunliffe, an Old Etonian gold speculator; Wilfred Bagwell Purefoy, an entrepreneur in various fields and a collector of rare orchids; Frank Forester, a fearless huntsman; and Edward Wigan, a pernickety little man with no sense of humour. The wide open spaces of the Hampshire Downs suited the Confederacy's secrecy requirements; not only was it eminently suitable for training racehorses but their stables at Netheravon on Salisbury Plain were well cut off from prying eyes and far enough from villages and pubs. Strict rules were imposed on stable staff, the trainer was well looked after financially and was of the kind to know where his bread was buttered. Probably their best coup was on a filly called Hackler's Pride, which had been selected by Holmer Peard. Having satisfied the Confederacy as to her merits by winning a reasonable contest at Hurst Park, she 'ran' most disappointingly in several subsequent races, which failures were duly noted by the handicapper. The horse, along with three others owned by the Confederacy, was entered for the Cambridgeshire at Newmarket towards the end of September 1903 and the Confederacy, headed by the 'put on' man Forester, using several different 'agents' such as a railway station master, a dentist and even a priest dotted round the country, started to back the horse from 25 to 1 down to nine to two favourite. Hackler's Pride made 'hacks' of the opposition and won the race by a very comfortable three lengths, the Confederacy collecting an estimated £10m at today's value. And, what's more, they repeated the dose in the same race with the same filly the following year, but by only a neck this time.

In those days there was not nearly as much racing as there is now and transport to racecourses was more complicated with journey times far longer. Most transport was by rail, with horses being led on foot from the training stable to the nearest railway station, usually several miles away. The lad travelling with his horse would be required to take with him all necessities for his horse including his feed, hay net, paddock clothing and any other special needs for a one-or-two-night stay away. On arrival the horse would be walked to the racecourse and allotted a box in the racecourse stables. For the same reasons, in order for trainers to determine the ability of horses in their care, 'trials' were frequently arranged between horses in their own stables and also with those of other neighbouring trainers; this was very much the case in the Stockbridge area with jockeys coming to stay for, say, a couple of days for specially arranged 'trials'. Here's when the secrecy element came into play: nobody apart from the trainer himself knew what weight his horses were carrying, not even the jockey. The trainer would saddle the horses himself and insert a weight 'cloth' under the saddle containing slabs of lead fitted into the 'cloth' compartments. Atty Persse was a past master at this. I inherited his trials book in which he noted the amount of weight carried by all the horses in trials. In the case of The Tetrarch, he had been 'tried' more than once with other older horses of a known calibre that had won high-class races and, giving away lumps of weight, had defeated them pointless. No wonder Atty and his cousin Dermot McCalmont, who owned The Tetrarch, felt justified in having a huge punt on the horse when he won on his first racecourse appearance at Newmarket. There is an interesting and little known postscript about The Tetrarch involving one of the members of the Druid's Lodge Confederacy mentioned earlier: the vet, Holmer Peard, so good at picking out promising-looking yearlings, had come to have a look at The Tetrarch as a yearling at his owner and breeder Edward Kennedy's stud, Straffan Station, in Co. Kildare. He liked him and struck a deal to buy him for £800. Kennedy asked Peard what he intended to do with the colt. 'Oh, I think I'll cut [geld] him and turn him away for a year or two because I think he'll make a great jumper one day.'

'In that case, the deal's off' replied Kennedy. Shortly afterwards Atty Persse, who had trained his half-sister, Nicola, to win in 1910 also came to see him and subsequently bought him at Doncaster Sales in September 1912 for 1,300 guineas. The rest, as they say, is history.

***

Back in the Lambourn Valley the search continued. All our friends and the racing community as a whole were most supportive and extremely sympathetic to our situation. In addition to Paul Cole and Ben Leigh, we had become very friendly with a young jumping trainer called Simon Morant who trained at Weathercock House in Upper Lambourn; his secretary, Emma Nicolson, shared our cottage at Inholmes with Duncan Sasse and a couple of others. A few years later she married James Bethell, with whom I had worked at Whatcombe. The marriage did not work out and, by a curious coincidence, she married, secondly, the adopted son of my neighbour in Cheshire, he who drank my whisky before I returned from my office in the evening and came for breakfast after I had left in the morning. I asked Simon if he would train New Brighton for me until such time as we found somewhere, which he readily agreed to do. Simon, a delightful Old Etonian with a lovely self-deprecating turn of phrase and a very acute sense of humour, had, unfortunately, a problem not normally associated with Etonians: a shortage of cash. The inappropriately named Weathercock House, too, had a problem: it leaked but not so the stables, which were of sound construction and the occupants lived in rather more luxurious conditions than their trainer. Simon happened to mention to me one day that perhaps I should do some research on a property called Berkeley House, also in Upper Lambourn and on its occupant, Ken Payne, and more importantly on Ken Payne's boss and actual owner of Berkeley House, one Krishna Maharaj. Most of the horses Ken (known as 'Window') Payne trained were owned by Maharaj or his nominees, and Simon had heard a rumour that all, perhaps, was not well with the arrangement. Maharaj also had a number of horses trained by Ryan Price (or Flying Rice to give him his *Private Eye* name). Could this possibly be a 'window' of opportunity? With a bit of stealth I got hold of his telephone number and called him. I told him my name, that I lived near Lambourn and that I would like to have a business meeting with him in connection with racing. He was a bit cagey but agreed to have lunch with me in London.

I was a member of the Curzon House Club, set up with a bang when gambling clubs and casinos were legalised in the mid-1960s. Plush and quite up-market, the Curzon House was not as smart as Crockfords and certainly not as exclusive as the Clermont but it had expert French-imported croupiers, baccarat, chemin de fer (chemmy), vingt et un (blackjack) and roulette tables plus a good restaurant. More often than not whenever I went, I would see people that I knew and it attracted a wide circle of people, including many from the world of show business. Little Davy Kaye, the compère and resident comedian at the Embassy Club, frequently appeared after his night stint at the Embassy was finished. The Club also had a few bedrooms and I sometimes used to stay there while on business in London when I was still working at RJ&N. It had another advantage as well: if one wanted to come in late in the evening accompanied by a young lady and did not want to be noticed there was a small door leading off the main gambling room which led to the bedrooms, which avoided taking the lift from the entrance

lobby. Anyway I thought it was a good place to entertain Mr
Maharaj. I came straight to the point after a drink and a few
pleasantries and told him briefly about the Budgett saga and my
riding days and stated that I was looking for a yard preferably
in or near Lambourn, that I had the funds ready to pay for it
and how about him selling Berkeley House to me? After all he
hadn't owned it for long, had only got Ken Payne in there with
pretty rubbishy horses and most of his horses were trained by
Ryan Price anyway, so what did he need Berkeley House for?
There was a lot of muttering, some haggling, some objections
but I could see that he was more than a little interested. In the
end, a bottle or two later, we came to a verbal agreement but I
was sworn to absolute secrecy and gave my undertaking that I
would not go poking my nose anywhere near Berkeley House.
The following week formal agreement was reached, after which
it was over to the lawyers. I did not, however, set foot in any
part of Berkeley House land, stables or the house itself until the
property had become mine and K. Payne had vacated. Maharaj
acted in total good faith and even left six horses for me to train
in my new yard. None of them turned out much good but I
wheedled them out, sold some for him and bought a few more.
We became good friends and I trained for him for a couple of
years or so until I noticed that his payment of training fees was
becoming slower and slower. Eventually he dropped out of racing
and I saw no more of him. Here, however, I must temporarily
fast forward about twenty-five years. I was sitting at home one
evening when the telephone rang; I answered it and a male voice
said that his name was Clive Stafford-Smith and that he was a
lawyer; he asked if I knew or had ever known Krishna Maharaj. I
replied that I used to know him but hadn't seen or heard of him
for very many years and why did he want to know?

'Because', he said, 'Kris Maharaj has been on death row in
a penitentiary in Florida for fourteen years for dual murder.'
Of course I had no idea and was absolutely flabbergasted.

Stafford-Smith went on to outline details of the case and that he was acting for him. He asked, as part of his plea to get Kris off death row, if I would be prepared to provide a written character reference and, if necessary, go to Florida to corroborate my evidence. I did write saying the period of time that I had known Kris and that our business relationship and friendship had been without blemish. Luckily I heard no more about going to Florida. Kris's business in England was based in Bermondsey and called West Indian Foods. I understood that his products were imported in tin cans from Trinidad. From time to time Kris's case has featured in television and newspaper reports. Clive Stafford-Smith did succeed eventually in reducing Kris's sentence from death to life imprisonment but after several more appeals having been denied, and despite very strong evidence that it would not have been possible for Kris Maharaj to have committed the crimes for which he had been charged, he is still to this day in prison in Florida.

Berkeley House, in the then hamlet of Upper Lambourn and about a mile out of Lambourn proper, was built in the 1930s by The Hon. Dorothy Paget, the daughter of the first and only Lord Queenborough. It was a mock Georgian style red-brick house with four medium-sized rooms on the ground floor, four bedrooms on the first floor and two attic rooms above. A later extension added mainly utility rooms and another large sitting room on the ground floor with additional bedrooms and bathrooms upstairs. The stable yard complex consisted of a lovely semi-circular south-facing row of thirty boxes, tack room, feed room with good storage space above with corn bins, the contents of which could be gravity fed to subsidiary bins below. Adjoining were a lads' hostel and separate flat. At the other end of the row of boxes was a Head Lad's house with its own entrance and small garden. There was a small top yard of six boxes with ample hay and straw space in a large barn. The property had 15 acres of paddocks, the house had a decent sized private garden and, curiously, there was a good swimming pool next to which was a separate secretary's office and an enclosed loose school.

Dorothy Paget was a very extraordinary lady: her mother Pauline Whitney was an American heiress and cousin of Jock Whitney, a hugely rich businessman and former American Ambassador to Great Britain. Dorothy was educated at Heathfield but grew up to be a singularly unattractive and most eccentric person weighing in excess of 20st, her only passions being racing and gambling. She owned the Ballymacoll Stud in Co. Meath, Ireland and had a long string of trainers with whom she fell out on a regular basis, including Basil Briscoe, Fulke Walwyn, Walter Nightingall, Gordon Richards, Owen Anthony and 'Frenchie' Nicholson. She owned many high-class and successful horses but the best and most famous was Golden Miller, the winner of five Cheltenham Gold Cups, 1932 to '36, and the Grand National. In the Gold Cup Owen Anthony trained him for the first and Basil Briscoe the other four but she fell out with both of them; the jockeys were Evan Williams, Gerry Wilson (twice), Billy Stott and Ted Leader. Golden Miller is the only horse to have won the Cheltenham Gold Cup and Grand National in the same year. Dorothy Paget also owned Straight Deal who won a wartime Derby in 1943 trained by Walter Nightingall and ridden by Tommy Carey. During the war all races normally run at Epsom were transferred to the July Course at Newmarket. A jockey who rode very successfully for Dorothy Paget post-war was Bryan Marshall, an Irishman from Co. Tipperary whose start in racing came when he was apprenticed to Atty Persse at Chattis Hill and, I discovered from the old man's gallop diary, could ride work at 7st. 3lbs. Increasing weight and the advent of the Second World War, when he was commissioned into the 5th Royal Inniskilling Dragoon Guards (the Skins) and demobbed with the rank of Captain at the end of the war, transformed Marshall into a jump jockey at which he excelled, becoming Champion Jockey in 1946/7. He won the Grand National on Early Mist in

1953 and on Royal Tan in 1954; one afternoon at Folkestone in 1948 he rode the first five winners on the card, all owned by Dorothy Paget who berated him soundly for finishing only second for her in the 6th and last race of the day. When Marshall eventually retired as a jockey Dorothy Paget was instrumental in arranging for him to set up as a trainer at Berkeley House. She hated men, therefore never married. It would be true to say that if she ever had any inclination to find a possible suitor, her advances were likely to have been rejected. She gambled hugely on her horses, betting vast sums, but bookmakers relished her business since her reasons for backing the horses were not always very sound. From a trainer's viewpoint she must have been a nightmare: on the one hand she spent lavishly on her horses and had a successful breeding operation at Ballymacoll but on the other hand you never knew where you were with her; she suffered from raging changes of mind and would think nothing of telephoning her trainers at any time during the night with instructions or counter-instructions. Frequently she would stay in bed all day and be up all night – just impossible – but she also had a kind and generous streak and donated large sums to charity: a group that benefited enormously from her generosity was Russian émigrés during the Stalin era. Dorothy Paget died aged only fifty-four in 1960.

As soon as the Berkeley House deal was signed, I put Inholmes Lodge on the market and it sold very quickly for £44,000, exactly double what I had paid for it only fifteen months pre-viously. It seems quite extraordinary now looking back some forty-five years how much property values have increased over this period. In 1972 the average UK house price was £7,374 and inflation was 6.4 per cent. In other main events a serious miners' strike led by Arthur Scargill was held in January and February, Bloody Sunday at Derry, Northern Ireland was on 30th January following which, after two Government investigations, it was concluded that the shooting of fourteen civilians was 'unjustified and unjustifiable'; the Munich Olympic Games was the scene of eleven Israeli athletes being murdered by Arab gunmen. In America the Watergate scandal broke, which ultimately led to the resignation to avoid impeachment of President Richard Nixon. A pretty torrid year but on a lighter note Harry Nilsson's 'Without You' was top pop song of the year. My year concluded by first setting foot inside Berkeley House in mid-December and, on 23rd December, Anthea and myself, two small children and a nanny moved in for what was a fairly chaotic Christmas.

Berkeley House

So, 1973 dawned and a new chapter started. I had already applied for and had been granted a Trainer's Licence for the new season starting in March having stated that (a) I had existing stabling and accommodation and (b) the use of the Lambourn gallops. What I was short of was horses to train and the staff to look after them. I struck lucky on the second of the above: when Atty Persse moved to Lambourn after the end of the war, he took on a man as Head Lad called Archie Hughes, who had been born and brought up on the Cheshire/ North Wales borders near Bangor-on-Dee and went to work at George Goswell's stable, from where he became a National Hunt jockey, having his last ride at Cardiff in 1939 immediately before the outbreak of war. When the war was over he was demobbed and joined Captain Goode in Lambourn before going to my uncle Atty, where he remained until the old man retired in 1954. He then took a position as private trainer to Lord Waterford in Ireland but Archie and the Irish didn't quite work out so back to Lambourn he came as Head Lad to Col. Peter Payne-Galwey. On the latter's death in 1971, Ken Payne, who had himself been apprenticed to Atty Persse in his younger days, invited Archie to come to Berkeley House so he was already in situ when I arrived. I snapped him up so he didn't even have to move house and I was very lucky to have a man of his knowledge and experience. In all the time that I was in Lambourn he never took a holiday or spent one night away from his house adjoining the yard. I also acquired as second in command and Travelling Head Lad Norman Mackness, who had been working for a short time for Ken Payne as well. Norman, who had been apprenticed to Peter Hastings, rode several winners on the flat and over jumps, the last two of which were on horses I trained. A loyal, good all-round horseman, he and his wife Jo became responsible and trusted members of my staff.

All the major yearling sales had passed by in the autumn and before I was sure about having anywhere to train them, but in January 1973, Doncaster Sales, in which my great friend Harry Beeby now played a prominent part, had a sale of horses just turned two-year-olds (as mentioned, all 'birthdays' of thorough-bred horses being officially on 1st January notwithstanding their actual foaling day). Doncaster had always been a major sales venue run by Tattersalls until, in 1957, that company decided to concentrate all their activities in Newmarket and did not renew their lease on the premises in Doncaster. In 1962, however, Willie Stephenson, having been approached by Doncaster Council, and Ken Oliver restarted Doncaster Bloodstock Sales. Willie was a highly successful trainer and the only man to train a Grand National and Derby winner, while Ken was a leading National Hunt trainer, former amateur jockey and head of an established agricultural auctioneering business based in Hawick, Roxburghshire. They recruited Harry Beeby, son of leading trainer George Beeby who trained, among many top horses, Brendan's Cottage, winner of the Cheltenham Gold Cup in 1939, ridden by George Owen, who in turn trained Russian Hero, winner of the Grand National in 1947, and my mentor in my riding days. I went to this sale and bought a couple of inexpensive horses that I liked in the hope of passing them on to owners for the coming season. At the end of one sales session I was in the bar buying a couple of drinks for friends when I was badly bumped into by rather a dishevelled man wearing an old Husky, the drinks spilling onto the floor. The man, somewhat the worse for wear, apologised profusely, and kindly replenished the drinks. That evening I received a telephone call at my hotel from a man who introduced himself as Billy McDonald and asked if I would like to have dinner with him. He explained that he was the man who had upset my drinks. Having nothing better to do I accepted.

Billy appeared, well scrubbed-up, neat and tidy, wearing a smart suit – very different from the scruffy drunk I had met earlier. It was almost as if he had come for an interview for a job, which in a way, I suppose, he had. It became clear that following the little incident in the bar, he had made enquiries about who I was and what I was doing at Doncaster. During the course of dinner he told me much of his life story, how he was born and brought up in Northern Ireland into a reasonably well-off farming family, learnt to ride and competed in local shows and gymkhanas and became interested in racing. With typical Irish charm he saw little point in saying a great deal about his education and it was difficult to pin down the success or otherwise of his competitive riding ability but it was the start of a close friendship, which lasted for many years; as it eventually dwindled I could sum him up by saying that I would send him across the world to sell a horse but not out of my sight to buy one.

He told me that evening that when he was in his later teens he fell in with an American who offered to take him to California and help him get a job, which indeed he did – selling cars, but not any old cars, rather Rolls-Royces, Bentleys, Lamborghinis and the like, limos, as Billy called them. Some of his stories, if they can be believed, were hilarious, involving of course the Hollywood stars he met and befriended, from Frank Sinatra upwards (or downwards, whichever way one looks at it). Anyway he told me that he had recently returned from the United States and had decided to renew his interest in racing using his American and Irish contacts. He was impressed, so he told me, by my racing knowledge and experience and that I was now setting up on my own, so perhaps there might be some mileage in our working together. I invited him to come and stay the following weekend at Berkeley House, during which we formed an unofficial liaison to cooperate on our respective contacts. I said that he could stay at Berkeley House whenever he wanted and come and go as he pleased; to help him with a bit of publicity, I said that when we were together at sales, I would allow him to bid on my behalf for horses that I was interested in.

By mid-January 1973 I had accumulated eighteen horses, including the six of Maharaj's, and recruited enough staff to look after them. Archie Hughes and Norman Mackness were well ensconced and Eric Cousins's daughter Wendy came down from Cheshire to become my secretary and to ride out daily. Fasig-Tipton, the oldest Thoroughbred Sales company in the United States, founded in 1898, were holding a Sale of unraced two-year-olds at Hialeah, Miami. Ocala, Florida is an important area of thoroughbred breeding in the US. Billy, Anthea and I decided to go to test the water. Henry Cecil's twin brother David, who was setting up a Bloodstock Sales Agency, came with us. I had known both Cecil twins for some time and David trained a few horses in Lambourn for a while before I arrived there. We also planned to go on to California after the Hialeah sale to meet up with some of Billy's contacts in the racing world.

This was my first experience of the American racing scene and very different it is to our own. All the tracks are similar left-handed ovals with all the training taking place on the racecourse complex with boxes, or stalls as they call them, being allotted to trainers for the duration of a meeting, which can last up to three weeks with races taking place on two or three days per week. Miami has two racecourses, one at Hialeah and the other at nearby Gulfstream and we went to both during our stay. At the sales I bought three two-year-olds, one for Bobby McAlpine, one for Kris Maharaj and one for David Cecil's business partner, Bobby Alexander. On the last night of the sale we rushed off as soon as possible because we had tickets for the World Heavyweight

Championship fight between George Foreman and Joe Frazier; however, by the time our taxi arrived at the stadium, we were too late, Frazier having been knocked out in the second round.

From Miami, we flew to Los Angeles where I had been before on wire business during my time at RJ&N, but this was very different and certainly a lot more fun. Where better to start meeting people than at the races, so on our first day we headed straight for Santa Anita, surely the most attractive of all American racecourses, having the beautiful backdrop of the St Gabriel Mountains rising from pretty countryside on the far side of the track. Racing first took place at Santa Anita in 1904 but the venture failed, and was not revived until 1934, when a movie producer named Hal Roach persuaded stars like Bing Crosby, Al Jolson and Harry Warner, of Warner Brothers, to invest in a brand new racecourse. At that time it was the only major track in California and ran such races as the Santa Anita Derby and Santa Anita Handicap. The famous horse Seabiscuit won the Handicap in 1940. Soon afterwards the racecourse was closed during the Second World War with the facilities and buildings used as an assembly point for Japanese POWs. Re-opening again after the war the course became increasingly popular, attracting vast crowds, and put on more top-class races with much increased prize money and now shares the Breeders' Cup races, which take place over three days each autumn with Churchill Downs, Keeneland, Belmont and one or two others. A feature of Santa Anita is the shute or spur of about a furlong, which provides an extra dimension to the standard oval track.

Through Billy's introduction we had been invited to lunch in the members' dining room by Charles Russell, past president of the California Thoroughbred Breeders' Association, and his wife. Charlie, or 'Boy' as he was known to his friends, was absolutely delightful, as was his charming wife, known as Sister – I never did find out her real name. Charlie had a 1,400-acre stud farm called Double H Ranch near Carmel, about a two-hour drive from San Francisco, and during lunch he invited us to extend our stay and to come and stay with him at the ranch in about a week's time to see the stud and breeding operation. It was an opportunity not to be missed. We met several of Billy's cronies during the afternoon but the one that stands out was an extrovert bloodstock agent called Albert Yank – yes, his real name but affectionately referred to as 'Alberto Pie, the good guy'. Albert Yank was a showman and a salesman par excellence. On another occasion I witnessed him in action selling a horse to a somewhat doubting potential purchaser. 'Tell me, Mr Yank' said he, 'Do you really rate this horse and think he can really run?'

'Can he run?' replied Yank, 'Why, it is just a matter of Goodbye Starter. Hello Judge.' Alberto was always dressed with at least one major piece of clothing being purple so was easy to spot, or indeed, to avoid.

The gambling metropolis and surreal city of Las Vegas was, we realised, only a one-hour flight from Los Angeles, and in a moment of madness we decided to go. Flights were heavily discounted, sponsored by the gambling cartels, and so was accommodation in the very smart hotels, so it was dirt cheap. The first thing one sees on leaving the plane is row upon row of fruit machines; likewise as soon as one steps into the hotel lobby. We booked in at the Desert Inn with sumptuous rooms and every comfort. I don't need to go into any great detail about Las Vegas being a complete one off, stuck as it is in the middle of the Nevada Desert, with every form of entertainment imaginable available pretty much within walking distance on The Strip, little more than a hundred yards away from which the desert takes over. At least that was the case in 1973; it's a little bigger now. Not that anybody seemed to walk anywhere: limos poked out of every opening. We only had time for twenty-four hours in this totally unreal fantasy land and were determined to make the most of it. Each hotel had a superstar show or entertainer: Dean Martin, Sammy Davis Jr, Andy Williams, the white tiger duo Siegfried and Roy and so on, but there was one who stood out – Elvis. I rang the hotel box office where he was performing: 'Four seats for Elvis Presley, please.'

'Certainly, Sir' came the reply, 'which year were you thinking of?' Undaunted, I went down to the Hall Porter's (Bell Captain, they call it) desk holding in my hand a $20 note clearly visible as I placed my hand on his desk. 'Four good seats for Elvis Presley tonight?' He relieved me of the $20 and I had the tickets in the same hand no more than a minute later. I can't remember the cost but it was immeasurably low. At the performance later in the evening we sat centre stage on a half-moon type banquette with a table in front of us for our drinks no more than 20 feet from where Elvis Presley performed for 1½ hours, singing all his well-known songs plus a lot more, every now and then mopping his brow with a white silk scarf, following which he launched it into the audience and it was replaced with another one. He was absolutely fantastic and it was a performance that I shall never forget. We were all completely mesmerised.

American gambling does nothing for me. Huge opulent halls which can be measured in acres with the constant noise and clanging of fruit machines operating twenty-four hours a day, roulette wheels by the score, with a double zero so there are 38 numbers to choose from instead of 37, tables of blackjack, trente et quarante and baccarat all with dolly bird croupiers dressed provokingly, plus many craps tables, all of which is a long way from the glamour and sophistication of the French equivalent. The vast majority of the players being dressed in all manner of ways just drags the scene down to resemble a check-in terminal at an airport rather than a place of entertainment and excitement.

San Francisco was our next stop. Just about my favourite American city in those days; cosmopolitan with a charm and atmosphere all of its own and geographically prevented from becoming a sprawling mass by being located on the side of an estuary, the scenery is outstandingly beautiful. The legendary

Golden Gate Bridge in the far distance crosses the bay to the quaint old town of Sausalito and in the bay lies Alcatraz Island on which the macabre and the now deserted semi-ruins of the infamous prison of still stand and earns income as a tourist attraction. Our primary object in coming to San Francisco was to pay a visit to Billy's former employer, a Norwegian American named Kjell Qvale, the primary distributor of British and European luxury motor cars but, of more interest to us, heavily involved with racing and with a stud farm about a hundred miles north of San Francisco to which we had been invited.

Qvale owned San Francisco's main racecourse, Golden Gate Fields. We drove up to the farm and were enthusiastically greeted by Mr Qvale, his softly spoken and charming manner fronted a very able and astute mind which became apparent as we toured his highly impressive breeding operation. It has to be said that California is not the ideal environment for breeding and rearing thoroughbred bloodstock. Yes, it's beautiful with fantastic scenery and wide open spaces but the soil is poor therefore the rich grass does not grow naturally. Totally different from England, Ireland and, for that matter, Kentucky. The California Thoroughbred Breeders' Association, though, has many members who do breed their own thoroughbreds and race them, Qvale being one and Charles Russell another. They have the land and the money to support their operations but substitutes have to be made to supplant the natural lack of what is found in the ground. Like anywhere else, the best quality hay and oats can be brought in but the natural goodness has to be in the form of vitamin and nutritional additives in nut form. During our tour and discussions, Qvale let on that he was in the process of buying Jensen Motors, a small but high quality marque of British sports cars which, like others in the motor industry, was under-capitalised and struggling. The factory was in West Bromwich and Qvale said that, as he would be spending a lot of time in England, would I like to train a couple of horses for him that he would send over? This was welcome news and I was delighted to accept.

Back in San Francisco, Charlie Russell said that he would send his own plane the next day to take us up to his ranch near Carmel, quite one of the prettiest parts of California on the Monterey peninsula. The 1,400-acre ranch was set back from the coast and up in the hills the main house, built in the 1920s by the Russell family who were major shareholders in Crocker Bank, was in Italian Mediterranean style with large rooms, some with cherry wood panelling and lovely stone arched verandas looking out onto beautifully kept gardens. The stable complex, about a five-minute walk from the house on slightly lower ground, was equally impressive with a wide circular range of adjoining wooden stables with tack rooms, feed houses, staff accommodation, many wooden-fenced paddocks spread over a wide area and a six-furlong oval training track. Charlie showed us the mares and foals and also some of the older horses and the just turned two-year-olds about to go into training. Of these he said that if I bought a nicely bred filly that he pointed out, he would send over an equally good-looking colt that we looked at for me to train for him. Neither of them looked to me like making early two-year-old types, but they were good-looking and well enough bred so the deal was done. Charlie flew us back to San Francisco and the next day we were off home at the end of a most informative and successful trip, during which I had acquired seven horses.

By the time I had moved into Berkeley House I had been in the Lambourn area, immersed in the racing scene, for some two and a half years and made many new friends but was still nervous at the start of the 1973 season, my first as a licenced trainer. At Aintree, Red Rum had won his first Grand National; ridden by Brian Fletcher he had caught the long-time leader, Crisp, ridden by Richard Pitman, in dramatic fashion just short of the line. We didn't have many early runners; the horses were, in the main, unknown quantities and I wanted to make sure that they gave a reasonable account of themselves when they appeared on the racecourse. The elusive first winner took its time in coming and it wasn't until 7th May that a horse called Close In, which I had bought very cheaply as a lead horse for the two-year-olds, won a small race. I did not even go to the meeting as I was elsewhere, at Wolverhampton – in those days a quite respectable minor meeting and many years before the introduction of all-weather tracks in England – running my first two-year-old, a filly called Sailors' Honey, who ran very well finishing fourth only two lengths behind the winner. She went on to win later in the season. Close In, however, broke the duck by winning easily by three lengths. Winners followed, not in a gushing torrent but more a steady trickle, but did include my first double, at Nottingham in August: Destiny Hill, the two-year-old I had bought for Bobby McAlpine at Hialeah won well, backed from 3/1 down to 9/4 favourite. I thought he would win, having run very well to be third, beaten by two necks on his first outing, but the other winner, a filly called Age Old, was a big surprise as she had badly disappointed when fancied on her previous race. Almost in desperation I had put a young and inexperienced apprentice jockey, Richard Watts, on her but she blazed off in front and just held on by a head. Watts had come to work for me from Arthur Budgett at Whatcombe, as did one or two other lads. Age Old was owned by an old friend of many years, Nick Robinson, who had a connection with the Newmarket Bloodstock Agency and started the racing magazine *Pacemaker*. Nick, as previously related, was largely responsible for Robert Sangster's interest in racing. In later years he started and managed Kennet Valley Thoroughbreds, a successful racing partnership and syndicate business.

I was exceptionally lucky that a number of my very best friends who were interested in racing and were aware of the appalling Budgett saga supported me by sending me horses to train or participating in taking shares in horses. Among those was my

Early days... Trouble?
What trouble?

Marieson (AJ
aboard) leads ...
and wins.

Formula 1-winning driver Innes
Ireland at Berkeley House.

Trainer at large.

Jeffrey Bernard at Berkeley House.
Probably the only horse that he ever sat
on – owned by Robert Sangster.

AJ, Anthea, Billy McDonald, Sweet Pea (unknown) and
David Cecil at Elvis Presley concert, Las Vegas.

Norman Mackness (Travelling Head Lad), Yves Saint-Martin (French Champion Jockey) and AJ with Funny Sunday, having won Prix Michel Houyvet, Deauville.

A Rolling Stone: Keith Richards and wife Patti at Maddox.

Maddox.

Tony Lewis, the only Welshman
to captain England at cricket ...
and (above right) Graham Gooch,
another English cricket captain,
taking good advice from AJ.

Charles Benson (below) and (right) Julian
'Screamer' Lewis posing for the chicks.

Barbadians all:
Garry Sobers,
Michael Stoute,
Wes Hall and
Charlie Griffiths at
Kensington Oval,
Bridgetown.

Michael Parkinson and Magsie.
(What is she thinking?)

Jemima at Maddox, 1989.

Robert (right) and Guy (left) Sangster
at Maddox party.

Top: AJ and Peter Hornby. Trouble in the outback: note huge boil on tyre.

Above: 16-foot crocodile seen in Kakadu National Park, Australia.

Left: Peter Hornby, Johnny Vestey and his daughter Torna in Sydney. All over … now playtime.

Arrival in Sydney – well done that car.

-25°C on Lake Baikal, Siberia (only another sixteen miles to go). Guide Alexei holding the reins, AJ beside, with Cilla behind the driver and William Gascoigne next to her.

Son Sam and grandson Charlie.

Son Simon and wife Marietta.

Cilla ... (isn't she lovely?).

super good friend Bryan Jenks, who I had known well since Cheshire days when he was living and farming in Shropshire. He had stacks of top-class horses both on the flat with Pat Rohan and Henry Candy and even more so under National Hunt Rules with Fred Rimell and Jack Bissill. I rode a few horses for him including Super Gay, on which I had won a hurdle race and been second in a flat race. Bryan very kindly asked me to buy him a horse at the end of season Horses in Training Sale at Newmarket, since he knew that I was looking for a horse with a bit of form and potential to go with the young stock that I would have to start with at Berkeley House for the 1973 season. I bought a good-looking grey colt called Tin Lid out of Jeremy Hindley's stable. He had been lightly raced as a two-year-old but had won and been placed and I knew Jeremy reasonably well enough since our riding days to trust him when I asked if there was any good reason not to buy him. Although a bit of a quirky character he seemed to have settled down all right in Lambourn, but after a couple of runs when he behaved in a bad and aggressive manner both in the paddock and in the races themselves I was very worried that I had bought a wrong-'un. However, we 'cut' him and turned him away for a couple of months which did the trick as we brought him back to racing fitness, and he won two races towards the end of the season, one ridden by George Cadwalladr, Eric Cousins's very underrated jockey, and the other by 'the long fellow' Lester Piggott in the good class St Anne's Handicap, carrying 9st. 6lbs and with twenty runners at Haydock at the beginning of November.

That win more or less wrapped up the racing for the season but the autumn and early part of the winter is a very busy time for trainers because all the major sales of yearlings take place at Newmarket, Doncaster and Goffs in Ireland at this time. The atmosphere at the sales was always exciting with each of them lasting three to four days; competition was intense, representatives of the racing world from all over the world were present, there were vets on hand to make detailed examination of horses shortlisted for potential purchases, transport arrangements to be made with the horse transport companies to take possession and care of purchases since they became your immediate property on the fall of the hammer and insurance to be secured if desired with the insurance companies, all of which had offices or booths at the sales ground. Frequently owners interested in buying yearlings would come to the sales so they had to be very carefully looked after in case they got captured by another trainer looking for a new owner. It was always fascinating to see the sea of bloodstock agents, trainers and general hangers-on crowded round any particularly well-known owner, hoping to pick up a crumb from under his table. And then there were the auctioneers, great characters most of them; at Doncaster there was Ken Oliver – the Benign Bishop, he was known as – with his deep and slow voice gently entreating bids as if hearing a confession, with his catchphrase coming out every so often when a particular horse was led into the ring: 'This is the one you've all been waiting for'; and my old friend Harry Beeby, precise, accurate, ultra polite and with a great supply of remarks: 'Only half its value, you know' when there was a pause in the bidding. At Newmarket, Tattersalls' senior partner, Michael Watt, was authoritative with perfect diction, like a schoolmaster addressing his pupils instructing them on the merits of the horse he was selling and expecting them to bid accordingly. He also had an acid comment to make if he spotted a transgression in his class, 'I wouldn't do that again if I were you.' In contrast there was Sir Peter Nugent with a loud, booming voice, seeming like a rugger second row forward charging relentlessly towards the line with the ball tucked under his arm. At Goffs in Ireland, Peter Nugent again and also David Nagle who with typical Irish charm could extract bids like a conjuror drawing rabbits out of a hat and Phillip Myerscough who could conduct an auction equally well in English or French, as I heard him do at Goffs Sales at Deauville.

In addition the Sales were highly social occasions, most trainers being friends as well as competitors. We stayed at the same hotels or, in Newmarket and Ireland, as guests of very hospitable home-based trainers; the talk, inevitably, was of horses but there was much hilarity, 'sledging' and high jinks accompanied by significant consumption of alcohol. In some peoples' eyes drinking and racing go together; while not claiming to be saintly, racing is part of the entertainment industry, at least from a large section of racehorse owners' perspective. After all, no owners, no racing. On the alcohol front, I learned my lesson many years previously; I had a gorgeous girlfriend and took her to Ireland one weekend for the Irish Derby for a fun and romantic weekend, having arranged to meet a friend, Jeremy Vaughan, and various others at the Shelbourne Hotel in Dublin on the morning of the race. Jeremy's horse Nicolaus Silver, trained by Fred Rimell and ridden by Bobby Beasley, had won the Grand National that year. We had a fabulous day's racing at the Curragh, drank a lot of champagne and were invited to a post-race party by Charlie Weld, father of the present-day trainer Dermot Weld who trained on the Curragh, close to the racecourse. Here the drink offered was whiskey; too late did I discover that champagne and whisky don't mix, with the result that the romantic part of the weekend went up the spout, or rather, down the loo. Luckily the relationship with the girlfriend survived and we had some very good times together over a longish period and have remained good long-distance friends ever since.

***

Generally speaking all purchases arrived in the yard by the following day and immediately it was a case of making them feel happy in their new and strange environment. This was the main responsibility of Archie Hughes, the Head Lad, and the senior staff who would start the task of breaking in each new yearling.

This has to be done very gently and with the utmost patience. They were all different and some took much longer than others but I liked to have them all broken in and gently cantering in small groups before Christmas. We looked like having a few more horses for the following season with some new owners, including a charming man called Freddie Wolff, who agreed to buy two yearlings that I had bought cheaply at Newmarket Sales. Freddie had won a Gold Medal at the Berlin Olympics in 1936 by running the first leg of our gold-medal 4 x 400 metres relay team (winning time a then European record of 3.09.0). His family business was Rudolf Wolff & Co., metal merchants founded in 1865 and among those companies who formed the London Metal Exchange, an organisation that I knew well during my years at RJ&N (Freddie was Chairman of the LME 1970–77). I had met him on a trip to the 1973 Arc de Triomphe at Longchamps won by Rheingold, trained by Barry Hills in Lambourn, ridden by Lester Piggott and owned by Henry Zeisel, all three of whom were winning the race for the first time and, apart from Lester, the only time. Rheingold had been second, beaten a short head by Roberto ridden by Piggott in the Derby. Zeisel, of Austrian extraction, was the flamboyant classically-trained violinist and owner of the Rheingold Club in London.

If Rheingold set Barry Hills up as a Classic-winning trainer, it was a horse called Frankincense who set him up as a trainer in the first place by winning the 1965 Lincolnshire Handicap. Hills started as an apprentice jockey with Fred Rimell before moving to Newmarket with George Colling, and then as Travelling Head Lad to John Oxley. By all accounts it was Hills who actually did most of the training and Frankincense was 'laid out' for the Lincoln. Hills, evidently, backed Frankincense at all rates during the winter to win £40,000, an enormous sum in those days and particularly so for a stable lad. With the proceeds he bought South Bank stables in Lambourn, setting up there with owners whom he had canvassed for a while. He was married to Maureen, the daughter of a jockey, Paddy Newsom, probably better known for being a very astute work rider. They had three sons, John who was an excellent amateur flat jockey before becoming a successful trainer also in Lambourn but who tragically died of cancer in 2014, and the twins Michael and Richard, both of whom became top-class jockeys. I remember them both as very small boys tagging on at the tail of Barry's string on their ponies. There was never much doubt where their future lay.

Following our successful trip to the States the previous year, Billy and I decided to go back to California for a sale similar to that in Miami but at Hollywood Park, Los Angeles, in January 1974. I also wanted to see Charlie Russell and Billy said that he wanted me to meet another friend who brought on foals and yearlings for sale. It would only be a quick visit as the sale was in mid-March, only a short time before the start of the season. Two others came with us: Michael O'Sullivan who I knew well and an Irish bloodstock agent, Cormac McCormack, who was scratching around for business and wanted to have a look at the American scene. O'Sullivan had recently formed a business in international transport of equine bloodstock, which he called Bloodstock Services (Ireland) Ltd based in Dun Laoghaire, Dublin. That was not his original occupation: before the legalising of casinos in the UK, Michael O'Sullivan derived the majority of his income running private games in London for his friends and acquaintances. These games used to run well into the small hours of the morning and so by the time Michael had deposited enough money into the banks' overnight deposit boxes to pay out those drawing their winnings when the banks opened, it was well past his bedtime. Hence he frequently didn't rise until lunchtime which became his nickname: Lunchtime or Lunch for short. With his new business he travelled the horse sales at all the major centres in England and abroad, which was the reason for him coming to LA. So there were four of us who assembled in the departure lounge bar at Heathrow for the Pan Am flight leaving in the late morning. Suitably refreshed we took our seats at the back of the economy class cabin for the 11-hour flight. Very soon Cormac explained that he had a problem; although he had rustled up enough cash to pay for the flight, he was now skint and had we any suggestions about how he was going to manage. The idea of lending money to Cormac did not appeal so we came up with another idea: collectively we bet him $500 to do a streak on the plane. He had no alternative but to agree and, in turn, we agreed that he could pick his time. He chose a time after lunch had been served and people might be nodding off. Now it is quite a long way from the very back of economy class to the curtain dividing first class from the rest. There was no business class in those days and only one economy cabin. Having removed all his clothes and started his dash up the aisle, he had only got about one third of the way when people were nudging their neighbours so by the time he turned round and came scuttling back like a leprechaun the whole plane was alive with what was happening and he was cheered as he dived into his seat and scrambled into his clothes.

The post-performance positives were manifold: we received free champagne as a party for the rest of the flight, there was a request from the first-class passengers for Cormac to perform a re-run, which he declined as there was no fee offered, and on arrival in Los Angeles the female ground staff attendant asked for the Streaking Party to come forward, so we were first off the plane and into the arrivals hall and US immigration checks without any queue. By the time we arrived at our hotel, having picked up our hired car, the news had overtaken us and we, or more particularly Cormac, were greeted as celebrities to such an extent that we had upgraded rooms and Johnny Carson made reference to the Irishman who was claiming the world altitude record for streaking on his show that evening. The next day I had arranged to meet Charlie Russell at the races at Santa Anita; as we were leaving the hotel, Cormac who had not come down off his cloud, picked up a telephone that was ringing at the Bell Captain's desk and proceeded to give a long dissertation on electronics to a poor woman whom didn't understand how to turn on her television. At the races I had a good meeting with Charlie Russell and filled him in about his horse, Uncle Joe, who had not arrived in England until well into the summer the previous year and, as I suspected, had taken time to acclimatise; I thought it wise not to rush him so we didn't get a run into him as a two-year-old but he had come on well during the winter, and would be ready for a run in the spring. Cormac was greeted as some kind of a hero by the racing fraternity, Billy having informed all his cronies who might not have heard about the plane streak. Albert Yank was in ecstasy and insisted that we go back to his house for a drink after the races, so by the time we were on our way back to the hotel we were physically and metaphorically in good spirits. Lunch was driving and suddenly a police motorbike overtook us and signalled for us to stop. A six foot three inch policeman bulging with muscle and guns approached us slowly, hips first with the rest of his body following. A large 30 mph road sign was a few yards away. The conversation between Lunch and the policeman went as follows;

Policeman: 'Do you know the speed limit in this area?'

Lunchtime: '30 mph officer.'

Policeman: '... and what speed do you think you were going?'

Lunchtime: 'Probably about 45 officer.'

Policeman (slightly taken aback by this admission of guilt):
    'Do you own this car?'

Lunchtime: 'No.'

Policeman: 'Who does own this car?'

Lunchtime: 'Hertz.'

Policeman: 'Can I see your driver's licence?'

Lunchtime: 'No.'

Policeman: 'Why not?'

Lunchtime: 'Because it is at my hotel, but if you would like to come there with me I'll be happy to show it to you.'

Policeman (bending down suspiciously): 'Say, have you guys been drinking?'

Cormac (from the back seat having pretended to be asleep):

'My man, I'm going to nominate you as detective of the year.'

By this time my mind was wondering how quickly we could summon the British Consul to get us out of jail, but the policeman stepped in: 'Do you know what date it is today?'

Lunchtime: '17ᵗʰ March, St Patrick's Day, officer.'

Policeman: 'My grandmother was Irish and if you are out of my sight by the time I am back on my bike, this has been your lucky day.'

We needed no second bidding.

Early the next morning Billy and I were at the sales ground at Hollywood Park racecourse examining the horses coming up for sale. Billy introduced me to a man who was making a name for himself by 'pinhooking', that is buying foals, taking them to his own farm and selling them on either as yearlings or keeping them a bit longer, breaking them in and getting them to the 'breeze up' stage before submitting them for sale again in their early two-year-old career. Among many very successful horses he bought a foal by Hoist The Flag, subsequently named Alleged, which was sold to Robert Sangster as a two-year-old for $175,000. Alleged ran in ten races, winning nine of them including the Arc de Triomphe in 1977 and 1978. Trained in Ireland by Vincent O'Brien, his only defeat was by Her Majesty the Queen's Dunfermline in the St Leger of 1977. This man's name was Marvin Roberts, commonly known as Monty, who became and still is the world-famous 'Horse Whisperer'. In earlier life Monty was a champion Rodeo rider and had held the world record time for 'bulldogging', that is dropping from a horse onto a wild steer, grabbing its horns and wrestling it to the ground. In the mid-60s Monty moved to Flag Is Up Farm near Solvang, about a three-hour drive from Los Angeles. For eighteen years he was a major consignor to the Hollywood Park Sale and today was no exception. As befits a Rodeo rider Monty was powerfully built and immensely strong but he and his delightful wife Pat were kindness personified and we seemed to strike a happy chord. I didn't buy any horses but Monty told me that three of his consignment had very high reserves which he doubted they would hit but that he was going to advise the owners, very well-off people, that he thought their pedigrees were suitable for British and European turf racecourses and that, if the owners agreed, he would suggest that they were sent over for me to train in England and that's exactly what happened. The next day, our last, Billy and I drove out to Solvang and spent the whole day with Monty and Pat going round the farm and seeing all the barns, dirt training tracks and facilities such as equine swimming pools and sophisticated veterinary equipment. Our flight home the next day was, by contrast, thankfully uneventful but everyone was happy – Lunch got the job of flying the horses back, Cormac made many new contacts, Billy renewed old ones and I had more horses to train. Quite an eventful five days.

The Valley of the Racehorse

Lambourn in the 70s was an exciting, fun, interesting and competitive place to live and work – if you were involved with horses and racing that is; if not it must have seemed like another kind of world. We worked hard and played hard and there was an unwritten rule: however late to bed, and for whatever reason, there was no excuse not to be out for first lot the next morning. Although nothing stays the same forever, I'm sure that the basics must exist today. Looking back, however, we must have seemed, and indeed were, incredibly insular. We talked, breathed and dreamt about nothing but horses twenty-four hours a day, seven days a week and eleven months of the year. For most of the twelfth month, January, we took a holiday but the strange thing was that frequently we went for holidays with our competitors, not just from Lambourn but from Newmarket and other racing centres as well. Two of Anthea's and my main friends in the early Lambourn days were Paul Cole and Ben Leigh, both near neighbours, both close friends with each other and complete opposites. Paul, tall, good-looking, the son of an army Major of uncertain background, one of whose chief interests was breeding fighting cocks which, the rumour had it, he used to take to France for contests. Paul had done his time in learning his trade with two tough taskmasters, George Todd at Manton and Richmond Sturdy at Shrewton. Inclined to be a bit chippy, he was very competitive and, it has to be said, somewhat jealous of the success of others, but was a very good friend to us newcomers in

Lambourn. He had set up on his own at a dilapidated stables and ramshackle house with his sister, Maureen, on the Folly Road. Ben, or the Honourable Benjamin Chandos Leigh, as he liked to be known, was one of the sons of Lord Leigh of Stoneleigh on whose land the Royal Show is held annually. Small of stature but tall of opinion, Ben was a former amateur rider who I used to see occasionally in my riding days. He did win the Grand Military Gold Cup at Sandown in 1965 on a horse called Rueil, trained by Tim Forster. If Paul Cole's yard and living quarters were dilapidated, they were like Claridge's compared to Ben's. Grandly named Neardown Stables, the boxes were held together with difficulty, a wing and a prayer and the house, a bungalow, could be compared unfavourably with an army Nissen hut.

The Pheasant pub, next to the cottage Anthea and I rented for £8 per week when we first arrived in the area, was frequented by racing folk from Lambourn, particularly at lunchtime. Here I met a youngish, svelte man, usually dressed in jodhpurs, by the name of Julian Lewis, an Old Wellingtonian a few years younger than me so we didn't quite interconnect. Always fascinated by racing, he'd had an interesting life having gone to Grenoble University with plenty of time to ski and have fun and then graduated into the racing world both in the USA and for several years in and around Chantilly, France where he had stints with various trainers including Henri van de Poele. He was a fluent French speaker, although the purists might not agree. On returning to England he had a spell with Walter Nightingall in Epsom before moving down to Lambourn where he rode out for a number of trainers and established his own Bloodstock Agency, specialising but not limited to Anglo-French trade. Julian was, and is, the most extrovert, impossible, bellicose, sexually explicit and loud person I have ever met. He was also, and is, an exceptionally good friend, with whom I have had as much fun – as well as a number of quite tricky experiences – than with anybody else … ever. Not for nothing is Julian called 'Screamer', possibly after the short-time pop star Screaming Lord Sutch, whom I once saw perform, but he was an amateur compared to Julian. He has a permanent love affair with the bottle but contrary to what the experts might say I would not class him as an alcoholic. Booze and his lifestyle did cause him to put on a great deal of weight and his face turned the same colour as the red/maroon pullover that he often used to wear.

A while after I first met him he married Caroline Dyson, a girl from a good north Midlands family who had been round the block a few times herself. She was also a competent rider and used to ride out for Paul Cole. Their wedding in London, which I attended along with many others, was an occasion not to be forgotten, during which the loudspeaker had to be turned off during the bridegroom's speech owing to the depravity of its content. An occasion I remember well came when departing from Ascot, a while after the last race on one of the days at the Royal Meeting, with Screamer in a very inebriated state, supported by Caroline on one side and me on the other. Having reached the main Ascot to Bracknell road outside the course, a very young policeman was standing in the middle of the road directing the heavy traffic in both directions. We had to cross the road in order get into the owners' and trainers' car park. 'Ossifer' called Screamer, 'I need to cross the road.'

The policeman raised his hands and stopped the traffic in both directions. Slowly but surely we manoeuvred Screamer as far as the middle of the road whereupon he proceeded to engage the policeman, hands still held high and no traffic moving, in detailed conversation about how he was feeling and why and thanking him for holding up the traffic for him. 'That's all right, Sir and don't worry' said the young policeman, 'I hope I shall be feeling just like you in about three hours' time.' Another incident at the main Goodwood Summer Meeting at the end of July inspired my friend, John Guise, a Jockey Club race starter, to compose the following limerick:

There was a young man called Screamer
Who had an unpleasant demeanour
Lord March got a shock
When he whipped out his cock
And pissed on the Goodwood arena.

The marriage of Julian and Caroline has lasted, to most people's surprise and through often tempestuous times, for over forty years. As has been said, probably nobody else could have coped with either of them but my hat is raised to both. It may be just as well that they had no children but Julian has been a very good and generous uncle and godfather. When Caroline was seriously ill some years ago the kind side of his nature came to the fore and he looked after her very well indeed. We don't see much of each other nowadays as they live in France for much of the year but Julian is one of those people who you can call on the telephone after a year, and it seems like you've seen each other yesterday.

My closest neighbours were also complete opposites. On the one side, Nicky Vigors, a kinsman of Tim Vigors who had come to my rescue by helping me when I flew back to England with a very badly broken leg skiing in Bad Gastein all those years before. Nicky was married, at that time, to Fiona, the daughter of the very well-known vet and bloodstock agent George Forbes of Epsom. Fiona later became a renowned equine photographer and received commissions to photograph many famous horses on both sides of the Atlantic. On the other side, separated by a lane, was Doug Marks, just about the most laid-back of men but as canny as any and not to be underestimated. At one stage Anthea was looking for a potential event horse and Doug asked me to come and have a look at a horse of his that had useful form on the flat but whose racing days were over. He took me across his yard but stopped a few yards short of the horse's box and said in a low voice 'This 'orse is very, very ugly but don't you tell him I said so.' Doug's house was called Lethornes, but when his wife left him he changed the name to Bleak House.

Peter Walwyn was 'king' of Lambourn in the 70s. Known among the racing community as Big Pete, he was Champion Trainer in 1974 and 1975 winning the Derby, Irish Derby and King George VI & Queen Elizabeth stakes at Ascot with Grundy, the latter race after a titanic struggle with Bustino, another super horse of his generation, owned by Lady Beaverbrook and trained by Dick Hern. After Grundy's victory in the Derby, ridden as in all his races by Pat Eddery, a riotous celebration party at Seven Barrows was interrupted by the wailing sirens and flashing lights of a police car, the chief policeman saying that they were responding to the report of a burglary: 'I'm not being burgled' said Pete, 'I'm having a party.'

'We've had a report that you are. We must search the property.' Just then a rather shamefaced P. Eddery appeared and explained that he had inadvertently pressed the panic button while giving the Walwyn children's nanny a good seeing to upstairs.

Other great horses that Pete trained at that time were the 1,000 Guineas winner Humble Duty; Polygamy who won the Oaks, English Prince, winner of the Irish Derby, and top performers Lucyrowe, Rock Roi, Oats and Crow. Pete, a pretty highly strung character, was very lucky to have the calming influence and nature of his wonderful wife, whose proper name was Virginia but for reasons going back to her childhood, and well before the nickname was associated with actions of a sexual nature, she was called Bonk. She was the sister of my old riding friend Nick Gaselee, and was always there at Seven Barrows, making sure everything was shipshape with the drinks cabinet suitably loaded and was wonderful with the owners both at home and at the races. She rode out with the string as much as possible and while appearing to be in the background she was actually at Pete's right hand. When he became agitated, which was frequently, Bonk was there to smooth him down. He hated anything mechanical such as a motor car, displaying violent rage at any fault with his vehicle or, indeed, vehicles driven by others which might possibly be in his way, and he treated such miscreants, whether human or mechanical, in a way totally contrary to the way he would a horse or his dogs, whom he loved dearly. Accordingly Bonk always drove. Everybody loved her and it was a racing as well as a personal tragedy when she died, quite suddenly, in January 2014.

Pete didn't suffer fools gladly and there is the story of a young trainer in the 70s who took himself rather more seriously than did others. He had a few moderate horses and even fewer winners. One morning, up on the downs, one of his horses got rid of its lad and charged off, causing havoc amid P. Walwyn's string. The young trainer rushed up, trying to blame Pete's horses for causing the rumpus; an altercation ensued, ending up with one of Walwyn's lads telling the young man to 'Fuck off, you cunt.' Incensed by this he tore off home, picked up his telephone, dialled Pete's number and was put through:

'One of your lads has just called me a cunt.'

'Well,' replied Pete, 'You *are* a cunt.'

Actually, of much more interest than the young trainer so labelled above was his ravishingly beautiful secretary, who all the Lambourn young blades were fancying rotten. She resisted most of them but along came Fred Winter's brilliant jockey, John Francome, the seven-time Champion Jockey in the late 70s and early 80s; he landed the spoils and married her – for a while.

Pete knew as much about racing and the training of racehorses as anybody ever, but that was his world and whatever went on outside it he regarded as not his concern. Foreigners, for instance, started at Calais. There was the occasion when Julian Lewis engineered the transfer of a top-class horse in France, Vitiges, from its French trainer to Pete in Lambourn. The French owner could not speak English and Pete's method of speaking French was to speak English – only very much louder. Julian had arranged a meeting between Pete and the French owner for dinner in a pub near Lambourn and by way of introducing himself Pete said 'Hello, I'm Peter Walwyn but I am always called Big Pete, Grand Pete, to you.' The Frenchman looked a little surprised that his very notable racehorse was to be trained by someone called Grand Pete, 'pete' being French for fart. However, all was well and Vitiges went on to win the Champion Stakes at Newmarket in 1976. Pete was always fiercely loyal to his jockeys, Duncan Keith for a long time until rising weight forced him to retire and Pat Eddery who was retained jockey for eight seasons. Pat's riding of Buckskin, who suffered from very flat feet, on firm ground in the Ascot Gold Cup of 1977 drew intense criticism from the horse's owner, Daniel Wildenstein; Pete strenuously defended his jockey, and that led to the Wildenstein horses being removed from Seven Barrows. Peter Walwyn retired in 1999 but remained actively involved with racing as Chairman of the Lambourn Trainers Association and other racing charities. Peter Walwyn died in December 2017.

The post-war history of Seven Barrows is quite interesting. It was part of a large block of superb downland bought by Derrick Candy, a friend of my father's at Oxford, when the Craven Estate came up for sale in 1961. The sale included Kingstone Warren where the Candys were already living and Derrick was training, so they leased Seven Barrows to David Hastings. Peter Walwyn was well ensconced at Windsor House in Lambourn but bursting at the seams and one day in 1964 the Candys, who were good friends, asked Pete if he would like to buy Seven Barrows from them, which he did, including 300 acres of land. Derrick was the father of Henry Candy who took over the licence when Derrick retired and has been there ever since, training with great success such horses as Time Charter, winner of the Oaks and Champion Stakes in 1982, the King George VI & Queen Elizabeth Stakes and Prix Foy in 1983 and The Coronation Stakes in 1984, and great sprinters like Airwave, Twilight Son, Kylachy and Limato. Henry, who was at that time assistant to his father, had become a good friend in Lambourn and it was to him that I turned at the time of the bust-up with Arthur Budgett; my father had a horse with Budgett that I had bought for him at the previous year's yearling sales. Naturally he didn't want to leave the horse with Budgett and so I arranged for the horse to go Derrick Candy, particularly since he and my father had been university friends.

The racing was ticking along quite nicely with a reasonable flow of winners, if not in terribly exalted company. In the spring of 1974 Monty and Pat Roberts came over from California and stayed with us at Berkeley House several times during their trip so that they could see our training operation and obtain a close-up of the English racing scene, which they enjoyed very much. Charlie and Sister Russell also came to stay and see their horses; we took them to see *Evita* in London with Elaine Page as Eva Peron and David Essex as Che Guevara as a kind of payback for the lovely times we had with them in Carmel. My other American, Kjell Qvale, now semi-based in England, came in and out on numerous occasions. Both of the two-year-old cheapies I had bought for Freddie Wolff won and, and as they had limited onward ability we sold them on at a useful profit, the colt to Belgium and the filly to South Africa where she became a good brood mare, producing several winners. We also had a bit of fun on the jumping front: I was introduced to an ebullient and enthusiastic character called Christopher Fleming who had been living in New Zealand where his family had strong farming connections as well as a stud farm where they stood Oncidium, the winner of the Coronation Cup in 1965.

Chris said that he had a horse that had showed a bit of promise but that had leg trouble and was turned out in a field. Would I like to come and have a look and tell him if I thought the horse worth putting back into training. He showed me his horse named Caille (French for quail), with a heavy winter coat and a distinctly thickened tendon, looking more like a shaggy mountain horse than a thoroughbred. But he had a good steely eye, an intelligent head and the tendon was hard and cold so I said to Chris that, if he would like me to, I'd have a go but couldn't guarantee if he would stand training or for how long. The horse had been placed on the flat and won a hurdle race when trained by Neville Callaghan but then broke down. He came to us in March and we took him very gently, hacking him around all spring and summer before stepping up his workload gradually during the early autumn. In early November I thought he was ready for a run so we took him to Uttoxeter.

Norman Mackness, my Travelling Head Lad, still had a National Hunt jockey's licence and since he had been riding Caille and schooling him, it was right that he should ride him in a race. He ran very well until he tired and tipped up at the last, unfortunately breaking poor Norman's collarbone. The race brought him on a lot so I took him to Exeter a couple of weeks later and got Jimmy Bourke down from Cheshire to ride him. I had known Jimmy well from my riding and permit holder days and he had ridden for me several times before. I thought the horse had a really good chance of winning at a decent price and I knew Chris was quite a serious punter so advised him accordingly. Caille was always going well, went to the front approaching the last and drew away to win by six lengths at 12/1 in field of eighteen. His next race was at Taunton in December with Norman, recovered from his broken collarbone, back in the saddle. He started favourite but the track was a bit sharp for him and he only finished third of twenty. However, he came out of the race very well and I entered him in a valuable sponsored race at Wincanton on Boxing Day. Norman rode him again and he won by 1½ lengths at 14/1 so Chris cleaned up again. But he had a hard race and, as I feared it might do, the leg flared up and he never ran again. It was also Norman Mackness's last winning ride as a jockey. Caille ran four times for us, winning twice and being placed once. Not too bad for a broken-down horse found in a field. Chris Fleming most generously said that he wanted to give me a present for training Caille for him and would I like a painting? He allowed me to choose a lovely Irish landscape with a fox running in the foreground by Ninetta Butterworth, which I have had ever since hanging in a prominent place. Unfortunately (for me!) Chris Fleming got married soon after Caille had won his last race; sadly his new wife didn't like racing and disapproved of gambling so he rather went out of my life but we had a lot of fun while it lasted.

I also had my old horse New Brighton back after injury. Before I renewed my jumping trainer's licence the season before, I had sent him to my very good friend Simon Morant down the road from me in Lambourn and he had won a race for him with Norman Mackness riding. Now I had him back and we ran him a few times, being placed twice, but the old boy was getting to the end of his tether so we retired him.

While on the subject of jumping, Lambourn in the 70s was just as much a training centre of National Hunt racing as flat racing, the senior jumping trainer being Fulke Walwyn, an elder cousin of Peter's. Fulke's twin sister was the formidable Helen Johnson-Houghton, one of the first lady trainers. Her son, also named Fulke, took over from his mother and had great success with horses owned by the American Charles Englehard, although Englehard's best horse, Nijinsky, was trained in Ireland by Vincent O'Brien. Fulke Walwyn won the Grand National as an amateur on Reynoldstown in 1936. He then turned professional but a bad fall at Ludlow in 1939 ended his riding career and prevented him from active service in the Second World War. After the war he set up as a trainer first at Delamere Stables and then at Saxon House in Lambourn. He trained four Cheltenham Gold Cup winners, two Champion Hurdle winners and a Grand National winner. One of his Gold Cup winners was the magnificent Mill House who had the misfortune of being born in the same year as Arkle, but for which he would undoubtedly have achieved even greater success. I didn't used to see a lot of

Fulke, being a junior new boy on the block, but he did come to Berkeley House one day to have a look at Charlie Russell's nice young horse, Uncle Joe. We had won a race with him but thought his future lay in jumping. Fulke liked him and paid top price for him at a forthcoming sale at Ascot. Snapping at Fulke's heels was the former Champion Jockey, Fred Winter, now turned trainer and having great success. I didn't see much of him either, probably no more than I did when we were both riding in the same race with predictable – but not quite always – results, but he had two pupil assistants. One was Steven – always known as Decies – Stanhope, the youngest son of Bill (Earl of) Harrington, whom I had met donkey's years previously while hunting in Ireland and staying with my elderly cousin Venice Price. 'Bollocky' Bill was a distinguished bloodstock agent at that time and bought the majority of horses for David Robinson who had built up and then sold a huge radio and television business, subsequently investing vast sums in racehorses and employing two private trainers in Newmarket, Michael Jarvis and Paul Davey. All the Harringtons seemed to have a bit of a mad streak in them and Decies was no exception. Always tremendous fun to be with, utterly fearless, he rode many winners during his time with Fred and partied like a dervish. I remember going to his 21st birthday dinner party given by his father at the Berkeley Hotel in London, which ended in a complete riot. Guests had started hurling bread rolls at each other until Bollocky stood up and demanded a halt to this disgraceful behaviour, only to sit down and throw a huge cache of rolls that he had been storing up.

The other Fred Winter pupil was Nicky Henderson, who has gone on to be a superb trainer at the very top of his profession and needs no introduction, save for a reminder that at the time of writing he has been Champion Trainer four times. He was the son of Johnny Henderson, who had been Montgomery's ADC during the Second World War before embarking on a distinguished career in the City, becoming first a partner of Cazenove, then leaving in 1982 to become Chairman of Henderson Administration. Racing was a major interest and he was instrumental in forming Racecourse Holdings Trust and getting together a group of investors to buy Cheltenham Racecourse, thus thwarting a group of property developers who had other plans. On leaving Eton, Nicky's first job was in the City but, rather against his father's wishes, he decided to make his career in racing and came to Fred as amateur jockey and assistant. We became very good friends with both Nicky and Decies. One year I had two rather slow horses which continually ran well into places but could not get their heads in front on the line. There were very few races for amateur jockeys on the flat but I found a suitable one and entered both horses and told Nicky and Decies that they could ride them and toss up who rode which; I can't remember who won the toss but Nicky's horse won the race and Decies' was second.

Nicky always wanted to train and having been with Fred Winter for five years had the opportunity of buying Windsor House and stables in Lambourn when Roger Charlton, who had been living there and running an equine swimming pool, was offered the job as assistant trainer to Jeremy Tree at Beckhampton. He was quickly successful, winning important races from the word go including the Champion Hurdle at Cheltenham three years in succession 1985–7 with See You Then. By the end of the 80s he was running out of room at Windsor House, which happened at a time when Peter Walwyn was considering downsizing at Seven Barrows, so they did a very convenient swap and Pete moved back to Windsor House, which is where he had started training back in 1960.

Anyone who has ever had anything to do with horses will know the importance of having a good and, if possible, friendly vet, from children's ponies upwards; from a racehorse trainer's perspective it is vital. While I was at Whatcombe, Charles Frank, the senior partner in the main Lambourn practice, was our man and very good he was too. When I set up on my own, I used the same practice but a different partner for no other reason than I felt that I was the Guv'nor now and needed to start afresh. Also I had got to know this delightfully whimsical Irishman with whom I got on very well and who was a superb vet, not only with racehorses but with eventers as well; he was on the panel of vets at Badminton for many years. His name was Frank Mahon and he became a very good friend. One day he told me an extraordinary story: when Bryan Marshall was training at Berkeley House many years before, Frank was his vet as well. Bryan rang him one morning asking him to come and have a look at a young horse that he was not happy with. It had won a race quite recently but was listless and definitely off colour. Frank examined the horse and after a few minutes removed his stethoscope from around his neck and asked Bryan if he knew the date of the next Ascot Sales. Bryan said he'd go and have a look but why? 'Because,' Frank said, 'you'll be lucky if this horse makes it to the sales. He has about the worst heart that I've ever listened to.' Not only did the horse get to the sale but he was bought by my father for 500 gns. His name was Dinner Jacket and he won a stack of races until he was fourteen. I rode him several times including round Liverpool.

For the first two seasons I didn't retain any particular jockey. During my time at Whatcombe I had got to know several of the top jockeys of the time, Lester Piggott, Scobie Breasley, Joe Mercer, Pat Eddery and the like. Geoff Baxter was a stable jockey who rode out every day unless he was away racing; likeable enough and a good rider but perhaps without real flair and anticipation. I used him from time to time. Locally, Paul Cook was all the rage and he rode quite a few for me but I found him a touch unreliable and usually looked elsewhere. Paul Cole had a good apprentice called Robert Edmonstone who had a meteoric rise but, owing to rapidly increasing weight, an equally meteoric fall and disappeared out of racing. Although out of reach of Lambourn, the jockey I liked and admired most and who was not in the limelight was George Duffield, who could do a handy weight, was very strong and fearless and who could always give a good and fair opinion of the horse he was riding. He was number one retained jockey for Mark Prescott for thirty years. I used him as much as possible and liked him a lot. His catchphrase was always 'I'll 'ave to ask Sir Mark but I think it'll be OK' whenever I rang him. Late on in his career he won the Oaks, Irish Oaks and St Leger on User Friendly in 1992, and the Eclipse for Aidan O'Brien on Giant's Causeway in 2000. He entered the *Guinness Book of Records* by winning eleven consecutive races (and thirteen in all) on the two-year-old Spindrifter, trained by Mark Prescott, in 1980. He retired as a jockey in 2005 but still acts as assistant to his trainer wife, Ann. A true Yorkshireman. Another northern-based jockey whom I held in high regard was George Cadwalladr who I remember as a lad when I used to ride out for Eric Cousins. He had grown quite tall but could still ride at a reasonable weight and I never thought that he had the opportunities he deserved. He rode winners for me and always gave a good account of himself.

But the star of the show locally was John (Kipper) Lynch, a real 'cheekie chappie' always with a smile on his face and some sort of a quip both in and out of the weighing room and an above-average jockey. Everybody in the trade loved Kipper; he'd go anywhere for you – I remember him going all the way to Carlisle and back for me one day for just one ride (yes, it did win). There was the time that he got a winter riding job for a trainer in Italy for which he was rewarded, in Lambourn anyway, with the name of El Kipporo. Sometimes he was regarded by owners as being a little too cheeky but that was just him and his happy attitude to life. Kipper's career ended tragically just after he had landed the plum job as first jockey to Bruce Hobbs in Newmarket when, driving back to Newmarket after a night out in London, his car crashed. Kipper was badly injured and never recovered full fitness. He had won the Dewhurst Stakes on Tromos for Hobbs not long before his accident. Then there were the ultra-lightweight jockeys, fully grown men who could ride at near enough 7st.; the likes of Sammy Millbanks, David East, Mickey Greening, Norman McIntosh, Ray (Sit) Still, Denis McKay, Taffy Thomas, and probably the best of them, Des Cullen, not, however, regarded as the brain of Britain. I recall him dismounting from a horse that I had saddled for Budgett and saying to the owner, 'Ran all right, Guv, but this horse needs six furlongs.'

'Cullen, that race *was* six furlongs' replied the owner acidly. They are a dying, if not dead, breed these days with the present minimum weight in handicaps having been raised to 8st. to take account of the rising weight of the British population, being 1lb every three years.

A trainer's routine in the build-up to the season, and indeed during it, is to have probably two days in the week when more serious 'work', i.e. gallops, is conducted with horses scheduled to run in the near future or as a means of testing their fitness. On such days it is most useful to have an experienced jockey to come and ride work, probably on several horses during the session, switching from one to the other and with two or three other horses taking part in each piece of work. Jockeys are not paid for this but are happy in the hope or expectation that they will be selected to ride the horse or horses when they come to race. Frequently they will go to more than one trainer in a morning with the timings of the work mutually agreed between the jockey and the respective trainers. I had a call one day from Trevor Rogers, a jockey based quite locally in Newbury, asking if he could come and ride work for me. I knew him slightly as a competent jockey so readily agreed that he could come but said that I couldn't necessarily promise him any rides but that we'd see how we got on. He rode very sensibly, followed the instructions given to him and gave helpful comments regarding each horse. He was also keen, polite and well turned out. After a few work sessions I gave him a couple of rides, one of which won and so began an arrangement that was to last a long time. He came to Berkeley House on three mornings each week unless he was away racing and I promised him the rides on our horses with the proviso that if I or any of the owners wanted a top 'name' jockey at any time, I would do so and he was not to take offence.

Generally speaking I was very lucky with those who so kindly sent me horses to train, some of whom I have already mentioned. Not surprisingly, none of those who I had known and whose horses I had looked after at Whatcombe sent any to me, but dear Tom Dowdeswell came over from time to time to ride work for me and repeat how sad he was with the way the whole episode had turned out. No people were more supportive than my own parents, who were affected and as distraught as I was about the Budgett fiasco. I bought a chestnut filly by Varona for my mother at Doncaster Yearling Sales in 1974. She wasn't expensive but I knew the breeder slightly in Ireland and so knew that she came from a good home. My mother named her Amore Mare and during the winter she had filled out and pleased me at home in her attitude so we gave her a run at Warwick where she finished a reasonable 5th of 15 without having a hard race. I knew my parents would love to have a runner at the Chester May meeting, their local course and the most prestigious meeting after the Newmarket Guineas meeting in the early part of the season. I thought she had come on quite a bit after her first race and that she would not disgrace herself at Chester so I booked Lester Piggott to ride her in the Sceptre Stakes.

The night before I stayed with Bobby and Jane McAlpine who always had a big house party for Chester, among whom was Brian Taylor, the jockey, who said he thought he had a great chance in the first race the next day, the same race as our filly. He asked who was riding mine and a slightly wary look came into his eye when I said 'Lester'. Brian was a really lovely man, great jockey and good friend. It was a tremendous tragedy when he was killed in a fall at Sha Tin, Hong Kong in 1984; he won the 1974 Derby on Snow Knight. At Chester the next day Lester was always prominent on Amore Mare, she led two furlongs out and won easily, much to the delight of her owner – and her trainer! She had started joint favourite with Brian Taylor's mount, more, I suspect, because of her jockey than her previous form. Peter O'Sullevan was very complimentary about her both in his BBC Television commentary and in his column in the *Daily Express* the next day. Sadly, however, although it cannot be said that she had a hard race, she never produced the same form again. Neither I nor the vets could find anything wrong with her and we gave her every possible chance with long layoffs, change of scene, everything. As can happen, it remained an unsolved mystery.

Owners come by strange and various ways. One morning, up on the downs, my near neighbour Doug Marks came up to me and said in his own droll way: 'Now listen to me. I have this two-year-old; she's probably not much good but might win a small race but would you like to have her?' Doug hated any form of confrontation and it seemed he'd had a minor fallout with the filly's owner. I hesitated, not wanting to get involved with a private feud, but Doug insisted: 'I'm going to tell the owner, Bill White, to call you.' Which he did that evening and arranged to come and meet me. A couple of days later a gleaming Rolls-Royce with the number plate WWW1 'rolled' into the yard and out stepped Mr White, his wife Shirley and rather pudgy son Paul, aged about ten. 'William Walter White' he announced, 'my word is my bond.' After another conversation later with Doug Marks, during which we exchanged pleasantries, I agreed to take the filly, named Ashen Light, which true to Doug's word did win a small race, but Bill White became if not a fixture then a regular, for whom we had some success, about which more later.

By way of contrast, an interesting, if relatively temporary, entry into the owners' ranks at that time came Michael Brudenell-Bruce, 8th Marquess of Ailesbury who had recently married his third wife Caroline. One of his ancestors was the Earl of Cardigan of the Charge of the Light Brigade fame in the Crimean War, but the Estate of Savernake, near Marlborough, was given to the Brudenell family by William the Conqueror. Michael had made over the estate to his son by his first marriage, David, Earl of Cardigan, and he and Caroline lived in a smaller house on the estate, the main house Tottenham House having been leased as a well-known prep school, Hawtreys, for many years. I had met Michael at a local party at which he expressed an interest in racing so I sold him a two-year-old filly I had bought on spec as a yearling. She was a grey, pretty, rather light-framed filly that I had called Butterfly Morning, and she won a race within two weeks of Michael having bought her. I wish it was always as easy as that. She was also later placed, but not being the sort likely to train on as a three-year-old so I recommended that Michael sold her on when we received an offer. Michael's interest in racing, as in other things, was short-lived; he and Caroline later divorced.

The summers of 1975 and 1976 were two of the hottest on record. In 1975, the year Margaret Thatcher took over as leader of the Conservative Party from Edward Heath, the temperatures in July and August were frequently over 85 degrees Fahrenheit, which came as a bit of a surprise since a fair amount of snow had fallen on higher ground as late as June. In 1976 it was even hotter, there being sixteen consecutive days with temperatures over 86 degrees and five days of over 95 degrees, the hottest in early July of 96.8 degrees. This was affecting us very considerably in two ways: first, no rain caused a drought and a control of water supply meaning that racecourses were very limited as to when, if at all, they could water the courses resulting in very firm to hard going with the knock on of very small numbers of runners per race. Fine, you might say, therefore easier to win races but in the vast majority of cases horses do not like galloping on rock hard ground and one did want to take a sound horse home, not a broken-down wreck. The other effect was that working outside in stifling temperatures was debilitating to humans and horses alike so, after consultation with Archie and the senior lads, to which they agreed readily, I decided that we would start work an hour earlier each day with first lot pulling out 6.30 a.m., meaning that the lads finished earlier and had more free time in the afternoon. Evenings were not affected; they came on at four p.m. as usual with me doing my rounds at 5.30.

At the opposite end of the scale to those two summers, Britain faced a series of strikes in 1974 and 1975, usually started by the miners under Arthur Scargill when Edward Heath was Prime Minister. The strikes spread and the Government declared a 3-day working week. The shortage of coal meant that the coal-fired power stations couldn't function properly, so power cuts were frequent and sometimes lengthy. It was also winter so, again, schedules and routine in racing stables had to be adjusted to finish work before dark. Yes, generators could be hired but they were expensive and not nearly so available or efficient as they are today; there was also a shortage of petrol to run a gen-erator or a car for that matter, with rationing for a time and long queues at petrol stations. Edward Heath called a General Election in February thinking that the country would rally round him to defeat the strikers but they didn't in sufficient numbers so he was very narrowly defeated and Harold Wilson became Prime Minister again. He of the infamous claim, broad-cast when Prime Minister in the 1960s and after he had devalued Sterling: 'that does not mean that the pound in your pocket has been devalued.' The future Prime Minister, Edward Heath, said in Parliament that Wilson's words 'will be remembered as the most dishonest statement ever made'. In October of the same year, Wilson, too, called another General Election hoping for a thumping majority which was also not forthcoming but he ended up with an overall majority of 3. He struggled on until, with the onset of Alzheimer's, he resigned in March 1976 to be succeeded by James Callaghan.

But enough of politics; I had a pressing little problem to deal with at home. I had noticed that Anthea was away often during the day and frequently well into the evening, and also that Frank Mahon was spending rather a lot of time at Berkeley House, not just on veterinary matters. I took little or no notice for a while; after all Frank was a friend, I liked him very much and loved his amusing Irish stories and way of expressing himself. But I did get annoyed one day when we had been asked to a dinner party by my very good friend and owner, Bryan Jenks, who had moved down from Shropshire to a very nice house close to a nearby village. By the time we should have left to go to the party, Anthea had not come home from wherever she had gone to and I had to go without her. Later, and halfway through dinner, she rang and said that she had been delayed at a horse show to which she had gone with Frank. Matters came to a head not long afterwards: I made a fleeting visit to California for a meeting with Monty Roberts, leaving on Sunday afternoon to catch the 11-hour night flight to Los Angeles, arriving there the following morning, local time. Picking up a hire car, I drove three hours to Solvang and Flag Is Up Farm, had a good meeting with Monty and Pat discussing the horses both he and friends of his had with me before driving back to LA to catch the next available flight. I arrived back in Lambourn in time for evening stables on Wednesday, admittedly rather earlier than I thought would be possible. Anyway, there, cosily ensconced, were Anthea and Frank and my suspicions, thoroughly aroused, were confirmed shortly afterwards when I tracked them down spending a night in a hotel near Chipping Norton.

That was the end really. I was very sad and I think she was too but I couldn't have my wife having an affair with my vet. None of us actually fell out in a major way, maybe because we all quite liked each other, but I made it clear that Anthea would have to leave. We had serious conversations; I insisted that Simon and Sam would be staying put at Berkeley House but that she must look for somewhere else to live, which I would pay for up to a reasonable sum. Understandably it took Anthea a while to come to terms with this and to agree, but about a month later she did. In many ways I felt sorry for her; I told her that Frank's wife, Eileen, who we both knew quite well (Anthea, a super rider herself and a very good teacher, had been teaching Frank's children to ride), was a very strict Catholic and would never divorce him, which turned out to be the case. Also, Anthea had not married a racehorse trainer: she had married a businessman with a sideline, which was at times demanding and dangerous, but only a hobby. So it was a major career change when it happened. Being a trainer's wife is not always a bed of roses; to start with her husband works from home and is there all day unless away racing, secondly it is a seven-day-a-week way of life for nearly all the year; thirdly a wife is expected to play an important supporting role, stretching as far as being involved with staff personal problems, sickness and management. She is expected to have a working knowledge of the horses in the yard so that she can communicate sensibly with the owners both when they come on visits to see their horses, usually at weekends, as well as on the racecourse; it often happens, during the season, that a trainer has runners at more than one meeting on the same day; in such cases, he will normally go to one and his wife to the other, particularly if the owner is due to be present. Owning racehorses for the majority is a hobby for fun and excitement; therefore a trainer is in the entertainment business as well as exercising his skill in making sure his charges are physically and mentally fit to run faster than all the others in a race. Anthea loves horses, dogs and all animals and has an excellent rapport with them; however, her background with horses was in other disciplines and she didn't really like racing very much so it was difficult for her.

The most important matter to be resolved was the children, Simon and Sam, still very young but who had started to go to a good day school just out of Marlborough. Naturally Anthea loved her children but she was not in the least bit maternal. She had wanted children but from birth onwards did not show the normal mother's love for them, hence my insistence that they stayed with me where they would be properly cared for and looked after. It was unusual but agreed in our divorce hearing that I should have custody, granting her access at her wish which she hardly ever exercised. My two elder children, Jemima and Richard, came to stay with me for two periods each year although it was sometimes a struggle to obtain Zandra's agreement on dates. In those now far-off days, it was essential to put one's children down for both prep and public schools at birth, especially the boys. I loathed my prep school but always liked the look of a nearby school, which I used to visit on the rare occasions that I was selected to play in a school cricket or football team. The school was Heatherdown, near Ascot and I knew several fathers who had sons there and spoke highly of it. When Richard was born I got in touch with the headmaster, James Edwards, straightaway and arranged to go and see him and look round the school and did the same for Eton and, indeed, my old school, Wellington. In the event all three boys went to Heatherdown but none to either Eton or Wellington. A sentence on fees: after my youngest, Sam, was born I thought it was sensible to make arrangements to pay for the children's prep and public school education, so asked for and received quotes from various sources giving exact dates, ages, period of education to be covered etc. I chose the firm of Save and Prosper which I thought offered the best but not necessarily the cheapest quote. I paid them a lump sum of £25,000, breathed a sigh of relief and relaxed in the knowledge that all my children's education had been paid for. As it turned out my payment of £25,000 made in 1972, many years before they started school at Heatherdown, ultimately paid for about one third of their education.

13

Racing: An Entertainment Business

I have to admit I was never very good at 'owner getting', in other words touting for people to send me horses to train. The king of that art was former jump jockey turned trainer Ben Hanbury, who never thought anyone would say 'no'. Good-looking, always immaculately turned out and married to the beautiful Chunky (which she wasn't), real name Moira, maiden name Pilkington, they made a very handsome couple and Ben trained in Newmarket for a lot of very wealthy owners, among them the shipping magnate Ravi Tikkoo, known in racing circles as Tik-Tok the Tanker Man.

I did pluck up courage once to use the Hanbury method; Henry Zeisel, the Vienna-born classically trained violinist, who owned a nightclub in Oxford Street called the Rheingold, had a number of horses all over the place with the majority trained by Barry Hills, including the horse named after his club in London and which was runner-up in the Derby before going on to win the Arc de Triomphe under Lester Piggott. I went up to him one day at the races and said 'Hello Mr Zeisel, my name is Antony Johnson. You have horses with pretty well every other trainer in Lambourn so what's wrong with me?' He gave a polite but nondescript reply and moved on. To my surprise, a few days later he turned up unannounced at Berkeley House. We had a drink, he ended up staying the night and bought a two-year-old filly that I had for sale, which he called Mozart Sonata. She won a couple of races, we had quite a lot of fun together and I expect he showed a modest profit by the number of guests that I took to his club in London. However, not very long afterwards his fortunes changed and he dropped out of racing. Another owner I acquired under strange circumstances emanated from one day coming home from Epsom; on the M4 I found myself sitting behind one of those maddening drivers who hog the outside lane. I gave him a couple of toots and flashed my lights but to no avail. He just sat there alternating between 50 and 70 mph: two children in his back seat kept putting their thumbs in their ears and wiggling their hands at me as the driver waved the V sign out of his window. I probably had a couple of drinks at the races and didn't want to take any chances so I stayed put, not wishing to overtake him on the inside, for a good forty miles until I made my exit at Junction 14, the turn-off for Lambourn, thinking no more about it. To my consternation, ten days later I received a police summons charging me with dangerous driving. Although this was later reduced to a less serious charge, I had at that time nine speeding points on my licence so couldn't afford any more; I instructed my solicitor to find me a proper barrister to attend the hearing at Newbury County Court, turning up with my heart in my mouth on the appointed day to search for my Rumpole. There was no sign of him. In a panic and no more than five minutes before my case was due to be heard, I approached a youth who was hanging about, whom I took to be a court official, asking him where clients were supposed to meet their lawyers. 'Who are you looking for?' he asked. 'A Mr Norris', I replied. 'I'm Norris' the youth answered.

My heart sank even lower; the boy looked no more than eighteen. But there was nothing I could do so I very briefly outlined my case before we were called in. Whereupon, after a few identification preliminaries, my accuser was put on the stand to be flattened, in boxing terms, inside of a round, by Mr Norris.

When it came to my turn Mr Norris asked me a few questions, including asking me to describe the sign my accuser was making out of his window. I replied that it was the same sign that had got Harvey Smith in a spot of bother at Hickstead about a week previously. This raised a titter in the courtroom, the Magistrates threw out the case saying that the police had wasted the court's time. William, as I now was allowed to call my barrister, and I repaired to the nearest pub where we remained for a considerable time, with the upshot being that I took him back to Berkeley House where he stayed the night and before bedtime I had sold him a horse named, perhaps rather appropriately, Hot Air, which sadly failed to trouble the judge on the racecourse. Thus began a friendship which lasted for very many years. William Norris is now an eminent QC.

I had known Gay Kindersley since my riding days and used to see his father, Philip, most afternoons of the week in Ladbrokes' cosy little sitting room cum office at Warnford Court, Throgmorton Street during my time at Lazards but I didn't meet Magsie, Gay's wife, until they both came to stay at Abbots Moss in Cheshire for the amateur riders race at Chester that I helped to organise in 1965, Gay being President of the Amateur Riders Association. Magsie was the daughter of Hugh Wakefield, a moderately successful character actor on the London stage in the 30s and 40s, limited to the kind of parts he could play: a little man evidently somewhat pleased with himself. Gay was the dashing Corinthian good-looking son of Philip and his first wife Oonagh Guinness, rich and making a name for himself as an amateur jockey with enough money to buy himself good horses, a place to train them and employ a virtual private trainer. He was tremendous fun with a happy-go-lucky attitude and a constant stream of beautiful, sexy girlfriends. He met Magsie while holidaying in the South of France, during which he was invited to a party on Chester Beattie's yacht when his daughter Sarah and her friend Magsie were among the guests. Immediately struck with her beauty and sense of fun, he made arrangements to see her again as soon as possible on his return to England and they embarked on a whirlwind courtship, culminating in his proposal and her acceptance at Kempton races the following January. The engagement did not meet with parental approval, particularly from Philip Kindersley who regarded Hugh Wakefield as a cocky little actor and his daughter a golddigger. He and Oonagh were long since divorced but there was still much enmity between the two of them. Valerie, Philip's second wife, naturally supported her husband. The upshot was an elopement which after two attempts, thwarted by officialdom and red tape in France and, surprisingly, Ireland, the union was legalised at Caxton Hall, London in the presence of the two mothers, Gay's half-brother Garech and a couple of others.

It didn't take Magsie long to discover that her husband suffered from CIS, Chronic Infidelity Syndrome, embarking on a series of affairs both in England and Ireland, especially from his mother's fairytale house, Luggala in Co. Wicklow, where riotous weekend house parties were commonplace. At one such of these Gay fell head over heels in love with Ann, then the wife of the Marquess of Queensbury. On returning home he considered asking Magsie for a divorce but by now she was used to her husband's erratic behaviour and pretended to take it in her stride and let it fizzle out which, indeed, it did. Until the next time… Gay was rich, Ernest Guinness being his grandfather, but the money was under the control of the professional Guinness Trustees who although tolerant to a degree were taking a firmer line on Gay's huge expenditure on horses and those of a more personal nature. They did, however, consider property a sensible investment and agreed to sell Hullers, an 80-acre farm near Dorking where Gay and Magsie had been living, and buy a farm at East Garston, five miles from Lambourn with around 1,000 acres and a very ordinary farmhouse named Parsonage Farm. Perhaps unwisely they gave Magsie full authority to make the alterations which she and Gay thought necessary, with the result that Parsonage, under Magsie's direction at vast expense, was transformed into a very splendid mansion with large, elegant rooms and bathrooms, swimming pool, tennis court, stables with staff accommodation, designer gardens … the lot, with a pub, The Queens Arms, at the end of the drive. Magsie threw all her energy into the work which took her mind off wondering what Gay was doing and with whom when he was not with her.

They eventually moved into the new Parsonage in 1962 by which time Magsie had produced three children, Robin born in 1956, Catheryn in 1958 and Kim in 1960, but these events had not cured Gay of his CIS which he followed with as much determination as he showed as an amateur jockey. Both pursuits were fraught with different forms of danger but both produced the adrenalin and stimulation of the chase, which drove him continually forward to the next race or conquest. A major one presented itself when Gay, at a very alcoholic party in December at a house overlooking the Thames, accepted a bet to swim across the river, which he did but ran into problems in the shape of an adverse current on the way back, and had to be rescued freezing cold and suffering from hypothermia. Later, still at the party but covered by thick blankets and rugs, he heard a lovely soft voice singing to a magical haunting instrument; it was Shirley Abicair, an Australian beauty and very much a cabaret queen at the time, playing her zither. He fell hook, line and sinker and made it his business to track her down, which only took him a few days, before he succeeded in engaging her to play at a New Year's Eve party he was organising. The affair stared then and went on for a long time until Miss Abicair, with a little help from her friends, demanded the equivalent of Gay's money or his life. He beat a hasty retreat back to Magsie armed with a bunch of roses and a magnum of champagne, but this time Magsie, with the work done at Parsonage and with a nanny to look after the children, had some free time on her hands and took a different view of the situation. She was attractive, they led a social whirl of a life with many friends in the acting and music world, frequently appeared in the social magazines and gossip columns with, as far as she was concerned, wrong conclusions suggested. That is not to say that she was deliriously happy: she wasn't and did turn to one man in particular who lifted her spirits, made her laugh and was socially acceptable. I first met Charles Benson some years before, in the late 50s, when he was very much on the London scene and married to a very beautiful girl called Carole Master. They had two children but the marriage fell apart largely because Charles was addicted to gambling, rather unsuccessfully both on the race-course and also in the casinos; he worked as a racing journalist on the *Daily Express*, first as 'Bendex' but eventually succeeding Clive Graham as 'The Scout'. Of course he knew Gay but also John Aspinall and all the 'Lucky' Lucan crowd. When Aspinall started the Clermont Club in Berkeley Square, he engaged the portly, Old Etonian, cash-deficient Benson as a 'house' player: someone with a large circle of friends, a gambler himself and very quick witted. For a considerable time he provided Magsie with something that was missing in her life.

It was about that time – September 1965 – that I first met Magsie when she and Gay came to stay with me in Cheshire. Five years later when I moved to the Lambourn area I didn't see much of them, certainly not during my time at Whatcombe and only at the odd party after Anthea and I had moved into Berkeley House. I was then totally involved with flat racing, therefore hardly ever went jumping, and they were the complete opposites. Gay had retired from race riding a while back and had taken out a professional National Hunt trainers licence, which meant that he had to resign from the Jockey Club as no one professionally engaged in racing was allowed to be a member. Gay's training was ticking along for a while without hitting many headlines and certainly was not making money, to the concern of the Trustees. A plan was hatched: why not emigrate to France, which would be an advantage tax-wise, and start training jumpers there? The idea of someone of Gay's age and temperament starting a jump-racing operation in France would have been an expensive non-starter, so Magsie was dispatched to stay with Oonagh who was now living in a fabulous house, La Tourelle de la Garoupe on Cap d'Antibes, to suss out the situation in France. How she was supposed to do that among the distractions of the South of France in the height of the summer season, goodness only knows. However, Magsie's absence suited Gay quite well: he had found a new girlfriend, Philippa Harper, who lived near Dorking and in a fairly short time they had become an item but were most careful to ensure that the children were not aware of the situation. Tania (Magsie's fourth child, born in 1967) was anyway with her mother in France. There was also another ace in the pack in the shape of Philippa's now former boyfriend, the hell raiser actor Oliver Reed, who also lived very nearby and who was more than a little miffed, when deciding to pay a late night call, to find the lovers already fully occupied. On another occasion, Philippa's birthday, he appeared stark naked at her door announcing 'I knew it was your birthday so I've come in my birthday suit.'

Magsie's absence in France may have been instrumental in Gay making the decision that the marriage was over. He there-fore determined to go to La Tourelle and formally tell her so, rehearsing his speech many times over. In the event, however, the tables were turned very soon after his arrival when Magsie discovered Philippa's name and telephone number in Gay's wallet; the balloon went up and at three o'clock in the morning Magsie rang Philippa, who sleepily answered 'Hello Darling' thinking it was Gay. An almighty row ensued, which probably would have happened anyway but maybe at a more civilised time of day; clearly it was the end and Magsie made immediate plans to return to England.

Back in Lambourn I had no idea of all these Kindersley goings on. The gossip, such as it was, was that Magsie had taken an extended holiday with her mother-in-law in France, that Charles Benson used to pop down for weekends and that Gay had a girlfriend called Dorking so it was quite a surprise to receive a telephone call – along with many others – from Magsie saying that she was back from France and had decided to have a party at Parsonage a few days later and would I like to come? Most Lambourn parties were thus arranged at short notice because trainers did not know whether they would be at Beverley or Bath for longer than that. It was a very good party, lots of friends, plenty to drink, buffet-type food, plenty to drink, disco dancing and plenty to drink. At another similar party several months beforehand in a different house Magsie had been pretty short with me for making the mistake of enquiring after Gay, who was not present, but this time she was much more friendly and we got on very well, probably rather too well so we made arrangements to meet again the next day. This, too, was most congenial, so much so that another date was planned; in what seemed no time Magsie was unburdening her problems with Gay and her marriage which was all over bar the shouting. For me, Anthea had only left finally about a month previously so we found ourselves, if not in the same boat, up the same tree.

We blossomed together, and Magsie started to come round to Berkeley House during the daytime. Her elder children had been told that there would be a divorce; Tania was back at boarding school, and Robin, Catheryn and Kim, aware for a long time that their parents' marriage was anything but normal, seemed to take it in their stride and were very pleasant to me. I had engaged a very sensible, experienced and thoroughly nice mature nanny for Simon and Sam called Isobel, and as long as I was not away racing I made sure I was at home as much as possible and certainly when they came back from day school until they were tucked up in bed in the evening. The configuration of the house was that both boys had their own bedrooms, but from one of their windows they both had a good view of the stable yard which was not entirely out of earshot, so they did pick up a certain amount of stable-lad language. Sometimes, when my parents came down from Cheshire to see the horses and stay the night, they used to take the boys to stay a few days with them. On one such occasion my mother took them with her to do some shopping; on the way to the nearest village she pulled out to overtake a car in front of her but, seeing another car coming the other way, pulled back again. Commented young Sam: 'Hmm, that's a pity, Granny, we'd have been OK if it wasn't for that other fucker coming the opposite way.' Note the word 'other'. She couldn't wait to relate the story to me on the telephone that evening.

On the racing front, things weren't going too badly. I had a stroke of luck thanks to the kindness of one man; Bill Payne, who trained a small string of horses at Eastbury, a village near Lambourn, wanted to retire. He had been a jump jockey before the Second World War but joined up and served with the Yorkshire Dragoons with the rank of Major. With Bill on his way to retirement, he very kindly suggested to some of his owners that they might consider sending their horses to be trained by me. Some of them were bold enough to do so, among them being a family from Highgate, north London, called Dollar. There was Mr and Mrs Dollar, both quite elderly, their son Robin and daughter Gloria. They had a business, I never found out the nature of it but their horses ran in the name of Tedwood Ltd. They had two horses with Bill and sent them both to me; Bill said that he didn't think they were much good but obviously the change of air or location stimulated considerable improvement because over the next two seasons they both won several races.

I discovered quite early on and by accident that Mr Dollar senior was very keen to have a proper tilt at the bookmakers: I had taken one of their horses, name of Brimps, in the hope of winning a small race up at Edinburgh which it did with some ease. On the strength of that, Newmarket was next in a better class race but I genuinely thought he had a fair chance of repeating his

Edinburgh victory and told Mr Dollar so, even though he was 20 to 1 in the betting forecast. In the paddock before the race, a rather breathless Mr Dollar came rushing up to me saying Brimps was 8 to 1. I asked him if he had had a bet and he said, 'Yes, £1,000 so far!' I was furious, not with him but with the way he had been manipulated by Ladbrokes, the bookmakers. The horse opened at 20 to 1 but Mr Dollar had gone to Ladbrokes saying the amount of money he wanted on the horse before asking the price. I knew Dickie Gaskell, the head 'railsman' at Ladbrokes, pretty well and told him that was no way to treat an owner of mine; in all fairness he didn't know Dollar or that I was his trainer but he apologised profusely and Mr Dollar was returned 20 to 1 for Brimps who won comfortably. Dickie was one of the last gentleman bookmakers but even he was never allowed, as a bookmaker, into the Royal Enclosure at Ascot. Johnson Houghton of Stafford & Co. was another until Staffords were taken over by Ladbrokes; a third was Archie Scott who traded under his own name. The other Dollar horse at that time was really only a pony, barely over 15 hands, beautifully bred by Royal Palace but on his day and with firmish ground he was pretty useful at around one mile, winning ten races. At one stage I thought he was losing a bit of interest so I popped him over some schooling hurdles, which he thought was great fun so I entered him in a novices hurdle race at Ludlow which he won and which gave him increased enthusiasm to revert to winning form on the flat. The Dollars were very lucky owners for me; in addition to the ones I inherited from Bill Payne, all the horses I bought for them won races, including one I bought very cheaply indeed as a yearling at Deauville. He was tiny, hence his price, but he had a bold eye and I knew the Dollars liked an early two-year-old on which they could have a bet. He was called Blackmanship; we gave him a run very early in the season when not really wound up, where he showed enough promise, so next time at Wolverhampton I told the owners we might have a bit of fun but on no condition were they to go anywhere near the bookmakers on the racecourse but to leave it to me. We had £1,500 to put on the horse expecting at least 20 to 1. Enlisting the help of my great friend Harry Beeby in Scotland we put the money on in small quantities in many different places. The Starter at Wolverhampton that day was my very good friend Sir John Guise; he had supervised the stalls loading of eighteen of twenty runners, including Blackmanship, when suddenly the stalls opened, leaving two horses that had not been loaded. Blackmanship won the 'race', then declared void by the Stewards, but they took the extraordinary step of ordering the race to be re-run thirty minutes later. Blackmanship had 'won' but had had a hard race, therefore was tired and, in any event, our 'cover' was blown so there was no way I was going to allow him to run again. I withdrew him, as happened with ten other horses. We had succeeded in getting all our money on at 33 to 1; he had actually 'started' at 20 to 1 but as the race was declared void, we did not lose our money. Neither did we win £1,500 x 33 = £49,500 which was a shame. The next day the racing press and national dailies were full of the story and critical of the Stewards' action in ordering the race to be re-run. 'THE STALLS VIBRATED, SAYS SIR JOHN' screamed one of the headlines. The verdict of the official enquiry was that the false start was due to 'mechanical failure'. Our little betting coup having been foiled, it was difficult to know what to do next with the horse as he was bound to start at a very short price the next time he ran because he was virtually a winner without a penalty. We put him on the easy list for a while as he took time to recover from his exertions at Wolverhampton. The rules of racing state that all horses should be allowed to run on their merits, and I never ran a horse that was prevented from so doing, but sometimes merits do vary and for Blackmanship's next couple of races he did not feature very prominently. I did, however, have a target in mind for him later in the season. At the York July meeting they used to have a valuable selling race for two-year-olds. The winner's prize money to the owners for this race was £5,000 with the winner to be sold by auction immediately after the race for a minimum of £2,000. I advised the owners that we should go for this race; Blackmanship was very small, had been a cheap purchase at 1,500 euros, would not have been up to carrying the heavy weights which he would have been allotted in handicaps and had served his owners well enough if he won this race. They agreed, we made this race his target which he duly won, ridden by Trevor Rogers who had been on him at Wolverhampton; the Dollars collected the good prize money, the horse was sold for £2,500 afterwards to the astute northern trainer, Harry Blackshaw, who had good Scandinavian connections and passed him on to a Norwegian client and they, the Dollars, had a good bet so everyone was happy. They had another two-year-old at about that time, which again I had bought for not much money by Decoy Boy, which they insisted on naming Rubber Duck; despite the name he won three races as a two-year-old.

As the yearling sales season in 1976 was getting under way, Robert Sangster asked me to train a couple of horses for him which I was delighted about. In England, Robert's main trainer was Barry Hills, my near neighbour in Lambourn, but he also had horses with Jeremy Hindley in Newmarket. Robert's marriage to the lovely Chrissie, unfortunately, broke up, Robert spreading his wings horse-wise to countries overseas and moving for tax reasons to the Isle of Man which, with all the constant travelling, didn't suit Chrissie who, although most attractive, decorative and fun-loving, was more of a stay-at-home bird. It didn't help either that Robert had fallen for the wife of Andrew Peacock, the then Foreign Minister of Australia. Her name was Susan, a rather brash, I always thought, and blonde lady, always known as The Sheila, who preferred the high life of a jet-setting rich British top racehorse owner to that of a politician's wife. Robert, instinctively, was a gambler, the higher the stakes the better: his father, Vernon Sangster, had started Vernon's Pools which is where the money came from originally and Robert maintained the family tradition by moving into the racing world in a big way. He was also a very good and hard hitting amateur boxer in his younger days, continuing to follow the sport and becoming a member of the British Boxing Board of Control. Staying with him once in the Isle of Man, I heard him pick up the telephone during a conversation we were having about his horses and place a bet of £9,000 at odds of 9/2 ON on the boxer Jim Watt to become world lightweight champion – which indeed he did. Robert loved the company of pretty women, but in conversation he was better in male company though he needed a crowd of congenial people. I introduced Billy MacDonald, who still had a room at Berkeley House whenever he needed it, to Robert and the pair of them hit it off very well, but the court jester in Chief was Charles Benson, not just a hanger-on but an essential member of the Sangster entourage. Charles had a huge circle of acquaintances, several friends and an excellent memory; he could make me laugh more than anyone else but it was always at somebody else's expense. His wit was sharper than a knife cutting through butter and his repertoire of embellished stories inexhaustible; likewise his skin was as thick as and his bulk comparable to the proverbial rhinoceros. He was Robert's man, confidant, alibi when necessary but above all, court jester. Of course it suited Charles down to the ground, as Robert picked up the tab for everything – flights, hotel and restaurant bills, ringside seats and, as frequently happened, bookmakers' bills. Some years after his divorce from Carole, Charles married Caroline Gerard Leigh, rather to the disappointment of her father Colonel William Gerard Leigh who commanded the Household Cavalry and was affectionately known as Polo Stick in Waiting to the Duke of Edinburgh; the Colonel rather hoped that his daughter might marry Prince Charles. I went to their wedding and listened to the bridegroom's speech, which started thus by addressing his new parents-in-law: 'Here's the bad news. I'm sorry that your daughter has married the wrong Charles. The good news is "Hello Mum and Dad."' Caroline,

rather unfairly I thought, was always known as Chubby, and was
– and is – a spirited lady, conscious of her own life, well capable
of taking care of herself, intelligent and certainly able to stand
up to Charles. But she liked and fitted into his lifestyle. Robert
had his own professional advisors and agents on the purchase
of bloodstock but occasionally he gave me a free hand and all
the horses I bought for him were victorious except one. He was
great to train for, never complained if things went wrong and if
a horse didn't make the grade he was the first to say don't worry
we'll send you another one. He was also a good friend: when he
married The Sheila he flew a party of us in a private chartered
plane to the Isle of Man for three days of celebration centred on
his lavishly furnished house, rather inappropriately named The
Nunnery, putting us up with various friends on the island.

Over the years Lambourn has collected as residents a large
number of eccentrics, almost always with a strong connection
with the equine world, but none more so than, direct from Soho,
the doyen of the Coach and Horses, Old Compton Street, Jeffrey
Bernard. Jeff, the son of an architect and opera singer, having
been asked to leave Pangbourne College at the age of sixteen, had
based himself at the Coach and Horses while finding employment
as a stage hand and actor for Joan Littlewood, a miner, barman,
professional boxer (when asked for his occupation, he replied
'pugilist'), navvy and evening companion for middle-aged ladies.
In the words of his biographer, Graham Lord in his book *Just The
One,* he had many wives, four of them his own. He loved, but
could not pay for, the big time and big time people so the Coach
and Horses, where many artists, actors and serious drunks like
Dylan Thomas and Francis Bacon used to congregate, was manna
from heaven to Jeff. Betting on horses was part of a day's work
and what money he had left after his daily stint in the Coach
and Horses went the way of the bookmakers. He found that by
going racing he could kill two birds with one stone: bet and get
close to the nobs. On racecourses, owners, trainers and jockeys

are easily approachable, with the first two groups frequently in the bar where their habits and mannerisms could be studied. Jeff, with his quick wit and mimicry skills, found himself a new home, one about which he could write in his own sardonic and cynical style. He was also very funny. He had, at times, regular columns with the *Sporting Life, Queen, Punch, New Statesman, Sunday Times Magazine, Daily Express, Sunday Mirror, Private Eye* and *The Spectator.* Most of the above resulted in dismissal either for failing to meet deadlines or for inappropriate content. One letter, which he had framed and hung in his loo, was from Alan Coren, the editor of *Punch*. It ran 'Dear Jeff, are you going to write the fucking article or not?'

One day in the Coach and Horses Jeff told me that he was moving out of London to a remote cottage at the end of a track high on the Downs near Lambourn. Jeff didn't drive, or at least he had no car or driving licence, but he devised a cunning method of getting down to the village for his daily tour of the pubs and/ or visits to trainers and friends: he wrote a letter to himself which meant that the village postman had to deliver it. On arrival, there was Jeff ready and waiting to ask the postman to kindly give him a lift down to the village. At the end of the day he always managed to scrounge a ride back up the hill to his cottage, having taken care to post the letter to himself for the following day. In 1976 he was hired for the *Spectator* by the then editor Alexander Chancellor, who pinched him from the *New Statesman* as their television critic, which was a bit of a waste of time because Jeff had just come off a two-year period of abstinence (of alcohol) so was always pissed when he turned on the television which sent him straight to sleep. Chancellor soon wised up to this but then produced a brainwave that was to last for the rest of Jeff's life: Taki Theodoracopulos – byline Taki – was writing a weekly column all about High Life. Who better to write about Low Life than Jeffrey Bernard? He could, and did, write about all the spivs, tarts and layabouts of Soho and characters of all ranges of those who frequented the racecourse, starting at the bottom and only working about halfway up. *Private Eye* was different: here his byline was 'Colonel Mad'. During the course of each week a little coterie consisting of Jeff, Julian (Screamer) Lewis, Michael Phillips, the racing correspondent of *The Times,* and me, plus a few others from time to time including Doug Marks, used to sit down over a lunchtime drink and decide who we wanted to be rude about in the world of racing. It wasn't vicious but was sometimes cutting, certainly as far as pomposity was concerned, and we didn't mind sending up ourselves on occasion since *Private Eye* readers had no idea who Colonel Mad was. As an example I reached the semi-final of the spoof 'Shit of the Year' competition only to be beaten by Daniel Widenstein who, in turn, lost to the Aga Khan in the final. Another is part of a spoof series of WW2 adventures, but instead of the real heroes we have the following:

The story so far: Germany is winning the war and the Cabinet decides on desperate measures. Now read on:

The tank landing craft nosed its way quietly through the fog. Soon they would be hitting the beach at Deauville. Capt. Antony Johnson checked the time on the luminous dial of his Asprey watch, and gave his Gucci service revolver a reassuring pat.

"OK, chaps," he whispered through the gloom and salt-spray, "time to check our equipment before the balloon goes up." His men murmured nervously. "Sergeant Sangster?" "Yes, sir. D Company's all accounted for. We've got £5 million and 6 cases of Vintage Krug." "Good. Corporal Walwyn?" "All present and correct, sir. £3 million and a dreadful little wog who says he wants to buy some yearlings." "Jolly good. Has anyone seen Private Benson?" Johnson drew nervously on his Davidos. He hoped to God Benson hadn't chosen this moment to ruin the show. "He's leaning on the stern rail, sir," said a muffled voice. "Says there's just time to catch some caviar before the flares go up." Johnson gave a sigh of relief. Tonight they'd show the frogs and jerries a thing or two...

Colonel Mad

Sporting Life

'I Was Rommel's Double' concluded:

*The story so far: **Capt. Antony Johnson** and his men have been captured during the daring raid on Deauville and sent to the dreaded Stalag 27 in Baden-Baden. Under the command of the notorious Obergruppenfuehrer Wildenstein they have suffered dreadfully but, thanks to the 'escape committee', morale is high.*

NOW READ ON:

Captain Johnson wiped the perspiration from his brow. He was incredibly tired and, as he forced the blade of his silver-plated Wilkinson Sword Edge spade into the clay of the tunnel, he paused to reflect that, if the Red Cross had any sense at all, they would have sent some Givenchy Eau de Toilette in their last parcel.

There were only a few feet left now and by tomorrow they should be out. He had already decided to make straight for St Moritz and he couldn't help smiling at the plans his NCOs had made.

Sergeant Sangster was intending to tunnel all the way to the Isle of Man so as to avoid paying tax on his way through France, and he doubted very much whether **Corporal Walwyn** would make it at all. His temper had attracted the attention of the Germans in recent weeks and, if he would keep hitting the guards over their heads with his shovel, then they were bound to keep an eye on him. No wonder his platoon called him 'Fawlty' Walwyn.

What worried Johnson most though was how to break the news to **Private Benson**. Both he and Sergeant Sangster had measured the tunnel several times since they had begun digging and there was no way in which Benson was going to wriggle his ample 17 stone through the narrow burrow. Never mind, at least it meant there was room to take the new arrival at Stalag 27. Only yesterday the camp guards had hurled a figure dressed in a Flying Officer's uniform into their hut. It had turned out to be the legendary air ace 'Concorde' Corbett, whose number had at last come up when he had been shot down over Nagasaki while attempting to drop Try My Best on Japan.

So now there were four of them and it was nearly zero-hour. Unbeknown to Captain Johnson at that moment, just 20 feet above him, in **Wildenstein's** private quarters, Private Benson was earning what was sadly going to be a posthumous Victoria Cross. There would be no wriggling along the tunnel for him, for Wildenstein, guessing an escape attempt was imminent, had been trying to break Benson for days.

The SS had served him lobster without mayonnaise, then they had made him drink a Chateau Mouton Rothschild 1927 with his Sole Bonne Femme. As he swallowed the last drop of a diabolically chilled vintage port, Johnson and his group were emerging from the tunnel and into freedom.

They gulped the fresh air, the first they had swallowed since the raid on Keenland years ago, and Corporal Walwyn threw himself on the ground to kiss it with gratitude. He straightened up almost immediately.

"Wouldn't you bloody well know it," he screamed. "It's on the soft side of good. How the f****** hell am I supposed to train horses on this?"

It was like old times again, Johnson reflected, and he set off in the direction of St Moritz and peace, pausing only in Gstaad at Van Cleef & Arpels to buy the kitchen-bound Maggsie a trinket.

NEXT WEEK: How Robert 'The Mole' Sangster got home 20 years later.

—

*   *   *

228

One of the greatest friends that I made, not just during the Lambourn years but ever, had nothing to do with and had no interest in racing – at least not with horses. He was, though, a winning Formula 1 motor racing driver named Innes Ireland who, with his wife Eddy, came to live nearby in the mid-70s. Sadly I never knew Innes during his racing days but he was in the era of Stirling Moss, Mike Hawthorn, Jim Clark and others who, similar to the last two named, didn't survive this most dangerous of sports. Innes was born in 1930, the son of a Scottish vet who moved the family back to Scotland when Innes was only a boy. Always interested in cars and engines, he trained as an engineer with Rolls-Royce but later was commissioned into the army with the King's Own Scottish Borderers and served with the Parachute Regiment in the Suez Canal in the early 50s. Demobbed, he ran a small engineering business which got him into racing sports cars so successfully that he was signed up by Lotus in 1959, for which he did very well for the next two years winning his first, and only, Formula 1 Grand Prix at Watkins Glen, USA in 1961. Shortly afterwards he was sacked by Lotus boss Colin Chapman in favour of Jim Clark.

Innes was a happy-go-lucky, daredevil, brilliant and fun-loving driver, one of the last of the *Ancien Pilotes* type of driver who raced for the danger, thrill and glamour; other things like money, although welcome and necessary, came second. Innes loved a party, pretty girls and whisky in any order and at any time. When he lost the job at Lotus he carried on for a few years but he never had a serious competitive car again so when the fun stopped, he stopped, went back to Scotland, bought a fishing trawler which he skippered until the excitement of that palled and he came down south to near Lambourn which is where I met him and his wife. He also had a son, Jamie, by his first marriage who became a great friend of Simon and Sam's. I had never paid much more than peripheral attention to motor racing, knowing roughly what was going on and being aware of the names of the top drivers, including Innes, so it was with interest rather more than anything else when I met him for the first time, but we seemed to hit it off very well, particularly when he regaled me, never without a glass of whisky in his hand, of the fun, danger and excitement that he had.

After he had retired from Formula 1, he took part in the first London–Sydney Marathon rally in 1968 with two former racing drivers and good friends, Mikey Taylor and Andrew Hedges, driving a Mercedes. Most of the world's top works rally teams entered but the Ireland/Taylor/Hedges team was entered privately and at the halfway point, in Bombay, they won the prize for the leading privately entered car. Sadly the Mercedes broke down irreparably in the middle of the Nullarbor Plain Desert – four times the size of Belgium – in South Australia where they were stuck for three days waiting for new engine parts, which put them out of the rally. Innes wrote a wonderful book on the rally entitled *Marathon in the Dust*, a copy of which he gave me, suitably inscribed, for Christmas in 1976. It was about that time when he rang me one day saying that he was testing an Aston Martin for an article he was writing for Autocar and would I like to come with him the next day for the final day of practice before the British Grand Prix at Silverstone. I'd never been to a car race, let alone Silverstone, so Innes picked me up in this fabulous Aston and off we set. I loved being so expertly driven in this ultra-smart motor car all the way to Silverstone, whereupon all hell was let loose: it was the first time that Innes had been back on the motor racing scene following his trawler skippering time in Scotland and he was feted and welcomed by all and sundry in the hospitality rooms of all the main works teams and by all the mechanics, directors, managers and general hangers-on wherever we went. The noise was horrific but we did not have a glass out of our hands from arrival at ten in the morning until we left at five in the afternoon to drive down some narrow lanes on our way back to Lambourn. I noticed that Innes was driving even faster than on the morning journey so I asked him if we were in any particular hurry. 'No', he replied, 'but there's this arsehole in a foreign car up my backside,' whereupon he put the Aston in a sideways drift so that it completely blocked the road and got out to remonstrate with the driver of the other car. After a while I thought I had better get out to support my friend, who was asking the foreigner what on earth he thought he was doing driving a poxy foreign car so fast along an English country lane. The argument continued so I said to this fellow that he must quieten down and gently pushed him on the shoulder; unfortunately he was off balance and fell into a deep ditch well planted with nettles at the side of the road. We got back into the Aston and continued, quite sedately now, along our way. 'Do you know that chap?' I asked Innes.

'Yes' he said, 'He's Emerson Fitipaldi.' A Brazilian, Fitipaldi was Formula 1 World Champion driver in 1972 and 1974. Innes went back to Silverstone the next day and made friends again with Fitipaldi, who remarked that he noticed he was without his bodyguard.

Magsie and I were married at Caxton Hall in London (her second appearance) in September 1976, her divorce from Gay having been finalised a few months beforehand, followed by a small, fun reception for family and close friends. There was no honeymoon as racing was in full flow with the yearling sales season fast approaching. The early part of the season had not been hugely successful with only a handful of winners in pretty moderate company, but the order book for yearlings was promising in numbers.

One of our first guests to stay after we were married was an old friend of Magsie's called Kenneth Rose, an acclaimed biographer and writer of an upmarket gossip (he would have hated that title) column in the *Sunday Telegraph* – Albany at Large. Kenneth's biographies included the lives of Curzon – *A Superior Person* – and King George V and, although from comparably humble origins, he lived a life of comfortable bachelorhood in Connaught Place and mingled with political nobility and the higher echelons of his selected society. He was a close confidant of the Duke of Kent. One morning at breakfast he announced that he was going to Spain: 'Why?' I asked. 'To see the King,' he replied. However, that is not the point of this little story. It was a lovely English summer weekend and Kenneth was taking an afternoon rest on a chaise longue, checking his column in the *Telegraph*, when my very small son, Sam, approached this, in his view, strange character lying down, his Panama hat shielding his bald head from the sun: 'Hello young man,' said Kenneth, 'and what are you going to be when you grow up?'

'I'm going to be a policeman,' said Sam, 'but by the time I'm a policeman, you'll be dead.' Seeing Kenneth's slightly shocked expression, he corrected himself, 'Well, nearly dead.' Slightly, and only slightly, on the same wavelength, the prominent French jockey who went to Australia to ride a horse in the Melbourne Cup and was introduced to the wife of the Governor General; his command of the English language was poor, most of it having been picked up by talking to English jockeys in Europe, so when asked by the Governor General's wife for his opinion of Australian racing he replied instantly, 'Fucking good.' Seeing the bemused expression on Her Ladyship's face he corrected himself grammatically, 'Pardon, good – fucking.'

There was never, or hardly ever, a dull moment in Lambourn. Characters attract characters from all walks of life. One such was Tony Stratton-Smith, who started as a sports journalist before graduating into rock music management and founded Charisma Records. Very keen on racing, more National Hunt than flat, he was always knocking around the pubs in Lambourn and, bumping into him in the village one day, and with the view of trying to sell him a horse, I asked him to come the following Sunday to go round the horses and have a drink afterwards. He said he had a couple of people staying so I said bring them along.

The couple turned out to be four but never mind. One of them was Graham Chapman, the Python, with a sycophantic boyfriend; Graham, a qualified doctor before switching to writing and performing with the Pythons, had played Jesus Christ/Brian in *The Life of Brian* and was good fun to talk to. Another of Tony's friends was an American to whom I was introduced but didn't catch his name, in typical English fashion; nevertheless he was fascinating to talk to in that he expressed such a keen interest in everything he saw to do with the horses, the establishment and the environment as a whole. In fact I spent more time talking to him than anyone else and it was several bottles later when they finally left. I thought no more about it except that it had been a pleasant way to spend the afternoon – until a few days later a large and heavy parcel arrived with RCA Records on the address label. Inside were fifteen LPs and a note saying, 'Thanks for a lovely day. Love, Harry.' It was Harry Nilsson and the records were all his own songs, plus songs written by others including the Beatles but sung by Harry. I had no idea that it was him to whom I had been talking for such a long time; he never mentioned music or himself at all. Of course I contacted him, thanking him profusely; we arranged to meet again in London and became firm friends. Later I met his third and last wife, Una, a charming quiet Irish girl who was devoted to him and put up with his quite extraordinary and frequently severely alcoholic life.

Harry Nilsson was a man of extreme talents whose voice and songs were internationally known number one hits, featuring in movies, but who never performed public concerts or tours. He wrote two songs for the movie *Midnight Cowboy*, the one selected, 'Everybody's Talking', and the other, just as good, 'I Guess The Lord Was Born In New York City'. One day he rang me asking if I would like to come with him to a musical play that he had composed and written and which was being performed at the Mermaid Theatre in London. The play was an adaptation of an American children's strip cartoon called 'The Point', all about the Land of Point in which all inhabitants had a pointed head: all excepting one poor man, our hero, who had no point on his head but was in love with the king's daughter. The king's wicked son banished our hero to the Pointless Forest in which he encountered various horrific dangers and adventures accompanied by his only friend, his dog, Arrow... As in all good fairy tales everybody lived happily ever after in the end, except the king's wicked son who, in turn, was banished. Bernard Miles, who owned the theatre, played the king, Davy Jones, lead singer of The Monkees, played our hero and the dog, Arrow was played – and danced – by Wayne Sleep. It was all totally enchanting, with lots of catchy tunes all composed by Harry, including the haunting 'Me and My Arrow', sung and whistled by our hero throughout his horrendous journey in the Pointless Forest. After the show Harry said 'Okay, what would you like to do next? I'm doing a recording session, would you like to come along?' We went to a studio somewhere in Soho where Harry had booked a group of session musicians and, for the next three hours, there was Harry in a sound-proofed cubicle recording an album. What an insight into another world – it was 4.30 a.m. when he finished. I continued seeing him sometimes when he was in England and we remained in contact but I hadn't seen him for a few years when he died in 1994. He was a great friend of John Lennon, including his adaptation of several Beatles songs in his albums; he was much affected by the tragic nature of Lennon's death, spending a lot of his time lobbying for changes in US gun laws. A short time after Harry died I met Michael Palin, another former Python who knew him well, at a party in a friend's house in London and asked what he died of. 'Everything' was his reply. It was Palin who played with John Cleese the famous parrot sketch: 'This parrot is dead'; 'Oh no, it's just resting' etc, etc.

Racing has always attracted people from the world of show

business and entertainment; at the races one day Charles Benson introduced me to Bryan Ferry, a Geordie and about the most charismatic songwriter and singer of the late 20th century. He led his own band, Roxy Music, and I remember going with Charles to a Ferry concert in London. Later that year Bryan asked Magsie and myself plus Charles and Chubby Benson to stay at his very super house near Goodwood for the big August meeting. I had a couple of runners so we were delighted to accept. Arriving through the lodged gates we drove up the drive to the most imposing house and lovely garden. Bryan had arranged a dinner party cooked and served by his staff. Early the next morning I wanted to check on the horses at the racecourse but, as it was such a beautiful morning, thought I had time for a quick swim in Bryan's pool first. There was a chap there sweeping the pool with whom I got into conversation; just then Bryan himself appeared and said, 'Oh, I see you have met my father!' It was he who was the gardener and lived in the lodge at the gate; the 'staff' the previous night had been Bryan's mother, the cook, and his sister who served. One of Bryan's first big romances was with Jerry Hall who dumped him for Mick Jagger, to Bryan's intense dismay at the time.

Another great character who I used to see racing a fair bit, particularly at summer evening meetings at Windsor, was the rubber-faced actor and comedian Mel Smith. Who can ever forget his sketches with Griff Rhys-Jones in *Alas Smith and Jones* and *Not The Nine O'Clock News?* He popped up in Lambourn from time to time and I remember him coming in for a drink one day and signing his name on the plaster on my son's leg which he'd broken skiing. Some years later I used to see him in Barbados where he used to spend much of the winter. He died of a heart attack in 2013 aged only sixty.

The season didn't end too badly and I had enough orders for yearlings as a starter for the sales season in the autumn but, again, for limited sums of money. Julian (Screamer) Lewis had a very good friend, an Englishman called Charles Milbank, who trained in Chantilly. I knew him too and that he used to take a selection of horses down to Cagnes-sur-Mere, on the coast near Nice, for a change of air and to run during their winter season from mid-December to early March. Julian knew the scene down there very well and suggested going down to take a look, which Magsie and I did for a long weekend including two days racing and fitting in a day's skiing at Valburg, only 1½ hours away. It was all very jolly and I discussed with Charles the idea of sending a horse of mine for him to train under his licence the following year, which indeed I did and it won a race. During this little break we all decided, that is Charles and his wife, Wendy, Julian and Caroline and Magsie and myself, to take a holiday on the French island of Guadeloupe in the Caribbean, taking in the sales at Hialeah, Miami on the way. Guadeloupe and the other main French Caribbean island of Martinique are departments of France with the same currency and laws as in the mother country. Charles and Wendy organised a lovely house on a beach to rent so we went in mid-January and had a marvellous time away from everything in the sunshine. One thing discussed was that, under French rules of racing, horses bred outside France are only eligible for entry in the top echelon of races but a French-bred horse, even if it is not owned or trained in France, is eligible to be entered and run in any race at a licenced French racecourse. Food for thought maybe.

The year 1977, the Queen's Silver Jubilee year during which Red Rum won his second Grand National and Virginia Wade won Wimbledon, also saw Jimmy Carter become President of the USA and marked the deaths of two distinctly different American show business superstars, Bing Crosby and Elvis Presley. In the air there was the tragic collision between KLM and Pan Am planes over the Canary Islands killing 583 people, and commercial flights on Concorde started between London and New York. I made my best start to the season so far with a flurry of early winners including a quite useful handicapper called Gold Streak, who won four races on the trot and was an unlucky second preventing a five-timer. On the social scene, Robin Kindersley, Magsie's eldest son, had moved in with us and his sister Catheryn was being pursued round London by the likes of Jamie Blandford (now the Duke of Marlborough) and Dai Llewellyn.

In August 1977 my father died. He had contracted shingles to his face and head the previous year and although incredibly brave and uncomplaining the illness really dragged him down and he never fully recovered. He had lived for very nearly thirty years following his racing accident in November 1948, which had initially rendered him totally paralysed, and although he regained some movement it was very limited, particularly on the right of his body. Curiously his left side became strong but he had no feeling in it. Internally the plumbing wouldn't pass building regs but as long as he was careful it was generally OK. He did, however, suffer near constant pain and it was only his amazing bravery and strength of mind that saw him through for so long, continuing to live as near normal as possible to the extent that he remained as Managing Director and Chairman of his company and various Trade Associations until his retirement in 1969. During the whole of his married life, and particularly after his accident, he was devotedly cared for and looked after by my mother. Although he did not want me to ride in races or to become a trainer, which he did not consider a 'Proper Job', he supported and encouraged me once it had become a 'fait accompli'. He had a fabulous sense of humour, adapted popular songs to his own words, was a good mimic and a limerick composer. One day in Barbados, he trotted out the following:

On Sandy Lane beach, Lady Hicks
Used to lie in the sun with no nicks
When asked for why, she said not to pry

But to see the effects on the gentlemen's pricks.

He seemed to have an obsession with titled ladies of a certain kind; for one such who, he said, kept a small country hotel, he provided her name and address:

> The Lady Florence Keeps,
> The Cock Inn
> Untillit,
> Wilts.

In June he became unwell with a stomach complaint and was eventually taken to the Nuffield hospital in Fitzroy Square in London in early August. My parents had a flat in Dunraven Street which was conveniently near to the Hospital so that she could be with him most of the time. I came up and down to London as much as possible and, after an operation, he seemed definitely on the mend. Late one evening, however, my mother rang and said that he had a relapse and could I come. I got to the hospital around 11 p.m. and saw him, my mother and the doctor, who said that nothing further could be done. He died at ten past one on in the morning of August 24th. I took my mother back to the flat and the next day, after the horrid formalities had been completed, she and I decided that she would come down to Lambourn. It so happened that I had a two-year-old filly of Robert Sangster's, called Lady of Man, running at Haydock that day; being before the days of mobile telephones and the internet, we listened to the racing results on the car radio read each day after the six o'clock news. The filly had won; we drove the rest of the way in emotional silence.

That summer, Kjell Qvale who had bought Jensen Motors with such enthusiasm a few years earlier and, during the course of this time, had sent me quite a few horses to train, got so fed up with the influence of the trade unions over his workforce that he decided that enough was enough, put the company into admin-istration and went back to California. Naturally he saw no point in racing horses in England any more but he thanked me for the enjoyment he had had and said that the company just started to produce a new model, a successor to the well-known Interceptor, when the balloon went up. They had only made twenty-eight of these cars and Kjell offered me one of them at a very discounted price, well below cost, as a sort of farewell thank-you. The car was quite a monster – on a good day. Unfortunately there were not too many of them; it was appallingly unreliable and spent more time in the repair garage than it did with me. However, I did succeed in driving it one night from Annabel's to Berkeley House in 48 minutes, admittedly at two o'clock in the morning.

At the yearling sales in Deauville the previous autumn I had bought two horses; one was Blackmanship for the Dollars which I've already talked about and the other was a very different type of individual that I bought for Bill 'My Word is my Bond' White, who wanted a horse of better quality than his first horse with me, Ashen Light, which had won two moderate races. The yearling was a good-looking son of the American-bred stallion Timmy My Boy, named Sunday Morning. I told Bill that he would probably not make a two-year-old and would need plenty of time to mature and a distance of ground. We brought him on slowly during the summer and towards the back end I told Bill that I would like to get one run into him before the end of the season just for education, so we ran him in a reasonable seven-furlong maiden at Lingfield towards the end of September. I told Trevor just to let him enjoy himself and on no account give him a hard race. To our intense surprise and pleasure he came a respectable second to a horse called Roland Gardens, our pleasure being considerably enhanced when Roland Gardens came out next time to finish first in the valuable and prestig-ious Horris Hill Stakes at Newbury, only to be demoted in the Stewards' room to third place for minor interference close to the line. The Horris Hill is usually a good pointer for the following season's Classics so we went into winter quarters with a possible top-class middle distance horse for the following year.

As I have said before, there was always plenty of mischievous mickey-taking going on in Lambourn; one morning up on the Downs Barry Hills came up to me with a twinkle in his eye: 'I've got Mr Bobby [McAlpine] staying with me.'

'Oh good' I said, 'Send him round after breakfast to have a look at his horses.'

'I'm not sure about that – he's got your ex-wife with him.' Although I did know that Bobby and Zandra were having a bit of a fling, it was no longer any of my business but I suppose Bobby might have found it embarrassing to bring her round to Berkeley House. Generally most trainers got along pretty well with each other and certainly that was the case regarding my nearest neighbours, Doug Marks on one side and Nicky Vigors on the other, but there was a little incident that ruffled feathers for a short while. I had bought a relatively expensive yearling filly at Newmarket for a new owner that I was very pleased with, but she was not an early sort and I made it clear to the owner that she would need time before she saw a racecourse. The owner had horses with a couple of other trainers as well and one day I received a call from him to say that he was calling in all his horses to an unknown destination for a 'veterinary inspection'. I told him that was fine but, if he wanted his filly to be examined by his own vet, why could this not happen at Berkeley House rather than interrupting her training preparation by taking her elsewhere? However, he was adamant so a horsebox came to collect the filly. I heard nothing for several days until Norman Mackness, my Travelling Head Lad, came to me and said that he had seen 'our' filly out with Nicky Vigors' string. I rang the owner who confirmed that he had sent the filly to Vigors without a word of explanation or complaint to me. I gave him a very strong piece of my mind in straight Lambourn language and put the telephone down. There is an unwritten rule in racing that if a trainer is asked to take a horse or horses currently being trained by another, the done thing is to speak to the other trainer concerned to discuss the matter. It could be, for instance, that the owner hadn't paid his bills or that they had just fallen out – any number of reasons but it was the polite thing to do. I had received no such call from Nicky, my next-door neighbour, so, next morning when I saw him up on the Downs I went up to him and said: 'Good morning Nicky. I wonder if you would like to come round evening stables with me this evening to see if there are any more of my horses that you would like to have?' The poor chap was so taken aback that he fell off his hack. However, he did have the good grace to come round for a drink the next day and apologise so all was forgiven and forgotten. For the record, something went wrong with the filly later on and I don't think she ever ran.

Bill Payne, the retired trainer who had so kindly recommended to some of his owners, including the Dollar family, that they send their horses to me to be trained, spoke to me during the winter to say his son, Pip, who had been working and learning about training in France for a while, was looking to come back to England to further his experience and wondered if I might have a place for him. Pip was thickset and heavy, therefore of no use as a rider, and I didn't really need an assistant but Bill had been so kind and indeed helpful to me that I thought it was the least I could do to repay him. Anyway Pip had gained useful experience in France, was very capable and well-presented so I agreed to take him on. He was married with no children and I had accommodation for them in one of two small houses that I had built for staff, with Norman Mackness and his wife Jo living in the other one. They moved in in the New Year and I appointed Pip as my assistant to work with Archie Hughes and to go racing when we had runners at two meetings on the same day. Wendy Cousins had left a while back to work as secretary at Manton for Robert Sangster and my new secretary was a very good girl called Clare Williams, whose husband Robert was a pupil assistant to Barry Hills.

The new season started pretty well again winner-wise but the main focus was to prepare Sunday Morning hopefully with the 2,000 Guineas in mind. All was going well and we ran him in a good class race at Newbury in early April in which he ran well but faded too quickly for my liking and was, frankly, disappointing. In his next piece of gentle work I thought I detected a very slight whistle in his wind as he came by me. His lad noticed nothing so next time I put Trevor on him but he, too, at that stage, noticed nothing but I was not happy and was fearful that he was making a slight 'noise,' so I asked Frank Mahon to come up on the gallops to listen to him. Frank confirmed the worst; he had a wind problem which could only get worse and ruled him out of training for any races, including the 2,000 Guineas to be run in early May. To make matters worse and rub in the disappointment, the 2,000 Guineas was won by Roland Gardens, the horse that I was convinced we could have beaten. Poor Bill White was just as disappointed as I was. I arranged for Sunday Morning to go to a vet specialising in a wind operation called 'hobday', named after F. T. Hobday, an English veterinary surgeon who perfected removing soft tissue from around the vocal folds to aid breathing.

On the other side of the coin and at the other end of the scale, we had a bit of fun with a filly by Decoy Boy that I had bought cheaply as yearling. I had had good success with another Decoy Boy offspring, a colt called Rubber Duck, that I had bought for the Dollars but this filly, which I named Final Act, showed nothing at home or on the racecourse as a two-year-old, which meant I could not recommend her to any owner so had to keep her myself. In racing parlance she was a proper cow, refusing to exert herself or even go on the gallops. I trained her mainly by trotting her up hills on her own and by sending her to Roger

Charlton's equine swimming pool. But I saw she had a modicum of ability if one could only unlock the door. As a three-year-old she did manage to be placed a couple of times but Trevor and other jockeys who rode her said that she could have won but was flatly refusing to go any faster. Blinkers and earplugs had no effect whatsoever; she was just a very unpleasant and bolshie female. Pip told me that he had once heard of a country trainer in France who had fitted earplugs to a horse and tied them together with shoe laces across the horse's head, instructing the jockey to reach forward and remove them during the race. He didn't know the outcome but we thought we'd give it a go. I entered Final Act in a selling race at Warwick, fitted the earplugs tied together and told Trevor to pull them out a furlong from the winning post when the noise of the crowd was increasing. Just in case we had a few quid on her at 7/1. So shocked was she at the sudden noise that she picked up and flew home to win. Trevor said that he was hard at work and getting nowhere until he pulled out the plugs. We repeated this plan on two further equally successful occasions, both times starting hot favourite. But our little ruse had not gone unnoticed by the Stewards. We had done nothing illegal: earplugs are a recognised method of calming a highly strung horse and there was nothing in the rules to say that they could not be removed. Anyway, the third time we fitted our gadget, the Stewards called for Pip before the race at Salisbury – I was not there – and asked him if we were fitting the plugs and if the jockey, Trevor Rogers, was instructed to remove them during the course of the race? Pip sensibly replied that the instructions to the jockey were that he should do his best to win the race. In the event he did remove them and Final Act (well named) did win. The racing press had a field day with such headlines as:

COTTON-PICKING WIN FOR FINAL ACT and SOUND PLAN WINS RACE.

Two weeks later the following notice appeared in the Racing Calendar:

EAR PLUGS

The Stewards of the Jockey Club give notice to trainers and riders that when any horse runs in a race with ear plugs of any kind, such plugs must not be removed during the course of the race.

I sold Final Act after the Salisbury race to Ken Cunningham-Brown for 1,700 guineas but she had only a few more unsuccessful races. Trevor told me after the Salisbury race that he thought she was getting the hang of the earplug game and doubted if it would have worked again, but it was fun while it lasted.

In the autumn of 1977, after Sunday Morning's very promising start to his racing career, I asked Julian Lewis who kept an eye on all French racing form and news to watch out to see if there was a yearling out of Sunday Morning's dam, Sunday Painter, coming up in the French yearling sales catalogues. Very late in the year, well after the main sales had taken place, he found what we were looking for: a chestnut colt by Exbury out of Sunday Painter. Exbury was bred by his owner Guy de Rothschild and named after his cousin's famous gardens in Hampshire; as a top-class racehorse, he was at his best and unbeaten as a four-year-old, winning two quality races in France, the Coronation Stakes at Epsom by five lengths and the Arc de Triomphe in 1963. As a stallion he was only a reasonable success, probably his best horse being Crow who won the St Leger and Coronation Cup. Anyway Julian rang me with the news that this yearling was coming at Deauville but that it was on the very next day. I rang Bill White and he agreed that we should have a go; accordingly Julian and I got in the car almost at once, drove to Southampton and caught the night ferry to Le Havre which is only about a two-hour drive from Deauville. The yearling, named Funny Sunday, was a totally different stamp of horse to his half-brother. Much lighter in frame and backward, which was probably why he hadn't come up for the main sales. However, he had a good eye and head with a very free and easy walk. Definitely an athlete but one which would need careful and patient handling. Bill said that he was going to fly over in the morning and catch a train to Deauville from Paris but by the time the horse had come into the ring, he had not appeared. It was not a very strong or large catalogue but Funny Sunday stood out and attracted a lot of attention both beforehand and when the bidding stared. It was difficult to know what to do without Bill being there but Julian and I liked the horse very much, we knew his half-brother had considerable ability so we went ahead and bought him for shade less than the equivalent of £10,000. Doesn't seem very much nowadays but it was a lot of money then. Bill turned up an hour later so we were able to give him the good (or bad!) news and at least show him what he was metaphorically taking home, all of which he took very well and was pleased.

In July 1978 my father's elder brother and my uncle Eric died almost a year after my father. He had lived a full and varied life, having been born in 1897, educated at Winchester, forgoing Oxford in order to join up, under age, and commissioned into the 16th/5th Lancers and won a very brave and good MC in 1918. Leaving the army he joined Richard Johnson & Nephew but didn't settle in civilian life and went cattle ranching in British Colombia, Canada, having had a row with his mother, my grand-mother, for exercising his horses on Christmas Day, as recounted in Chapter 4. Returning from Canada in 1930, he trained his own horses under permit at Ashton Hayes until the outbreak of the Second World War when he joined up again and served in an administrative and training role as a Major at Catterick. After the war he went into politics, standing unsuccessfully as a Liberal, but then as a Conservative he captured the Labour-held seat of the Manchester constituency of Blackley, which he held through various General Elections until 1964 when Harold Wilson became Prime Minister with a House of Commons majority of 4.

Eric devoted much of the rest of his life to charitable work, chiefly for BLESMA (British Limbless Ex-Servicmen's Association) and his own Regimental Association. He never married, most of his girl/lady friends having been firmly rejected by his mother who, as I have recounted previously, was a very formidable Irish matriarch who lived to the age of ninety-five. Since becoming an MP and indeed for the rest of his life he lived in a permanent suite of rooms at the Cavalry Club, which is where he died from a heart attack, aged eighty, having suffered from crippling arthritis in his later years. He was always helpful and supportive to me, never more so than in the Budgett war.

For many years my parents owned a ground-floor apartment in an old beachside house on the west coast of Barbados, which had been converted into four separate units. They used to go after Christmas and stay until about the end of March, quite often asking me for a holiday in January, which I loved very much to do, usually alternating between going to Barbados one year and skiing the next. After my father died, my mother continued spending time in Barbados, asking friends of hers to come out at varying times. In the winter of 1978–9 she very kindly allowed me to have the apartment to myself and invite friends to stay. At that time Magsie and I were good friends of Gerald Harper and his wife Carla. Gerald was a well-known actor having stared in many West End productions and two long-running television 'soaps', *Adam Adamant Lives!* and *Hadleigh*, in the latter of which his mother was played by a very good friend of my parents, Ambrosine Phillpotts. The Harpers and us, plus Magsie's youngest daughter Tania, flew out together and we survived a very close shave on arrival in Barbados. The British Airways jumbo jet landed and was immediately being refuelled for the next leg of its journey when the coupling connecting the fuel tanker hose and the plane failed, spewing out high octane fuel over one of the engines which had scarcely been shut down. The engine immediately caught fire and within a few seconds the whole of the interior of the plane was thick with dense smoke. Some passengers had already disembarked but not any of us; with amazing speed the emergency chutes were lowered and we felt our way to the emergency exits, slid down the chute and ran away from the blazing plane. Quite incredibly no one was killed and the only serious injury, apart from smoke inhalation, was a man who broke his leg. The fire was eventually put out but the plane remained where it was for many months. Luckily our luggage in the hold was undamaged and we managed to retrieve it the following day – quite an exciting start to our holiday.

Our next guests were also what you might call from the entertainment world, in the shape of Jeffrey Bernard and his then wife Sue. Sue, tall and good-looking, with long hair, was a delightful, amusing guest; Jeff spent a lot time sampling and consuming large quantities of the many different labels of Barbados rum, on one occasion emerging from a local bar with a huge smile proclaiming that it was cheaper to drink rum punch than grapefruit juice. During the whole time he spent with us he never got wet in the sea above his ankles, but one day a very strong wind got up, with the resultant very rough sea. Sue wanted to swim but, knowing the beach and current in rough weather, I told her on no account to go out of her depth. She did and couldn't fight back against the current, not being a strong swimmer. I went in after her and although I could get back myself, I couldn't tow her as well. Telling her not to panic I said we should allow the sea to take us out further where the waves were not breaking and that we should swim gently along the coast to a place where I knew we would be able to make the shore. Sue quickly became tired and very frightened so I told her to lie on her back and I would pull her along by her hair. Sounds daft and painful but it wasn't. A group of local boys realised that we were in a bit of trouble and swam out wearing masks and flippers together with a long rope, giving us the rope to hang onto so we could pull ourselves onto the shore. Unfortunately they had failed to attach the other end of the rope to anything on the shore so that little exercise failed and they disappeared. The good news was that we did arrive at the area that I knew would be safe and I managed to push, tow and heave Sue onto the shore, but by this time she was seriously exhausted, petrified with fear, very cold and passed out on the sand. Luckily help was at hand and after a few hours' sleep, fortified by a tumbler of rum supplied by Jeff – the only part he took in this drama – she was OK.

On his return to England, Jeff made hay in his Colonel Mad column in *Private Eye*, with lurid tales of misbehaviour amongst the contingency of racing people holidaying on the island, including his host and hostess, Michael Stoute visiting his homeland, BBC racing correspondent Julian Wilson, Robert Sangster, Charles Benson and Henry Cecil and his then wife, Julie.

14

The End of the Rainbow

In all the years that I trained horses, from my time in Cheshire onwards, the feeling of training a winner never failed to be an extreme high, whatever the class of race. I suppose that perhaps having bought a 'baby', i.e. a yearling, and trained it on to win, comes out on top because it is not just the physical side but the cultivation in the mind of a horse of the desire to succeed and run faster than all the others – that is the ultimate. Seeing a horse come into the winners enclosure at Ascot or Wolverhampton and the glint in its eye saying 'I did it didn't I?' is quite wonderful. I am absolutely certain that horses know that they have done well, just as one would do oneself.

The 1979 season again started brightly, with winners – plenty of winners – coming in the first couple of months. I suppose my main hope was that Sunday Morning's wind operation would prove successful and that he would reproduce the form of which I knew he was capable. Unfortunately this proved to be only partly the case; the horse was tremendously well in himself but a 'noise' was still there and I knew it would get worse again instead of better; he was second a couple of times but we then put him on the easy list for a while before deciding on his future. On the plus side, his half-brother, Funny Sunday, whom we only gave two very quiet runs to at the backend of his two-year-old career, was starting to develop into a very handsome colt and would stay 1½ miles plus. He won his second race as a three-year-old, ridden by Trevor Rogers, after which we upped him considerably

249

in class and, ridden by Walter Swinburn, he won a big sponsored race, the main race of the day at the Newmarket July meeting, comfortably by two lengths beating a very useful horse of Henry Cecil's, the odds-on favourite, that had won its previous three races. Needless to say I and, more importantly, Bill White were tickled pink that he had justified the confidence that we had placed in him. What to do next? An idea came to me: in France all the Paris tracks close down in August and the racing scene shifts to Deauville for the month, during which many of France's top-class races take place.

Deauville, in Normandy, is a coastal resort separated from the next-door town of Trouville by a small bridge over the River Touques, but the physical difference is huge. Whereas Trouville has a fishing and holiday atmosphere in the summer with small restaurants, cafés and boarding houses dotted all round the harbour and seafront, Deauville is chic and elegant with splendid hotels such as the Normandy and Royal, the magnificent casino, the harbour with super yachts and ocean-going gin palaces à la St Tropez moored along the quayside, smart restaurants, wonderful golf course, polo grounds and, of course, the racecourse with a convenient airstrip nearby. The town really comes alive in August when the international racing community with their well-heeled hangers-on, beautiful ladies and 'poules' dressed in best Parisien finery descend like bees round a honeypot. The Normandy bar is the accepted meeting place to start the evening followed by dinner either in one of the top hotel restaurants or in any one of several specialised restaurants, eating outside in lovely courtyards, weather permitting, then on to the casino, black tie obligatory in the salle privée, or a nightclub for dancing to fashionable bands with international cabaret artists. On one occasion, having accomplished most of the above itinerary, I was invited for a late-night drink, as if one were needed, on a smart gin palace in the harbour. I had driven my car alongside when my companion advised me to stop; on alighting from the car, this proved a sensible decision. Had I gone one foot further it was a vertical 10-foot drop into deep water. Another time I was summoned to dinner at the Royal Hotel by a very rich American Jewish owner for whom I was training; it was, however, on a Saturday which meant that he could neither eat nor drink until the sun had disappeared over the horizon. This was mildly inconvenient because I was (a) thirsty, (b) hungry and (c) had other plans … but duty called. He was a splendid chap with a sense of humour so, during the course of our rather late dinner, I explained to him that, in England, many of our better races were run on a Saturday and asked how that might affect him if he wanted to see his horse run. He explained that if he happened to be in a car going past the racecourse and as long as he didn't have to pay any money to enter the course, it would be perfectly permissible to watch it run. Likewise, if the race was on television and if he passed by a television that had been tuned into the race, that, too, was OK.

Close to Deauville lies the small town of Clairefontaine with an attractive lower-scale racecourse but also good holiday atmosphere. If Deauville can be compared to Goodwood, then so can Clairefontaine be with Brighton from a racing perspective. Deauville in August was always very special.

I remembered what Charles Milbank had told me – that French-bred horses were qualified to run in all French races. Of course Group races and the like were open to all comers, but one scale down it was French-breds only. Funny Sunday was close to Group class and rated pretty highly a little down the scale. I got hold of Screamer Lewis and we found a race ideal for Funny Sunday in the Deauville programme and, what's more, a low class but nevertheless quite valuable race, with over £4,000 to the winner, for Sunday Morning. The question was who to ride him? Obviously we wanted the best and with no disrespect to Trevor, who had not ridden at Deauville or indeed in France, I rang Lester Piggott who agreed. A couple of days before the race, Susan, Lester's wife, rang to ask how we were travelling to Deauville. 'My owner has chartered a plane,' I told her.

'Oh,' she replied, 'would there be room for Lester?'

Bill was very excited about the whole plan and delighted that Lester was coming with us. I had a French lad working for me at the time who looked after Sunday Morning so I sent him over with the horse and Norman Mackness, my Travelling Head Lad who spoke not a word of French. On the morning of the race we took off from Biggin Hill, Bill White, his wife Shirley, Paul, the son, Lester puffing a cigar and reading the *Financial Times* and me. On arrival, a car and driver whisked off Lester, I deposited Bill and family in another car at the racecourse and made my way to the racecourse stables where I had arranged to meet Norman and the French lad. Having checked the horse over I took the lad on the 15-minute walk on exactly the route he was to take with Sunday Morning an hour before the race, leaving him to go back to the stables while I joined up with the Whites. There was a moment of panic before the race because the stupid lad had taken someone else's advice on the route to follow and was very late in bringing the horse; I had visions of Lester, me and the owner standing there having flown from England but no horse. However, at the last moment all was well. The race was what was known as Claiming Race, in other words the winner can be 'claimed', i.e. bought, by anyone after the race for a listed sum of money, in this case 20,000 francs (then approx. £2,345). I told Lester about the horse's wind problem and that he should conserve as much energy as possible until the last second which he did and in a pulsating and driving finish in which we all had our hearts in our mouths, he prevailed and won by the shortest of short heads. In fact the first four horses were separated by less than half a length. I was not convinced that he had won until the announcement was made, although Lester was confident. The aftermath was that Sunday Morning was claimed so Bill netted about £6,500 for the race. I believe, though, via Julian's French spies, that the new owner was not at all pleased to discover that his new purchase made more of a noise than the *Flying Scotsman*.

A week later it was Funny Sunday's turn and we followed the same plan, although this time without L. Piggott. He couldn't come to Deauville on that day so I asked Julian to contact Yves Saint-Martin, the internationally known French Champion Jockey, to ride him, and Yves willingly agreed. The day went without any hitch and totally according to plan. Funny Sunday won a high-class race, the Prix Michel Houyvet, comfortably by a long length. It was all very exciting and gave me a 100 per cent winning record at Deauville – two runners, two winners with half-brothers.

There was a funny little sequel to the Deauville story: about a fortnight after Sunday Morning's triumph, a small brown envelope arrived, handwritten and addressed to 'The Secretary, Berkeley House Stables, Upper Lambourn'. Inside was a bill headed 'Dr to L. Piggott. To Transport Expenses, Deauville 15th August 1979. £150.00.' I saw Lester at the races a few days later and told him to pull the other one. 'Well', he said grinning, 'worth a try weren't it?' Having said all that, no other jockey could possibly have won on the horse, he was quite brilliant and the most superb jockey; it is near impossible to make comparisons with top jockeys of different generations but I'll never see a better jockey than Lester. He won on each and every horse that he rode for me, if not the first time, then the second. And what a character and what strength of body and mind.

Stories abound about Lester so here's another one: he had a retainer to ride for Charles St George, one of the leading owners in the 70s, and Charles used to invite him for a holiday to his house in Nassau, sending him, Lester, a first class return air ticket. One year a friend of mine was travelling out with Lester and they agreed to go to Heathrow together. Lester said that he wanted to get to the airport much earlier than he need have done but, on arrival, instead of going to the check-in counter, he went to British Airways ticket desk, produced his first class ticket but said that it was a mistake, he didn't want to go first class and please could he have an economy ticket and a refund for the difference. The ticket clerk obliged and Lester then went straight to the check-in section, produced his economy ticket saying to the attendant, 'I'm Lester Piggott so any chance of an upgrade to first class?' It was granted.

Funny Sunday's next race was the Newbury Autumn Cup towards the end of October. I really fancied him for this race in which he was 'napped' by Peter O'Sullevan who also commentated on the race for the BBC. Walter Swinburn rode him again and he finished fourth in a big field, beaten by only two lengths, the first four finishing well ahead of the rest. Even though it was a high-class race I was rather disappointed but the reason wasn't long in coming. The next day he had heat in his near foreleg and had strained a tendon. Undoubtedly he would have been feeling this in the latter stages of the race, but in any event the recovery for an injury of this nature is the best part of one year and I am convinced that, like his sire, he would have been at his best as a four-year-old. To make matters worse, I had received a very substantial offer for a half-share in the horse with the promise that he would stay in training with me for the remainder of his racing career before going to stud. Bill White had accepted the offer which, of course, was withdrawn after his injury was made known. He was the best horse that I trained, but never ran again.

Funny Sunday apart, the last third of the season was a bit of a damp squib with a nasty cough running through the yard, so we had very few runners or winners. I had managed to separate Funny Sunday to a small row of boxes in what we called the top yard so now it was all systems go for the yearling sales season and to look forward to 1980. I had a reasonable order book and, as usual, bought a few extra to pass on to owners during the winter. Robert Sangster sent me a very nice filly that his own team had bought so I was reasonably happy going into winter quarters. Sadly I never landed my rich Arab Sheik; the nearest I got to it was indeed an Arab but a commercial one which doesn't really count. His name was Dr Omar Zawawi, a doctor of what I never discovered but he came to me through the offices of my bloodstock agent and good friend, Tim Bulwer-Long, known as The Captain, an Old Wellingtonian like myself but a shade younger so we didn't quite overlap. The Doctor had a most unlikely partner in some of the horses sent to me in the shape of Bobby McAlpine, who normally had at least one of his own with me anyway. All the Doctor's horses he had with me won but the best was a filly/mare named Skin Deep. Unfortunately the Doctor liked her to run at the top meetings like the Royal Meeting at Ascot, but for which she would have won many more races. As it was, she won a decent race at Kempton ridden by Steve Cauthen, was just touched off second in photos at the July/August meeting at Goodwood in consecutive years and ran very creditably in the Wokingham Stakes and Royal Hunt Cup at Ascot. Of his other horses, there was colt called Malpaso who stayed all day but was very slow. I won four races with him, all over two miles and all at Beverley, a very stiff track with a long uphill straight so that all the other runners became even more tired than he did. He was unbeaten at Beverley and they should have named a race after him.

Another most enjoyable winter holiday in my mother's house in Barbados in January started off the year of 1980. We had guests for part of the time but among all the fun and frivolity of the racing scene, with people who were very good friends as well as being competitors at home, I had time to sit back, reflect and take stock. I'd had ten years in Lambourn, wouldn't have missed any of them, enjoying the successes and putting the disappointments behind me as is right and proper. But I had to look to the future: the fact was that, as a business, it never made a worthwhile profit at any stage and I came to realise that my top order on value was only the average sale price realised at the main yearling sales for autumn 1979, and all the others were well below this figure. Now, I'm not saying that the most expensive horses are always the best; after all many top horses are home bred and never pass through the sales ring but you need to have a few up there to be in with a shout of acquiring a top quality horse. Without blowing my own trumpet, I was pretty confident of my own ability with the material that I had. No horse ever left Berkeley House and won a race for any other trainer except those that, on my advice and with the agreement of the owners, we sold to go abroad, usually to a country with lower class racing. Also I never once had a horse that refused to go into the starting stalls; sure we had some difficult ones but I would spend some-times hour after hour with them at the trial stalls at home very patiently, talking to them all the time saying such things as 'I can be here all day, if that's what you want. I'm in no hurry and, if necessary, I'll have my lunch sent up here but there'll be nothing for you.' When, eventually, they got fed up and went through, I'd say 'OK, well done, now that you've done it once, you can do it a few more times just so that you don't forget.' When it was all over they'd get a big treat – usually most of a packet of polo mints that I used to keep in my pocket. On the other side of the coin, I won plenty of races with other peoples' castoffs, Caille for one, Tin Lid another and a horse called Machine, which he certainly wasn't but left his previous trainer scratching his head wondering if it could be the same horse when he heard that it had won a race. The most extraordinary horse I ever trained belonged to my Arab doctor, not bought by me I hasten to say. None of its legs was straight, they all seemed to push in different directions with little effect. I put one of my apprentices on him for the experience, did not go to the race and didn't believe it when the lads in the yard told me that it had won, until I read it in the *Sporting Life* the next day. It was the slowest horse I ever trained.

I loved my job and everything about it; it was, however, a conundrum and I had four children to educate. Of the many

Barbadians that my parents had got to know and were very good friends with was a man called Nick Parravicino. As the name sounds, he was and is of Italian extraction, his father or grandfather having come to Barbados on a visit and never left. Nick was a tremendous racing fan, owner and very prominent member of the Barbados Turf Club which controls racing in Barbados, which takes place on the course known as the Garrison Savannah. Nick was also the leading equivalent of an estate agent on the island and I happened to say to him one day that if he came to hear of a good property that might become available at some time in the future, he might let me know. It was more of a throwaway line and I thought no more of it.

Back in England, at the start of 1980 Margaret Thatcher had been Prime Minister for nine months. She had been leader of the Conservative Party since 1975, having ousted Ted Heath. In early 1980, with high unemployment, the aftermath of 'the winter of discontent', struggle with the unions and a recession, the popularity of the Iron Lady, as she was known, had sunk low, with polls saying six people out of ten were dissatisfied with her. But she was to continue as Prime Minister for ten more years, and became the longest serving Prime Minister of the 20th century. Such is politics.

In racing, Prince Charles became a jockey, having a horse trained by my friend and neighbour Nick Gaselee, on which he had a few rides being placed a couple of times but sadly without entering the winner's enclosure. Of course Gaselee came in for a lot of Lambourn ribbing in particular when, later in the year, it became known that he and his wife Judy had been invited for a weekend to Balmoral. On the day of their departure and by a manoeuvre of which the SAS would have been proud, access was obtained to their luggage for the weekend. On the assumption that such things as unpacking would be taken care of at their destination, certain 'things for the weekend' and copies of *Men Only* and *Penthouse* were prominently placed in Nick's suitcase.

The flat season started as usual at Doncaster towards the end of March and so did the winners, in a steady trickle and mainly, it has to be said, in less than exalted company and without a potential star in the yard. My mind kept returning to my holiday thoughts and also to the fact that even though the training operation was not adding to the family coffers, the opposite was the case as far as the property was concerned, showing a very substantial gain on paper since the purchase date. I decided to take soundings. Antony Brassey, who worked for Lane, Fox and Partners, I knew and had a quiet and discreet word with him. He put me onto his senior partner Mickey Wiggin who was an expert on equestrian properties and a keen racing man and to whom I spoke, emphasising the strict confidentiality of our conversation. In the front of my mind was the hope that I would hear no more, but one week or two later he rang me asking to come to see me. He had a foreign client, he said, who was prepared to pay a substantial sum for a racing yard where he wanted to install his own private trainer. For obvious reasons it was very necessary that no news of this possible plan became known – I had still by no means made up my mind. It would be catastrophic if a rumour got out before I had informed my owners, staff and the racing press but time was not on my side; something was bound to leak out. First of all I had to be sure of the identity and credentials of Mickey Wiggin's client; this knowledge, when I received it, was not totally reassuring: he was a petrochemical engineer from oil-rich Venezuela named Dr (another one) Sahagun. Mickey, very well-off himself, was a very experienced and shrewd operator who confirmed to me that the money was available and in England so it was time for me to get the lawyers on the job. Then a most extraordinary thing happened.

It was May by now and we'd had about ten winners at that stage; I took a telephone call one day: it was Nick Parravicino calling from Barbados. He told me that he was the Barbadian executor for the late very famous theatrical stage and fashion designer, Oliver Messel, who had died approximately eighteen months previously. Oliver had lived in Barbados from 1964 until he died in 1978 in a most beautiful house called Maddox on the west coast of the island, which he had converted from an ordinary farmhouse. He had left the house in his Will in the main to his nephew Lord Snowdon, with a minority interest to his other nephew Thomas Messel. Tony Snowdon, while he was still married to Princess Margaret, used to come and stay quite often with his uncle at Maddox and I had met him a few times at parties, and Thomas, who I had never met, had decided that the house should be sold and Nick asked, bearing in mind our conversation in Barbados a few months previously, whether I would be interested before the house went on the open market?

This was a very serious bolt from the blue, which made up my mind for me in several directions: one, I was very worried as to what to do next if I sold Berkeley House. I loved training racehorses and everything connected with it but I had no wish to go into administrative jobs in racing like working for the Jockey Club as an official, stipendiary Steward, handicapper or the like; therefore, two, I wanted to get completely away into something utterly different and, three, things on the home front were not great and I thought that getting Magsie away from the racing scene would help our marriage. Added to this I had been going to Barbados on and off since the mid-50s, had got to know many friends of my parents and loved the island. And Magsie was very enamoured with the idea of going to live there. Nick was coming to England anyway for Ascot so we arranged to meet in London. He contacted Tony to say that I was interested in a deal and set up a meeting in his house in Launceston Place. At the meeting Tony was rather theatrical so it was more of a general conversation than a business meeting; he didn't want to talk about sordid things like money, he was more concerned that the house be sold to someone who understood how important it was to him to continue the Messel image. He made great play that he was sure that, if he put the house on the open market, the price would be higher but he might not like or approve of the purchaser and so on and so on. He might well have been right on all counts. Evidently I passed the test but the next meeting with, it seemed to me, Tony's rather pompous high and mighty solicitor, who appeared, to begin with, to dislike the whole plan, was in a very different key. On our side I had a partner of our family solicitors plus Nick Parravicino and me. The meeting swung both ways for a good two hours but eventually an agreement in principle was thrashed out.

The preparation of documents for both contracts – the sale of Berkeley House and the purchase of Maddox – took several weeks during which time I continued training the horses and running the business in the normal way, but always with the unpleasant shadow of guilt and deception towards my owners and the staff hanging over me. Winner-wise we were well on the way to having the highest total ever in number but, as previously said, they were in moderately classed races. At last it was over and I contacted all the owners personally to inform them of my decision. Being very sentimental, I hated doing this; they had all become friends and I promised I would make recommendations as to who I would suggest to take over the training of their horses. Next, the staff who were all given plenty of notice; the lads, I knew, would all find it easy to find jobs elsewhere: good lads were always at a premium but the senior staff was more difficult. Norman Mackness and his wife, who also worked full time as a stable girl and was a very good rider, and Pip Payne and his wife all lived in houses belonging to me on the property, as did Archie Hughes and his wife. Pip went to stay temporarily with his parents before moving to Newmarket and setting up training on his own, Norman decided to have a break from racing and went back to London where he came from and for Archie, by now well past retirement age, I bought a house in the local village of Eastbury where he lived until he died. Knowing that as soon as I told the staff the news would be around Lambourn in a flash, I rang Charles Benson on the *Daily Express* to give him the 'scoop' so far as the racing press was concerned. The horses went in dribs and drabs and the yard, devoid of all the hustle and bustle, chit-chat, empty of horses with their heads over the box doors, their constant smell and that of tack in and around the tack room … the whole place seemed ghostly and sad. Going outside into an empty yard and stables on a summer's night was eerie and left me feeling very lonely. However, I also had the knowledge that I had done the best possible job with the horses that I had bought or had entrusted to me, plus I had provided a lot of excitement and fun and enjoyment to my owners. Of course there were heartbreaks, setbacks and hard luck stories but so there are in any walk of life. I held a sale of all tack, stable equipment and machinery, horse clothing, even my battered old Land Rover. The poignancy of all this was slightly relieved by Jeff Bernard's Colonel Mad column in *Private Eye* really camping up the whole thing. (See overleaf.)

Sporting Life

It is with a heavy heart and a deep sense of loss that I take up my pen to record the end of an era. The early retirement and forthcoming exile of the valiant **Captain Antony Johnson** VC DSO Croix de Gucci is as tragic as was Napoleon's retreat from Moscow and the exile of my own dear great-great-grandfather Lord Byron.

At the recent dispersal sale at Berkeley House, Upper Lambourn, as the Sotheby hammer rained down time and time again, hardened racing men such as **Fred Winter** and **Henry Candy** openly wept. As the relics of racing's Golden Age changed hands it was impossible not to think with genuine sadness of the Captain's feats. Even the Russell & Bromley shoes that he wore when he made the Deauville landing were for sale, and they were knocked down to a snivelling wretch of a stable lad who procured the priceless relics for a mere 50p.

This column has lost not only a true friend but a wonderful host and almost bottomless mine of vodka, havana cigars, scintillating conversation and bed and breakfast. (*Who the hell are you going to write about in the future? Ed.*)

It may interest readers to know to whom some of the more interesting Johnson chattles went, and I marked the catalogue, albeit through tear-blurred eyes, making notes as the vultures of racing closed in on the now penniless Captain and his wife. (Incidentally, you will be relieved as I was that the gorgeous **Maggsie** failed to reach her reserve. God knows into whose evil hands she might have fallen.) Lot No 94, three fire extinguishers, went to **Sammy Millbanks.** Lot 114, two dust bins to **Jack Logan.** Lot 116, medicine cupboard, to W.A. **Stephenson** at £100,000 after fierce bidding against **Maurice Zilber.** Lot 149, hen house, to

the **Marquis of Tavistock.** Lot 190, another lot, to **Franca Vittadini.** Lot 180, two summer rubbers, to **Sir William Piglet-Brown.** Lot 340, three night caps, to **Bill Marshall.** Lot 392, corn bin, to **Dick Francis.** Lot 354, pair of blinkers, to the Jockey Club. Lot 367, skull cap, to **Sir Douglas Marks.**

Meanwhile, back in the now almost empty and deserted house, the Captain and a group of close and intimate friends that included myself, **Lord Howard de Walden, Lord Porchester** and **Jim Stanford,** reminisced over the few remaining bottles of Dom Perignon which the servants brought up from the vast cellars. Through the windows I caught sight of **Charlie Dingwall** — who has himself had a Sale of belongings and stable girls — in the company of his adviser **Adrian Clegg.** It had come to this, I thought, that two such evil men could prowl the lawns of Berkeley House. It was unthinkable.

Reading my thoughts, Lord Howard placed an affectionate arm around my shoulder and asked, "Where will you go for Sunday morning cocktails now?" "Your place," I replied.

The champagne finished, the sun setting behind the cedars, the last Lot, a tongue bit, fell to **Peter Walwyn,** buying for **Screamer Lewis** in his absence. Solemnly we shook hands with the Captain and it was then I noticed the label on an enormous Rembrandt that the removal men were taking from the house. Barbados, Not Wanted on Voyage. As I looked into the Captain's eyes I realised, not for the first time, that you can't keep a good man down.

★   ★   ★

15

Island in the Sun

The English-based Dutch Van Geest family started importing
Dutch flower bulbs to England in the 1930s but in 1953
and at the request of the British government began importing
bananas from the Eastern Caribbean islands, taking general
cargo on the outward journey. They had about half a dozen
purpose-built ships operating on a weekly service equipped for
carrying bananas at the right temperature for final ripening so as
to be ready for sale by distributors within twenty-four hours of
arrival. The ships also carried about twenty fare-paying passengers in comfortable, spacious cabins with steward and bar service
and all meals served with the ship's officers. The packing up and
distribution of contents at Berkeley House was complicated and
time consuming – a few things to be sold but the vast majority
to either go into store or to be shipped to Barbados but on 21st
September two huge containers, one Ford Estate car, Magsie and
myself embarked on the *Geest Star* at Barry, South Wales docks
en route for Bridgetown, Barbados. Since we had a large amount
of cargo as well as ourselves, we were allotted the smart owner's
suite on board at no extra cost, all of the other passengers being
on a return trip cruise. Although the *Geest Star* was essentially
a cargo ship it was well equipped with plenty of deck space for
games and exercise machines, the other passengers congenial if
not madly exciting, we made good friends with the captain and
the weather improved every day. We passed by very close to the
Azores but really it was very relaxing after the turmoil of the

previous three months or so. Pods of dolphins kept pace with us from time to time and the amount of bird life was surprising even when a huge distance from any land mass. The voyage took eight days but was prolonged by one day because we had to make a detour to St Lucia for a day owing to a hurricane warning, the storm luckily changing course. The local hurricane warning rhyme goes 'June too soon, July stand by, August a must, September remember, October all over'. We docked at the very pretty small semi-circular harbour in Castries, St Lucia which has hardly changed from that day to this, had a very pleasant day wandering through the town and having lunch at La Toq, then a smart, old-fashioned, Caribbean-style wooden hotel with wide colonial verandas. In the evening we left for Barbados giving me my first glimpse of the twin peaks of the Pitons off the coast of St Lucia.

At around six a.m. on the morning of 1st October 1980 the *Geest Star* docked at the quite new deep-water harbour at Bridgetown, Barbados. Prior to the early 60s all ocean-going cargo and cruise ships had to anchor in Carlisle Bay with passengers and cargo having to be transported to shore on lighters.

Fragments of civilisation have been found in Barbados dating to the second millennium BC but definite traces of a tribe known as Amerindians exist, showing their occupation of the island between 350 and 650 AD. Around 800 AD the Arawaks who originated in South America came to Barbados and other Eastern Caribbean islands, followed in turn by the Caribs in the 12th century who were more intellectually and politically powerful than the Arawaks who faded from the scene, as did the last remaining Amerindians who were captured and transported as slaves by marauding Spanish pirates. Although there were reports of earlier English vessels landing, the first recorded was in 1625 when a ship commanded by John Powell landed at Jamestown (now Holetown) and claimed the island on behalf of King James I of England. Two years later, Powell's brother

Henry landed with eighty settlers and ten labourers, all indentured servants. In those days indentured servants were freed of
their indentures after five years and given £10 and between five
and 10 acres of land. Their successors in title would be very rich
now if they'd hung onto their land. In 1639 there were 44,000
settlers in Barbados compared to only 23,000 in New England.
In the same year James Hawley was appointed Governor of the
island and formed the House of Assembly on the same lines as
the House of Commons at Westminster.

Over the next 100–150 years tracts of land were given by the
Crown to various beneficiaries as rewards for services rendered,
with most of them turning to the production of sugar cane,
first introduced from Brazil in 1640 and with the crop rapidly
increasing by many hundreds of percentage points. In order to
support the industry, slaves were imported from West Africa and
by 1660 Barbados was producing more export trade than all other
British colonies combined. By 1680 over half the arable land was
owned by 175 planters, each owning about sixty slaves, and most
of whom having good connections at Westminster. Slaves frequently took the names of their owners and, to this day, names
like Cadogan, Harewood, and Cumberbatch feature prominently
in the Barbados telephone book. In 1713 Bridgetown was one of
the three largest cities in this part of the Empire, the others being
Boston and Port Royal, Jamaica. The slave trade was abolished
by an Act of Parliament in 1807 but it took several years for
the actual transition to gradually take place, which was finally
accomplished in 1834 and this was followed by a long period of
severe industrial unrest and unemployment.

In 1881 a call was made throughout the Caribbean and elsewhere for labour to work on the largest and most important
engineering project of the 19th century: the construction of the
Panama Canal. Many thousands of Caribbean nationals, including a huge number of Barbadians, were recruited to work on the
project and were shipped to Panama. The original contract for

the Canal was awarded to a French Consortium headed by the engineer Ferdinand de Lesseps, the man who had supervised the construction of the Suez Canal between 1859 and 1869; however, the climatic, terrain and geographical conditions were totally different to those in Egypt. Between 1881 and 1889 work continued under appalling conditions and with huge loss of life caused by, in addition to fatalities from the construction work, venomous snake-, insect- and spider-bites and epidemics of yellow fever and malaria. The long rainy seasons of approximately eight months per year caused the river Chagres to rise by 35 feet into raging torrents. By 1889 the French Consortium went bankrupt and work ceased for fifteen years, during which the US became more involved, enormous political differences between Panama and Colombia were settled and a new US consortium was put together to continue constructing the Canal, which was eventually opened in 1914, 400 years after the Spanish explorer Vasco Núñez de Balboa first explored and established a possible route between the Atlantic and Pacific oceans. It is estimated that between 150,000 and 200,000 Caribbean immigrants were employed in the whole project, many of whom never returned to the Caribbean, and that the total loss of life was 27,000.

In the 17th and 18th centuries many of the plantation owners built large colonial coralstone mansions to accommodate themselves and their families; some of these, known as Great Houses, still exist in one form or another but many are mere shells and ruins. One of the best known is Farley Hill built by Sir Graham Briggs in 1818 but added to substantially over the following fifty years. It was the setting of the mansion in the film *Island in the Sun* in 1957 but was subsequently very badly damaged by fire. I remember visiting Farley Hill in the mid-50s, unoccupied and empty except for one picture hanging lopsided from a wall; it was a framed print of Cicero with Danny Maher up. Cicero, owned by Lord Rosebery, won the Derby in 1905. Now Farley Hill is a ruin set in a National Park and a noted tourist attraction.

Much earlier are two Jacobean houses, Drax Hall, still owned by the Drax family, and St Nicholas Abbey, both built around 1660. St Nicholas Abbey isn't an abbey at all and has no religious connection. The original owner of the house was killed in a duel with his neighbour who promptly married his widow. The house passed into the Cave family, the last of which, Stephen Cave who I knew very well, was a highly respected authority on the sugar industry and lived in the house from 1977 until his death in 2003. It is now the property of Larry Warren, a very well-known Barbadian architect. St Nicholas Abbey and Drax Hall are two out of only three similar Jacobean houses remaining on the combined land mass and islands of the American continents, the third being Bacon's Castle in Virginia.

Sam Lord's Castle is another Great House with a history: built by one Samuel Lord who lived from 1778 to 1844. Sam Lord derived (earned is not the right word) his fortune by hanging lanterns on the palm trees bordering his beach to lure sailors who mistook the lantern lights for the port of Bridgetown. Two hundred yards off shore, however, was a vicious reef on which the ships foundered. Lord had his men armed and ready in rowing boats to plunder the booty from the wrecked ships. A very well-known calypso *The Legend of Sam Lord* was written to record these events. The Castle was restored at great expense and turned into a five-star hotel but was mysteriously destroyed in a fire some years ago and is now derelict. A lovely grand plantation house with fabulous views in the centre of the island is Villa Nova, built in 1834 in place of an older house that was demolished by a hurricane, hence its name. Over the next 100 years the property passed through two families until it was bought in 1965 by the former British Prime Minister Anthony Eden (the Earl of Avon) who referred to it as The Garden of Eden and spent the last four winters of his life there. Following his death it became the home of the prominent Barbadian Hunte family, until they sold it in 2000 to be transformed at vast expense into a twenty-eight-suite super luxury hotel, which sadly was a disaster and it closed in 2005.

The first time I came to Barbados, in about 1955, apart from the wonderful warm sunshine, I noticed the happy-go-lucky, carefree atmosphere that prevailed everywhere. I stayed with my parents who in those days rented a wooden bungalow raised on stilts about four feet from the ground which, along with three others of similar construction, formed part of Paradise Beach Club on a well-named beach of the same name. In those days there were just four hotels along the whole of the west coast of the island: Paradise Beach owned by the local Ward family; Coral Reef Club, owned by an Englishman and his wife, Budge and Cynthia O'Hara; Colony Club owned by the Mitchell family; and the Miramar Hotel, owned by the 'Queen' of Barbados, Victor Marson. You will notice the prefix 'Club'. In theory this meant that you had to be a member which, in turn, meant that the owner of the 'Club' could refuse your application for membership. There are obvious connotations to this which were made much of by sections of the press; the insinuation was that this was by now out of date and the word 'Club' was soon dropped, but personally I never saw nor heard of any victims who were excluded from any hotel or 'Club' of this nature. Going north along the seaside road from Bridgetown, cane was grown down to the roadside on the right and there were a few hamlets, each with its rum shop. The site of the present Sandy Lane Hotel was a rum distillery. In bustling Bridgetown, the Marine Hotel was the old-fashioned, staid hotel where ladies used to meet for tea and gossip, the Yacht Club was the height of formality, most of the shops in Broad Street were made of wood, the Houses of Parliament and St Michael's Cathedral were as they are now and the Bridgetown Club made White's seem like a village pub.

It was also the fairly early days of the steel band and calypsos. Little groups of steel band players or single itinerant guitar-playing calypsonians would wander around in the evenings, always with broad grins and wearing their own scruffy identifiable hats, play and sing for a few cents and wander off again. They would sing topical calypsos such as 'Shame and Scandal in the Family' – mother to son: 'Your Daddy ain't your Daddy but your Daddy don't know.' One of my favourites was 'The Queen's Canary'. It is quite long but I'll precis it as best I can. It revolves around a Clean Up Campaign issued by the island's Governor, who decreed that it was a punishable offence to leave litter and rubbish of any kind lying about so… 'Up comes Mr Powell who wanted to do something in his bowel / So stopped by the side of the road and there put down his load.' Seeing a policeman approaching, he hurriedly whipped off his straw hat and placed it over what he had done, explaining to the policeman that 'the Queen's canary fly away but I have it covered down there.' The policeman, aware that there would be a hefty reward for capturing the escaped Queen's canary, told Powell to scarper and that he would deal with the matter. Curiosity getting the better of him, he bent down to retrieve the canary from beneath Powell's hat, the last line of the calypso being, 'The nasty canary is dead.'

Of course during the intervening years, from 1955 to 1980, there were many changes. Hotels were springing up as were supermarkets, shops and banks. Ronnie Tree, one of the first important settlers post-war, built the magnificent Heron Bay house, a near copy of an Italian palazzo, on the beach a little further north of the Coral Reef Club. Ronald Tree, whose mother Ethel was the daughter of the American Marshall Field, the entrepreneur and founder of the famous department store in Chicago, was a Conservative politician and one of the first to recognise the danger of the increasing popularity of the Nazi Party under Hitler in the 1930s. He became one of Winston Churchill's staunchest allies and was a principal advisor to Churchill throughout the war. His house, Ditchley in Oxfordshire, became a regular meeting place of the War Cabinet and for secret conferences. His wife, Nancy, was the widow of

Tree's cousin Henry Marshall Field; they had two children, one of them being a son, Jeremy, who became a successful trainer at Beckhampton where his long-time assistant, Roger Charlton, took over as trainer on Jeremy's death in 1993. After the war Ronnie and Nancy divorced, Ronnie sold Ditchley and went to live, after a short time in New York, at Heron Bay having married his second wife Marietta Peabody. He was a client of Lazards and discovered that a large plot of land to the south of Heron Bay, on which a rum distillery stood on a beautiful wide beach, was for sale. He contacted Lazards and suggested that a small group of clients should combine to buy the whole property, build a hotel on it, each keeping an area of land on which to build their own house. My father, being a client of Lazards, was offered one such property. But, conservative as always, he declined to participate. A pity! There was a logistical problem in that the main south to north road, called Highway 1, ran straight through the property and about 30 yards from the beach. Ronnie arranged a meeting with the Prime Minister, a splendid man called Errol Barrow who had served as a navigator with RAF Bomber Command during the war. 'We'll move the road' said Barrow. And he did, a substantial half-moon shaped diversion of a good half mile. The original Sandy Lane Hotel was therefore built by Lazards clients and opened in 1961. Ronnie and Marietta Tree's marriage was a strange one, she being twenty years his junior; eventually they separated and she had a long-standing affair with Adlai Stevenson, the American politician and Presidential candidate. In fact they were walking together in Hyde Park when he collapsed and died from a heart attack in 1965. Ronald Tree died in 1976. Heron Bay is now the Barbados home of Anthony and Carole Bamford who have looked after and maintained it immaculately.

In 1962, while Zandra and I were married, we and two other couples rented a beautiful house on Glitter Bay beach. Glitter

Bay house was an old plantation house standing some way back from the beach, which once belonged to Edward Cunard; he built this delightful coralstone folly with a wide balcony on the first floor overlooking the garden and ocean no more than ten yards away. Fully staffed with a butler, cook and two maids we paid £150 per week, £50 per couple per week. The others were Tim Summers from the steelmaking family with his lovely girlfriend Sally Priest, who we called the Priestess, and Tim's younger brother Mark and his wife. Mark was a keen polo player so we met many of the Bajan players and through them four young very talented musicians all from respected Bajan families who had formed themselves into a band calling themselves The Merrymen, playing and singing calypsos and folk songs adapted to their own style. The leader, main arranger and composer was Emile Straker and the others were Robin Hunte, Chris Gibbs and Stephen Fields. At that stage all had 'proper' jobs but got together in the evenings to entertain their friends and play at local hops. During our holiday we had so much fun with a great amount of hospitality so, before we left, we had a party for all our new friends at our house, inviting The Merrymen to play. It was an outstanding success; The Merrymen played virtually nonstop from nine o'clock in the evening until about three o'clock the next morning. We paid them the equivalent of £25. The point of this story is that The Merrymen, apart from becoming good friends, went on to great international success, becoming the best band in the Caribbean as well as playing in huge concert auditoria all over Canada, the USA, England and Australia. In England they played at the Albert Hall and performed summer seasons and on tour.

During the Lambourn years, I came out to Barbados, not every year but more or less every other, staying with my parents in their house, Las Palmas on the beach close to Holetown, which they had bought after the hut on stilts at Paradise Beach. After my father died, my mother sometimes kindly let me use the house in January. It was during that period that many people from the racing world had started to make Barbados their regular winter holiday, so much it was referred to as Newmarket-on-Sea. Robert Sangster bought the lovely holiday house of Jane's Harbour just north of Sandy Lane; it was called Jane's Harbour by its owner Jane Warner, her having been given the land on which the house was built by her husband, one of the Warner Brothers, makers of magnificent movies. At about the same time, his big racing partner and Vincent O'Brien's son-in-law John Magnier started to come each year, renting a house called Laughing Waters owned by someone I knew quite well, Julian Byng. The house was soon renamed Passing Waters by us; John eventually managed to buy it from Julian after a lot of negotiation between two master tacticians. During this period, with Barbados acquiring the reputation of an upmarket destination, the number and quality of hotels increased, matched by good restaurants appearing on the scene. One such was the Bagatelle, another old plantation Great House up on the first ridge above the west coast; it was taken over and transformed into an attractive restaurant and bar with a special ambience by a larger than life character called Nick Hudson, who had run a popular fashionable restaurant in London called Nick's Diner. Nick, suave with long flowing golden hair, used to wander about in a kaftan but, smooth as silk, ran a very good show with excellent food and wine in a romantic, classy setting. I was always slightly suspicious that he might have been the villainous Nigel Dempster's Barbados correspondent, from whose poisonous pen I and countless others had suffered from time to time.

So, back to 1st October 1980 and arrival in Barbados, not as a holidaymaker but to live. Nick Parravicino came on board ship to welcome us and to help with landing formalities which were long and tedious even though everything had been planned, agreed and rubber stamped. The passport control man had no idea what to do. 'How long you stay in Barbados?' he asked. 'Indefinitely,' I replied. This foxed him. There was no box with this word on it for him to tick. Eventually all was sorted and the unloading of the ship's cargo commenced, starting with my car, a Ford Granada Estate. The two containers would clearly take a long time and then, of course, there was customs clearance and not for just a couple of suitcases and a bag of duty free. Nick arranged for the containers to be brought on a lorry 'presently'. Presently turned out to be ten days. The car was immediately impounded for customs valuation; I had foreseen this and obtained a certified valuation from the main Ford dealer in Newbury. The Newbury firm's name did not appear on the Barbados customs list so that was a non-starter and a taxi was summoned for us and the small amount of luggage we had needed on the ship. Everything in the car was excluded. We proceeded by taxi with me giving the driver directions and Nick following behind in his car. We entered the gates of Maddox, drove up the short gravelled drive and dismounted to be welcomed by the staff all dressed in their smart uniforms consisting of the butler, cook, laundry maid, two housemaids and the gardener. We went in through the colonnaded entrance, past a small cultivated courtyard with a fountain and into the main part of the house. For the second time in my life I entered my new home without having ever set foot in it beforehand. It was all rather overwhelming. We went round the house with the staff, in a line of seniority, following. It was truly wonderful and magnificent, just as Nick had said it would be. We said goodbye and thanks to Nick, who went back to his office saying that we would keep in close touch regarding developments. There was time for a swim by going down the few steps at the end of the garden and into the sea on what was virtually our own private beach, about 70 yards long and protected by high coral rocks at either end which dissuaded any beach walkers from climbing over them. Lunch was elegantly served in the dining room, which consisted of three sides with the fourth open to the garden and sea. The drawing room was similarly constructed, giving onto a large terrace with two steps further down onto the lawn. There was the ground-floor wing with a double bedroom and bathroom; upstairs via an outside balustraded staircase, a wide-roofed balcony overlooked the garden and led to three bedrooms with two bathrooms. Downstairs again, the drawing room opened into a large inner L-shaped hall which was the core of the original house and which also could be entered from the entrance colonnade. Beyond the hall, on the eastern section of the house, was a large, airy morning room, two sides of which were glass louvered windows with jalousie shutters. Two large openings led into the hall. There were no doors on the ground floor; they were just not necessary. Large floor-to-ceiling folding shutters sealed off the hall and morning room last thing at night, but otherwise it was an open space determined only by thick coralstone walls defining the separate rooms. In the garden, about 40 yards from the main house there was a delightful coralstone cottage consisting of a large double bedroom, bathroom, small dressing room and kitchenette. The main kitchen and service areas were spacious with two staff resting rooms and a laundry room but with an absence of any modern appliances. The cooker was heated by big Calor-gas bottles replaced when necessary. In all the years that I lived at Maddox I never had a washing-up machine but at some stage I did install a clothes washer. Outside, large mahogany trees lined the drive and entrance area with a complex of garage, garden sheds and a potting and seeding area next to the entrance gates. The lawn areas were dotted with a variety of trees, mango, shaddock (large grapefruit-type fruit), breadfruit, avocado, lime, a lovely ylang ylang which gave out a marvellous sweet-smelling fragrance in the early evening, large bougainvillea bushes, a huge manchineel, surprisingly non-poisonous, which provided shade over a large terrace overlooking the sea at the bottom end of the garden, frangipani, heliconia, about a dozen coconut palms and a very rare teak, together with hibiscus and plumbago-lined paths leading to another set of steps down to the sea at the northern end of the garden. The borders round the house and the inner courtyard were planted with ixora, plumbago and hibiscus and bird of paradise plants. The decorative balustrades round the outside balconies to the north and south on the upstairs floor were smothered with allamanda and other tropical foliage. It was all very theatrical and beautiful. The whole area was only about 1½ acres. Nick Parravicino had very kindly put enough provisions, both solid and liquid, in the house to last us a few days. That first evening Magsie and I sat in the drawing room having a drink; she was sitting opposite me and I said to her: 'Very slowly and carefully look behind you; there's quite a large monkey sitting on a side table taking careful note of what you are doing.' She did and we both engaged eye contact with the monkey who was quite unperturbed until he got bored and hopped off into the garden. He was one of a family living in our trees but they were quite tame and would come close enough to take bananas out of my hand.

After a great deal of officialdom I was allowed to collect the car five days later, having parted with about four times the value placed on it by the Newbury dealer, but as the customs official succinctly put it: 'No pay, no car.' I would have done much better to sell it in England and buy a new one in Barbados. The two containers of furniture and household goods were a different matter: the gates into Maddox were non-ostentatious and wide enough for normal commercial traffic but the huge lorry on which the containers rested provoked a crowd-raising problem, with traffic backing up both ways like the M20 when French dockers are on strike. Verbal assistance as well as threats of assassination came from all quarters before ultimate success was achieved. The two uniformed customs officers were not amused and there began a minute inspection of every last piece of furniture or article of clothing. Anything which looked vaguely new – nothing was – was scrutinised even more closely and with great suspicion whereas the better and more valuable furniture was allowed to pass without comment. Then it started to rain which was too much for the customs men who decided that their working day was over, locked the containers leaving some items in the open and cleared off for the day. The next day they returned and I decided on a different tack by greeting them with a tray on which were two glasses and a bottle of rum. It worked like a miracle and they tottered off quite happily having accomplished their task perfunctorily and without a demand for any duty to be paid.

We had only been in residence for three weeks before our first guests arrived, none other than Tony Snowdon who brought with him his utterly charming daughter, Sarah Armstrong-Jones as she was then, aged seventeen. There were a few loose ends and details to tie up. Tony had been really helpful over one important matter on which we were both advised by Nick Parravicino: non-residents of Barbados had to pay a non-residents tax if they wished to purchase property on the island. Nick suggested and Tony kindly agreed that the sales contract for Maddox should be drafted in two sections, one being for the purchase of the house and land and the other for the contents of the house. For convenience purposes these sections were split half and half. It was agreed that I should buy and pay for the contents, which were not subject to tax, before leaving England and wait until my residency was established before paying for the house and land thereby avoiding the non-residents property tax. This made a pretty sizeable difference for which I was very grateful. Tony and Sarah arrived with considerable pomp and importance. Although no longer a member of the Royal Family, he was nevertheless well-known as Oliver Messel's nephew and due to his frequent visits with Princess Margaret. I was instructed to drive my car onto the tarmac at the airport and right up to the plane; any inspection of their passports was made on the plane and such things as customs inspection were waived. Luggage was unloaded into the car and we drove straight home. All the staff, whom he knew well, were delighted to see him. It was a slightly sensitive situation; he knew Maddox better than I did and couldn't help harking back to when his uncle, to whom he was devoted, lived there but his visit was certainly a success with Sarah being a great asset, standing no nonsense or pomposity from her father who was, from time to time, inclined to play the Royal Card particularly when he wanted to visit other houses designed by Messel, insisting on just driving up to them unannounced whether their owners were there or not. There were a few items of furniture that were specifically excluded from the sale so some time was spent in making arrangements for them to be shipped back to England. Actually the 'few' items turned into rather more than a few but it was not worth making a fuss about it. They stayed for about a week and no sooner had they left, again driven right up to the steps of the plane, than Oliver Messel's other nephew, Thomas, arrived to stay for another week. I had not previously met Thomas but what a delightful man he turned out to be and still is for that matter. No pomposity there but rather a wonderful sense of humour, no airs or graces and he dealt with all matters in a far more methodical and business-like manner than his cousin. He is an outstanding and successful designer of high-class modern furniture. A few years ago, in conjunction with Rizzoli International Publications, Thomas produced and edited a marvellous book on his uncle's work and life entitled *Oliver Messel: In the Theatre of Design* of which he very kindly gave me a copy. Naturally Maddox features prominently in the book.

It wasn't too long before a few chinks in the idyllic armour of Maddox started to appear. Although the house had been let for short periods during the two years since Oliver Messel died – once to Paul McCartney – it had been otherwise unoccupied and no attention paid to any maintenance. Oliver Messel was a fantastic designer with an incredible sense of what was perfect from a theatrical point of view, but he was not an architect. Drains, for instance, should really run downhill as far as possible and without obstructions en route; plants and roots grow quickly in the tropics. The electric cables and wires had been installed and concealed with the minimum amount of fuss and with none of the regulations or inspections required, say, in England. Now that the house was occupied on a full-time basis things began to go wrong. Nothing that could not be put right but, through neglect, very expensive. I found a wonderful plumber, tall, thin and dentally challenged; I christened him Inspector Clouseau because trying to fathom out drainage routes at Maddox was worthy of a Pink Panther film. A very serious problem was caused by termites. I thought termite damage was confined to wood and trees; not a bit of it. They are more than happy eating through stone work and thereby destroying buildings. No wonder Rentokil had a flourishing business in Barbados; it took them a good five weeks of drilling with resulting noise and clouds of dust to put matters right. The garden too, however beautiful, had, owing to the lack of supervision, been allowed to run away and was in need of a pretty severe haircut; this was too much for the gardener who expressed the view that Mr Messel would not have approved. He may or may not have been correct but I suspect that it was more to do with some intense physical effort to which he was not accustomed; his mood was not helped because I joined him in his labours showing more stamina than he was prepared to give. Anyway he had to be replaced, which he was by one Clarence. Clarence and I hit it off quite well; he called me Chief. He, too, had his limitations and had a long-time love affair with the rum bottle which from time to time got the better of him but his heart was in the right place. Whenever he considered a task too much for him he suggested obtaining help from 'some person', who turned out to be a rum-consuming friend of his called Luis who was utterly plumb useless but occasionally I had to put up with Luis to keep Clarence happy.

By the time all this first instalment of the restoration of

Maddox was completed, Christmas and the arrival of the first lot of family and guests was upon us. My mother came with my two young sons, Simon and Sam, for Christmas followed by a succession of others including my dear old friends Michael and Joanna Kelton who became annual regulars. Michael used to stuff his golf club bag full of pheasants thinking, quite rightly, that they might be in short supply in Barbados. We had the first proper party at Maddox on New Year's Eve when the racing team from England had started to arrive, headed by the Newmarket trainer Jeremy Hindley and his wife Sally, who owned a perfect holiday beach house on Gibbs Beach, a mile or so north of Maddox. Staying with them were Michael (Lunchtime) and Margie O'Sullivan. Robert Sangster and The Sheila were in residence at Jane's Harbour with chief guest and court jester Charles and Chubby Benson, so for the next three or four weeks there was a steady round of beachside lunch and dinner parties. Of the non-racing winter residents, Bill and Philippa Tyrwhitt-Drake had a super house a little inland on the then only polo ground on the island at Holders. On the other side of the ground Johnny and Wendy Kidd owned an old plantation house bought and converted several years previously by Johnny's mother Janet, the daughter of Lord Beaverbrook, the Canadian owner of the *Daily Express* and a great wartime ally and friend of Winston Churchill. Johnny, at that time, was a prominent member of the English show jumping team.

A most unlikely person to become a very dear friend – his own words – was Simon Foster, a designer and maker of ladies' dresses, undoubtedly homosexual but not flauntingly so. Simon had been a good friend of Oliver Messel and as I was now living, not only in Barbados but in Messel's old home, there was a natural interest on Simon's part to see who was living there now. I began to notice him more and more at drinks and dinner parties and to listen to his delightful mimicry and very funny stories showing a wild sense of humour. The ladies, young and old, loved him and flocked to his ramshackle chattel house studio to be fitted into highly coloured floating-like summer dresses. He was altogether an enormous and very much loved contributor to the community. Many stories he would tell with himself being the fall guy; for instance once, on a visit to see Oliver at Maddox, he found him gently sleeping on a chaise longue on the terrace. On hearing steps approaching, he opened one eye; saw Simon standing there and said 'Oh! I'm in love again.'

Simon was a fixture at parties, as a person not just as a spare man. He was an irreplaceable piece of Barbados and a huge loss to the island and to so many friends from home, near and far away, when he died suddenly of a heart attack when walking home from his studio in 2013.

When I started going to Barbados, water skiing on the warm Caribbean sea was the number one thing to do. So, arriving to live there, I bought a boat for which I put down a mooring about 100 yards off Maddox. Quite powerful with an inboard engine, it was ideal for skiing or going for trips up and down the island. I put out a flyer to most of the hotels along the west coast and to the house agents for them to place before their guests advertising my availability as boatman and water ski instructor. Soon I began to receive 'bookings', so I used to drive the boat to appointments. For the most part it was not madly exciting but there were one or two goodies with fun, interesting, and, let's face it, attractive people. One morning I received a call from Pamela Harriman who, with her husband Averell – very considerably older than her – had rented a house on Sandy Lane beach. She asked if I could give her a skiing lesson and was waiting on her beach alone when I arrived. Surprisingly she was no expert but after a couple of attempts she got up and wobbled rather insecurely round the bay. That, she said, was enough but asked if I was in a hurry, to which I replied that 'hurry' was not a word commonly used in Barbados. 'Good', she said, 'let's go for a little trip up the coast.'

Here I was with Pamela Digby, an aristocratic West Country girl, daughter of Lord Digby, whose first husband was Randolph Churchill, son of Winston, and having divorced him had affairs with such as Ed Murrow, the famous broadcaster and journalist, Jock Whitney, entrepreneur, businessman, American Ambassador to the UK, prominent racehorse owner and among the ten richest men in the world in the 1970s, Aly Khan, Gianni Agnelli by whom she was alleged to have had an aborted pregnancy, Edie de Rothschild of the famous banking family among others. Taki, in his weekly *High Life* column in the *Spectator,* described her as knowing more about rich men's ceilings than any other living lady. Actually her first affair was with Averell Harriman, a man twenty-nine years older than her and whom she was, much later, to marry. In 1959 she married, as his fifth wife, the Broadway producer Leland Hayward whose most successful production was *The Sound of Music,* having had her proposal/ultimatum to Edie de Rothschild rejected. They remained married until his death in 1971. Within six months of his death Pamela had resumed her relationship with and married Averell Harriman, then aged seventy-nine, so when I met her in 1981, her husband was eighty-nine and she in her early 60s.

It was clear that she was bored and wanted a bit of free time. She was utterly charming, eager to ride the waves and talk, not so much about herself but about life in general, although she did say that she had a very bad marriage to Randolph but greatly admired his father, which feeling was reciprocated. She asked if I could come again the next day and for about the next week I brought the boat to meet her at 11 o'clock and we went up and down the coast dropping in at beachside bars for a drink or light lunch before taking her back in mid-afternoon.

During one conversation she talked about a book by Truman Capote called *Answered Prayers*, which contained references to herself. The book remained unfinished at the time of Capote's death in 1984, only a year or so after my days with Pamela. The book is a salacious namedropping account involving the glamorous high-living stars and socialites of New York society, their affairs, secret business deals of enormous proportions of the 1950s (including how Aristotle Onassis managed, as a non-US citizen, to buy ten US surplus T2 Tankers for $1.5m each, forbidden to foreigners).* Some of the characters in the book are real and others are thinly disguised by pseudonyms. A case in point is Kathleen (Kick) Kennedy, Jack (President) and Bobby Kennedy's sister and daughter of Joe Kennedy, the ambitious, social climbing and ruthless US Ambassador in London.

Aged eighteen, Kick came out as a debutante in the 1938 London Season in the same year as Pamela, of whom she was a very close friend. In the book a principal character is the fictitious Lady Ina Coolbirth. A description takes place where 'Ina Coolbirth' is staying in a house party hosted by the Kennedys; in the middle of the night Joe Kennedy came into her bedroom. The next morning he showed no emotion nor made any reference to what had taken place, much to 'Ina's' disappointment and anger, having expected at least some kind of memento of the event.

During a later meeting with his friend Joe Fox, the editor at Random House who had paid Capote a large advance to publish the book, Fox suggested that Capote had based 'Ina Coolbirth' on Pamela Churchill. Capote replied: 'Not based on Pamela Churchill; she IS Pamela Churchill.'

There is no doubt that Pamela came out of all her affairs considerably better off than when she entered them.

One morning she greeted me saying 'Look, I've been asked to lunch with Claudette Colbert but have arranged for you to come too if you'd like to.' Claudette Colbert was a very well-known French Hollywood movie star of the 30s and 40s and owned a

---

* Onassis was later fined $7m in exchange for having all criminal charges against him dropped.

house on a beach close to Speightstown where she spent several months in the winter. Of course I said yes, parking the boat just off Claudette's beach. It was fascinating listening to the two of them reminiscing about Hollywood and the times they had together. They had been great friends all the time that Pamela had been married to Leland Hayward. I did see Claudette a few times subsequently and when she died in 1996, aged ninety-three, a sale was held in house and I bought two Caribbean oil paintings which I still have. Averell Harriman lived for another five years, dying in 1986 at the age of ninety-five; I never saw Pamela again; after Averell's death she turned all her energies to the Democratic Party, having been a United States citizen since 1971. President Clinton appointed her US Ambassador to France in 1993 and it was in Paris that she died from a brain haemorrhage in 1997 at the age of only seventy-six. But what a life she had led.

It was at this time that I heard from Jeffrey Bernard again; he had been commissioned to write an article on Barbados with all expenses paid and so was ensconced at the Coral Reef Club. It was some time after Keith Waterhouse's play *Jeffrey Bernard is Unwell* had been a box office success in the West End, with Peter O'Toole playing Jeff. We had some friends staying so I told them I had a friend coming round for a drink. Jeff arrived, had several drinks, held my other guests in awe with lurid tales and stories and tottered off again. 'Well,' the others protested, 'You might have told us that your friend was Peter O'Toole.' Not long after we had arrived at Maddox to live, I heard from Jeff by way of a personal letter in the form of his Low Life column in the *Spectator* as reproduced below:

Back in town

Jeffrey Bernard

27 November
Kentish Town, London NW5

Antony Johnson,
St James, Barbados

Dear Antony and Maggsie,
Thanks very much for your letter. Glad to hear things are all right with you. The house sounds marvellous and your almost private beach has me green with envy. I still think of those two weeks with you last February as being the best holiday I have ever had. Meanwhile, like you, I've left Lambourn for good and I had the amazing luck to find a flat from which I write to you. We're not exactly lolling about in the sun sipping rum punches here in Kentish Town, but the population is much like yours, give or take a thousand or so Irishmen. The actual move from Lambourn would have amused you if you had seen it. I was very kindly assisted by a motley bunch – the 'wild bunch' in fact – comprising a farmer from Baydon, Phil the Wantage dustman and 'Mad' Jock, and in London we were joined by Mick, an ex-Royal Navy stoker who once went the distance with Randolph Turpin.

Before loading up at the Lambourn end I took the wild bunch out for a farewell pub crawl. ¿I gather from your letter that you have already heard about my being thrown out of The Swan. We walked in and the new guvnor – he takes himself very seriously and is dying to get the custom of the likes of Barry Hills and the Walwyns – said: 'You're barred. I don't like people who walk into my kitchen, cut themselves a slice of cold roast beef without asking and then tell me I'm a four-letter name.' Of course, I thought it was very funny. Later on that evening, we went to our friendly dustman's house. It was quite extraordinary, like something out of Hogarth. In the tiny kitchen sat his wife and no less than six children all stripped to the waist. They also had a three-legged greyhound, would you believe. He swore it could go like the clappers which must be a strange sight and I gather it assists him with his poaching activities.

Anyway, it took three days to load up the enormous trailer the farmer lent me because we kept having 'tea' breaks to say goodbye to various people. I gave Flo from the Red Lion my Waterford crystal fru bowl and that was a moving farewell (sh frequently, over the years, nursed m through several self-inflicted illnesses Then we had a session in The George, no easily the best boozer in the area. I sha miss those mindless morning sessions tall ing horses and racing to the lads whil listening to Ruby moaning behind the bar a she adds up my slate. I suppose what I like most about the place was leading a doubl life. Sunday lunch with your posh traine and the next minute watching one of Barr Hills's lads falling off his bar stool.

Of course, it could happen here Although I am having lunch at the Savo today I haven't neglected my own manor. I fact I've been doing some scouting aroun Kentish Town and there are some strang pubs here, I can tell you (I think 'down t earth' is the phrase). Bang in the middle o it all I was surprised to find a French bistr and some very civilised shops. Also I'm wel in with the only other bloke in my house Since I tipped him a winner and he saw a photograph of me with Lester Piggott h damn near tugged his forelock right off. (H is a nightwatchman and quite brilliant a extracting £1 out of you for a drink.)

Apart from that there's not much news Fred Winter's having a fractionally bette season than I'm having and, as you may imagine, all our old mates are getting legles at the Newmarket Sales. What I still haven't got used to is the wonderful abundance of women in London. They're all over the place and an amazing number of them seem to be quite agreeable in spite of the feminist movement. I sometimes think that they really do like men on the quiet. Which reminds me. There's a lady here who says she would pay my fare to Barbados next January or February to come out and see you for two weeks if she could come with me. The only thing is I don't know how you'd get on with each other. She's a member of the London branch of the wild bunch.

That's about it for now. I'm off to Chelsea to write something for *Pacemaker*. You'd think that a magazine owned by Robert Sangster might pay moderately well, but you'd be wrong. I could scratch a hole in my head trying to think up jokes about an activity as boring as National Hunt racing, but there we are. So keep the rum punches going, don't get sunstroke and write soon.

Love, Jeff.

Racing has been taking place on the Garrison Savannah, Bridgetown since 1845. This area of open ground was the Headquarters of the Imperial Forces with surrounding military barracks and admin buildings constructed around 1780. The right-handed grass track is six furlongs round, making Chester seem like a wide open galloping course. Bajans from all sections of the community love horses and racing. Many of them are also extremely knowledgeable about thoroughbred breeding lines in Europe and America; in Barbados there are several thoroughbred stud farms with either home-bred stallions or those imported from England or the USA. One of the top trainers in England, Michael Stoute, is a Barbadian who I first met as a young man who had come as pupil assistant to Pat Rohan at Malton. His father Ronald was Chief of Police in Barbados. There is a totally unfounded rumour that when Michael was knighted in 1998, as recommended from Barbados, that the wrong first Christian name was put on the form – Michael instead of Ronald, his father, for services to the Barbados Police Force – Michael's second name being Ronald. Michael's commendation is for 'services to tourism in Barbados'. Not so sure about that but he hasn't done badly as 'services to British Horseracing Industry' having been Champion Trainer ten times to date. When I used to go to Barbados for holidays I always had at least one day at the races and was astonished at the depth of knowledge of the locals. There was a chap who always made a beeline for me to park my car at the racecourse who professed to know more about my horses in England than I did so one day, early in the morning, I went down to a very scruffy area of Bridgetown to a street consisting almost entirely of betting shops all tuned into English racing with board prices, commentaries, analyses, the lot; there, in one of them, was my car parking man. In my last season in England I had a two-year-old called May Go Twice in which I had a small share. He was sharp little thing by The Go Between who had won a small race and been placed. Nick

Parravicino, who always had quite a few horses trained by his son Roger at the Garrison, said he was looking for another horse so I bought out the other partners in the horse and shipped him out to Barbados, with Nick and I having a half share each. The only record he held in Barbados was not for winning but for finishing second – sixteen times I remember, only winning twice but we had a lot of fun. David Seale, who owned one of the main supermarket and importing agencies in Barbados, R. L. Seale & Co, had probably the largest and most efficient bloodstock breeding operations on the island. All the training was done at and around the racecourse, with operations starting at 5 a.m. each day; the horses were very well looked after with 'lads' and stable staff being kind to their charges and very conscientious; if I had a criticism it would be that the horses were over-galloped. During the racing seasons horses quite likely ran nearly every week and once a horse is racing fit, the main object is to keep them on the boil and not over-gallop them. The Garrison is only a few minutes' walk away from the sea; horses love swimming and the more astute trainers took full advantage of taking their horses – and lads – down for a lovely morning dip in the ocean. My old friend Scobie Breasley, the Australian former Champion Jockey in England turned trainer, had retired from England and came to settle in Barbados where he set up training a few horses as much for fun and for something to do as anything else. He was a lovely man with a fund of knowledge and wicked sense of humour; he lived quite close to Maddox and I used to see a lot of him and his wife May. Another, quite different, English trainer who came to live and train in Barbados was Bill Marshall. Bill, born at the end of the First World War, left home on a Sussex farm in his teens for Australia, rode as a jockey for a short time, trained a few horses before moving to South Africa where he was similarly occupied until the outbreak of the Second World War when he returned to England and joined the RAF, learning to fly Spitfires. Returning from an operation over France, he was late for an assignation with a girlfriend so diverted himself to Marlow, flying his Spitfire under Marlow Bridge to remind his girlfriend, who was waiting for him at the Compleat Angler, that he was on his way. Avoiding a Court Martial 'as it was wartime' he fought in the Battle of Britain and also in North Africa. He was shot down twice and awarded the DFC. At the end of the war he started training again with much success at, among other places, Whitsbury before moving to Newmarket. Soon after I got to know him, I had a runner at Warwick in the same race as one of Bill's. I climbed up the stands with my owner and found myself standing next to Bill, hearing him say in a loud voice to his owner, 'You watch yours. I'm going to watch the one I've had a few quid on.' At about that time, 1972, he, his wife Pam, the jockey Joe Mercer and one of his owners had a crash in a light plane taking off from Newbury racecourse on their way to France. The pilot was killed, and all the others seriously injured, except Joe who was thrown clear. It was on a Sunday, just before the Royal Meeting at Ascot at which Joe Mercer was due to ride Brigadier Gerard in the Prince of Wales' Stakes on the Tuesday, among other top-class rides at the meeting. Although feeling very shaken and traumatised, Joe took the ride with the horse giving a scintillating performance, winning by six lengths, but Joe felt very unwell afterwards and did not ride again at the meeting or for sometime afterwards.

At the end of the 70s Bill Marshall got fed up with what he considered petty restrictions in England – the compulsory wearing of seat belts in cars being one of them – so upshipped to Barbados where he became Champion Trainer eleven times and won all the top races a record number of times, continuing to do so until his death aged eighty-seven in 2005. A truly remarkable man whom I was lucky enough to know.

In 1981, Nick Parravicino proposed me for membership of the Barbados Turf Club, an honour I was delighted to accept. At the races, going to church, accepting an invitation to Government

House or to a meeting with a Cabinet Minister were the only occasions that I found it necessary to wear a tie in Barbados. Nick also asked me if I would act as judge at the annual Thoroughbred Show, the equivalent of the Royal Show in England. This was a monumental and difficult task at which I don't think I excelled. There were classes of foals, yearlings, two-year-olds, brood mares and stallions with, apart from the stallions, at least twenty to twenty-five in each class. I had to select the first six in order in each class. As it was the only Show of its kind, there was no 'form book' to help and a lot of competition between the owners. I am sure I upset a lot of people.

Way back in the 1950s an Englishman named Jack Teller came by sail to Barbados, fell in love with the island, its people, its happy-go-lucky atmosphere and never left. He was artistic, imaginative, entrepreneurial and had a flair for entertaining, cooking and music. He bought an old medium-sized planta-tion house just back from Gibbes Beach, a mile or so south of Speightstown, and another smaller house across the road directly on the beach. He turned the main house into an elegant small hotel with fifteen duplex suites in four well-designed blocks, each on two floors, clustered round a lovely swimming pool with bar and restaurant on one side. The beach house became a lunchtime beach bar and restaurant either in an open but roofed area or on the lawn backing onto the beach. Jack knew his stuff and both restaurants soon became THE places to go on the west coast both for gourmet, well served food and for entertainment. Jack called his establishment Greensleeves, which he and his wife ran most successfully for a good twenty years before handing over to his son Nick, whose main and pretty well only claim to fame was to marry, briefly, the 60s pop star singer Susan Maugham whose No. 1 hit was the song 'Bobby's Girl'. Sunday lunch barbecues at the beach bar with steel band accompaniment were immensely popular and it became a regular feature for many of us in the racing world. Jack knew his clientele also so, even though it was normally essential to book, Jack always kept a large beachside table for about fourteen of us during the months of January and February. Vividly do I remember one such lunch attended by Barry and Penny Hills, Bobby and Angela McAlpine, Robert Sangster and The Sheila, Charles and Chubby Benson, Lunchtime and Margie O'Sullivan, Billy McDonald, the American jockey Steve Cauthen and a few others. At the same time Frank Sinatra was staying practically next door with Claudette Colbert. We were also mobbing up Billy about his self-confessed knowledge of Hollywood stars, so after a couple or so rum punches Billy was persuaded to go down the road to 'fetch' Sinatra, which he failed to do but brought back as substitute Sinatra's bodyguard who was bored to tears with nothing to do. His name was Jilly Rizzo and he appeared wearing clean blue T-shirt, blue shorts, shoes and socks, blue-rinsed hair and carrying a small blue leather handbag. Straight out of Damon Runyan in looks and speech, he could have stepped off the stage of *Guys and Dolls*.

'Dat Frankie, he does nothing all day but talk to that that old broad.'

'What have you got in your handbag?' I asked him.

'Dat's where I keep the heater' was his reply, adding, 'it's repeater heater, six shots – four for the tyres and two for the guy.'

'Let's have a look?'

Unzipping the handbag, out came a beautiful tiny revolver with a pearl-studded handle.

'Do you have to practise?'

'Oh yeah. I shoot at the birds or the leaves on the trees – dat is if there ain't no niggers around.' Jilly was alleged to have successfully defended his boss with his 'heater' on a number of occasions. He was killed by a drunken driver in his home town of Palm Desert, California in May 1992.

During the winter months many 'marvellous parties', to quote Noël Coward, were held and none better than those given by Anthony and Carole Bamford at their house Heron Bay. At one such party, which as always had a fistful of international stars and characters, I saw Joan Collins who at that time was being escorted by 'Bungalow' Bill Wiggins, sitting not on her own but surrounded by a clutch of sycophantic men less than half her age. Plucking up courage I asked her to dance. Pointing at the dance floor she said that no one else was dancing. 'Leave that to me for one minute,' I replied. I had a house party myself staying at Maddox, so 'You, you and you, on the dance floor now and quick.' Getting the message they responded. 'Now, Miss Collins?' We had a lovely dance and everything, as far as I could tell and see, was real. On a different note Robert Sangster rang me one day saying that Edward Heath was coming for a drink and could I help swell the numbers. He came, one hour late, wearing very scruffy shorts and a T-shirt, and disappeared having made no effort whatsoever with his host or other guests.

In the 1980s the West Indies dominated world cricket; England, along with all other cricketing nations, suffered inglorious defeats. The West Indies, first under the captaincy of Clive Lloyd, demonstrating feline activity in the field and controlled aggression with the bat, then the monster himself, Viv Richards, boasted the marvellous opening pair of Gordon Greenidge and Desmond Haynes, followed by the likes of Richie Richardson and Larry Gomes, the wicket keeper/batsman Jeff Dujon and then the fearsome fast bowlers: Michael Holding, Joel Garner, Malcolm Marshall, Courtney Walsh. I was at the Kensington Oval to witness the incredible opening over Holding bowled to Geoffrey Boycott in March 1981. I swear he knew nothing but instinct for the first five balls but even instinct failed to save him on the 6th, which saw his stumps go cartwheeling out of the ground. Test cricket in the islands brings visitors who come not just to watch cricket. Some of the players wanted to have fun as well, Alan Lamb, Ian Botham and 'Freddie' Flintoff being some of them, but it also brought some of the older brigade who came under various descriptions. Among those was the delightful

Welshman Tony Lewis, accompanied by his wife Joan. Not many Welshmen play Test cricket for England and none, apart from Tony, rose to be captain, which he did making his Test debut as captain in the five-month long tour to India, Pakistan and Sri Lanka in 1972/3. Altogether he captained England in nine Test Matches, scoring a century in one in which he was Man of the Match. He was actually asked to captain England in the 1973/4 series in the West Indies but broadcasting, cricket commentating for the BBC and writing had taken over. Many top-line cricketers of all nationalities have an affinity with racing and Tony was no exception. In 1987, the bicentenary of MCC, Tony wrote *Double Century* and he served as the Club's President, most unusually, for two years, 1998–2000. When I proposed my son, Simon, for membership, Tony Lewis very kindly agreed to second him. We saw a lot of him and Joan. From the world of television there was Michael Parkinson and his wife, Mary. Great fun off camera, Parky, son of a miner, left school in Barnsley aged fifteen with visions of becoming a professional cricketer, but got no further than opening the batting with 'Dickie' Bird for Barnsley CC before losing his place to Geoffrey Boycott. One day Robert Sangster and I hatched up a plan to repay Tony and Parky for some of the fun we had been having with them by chartering a plane to go to Mustique for the day. The party consisted of the two of them plus their wives, Robert and The Sheila, Magsie and I. Robert and I tossed up as to who was to pay for the plane or playtime in Mustique – drinks at Basil's Bar and lunch at the Cotton House. I won the toss and selected the latter; halfway through the day I was convinced that I had backed a loser but at the end I might have finished just in front. It was a memorable day and the plane was expensive. One of the joys was to see two people, Tony Lewis and Michael Parkinson, both of whom very well-known in their respective spheres and instantly recognisable, showing such great affinity and genuine affection for their long-time spouses and behaving in such a normal and happy manner.

In my earlier days in Barbados my parents had befriended the English cricket pundit and journalist E. W. (Jim) Swanton and his wife Mary, who had a house near Sandy Lane. There's no doubt that he lived for cricket but I thought he always sounded rather pompous and serious on the wireless and television, which having met him is being just a little unkind. He was a very devout man with high principles. He had his own private cricket club called the Arabs. To play for the Arabs was by personal invitation only by Jim S; he used to bring a team to Barbados to play against local club sides. The players included some who, on coming to the West Indies, had one or two plans on their minds other than just to play cricket. Two such players were Colin Ingleby-McKenzie who captained Hampshire and Ian Lomax. Ian was a very good cricketer but also an MFH, as well as being married to Rosie who trained racehorses including Precipice Wood, ridden by Jimmy Lindley, winner of the Ascot Gold Cup for my friend Bobby McAlpine in 1970, beating the previous year's Derby winner Blakeney in the process. Ian turned down an invitation to captain Somerset lest it might interfere with early season cub hunting. In Barbados for the Arabs, Jim Swanton informed his team, the evening before the first match of their tour, that he expected all the team to be in bed by 10 o'clock. Both Colin and Ian said that they needed a bit more sleep than that, pointing out the game was due to start at 11 o'clock. There was a very lovely American lady who, having divorced her husband on the grounds that he couldn't pay his backgammon debts to her, upshipped to Barbados and a house very close to Maddox. In later years she became a very close friend but at the time of the Arab cricket tour she attracted the attention of Ian Lomax, with whom she had a lovely time for the duration of the tour. Her name was Margot Walsh and she was later to tell me in her rather deep and gravelly voice that she knew more about cricket than any other American and could tell me precisely the position of silly mid-on.

One other amusing cricket story, some years later, witnessed at first hand: during the apartheid era South Africa was officially banned from international cricket although a few rebel tours did take place. In 1992, after the lifting of the ban, a South Africa cricket team made its first overseas tour of the West Indies, playing several island and ODI games, but only one Test Match which took place at the Kensington Oval, Barbados. The South Africans fielded a pretty strong side captained by Kepler Wessels and including the very fast bowler Allan Donald, the brilliant fielder and middle order batsman Jonty Rhodes, the later disgraced Hansie Cronje and top batsmen Peter Kirsten and Andrew Hudson. The West Indies, too, had a good side but one of their top line 'quicks' was hurt and unable to play. In everybody's mind the natural substitute, particularly as the match was to be played in Barbados, was a Bajan fast bowler named Anderson Cummins. For reasons best known to themselves, the selectors did not pick him, preferring Kenny Benjamin from Antigua. This promoted a storm of protest from the fans, huge numbers of whom paraded up and down round the Oval with banners proclaiming No CUMMINS, No GOINS. The match, a thriller, was played to a half-empty stadium. South Africa established a good first innings lead and, in their second innings, needing only 201 to win, at 123/3 looked all set to do so. However, they collapsed and were all out for 148 with Curtly Ambrose taking 6/34 and Courtney Walsh the other 4, leaving the West Indies the rather lucky winners by 53 runs.

Domestically the storm clouds had been gathering for quite a while. It was just not working out, Magsie spending about as much time back in England as she was in Barbados. I had hoped that the complete change in lifestyle and even country would have saved matters but the plain fact was that we should never have married in the first place. It was the classic case of rebound: her from Gay and me from Anthea. Deep down, Magsie never really fell out of love with Gay but she, understandably, could no longer accept that he was a serial adulterer, however charming, fun and kind-hearted. We fell into each other's arms and after a period of comfort, support, love and sex should have fallen out of them and gone our separate ways with no recriminations, remaining as friends. Sadly Magsie found it difficult to settle, always looking over her shoulder; she had three husbands after me, the last one being an old friend of mine who I hope and think did his best for her for the remainder of her life.

After she left, I didn't mind spending time on my own. Socially it was a quiet time of the year and I busied myself both mentally and physically on repairs and the maintenance of Maddox. Much of the more menial and unskilled work I could do myself so I was up and down ladders stripping and painting wooden window sun shields, scrubbing and cleaning coralstone walls and stripping and re-painting the enormous amount of decorative metal balustrades, stair banisters and terrace furniture, all of which had been designed by Oliver Messel. He had invented his own special shade of green and Tony Snowdon told me that he had done this in conjunction with Berger Paints. It so happened that I knew the new manager of Berger Paints in his days as 'roadie' for The Merrymen so I went to see him and, between us, we found the old formula for Messel's special green, which he called Mustique Green and which he used for many of the houses he had designed in Barbados and Mustique. As I needed many gallons of the stuff, my friend at Berger's, Ralph Johnson, agreed to make it again for me. The huge mahogany trees on the short drive leading up to the house also needed attention, with some seriously heavy branches coming dangerously close to the walls of the house. This was too much for me to handle but, again, I was lucky in that the 'day' job of Chris Gibbs, the base guitarist of The Merrymen, was as a tree surgeon so he and his team came and did the necessary.

A little later in the year my mother was due to have a hip replacement operation in London. Although not rare, hip replacements were not so commonplace as they are now so I arranged to fly to England so that I could be with her. A couple of days before leaving I went to a small drinks party at the Coral Reef Club given by David Heimann who had a house on Mustique but was also en route to England. At the party I was introduced to a young lady called Gaie Lee who was staying with friends of hers at Coral Reef. During conversation it transpired that she was going back to England on the same plane as me so I suggested that I picked her up and took her to the airport. We managed to get seats next to each other and spent most of the night flight talking and getting on rather well. She told me that she was in the middle of a divorce from her husband, had three children and lived near Henley. I was only going to be in London for a week but arranged to take her out to dinner on my last night, assuming that my mother's operation went well and that she was on the road to recovery. She was; Gaie and I spent the evening together which was the start of a love affair. I flew back to Barbados with a heart light with happiness but heavy with separation from my new love. Gaie told me that she was from a Jewish family and, frighteningly, that she was very rich. Her grandfather, Michael Sobell, had made a fortune in pioneering radio and television. He also owned racehorses, the most notable of which was Troy who, trained by Dick Hern and ridden by Willie Carson, won the Derby, Irish Derby and King George and Queen Elizabeth Stakes in 1979. Michael Sobell had two daughters: one, Netta, married Arnold, Lord Weinstock and the other, Hilda, married Gaie's father Stanley Rubin. Weinstock worked for Sobell and eventually the company merged with GEC, with Weinstock becoming Chairman and the Sobell family the largest shareholders in GEC. Hence my being rather frightened. I had never had anything romantically to do with a rich lady and was determined to make sure that it could not be said that I was after her money. Our love affair was, to start with, carried out at long distance, letters, telephone calls and all that, but we managed to find opportunities to meet, for instance in New York where she came, chaperoned most discreetly by her mother. Another time I had a reason to go to Ireland and we met there and after a while she made her first visit to Maddox. Altogether, for three years, although we never formally lived together, we spent a great deal of time in each other's houses. She had three lovely children, Julian, the eldest, Tara and Sebastian and she got on very well with and was very kind to my two youngest, Simon and Sam. We all had lovely times together at Maddox and skiing holidays in Verbier and Val d'Isère. Her house near Henley was extremely comfortable and liveable with a swimming pool and all mod cons. Gaie was a good rider, loved hunting and I managed to have the odd day with the Bicester when I was staying with her in England. But there were overriding and, in the end, insurmountable problems. I got on fine with her mother but her father was, I thought, a horrible little man: one of those bigoted Jews who thought the whole world, and me in particular, was anti-Semitic, even writing a silly letter to my mother to that effect. My youngest son has a Jewish wife. One thing I've always thought is that the Jews – which Gaie's father was – and the Irish – which I mostly am – have one thing in common: an ability to laugh at and make fun of themselves. I've seen and met so many of both to have reason to believe this to be true; but not Stanley Rubin. He was rude, unpleasant and jealous; I always suspected that he traded on being Arnold Weinstock's brother-in-law. I was never allowed to meet 'Uncle Arnie' as Arnold Weinstock was known in the family; probably Uncle Arnie never wanted to meet me. I did, however, meet his son Simon on several occasions. Apart from being a director of GEC, he looked after and managed the family's racing interests. I found him rather shy but absolutely charming in every way, very knowledgeable on thoroughbred breeding lines and racing in general. Very sadly he died all too young aged forty-four. Luckily I know and have known enough Jewish people to be aware that the likes of Stanley Rubin are in the minority. Anyway, in the end the family won and we were both sensible enough to part, very sadly from my point of view, as friends but no longer lovers and remain so. I look back with great happiness on the time we had together. One little story: at the height of our time together Gaie gave me a gold chain to hang round my neck; I've never been one for male jewellery but I was proud to wear this chain because, attached to it, was a gold whistle with the inscription BLOW ME AND I'LL COME. When we parted I gave it back to her. She wasn't going to come any more. A year or so afterwards Gaie married a nice man with Jewish and Greek connections called Philip Scoular who rode in point-to-points. Tragically he died of cancer some years later.

16

The Magic of Maddox

Barbados since the end of the Second World War had experienced huge changes. It had developed from a sleepy backwater dominated by the growing of sugar cane virtually controlled by the plantation owners to a gradually increasing tourist destination, which was lucky because sugar production could no longer compete with modern and more economic methods of production in other areas of the world. In Barbados, plantations were small by international standards – a plantation of 300 acres was considered large with cane being cut by hand in tiny areas of sometimes steep land totally unsuited to modern machinery used on flat land in parcels of 1,000 acres plus in, say, the USA. From the mid-50s when I first went there, on the west coast from the Eagle Hall area just north of Bridgetown up as far as Speightstown and beyond, ever increasing hotels sprouted, with a matching supply of supermarkets and restaurants of all types, occupying space which had formerly been cane fields growing down to the water's edge.

Barbados is governed by the House of Assembly, consisting of twenty-one Senators and thirty Members of Parliament representing all the constituencies of the island. It is one of the very oldest in the Commonwealth, its first sitting having taken place in 1639. Nowadays Barbados has a two-party system with the Senators being the equivalent of the House of Lords in Westminster. Parliament in general is run on the same system as in Westminster. The main change since the end of the war has been the transfer of power from the white landowners and settlers to the black majority of the population, many of whom are descended from the original slaves imported from West Africa. Education is very good with a near 100 per cent literacy rate. Many students graduate and win places to all the major universities in the western world including Oxford and Cambridge. It is, perhaps, surprising that the franchise to women was granted only in 1942, which is a demonstration of how so little progress was made pre-war and how much post-war. There are three dominant politicians who have helped hugely with this progress. The first was Sir Grantley Adams, born in 1898 and a promising cricketer in his young days playing for Barbados. He won a scholarship to Oxford. On his return to Barbados he formed the first Barbados Workers Union before entering Parliament and leading his own party, the Barbados Labour Party (BLP). He was a staunch monarchist and was very instrumental in paving the way between the old and the new. From 1958 to 1961 he became the first and only Prime Minister of the ill-fated Federation of the West Indies, which lasted only a short time due to the ultra-nationalistic tendencies of the member islands. EU take note. He was Premier (Prime Minister) of Barbados from 1953 to 1958 when he was succeeded by Hugh Cummins. In 1961 Eroll Barrow, a former protégé of Grantley Adams who, as I have mentioned earlier, rose to be a flying officer and navigator in the RAF in the Second World War, departed from the BLP to form his own party, the Democratic Labour Party (DLP). Errol was also a monarchist but, twenty-two years younger than Grantley Adams and with the experience of war behind him, captured the mood of the people and became Premier in 1961. Barbados became an independent member of the British Commonwealth in 1966, the ceremony and handover being conducted by the Duke of Kent with the title of 'Premier' being changed to 'Prime Minister'. Barrow continued in this post until 1976 when he was defeated by the third influential Barbadian politician, Grantley

Adams' son. Always known as 'Tom', his actual names were Jon Michael Geoffrey Manningham Adams, born in 1931. Like his father he won a scholarship to Magdalen, Oxford and trained as a lawyer. He served as Prime Minister from 1976 to 1985, was conservative in style and an admirer of both Margaret Thatcher and Ronald Reagan. Following the Falklands War, he was instrumental in encouraging both Thatcher and Reagan to intervene militarily against the Communist and Cuban-led riots in Grenada.

Grenada at that time has been described as a smouldering volcano under the self-believing, nobody-can-touch-me spiritual guidance of Prime Minister/Dictator Eric Gairy. Enter the left-wing, rabble rousing, crowd-pleasing, English/East German experienced, Communist-inclined Maurice Bishop. Violently anti-British, he travelled to Cuba and made friends with Fidel Castro. In 1979 Bishop stood against and defeated Gairy, becoming Prime Minister of Grenada. But he had a rival and acquaintance since school days in Bernard Coard, who had gone to the USA at the time Bishop went to Europe. The final factional clash came and Bishop was deposed by Coard and summarily executed by firing squad. Castro couldn't care less if Communist infiltration came about through Bishop or Coard, so he supported Coard's Leninist/Marxist faction as an excuse for establishing a base and airport in the Eastern Caribbean, which was the reason President Reagan (supported by Margaret Thatcher, who was only just getting over the Falklands War and did not want to be actively involved in another), committed American forces to invade Grenada and restore order. Tom Adams supported this invasion and allowed the US to use Barbados as an intermediate transit station for troops, aircraft and military equipment. Barbadians, peace-loving people, were not entirely happy with this plan but Adams stuck to his guns reasoning, quite rightly, that Grenada was only a step away and he did not want any escalation of Communist ideals to spread any further.

The invasion, condemned by the UN General Assembly, was a success. It also, ultimately, gave Grenada a free boost to its Tourist Trade by having a brand new airport with a long runway built by the Americans. In 1980 Nicholas Braithwaite was appointed Prime Minister of an interim administration by the Governor General Sir Paul Scoon.

In Barbados, Tom Adams died suddenly from a heart attack in 1985 to be succeeded by his deputy Bernard 'Bree' St John, a thoroughly likeable and good-natured lawyer who did not have the dynamic thrust needed from a Prime Minister, perhaps not helped by his socially mobile wife, Stella. He lost the General Election the following year by a wide margin, allowing Errol Barrow to return as Prime Minister, only for him to die also of heart failure a year later.

So ended a very eventful period of Barbados politics, but a final word on the subject: the Head of State is called the Governor General. He or she is the Queen's Representative, appointed by Her Majesty on the recommendation of the Prime Minister of Barbados. The two political parties, the BLP and the DLP, are not too far removed from each other and generally it is the strength, leadership qualities and policies of the party leader that determine the result of a General Election, rather than a dogmatic attachment to either party on the part of the electorate. The official residence of the Governor General is a very splendid mansion, Government House, built in 1702, which stands on a hill close to the racecourse and not far from the city centre. Many official functions are held at Government House and it is where members of the Royal Family and dignitaries of foreign countries stay if on official visits.

The Governor General also holds less formal lunches and dinners. The Governor General who I got to know best was Dame Nita Barrow, the sister of the late Prime Minister, Errol Barrow. Her basic training as a nurse led to many senior appointments to nursing organisations worldwide and in the YWCA. Prior to her appointment as Governor General in 1990, she had been Barbados' Permanent Representative at the United Nations in New York from 1986 to 90. Occasionally I was invited to her more private lunches at Government House. Although informal they were quite smart occasions, always with around ten to twelve guests with Dame Nita accompanied by her faithful ADC, one Captain Daniels, resplendent in her Barbados Defence Force uniform. At one of these lunches Lord and Lady Forte were among the guests. Forte was Chairman of Trust House Forte which owned, among several others, the Savoy Hotel in London and, at that time, Sandy Lane Hotel in Barbados.

I seemed to get on quite well with his Lordship, a very small man with a distinct lack of sense of humour. Anyway the next day I received an invitation to dine with Lord and Lady Forte at Sandy Lane Hotel. I explained that I had two very great friends, Jamie and Carole Guise, staying with me at Maddox whom I didn't want to leave behind as they were guests. Slightly grudgingly, I thought, I was told that I could bring them. The next mistake was that we were ten minutes late; his Lordship and Lady Forte plus a daughter, Olga Polizzi, were sitting stone-faced on a bench in the foyer of the hotel from which he rose and without a word led us to the centre table in the hotel restaurant. An icy silence pervaded. Carole, placed next to his Lordship, did a wonderful job on him with almost nothing in return, while I did my best between her Ladyship and the daughter, herself a well-known hotelier, but it was a very sticky evening. At the conclusion of dinner the head waiter exclaimed with a flourish that he would escort the party to the best table for the floorshow, but that was too much for his Lordship who announced that he was going to bed and beckoned his wife to follow. She had other ideas and stayed with us to watch the limbo dancing, which provided a bit of light relief for all.

17

Greensleeves

After Gaie and I split up I needed a new project. Maddox was up and running with new wood shingles on the whole roof into which I had fitted concealed solar panels in the gables. Nick Teller, son of Jack, had finally quit Greensleeves. One of my last occasions there was when he lost his temper with staff and guests and was shouting to everyone to leave. Assisted by a slight nudge from me, he fell into his swimming pool. Emerging dripping wet he ran to his office, returning waving a gun, making it worse for himself when everybody laughed at him. He called the police who scratched their heads, had a drink and left. No charges were pressed and soon afterwards he sold the place and disappeared to run a bar and liquor store which he closed at 6.30 p.m. A quite short-lived venture. The purchaser of Greensleeves, a Scotsman, only kept it for a year or so, leaving it in an almost derelict state. By chance I met two other Scotsmen, quite delightful, who told me they had bought Greensleeves for a song – sorry for the pun but they were playing partners in an Edinburgh jazz band – but had no idea what to do with it. How, an hour or so later, I found myself in the position of having taken on the job of renovating and re-opening Greensleeves as an up-market hotel goodness only knows. I knew as much about the hotel business as running an illegal crap game in New York but there wasn't really a great deal to lose; I paid the Scots no rent and, for a while, they agreed to pay the skeleton staff consisting of a splendid barman and/ or head waiter called Horace, an excellent gardener with a very basic knowledge of plumbing and electronics called Ervin, a lovely receptionist and bookkeeper called Gwen, who we called Aunty and who agreed to be temporarily laid off since there were no books to be kept and no customers to receive, and a couple of maids to keep the place clean. The sixteen accommodation units were all spacious well-designed suites in blocks of four – two up, two down in each block – and the furnishings were only in need of a good clean, These apartments, plus the bar and restaurant space and a couple of offices, surrounded the empty swimming pool. The entrance to the hotel was along a 100-yard drive off the main road, up a few steps and into the good lobby and reception area. On the other side of the road was the beach bar and restaurant which was leased out to a couple of local likely lads, Frank (Corbin) & Trevor (Harris). Backing onto the main building on the land side was an open plot of 8 acres leading directly from the road side. It was for sale at a reasonable price so I bought it, thinking, quite rightly as it turned out, it would be a very valuable addition to the property as a whole and useful for a gem of an idea that I had in mind. In the early 80s, Health Spas were starting to become fashionable. Places like Forest Mere and Champneys in England, and even more so in the USA; personally I could think of nothing more miserable than to go to a very comfortable and luxurious establishment to be wuffed, coiffed and pampered without a proper bar and restaurant to follow, so how about mixing the two? Having decided to have a real crack at the plan, which was clearly going to take some considerable amount of time, I let Maddox for a period of months so that I could live over the shop, it being very empty. I went for a visit to England to sound out my idea, look for possible sources of finance and to find a company associated with the hotel industry that could produce a weight-carrying Feasibility Study on the potential of Greensleeves. I had another little idea too: cosmetic plastic surgery was becoming quite an industry, particularly in the USA. Why not build a smart plastic surgery unit on my

8-acre plot, sell the idea to a few New York plastic surgeons to come for, say, one- to two-month stints in turn, encourage their well-heeled female middle-aged clients to have tucks and whatever else is done in the plastic surgery unit and then shift over to the luxury hotel side to be joined by their rich husbands and/or boyfriends to find their newly MOT'd ladies?

While in England I bumped into an ex-girlfriend of my dear friend Innes Ireland, named Frances Loudon, whom I had known when she and Innes had been together. She was at a bit of a loose end in a very boring job and on her own, as was I in a manner of speaking. I told her why I was in England and what I was doing. The next day she rang asking if it might be possible to come and work with me on the project. We met again and it was agreed that she could on the basis that we were both entirely free agents to lead our own lives. Frances had a business brain and we got on well together, I found what I was looking for in the shape of help from a small venture capitalist organisation which was prepared to compile the feasibility study partly from sources in London but also on the ground in Barbados. We started to prepare a Business Plan and before returning to Barbados started to see the first round of possible investors. The first question asked by all was 'What's your own investment in the project?' I could turn quite truthfully to the fact that I had more than doubled the size of the property by putting in an area of eight acres of prime open beachfront land. Frances, from a Scottish family but a product of the London Swinging sixties, came back to Barbados with me, and the arrangement suited us both.

Back at Greensleeves, it was all hands to the metaphorical pumps on a massive clean-up and restoration exercise. In charge of the manual bit was Ervin who roped in several of his mates. From my work at Maddox I had made good friends of electricians and called upon Inspector Clouseau to solve some of the plumbing mysteries and even became a dab hand at shifting a lavatory from one apartment to another in cases of emergency.

Looking back I could have written several episodes of *Fawlty Towers*. A plan of works was formulated with deadlines – not a word much liked in Barbados and certainly never achieved. At one stage when everything seemed more or less under control, Frances and I flew to New York to see potential investors and to talk to plastic surgeons, one of whom we had preliminary telephone conversations with and who was taken with the idea – so much so that he lent us an apartment in Manhattan normally occupied by his mother who was away at the time. It was August and stiflingly hot and humid. We did the rounds, sowed the seed which was well received subject, of course, to the project seeing the final light of day. The completed Feasibility Study, a large and heavy bound document, was bullish and the Business Plan showed that we needed $8m. On the investor front the main interest came from one of the large American hotel chains where we got in front of the CEO and family shareholder who confided that he loved the idea and would put it to his main board with his recommendation to proceed. We flew back to Barbados quite excited. All this I reported to the Scottish jazz band owners.

We planned a grand opening of the new Greensleeves to coincide with the start of the main winter season in the middle of December. Shortly beforehand I got in touch with a contact at CBC – Caribbean Broadcasting Corporation – who compiled a weekly business programme. He brought a camera team out to Greensleeves and conducted an interview with me on the project which generated good publicity. In early December we were nearly ready; with new electric pumps and mechanisms to the swimming pool, all that was needed was to physically scrub the shell, removing remnants of repair work, so Ervin and I got busy with bleach and cleaning materials and scrubbed away for three full days until it was gleaming white. We just needed to fill it with water. It was so obvious that nobody had thought of it. I knew a fireman in the fire brigade so I rang him. He exploded with laughter and half an hour later a fire engine with lights flashing and sirens screaming arrived at the hydrant close to the entrance to the hotel. Firemen sprinted across the field in front of the hotel, put the end of the hose in the pool and pressed the button. Nothing happened, not even a trickle. However, the whole field was being beautifully irrigated through the holes in the rotten hose. They thought it quite hilarious, hooting with laughter and jumping up and down with delight. An hour later they came back with a brand new hose and this time water came gushing out of the end. The only trouble was that it was dark brown in colour. The hydrant and irrigation pipe had clearly never been used. In four hours the pool was full of dark brown water and our hotel opening was the next day with the party and invited guests coming. What to do? I got hold of a friend who had a printing business; he rushed up a large laminated notice which I had fastened to an easel by the side of the pool which read:

WELCOME TO THE NEW GREENSLEEVES AND WE HOPE YOU ENJOY THIS EVENING. AS A HOTEL NOVELTY WE CHANGE THE COLOUR OF THE WATER ON EVERY THIRD DAY. TODAY YOU WILL NOTICE IT IS BROWN, NEXT TUESDAY IT WILL BE BLUE AND ON SATURDAY IT WILL BE GREEN AND SO ON.

There were comments but no complaints; people thought it was a bit of fun. I rang the pump and chemicals people and a couple of days later the water was crystal clear blue.

With Aunty Gwen installed back behind her reception desk, and me and Frances playing our Basil and Sybil parts, a steady if not tumultuous trickle of guests started to flow through the doors. Ervin made a very good porter, waiter and handyman. Horace, however, bore no resemblance to Manuel: quite tall, decidedly plump in his uniform of black tie, white shirt and neatly pressed trousers, Horace never moved very fast but with an air of solemnity that hid a wicked sense of humour and sharp repartee, which he used when and if, in his opinion, it was necessary. He was also a very good and jovial barman. I had taken on a couple of extra maids, Sherry and Belinda, both of whom performed their duties well until one day Belinda didn't show up. I asked Sherry where she and was anything the matter. If Sherry could have blushed she would have done so: covering her face with her hands and cringing away she said 'Oh, Belinda not coming anymore; she gone on de game in Bridgetown.'

We had a very jolly group who had won a major merit prize of a holiday in Barbados, presented by the London Fire Brigade, with their wives or husbands. Their leader asked me most politely if I minded if the ladies sunbathed topless round the swimming pool and in the garden. As most were quite attractive I said that it would be perfectly in order. But the first major excitement was that the Rolling Stones were recording an album at the Blue Wave Studio in Bridgetown of Eddy Grant, a Guyanese-British musician who wrote and performed a long series of hits including *Baby Come Back*. The Stones were looking for accommodation for their backing team, they themselves having taken a house near Greensleeves. I invited their roadie to come round and have a look. An hour or so later, not the roadie but Mick Jagger and Jerry Hall came into the hotel, liked what they saw and we looked after their team for the length of their stay. Both could not have been more charming although my first impression of Jerry Hall was that she looked better in photographs than she did in real life.

Over the next few years I saw a fair amount of them. Mick bought a house on Mustique where he spent a lot of time but I saw him and Jerry while they were together when they came to Barbados, as well as 'Keef' Richards and Charlie Watts, who frequently moaned about why he was in Barbados when could have been on his farm in Somerset. Contrary to general public opinion, Mick was and I'm sure still is very good company, highly articulate and intelligent, loved cricket and is a great authority and collector of antique silver. I had moved back into

Maddox and they were frequent visitors. Many years later, I was in Rio de Janeiro with a party of travel clients staying at a hotel on Copacabana Beach next to the ultra-smart and expensive Copacabana Palace Hotel: the mayor of Rio had decided to give a free concert by the Rolling Stones on Copacabana Beach. The Stones were provided with a whole floor of the Copacabana Palace Hotel and a temporary gantry had been built over the four-lane highway connected to their floor for them to cross directly onto the stage to perform. For four days I saw the stage being built; 1¼ million people attended the concert, all for free with huge screens and amplifiers having been erected at 100-yard intervals along the beach. For the concert itself, which was quite fabulous, I had a perfect view from my hotel room balcony.

The deal from the American hotel group fell through, the young CEO having been advised by the senior family shareholders and the main board that a highly speculative investment in an uncharted territory (as far as they were concerned), having been put forward by an unknown and inexperienced proposer in the hotel industry, was not for them, however romantic it might sound. And who could blame them? The next one up was a British entrepreneur in the retail and property market who came, with his wife, to Barbados for a holiday. I met him at a drinks party and he was tickled pink with the idea, saying that he was on the lookout for a new project. We went through the rounds of meetings, discussions on the Feasibility Study, meetings with our lawyers and accountants in Barbados, all of which went well. He took a copy of the Feasibility Study back to England to discuss with the authors, again with favourable results so our hopes were high. Ultimately they were dashed, mainly due to the fact that our Mr Big was quite elderly, and his wife was perturbed that he was embarking on a major, risky project which might cause him too much worry and anxiety. Coupled with all this there may have been a thought in his mind that the whole idea might have seemed good at the time in the lovely Caribbean climate and lifestyle but perhaps not the same at the end of a cold English winter. There were quite a few others, not more than sniffs, but a major interest came from an Austrian hotel group headed by one Stefan Tomek. The approach and first meetings from this group took place in London, Frances and I went to their flagship hotel in Bad Gastein, Austria (the scene of my badly broken leg in the 50s) followed by Mr Tomek coming out to Barbados, being very taken with the property plus my additional land and sending a team of three of his directors and senior employees out for a very detailed inspection and meetings with the professionals in Barbados. It was, it seemed, all systems go. They asked for Horace to go for a month's training to Bad Gastein, paid for by them, and also for Frances to go for about two months to learn the administrative ropes. During that time I had been promised that a draft contract was being drawn up by their lawyers and that it was 'on its way' for inspection by me and my lawyers in Barbados. It never came; I was told that there were 'financial difficulties' at their end and that the deal, therefore, was off. Frances came back to Barbados but I decided that enough was enough. I had, at various times during whole exercise, been promised up to $6m of the $8m required and Tomek's group had promised to finance the whole operation. I certainly was not prepared to go on risk for the extra $2m so I had to say to the Edinburgh jazz band that I was pulling out and handing the property back to them, but in much better condition than when I took it over.

On 5th March 1987 my mother died, quite suddenly. Although we spoke regularly once a week, frequently more often, I hadn't seen her for a few months. She used to come out to Barbados about twice each year and had planned to come again in the spring. I had already arranged to come to England, pick up Simon and Sam from their schools and bring them up to her in Cheshire where we would all stay for their half term. I telephoned her as soon as I landed in London just to say hello and agree our time of arrival the following day. She sounded well and we were both very excited about seeing each other. She said that she had a routine dentist's appointment that afternoon but otherwise would be at home. Later in the day I received a call from my cousin John Bromley-Davenport, who also lived in Cheshire, with the devastating news. Evidently she had returned from seeing the dentist, had sat down in a big armchair in the drawing room, had a snooze and never woke up. She was found by her devoted couple Lottie and David Read who had been with my parents for some thirty years. Although not in the very best of health, she had a slight heart problem that, we were assured, was not serious and under control with medication but she also had very painful arthritis, particularly in her hands. For this she received painkilling drugs and, from time to time, cortisone injections. She was always very brave, uncomplaining and determined. A wonderful loving mother to me, grandmother to my sons and wife to my father whose own death I don't think she ever really got over. She died ten years after him. I had to break the news to both boys on arrival at their schools the next day and it was a very sad, silent and sorry carload that made its way northwards. Simon was seventeen and Sam fifteen. The funeral was in our local church of Lower Peover which I had attended all my younger life and where my father was buried. My mother wished to be cremated and her ashes were interred on my father's grave with a shared headstone. I had to go back to Barbados at the end of the boys' half term but arranged to come back some weeks later to pack up Sculshaw Lodge. It was a very difficult family decision to make as regards Sculshaw: I was living abroad, the boys were very young with their whole lives in front of them and there was no one in the family that needed or, indeed, wanted it. In the short term nothing was to be done until Lottie and David had decided what to do next and had found suitable employment and living conditions but the heartrending decision was made that it should be sold.

After I had called off the Greensleeves project, Frances asked if she could move back into Maddox with me. I slightly demurred about this; after all the project that we had worked on together was at an end but considered it churlish not to agree. A mistake it turned out to be.

Although not a plantation Great House, Maddox was, by Barbadian standards, quite large, in the centre of the prime location on the west coast of Barbados with the garden leading directly down a few steps onto what was, in essence, a private beach with large coral rocks jutting well into the sea at either end. It was also expensive to maintain to the standard set by its previous owner and designer, Oliver Messel. During my time at Greensleeves I became a member of the Barbados Hotels Association, attended many meetings, met the owners/managers of other hotels and also owners/managers of businesses associated with the hotel industry. Maddox was my principal asset and I needed to make it work for me; I formed an idea of making it do so whilst remaining in occupancy. Many large multinational companies operate Reward Schemes for their top employees at senior management level by taking them with their wives/husbands/girl and boyfriends to exotic places round the world for a week's hooley. Some companies do a similar exercise to launch a new product to their main distributors; they put them up at smart hotels but frequently have one day or evening as their 'special' or gala. All this I found out from my colleagues in the Hotel Association. The notion is known as Incentive Travel. Why not, I thought, promote Maddox as the location for their special day working in association with the specific hotel where the group were staying or with the agents appointed by the companies themselves? I could easily seat up to 150 people in comfort using round or rectangular tables and the kitchen quarters were big enough to cater for this amount of guests. Or I could provide for small, more intimate, parties of, say, fourteen to twenty. I had access to all the top bands and solo entertainers on the island and the layout of the house, thanks to Oliver Messel, was distinctly theatrical. There was another feature that appealed particularly to American potential customers: the Royal Card. The fact that Princess Margaret often used to stay at Maddox and that Her Majesty the Queen had been there was a great draw. I have to admit that one idea came from a very successful play in London called *Lettice and Lovage* by Peter Shaffer starring Maggie Smith, which featured the heroine as a guide in a large English country house who gets bored with telling the same story over and over again so decides to embellish it. I had a very imposing upholstered and carved armchair in the interior hall which I had inherited from my father and I used to say to American clients that this was where the Queen sat when she received local dignitaries. I even had a couple of genuine Zulu assegais that on occasion were alleged to have been used in performing Royal duties.

The word soon got around, working with two Incentive Travel agents in conjunction with the hotels. We were getting on average two bookings per month of varying sizes, mainly from British and American companies, a number of them from the Life Insurance world which seems to offer very large rewards to their salesmen that perhaps might have been better directed at increasing the death payouts to descendants of the deceased. We did a very large event for Austin-Rover; they hired the enormous *Windstar,* a beautiful five-masted motor/sailer with computer controlled sails. For the first time ever they persuaded the Port Authority to allow the *Windstar* to anchor off Maddox beach and sent their immigration officers to stamp passports allowing the Austin-Rover clients to come on shore into the garden where a fleet of thirty mini mokes were waiting for a treasure hunt round the island followed by a slap-up lunch in the garden with steel band and limbo dancers for entertainment. Another time we had a party arranged for sixteen American Senators and their wives doing a 'fact finding' tour of the Caribbean. Somehow this had included Cuba, a country from which US citizens were virtually banned at that time … but as for 'fact finding' Senators…? The male members of the party were even invited to a dinner party with Fidel Castro at which they were each presented with a box of Havana Cigars and … a packet of Viagra. Their evening at Maddox was a great success, so much so that their leader invited me plus Michael and Jo Kelton who were staying with me at Maddox, to dinner with them at Cobblers Cove, a very good beachside hotel near Speightstown, owned by the English Godsal family. Late in the evening this party got rather out of hand with the leader's wife, a High Court judge, becoming more than displeased at the amount of attention her husband was paying to another female member of the party while frolicking in the sea at around midnight. 'Take your hands off my husband, you bitch!' The damage bill to their suite was huge.

One of the best social and cultural events of the year in Barbados is the annual Holders Festival in March founded originally by Johnny and Wendy Kidd at their lovely old 17th century Plantation House, Holders, half a mile inland above Sandy Lane beach which Johnny had inherited from his mother, Janet Kidd, the daughter the first Lord Beaverbrook. Johnny, who had been a prominent member of the British Showjumping Team and Wendy, the parents of the models Jodie and Jemma, started the week to ten-day-long festival in 1993, attracting internationally known artists mainly from England and the USA as well as local artists from the Caribbean, staging operas, plays, concerts and individual performers all in the open air. In the later 90s Luciano Pavarotti gave a concert at the Festival. In one of the early years among the artists appearing were Judi Dench, her husband Michael Williams and daughter Finty; also Christopher Biggins and the cabaret act Kit and the Widow. During the run-up to the Festival, I got to see most of them at parties including one we had at Maddox, particularly Kit Hesketh-Harvey. One evening there was a fringe event at Sandy Lane Hotel at which Kit and the Widow were performing. A day or so beforehand Kit took me on one side and said he was going to include in his act a send up of Cole Porter's *Let's Do It* featuring well-known personalities on the island and could I help? I supplied Kit with names and some stories for him to have fun with, including the diminutive Lord Forte as it was not long after our disastrous evening with him. Knowing what was coming, when Kit came to 'Lord Forte, standing on a chair, does it' I had his Lordship firmly in my sights; not one flicker of a smile creased his face although the rest of the audience were in stitches.

The Incentive Travel work continued to tick over satisfactorily at Maddox with weddings becoming quite a regular feature. I befriended the vicar of the northern parish of St Andrew, a rather remote area around the rough seas of North Point, who was not terribly busy with his parishioners and on the lookout for a bit of extra cash. The wedding ceremonies took place in the garden, or sometimes on the beach with the sound of the softly breaking sea providing a soothing and romantic backdrop. Depending on the budget, the reception afterwards was either a stand-up cocktail party with champagne and canapés or a full blown sit down and served lunch or dinner with a crooner to serenade the happy couple. Always they wanted a video, the finished article accompanied by rather sickly naff music. One had the feeling that they all started their married life well and the money was good.

From time to time stories appear in the British press about the high level of crime in Barbados. On the whole that is nonsense – or at least it was in my day. Any serious incident received major headline news in both the local newspapers, *The Advocate* and the *Nation*. In Brixton it would probably go, if not unnoticed, unreported in the press. Maddox had no doors and hardly any windows on the ground floor and I had no live-in staff. At various times I was entirely on my own, sometimes for weeks on end. Whenever I went away I left everything exactly where it was so from the late afternoon until the following morning the whole property was empty and unoccupied. I never lost anything or even took the key out of my car. Two funny stories, however: I had a wireless alarm that used to go off to the signature tune of the BBC World Service at seven a.m. One morning when I was alone in the house, I went down for my early morning swim having heard the BBC news headlines, to find a youngish white man asleep on a sofa wearing only swimming trunks. I woke him up and asked what he thought he was doing. 'Oh' he replied, 'I live here.' I informed him that he was incorrect in this assumption and invited him to leave. He declined and so I called the police. Two uniformed policemen arrived but by this time the young man had gone down to the sea and was bobbing about in the water. The policemen, unwilling to let the sea spoil the brilliant shine on their boots, were hopping up and down calling him to come in but to no avail. They asked me to telephone for reinforcements; soon a police Range Rover with siren blaring arrived, disgorging six heavily armed policemen who succeeded in apprehending the young man who was led away in handcuffs. About a week later another policeman turned up carrying a pair of swimming trunks which he offered to me. They were the ones worn by the young man which I had left to dry overnight on a balustrade. I considered that their life was over as far I was concerned and consigned them to the bin.

The other incident came very early one morning when I was woken up by barking, shouting and clamouring going on outside. I looked down and saw my dog, Lucky, who was a racist, attacking two policemen in the garden. I called him off and went down to see what was the matter. The policemen told me that they had tracked down an escaped criminal to a nearby chattel house where he was in bed with his girlfriend. However, he had eluded them by jumping out of a window, coming, they thought, in my direction. Together, and with Lucky's help (having partially accepted the policemen but excited about the prospect of sinking his teeth into another black man), we searched the whole premises but found nothing. The policemen then gave me a detailed description of the criminal in case I might see him, with a throwaway line as they departed: 'By the way, he naked.'

In August 1989 my cousin Jane Bromley-Davenport and her son Edward were staying and Simon and Sam were out for the summer holidays. Bobby McAlpine and his wife Angela had taken a house nearby also for a summer holiday. Bobby's first wife, Jane – a super person and great friend – had died of a brain tumour a few years earlier. Sadly they had already divorced. Angela Langford-Brook was the daughter of friends of my parents in Cheshire and, curiously, I had employed her as a young eighteen-year-old to help look after my two elder children, Jemima and Richard, when they were small. I asked Bobby and Angela to a barbecue lunch on the bottom terrace at Maddox overlooking the sea, together with a few others including a German friend and his American wife and an English friend, Chris Curtis, who lived in Paris with his devastatingly attractive Malaysian wife Judy; not only was she very pretty but also highly intelligent and an international bridge and backgammon player.

Carl, the German, lived and worked in Caracas, Venezuela but had a beachside holiday house quite near me in Barbados. He had just bought a new boat and came to lunch in it, anchoring just off the beach. After lunch, later in the afternoon, Carl asked if anyone would like a ski behind his new boat. Edward said he would love to so we went down to the beach: Carl drove the boat with one of the others sitting beside him as a lookout with my son Sam and I sitting in the rear-facing stern seats observing Edward who was skiing. We were making a lap of the bay when the boat made a sudden turn followed by a big thump. I looked behind the boat and saw a body floating. It was Angela; Sam and I were the first to get to her in the water. She was conscious but clearly very badly injured, the water all round her being blood red. We all shouted to the shore to get help, summon a doctor and ambulance. Luckily the sea was flat calm while we handled her slowly and carefully to the shore. The ambulance and paramedics came amazingly quickly but while waiting I dashed to the house and called my very good friend and the most skilled and respected doctor in Barbados, Jack Leacock, and told him what had happened. He immediately rang the Queen Elizabeth Hospital and arranged for the top orthopaedic surgeon to be waiting to receive the ambulance, which I followed by car with Bobby. What had happened was that Angela had decided to go for a swim; it was quite late afternoon and the sun was well down in a cloudless sky and shining directly into Carl's eyes, and he could not have seen her in the water. He was naturally totally distraught.

It was the most terrible, freakish accident; the sort of thing that one hears about and now had experienced. We had followed all normal safety procedures. Perhaps Angela could have mentioned to someone that she was going for a swim but it was impossible to apportion blame. Angela had a very long operation lasting most of the night with the team of surgeons extracting every grain of sand that inevitably had got into her wounds. One leg was worse than the other and it was questionable for quite some time whether or not it might have to be amputated. Bobby's first, and totally correct, wish was to get Angela back to England as soon as possible. I knew the local British Airways manager and he arranged for enough seats to be available for Angela to lie flat plus room for Bobby and a senior nurse from the QEH to travel with her, which they did five or six days later. Poor Angela did keep her leg but was in and out of hospital for a good two years, having a multitude of operations on both legs.

Domestically, Frances continued to base herself at Maddox. She was not, however, a Resident of Barbados or property owner as I was, and therefore not allowed to work or be employed on the island or to remain for more than three months at a time. She came and went as she pleased. One evening I had a call from Chrissie Sangster (that was), Robert's first and by far his best wife; she and Robert had an arrangement whereby he allowed her to have one holiday per year with her new husband and family at Jane's Harbour. After a disastrous second marriage to the not universally popular Daryl Carey, Chrissie had met and married a steady, reliable and all-round good egg called Iain Gordon; she and Iain plus some friends were ensconced at Jane's Harbour and Chrissie rang me to say that she had two single ladies staying and would I like to come to dinner? 'That would be lovely,' I replied. There were nine or ten for dinner and I was placed between the two single ladies, one of whom had a mild attack of flu so was not on top form; I got on pretty well with the other one whose name was Pamela Codrington. It was a very jolly evening and I went home, having arranged to play tennis the next day with one of the men plus two others who I knew would like to play. The following afternoon who should turn up to watch us play tennis but Chrissie, Iain and a couple of others from the previous night's party including Pamela Codrington. After the tennis they all came back to Maddox for a drink and I was asked to lunch the following day; Pamela and I hit it off well, we went water skiing in the afternoon and that was the start of the romance which continued for the rest of her week's holiday and thereafter...

Frances, who had been away, came back a few days later by which time I had other friends also staying at Maddox, which made it a little difficult to have a quiet talk to her in as nice a way as I could about the change in circumstances. However, I managed it; very much to my surprise she took it all rather badly which was not at all what I expected. Our arrangement, agreed between us, was that it would last as long as it suited either of us with no recriminations from either side if and when it ended. In hardly any time I received a legal document from a Barbadian lawyer who I knew very well – he was Simon Foster's brother-in-law – saying, in effect, that Frances had been living in my house, co-habiting, as he put it, with me and therefore was regarded as my common-law wife. This put a totally different complexion on everything, making it a great strain to be living under the same roof. I had hoped and expected that we would have remained friends and that I could have helped her morally and financially without the legal expenses and unpleasantness. I ended up having to pay her a large sum, albeit less than half what she demanded to my face.

A month or so later I went to England really to test the water and to be sure that it had not been just a holiday fling with Pamela. It hadn't. She took me to stay at her quite large but rather run-down Georgian house in Gloucestershire, just off the M4 and near Chipping Sodbury. Born Pamela Wise in 1937, she was the daughter of a builder in Kent and his Scottish wife. Soon after the outbreak of war her father had joined the army in an administrative role and received postings to many different places. In the early to mid-50s the family was in Tripoli, Libya, and aged eighteen, Pamela met a former Coldstream Guards officer who was running a watersport diving school and club. His name was Simon Codrington, and he had seen active service in the Second World War Italian campaign. The heir to a baronetcy and a magnificent stately home in Gloucestershire, Simon was married to a lady considerably older than himself. He and Pamela had an affair, Pamela became pregnant but Simon's divorce from his wife came through just in time for them to be married before their son was born, thereby entitling him to succeed to the baronetcy in due course. After the birth of a second son they returned to England, taking over the family home of the James Wyatt house, Dodington which they succeeded in turning into a major tourist attraction with thousands of visitors annually. The marriage eventually fell apart and they were divorced in 1979, one day before Simon's father died, therefore preventing Pamela from becoming Lady Codrington. What a difference a day makes.

I didn't stay in England for long as I had bookings at Maddox to attend to, but Pamela followed soon afterwards and stayed for the whole summer during which time all our respective children came at various times, except for my daughter Jemima who had come the year before but had now become a very successful Three-Day Event rider with her own stable, partly sponsored by Asprey's. She was a member of various British teams and competed at the highest level internationally. To this day she is recorded each year in the programme for Badminton Horse Trials among those riders to have completed the course for a specified number of years.

In October 1990 Pamela and I were married in England. She had made it clear that while she was very happy to spend a lot of time in Barbados, she did not want to live there on a full-time basis, which view I respected. We agreed on three-month spells in either country, meaning half the year in each. Of necessity this changed my lifestyle and business arrangements at Maddox. Obviously I didn't want – and couldn't afford – to leave it empty for long periods so, in consultation with Nick Parravicino whose company, Realtors Ltd, would handle the lettings, we set about letting it to upmarket clients for much of the year when we were not there which, for marketing reasons, meant the winter season from mid-December to mid-March and the summer July, August and September. Most importantly everything had to be spot on, both so far as the state of the house and garden and the staff. Regarding the latter, it was different from just having friends and family to stay with a quite free and easy atmosphere: apart from Clarence, the gardener, I employed only female staff, finding that it worked better that way. I engaged a manager, Rachel Wilkie, the highly efficient daughter of the vicar of St James, Andrew Hatch, and his English wife Sheila, both of whom had become very good friends. Rachel was recently divorced and looking for something that she could get her teeth into. Sherry, who I had brought from Greensleeves, I promoted to housekeeper and head maid; Greta was the cook, there were three to four other maids with Hyacinth being the one i/c, plus Frank the night watchman, who I employed only when the house was let. One problem about all female staff is that they kept having babies: Greta, a delightfully outgoing person, had two. She came to me after the second one was born and said 'Mr Johnson, I not having no more babies until I get married.' Sherry, a more authoritative person, disapproved of all this and would have none of it until it happened to her, when she said that she couldn't understand how it happened and it was not her fault. I got a professional photographer to photograph all aspects of the house for an excellent brochure and engaged a delightful couple from New York to make a promotional video, giving them a week's stay in the house in lieu of payment.

Pamela's house in Gloucestershire, The Old Hundred, was originally part of the Codringtons' Dodington Estate consisting of very many thousands of acres which had been whittled down through various generations to Dodington House itself and 800 acres of parkland around. The Old Hundred with about 25 acres of land was Pamela's divorce settlement from her husband Simon, valued in 1979 at £140,000. During the next two to three years we settled into the three-month routine in England and Barbados. Pamela had lived in Gloucestershire for about twenty-five years and had a wide circle of friends, some of whom I also knew, among them being Sheira and Roddy Brinckman from my connections with them in Barbados and the Guise family.

(Sir) John Guise was my old friend from racing days, a Jockey Club starter who had been the starter for the Blackmanship incident at Wolverhampton. John had also been Chairman of the Turf Club and had kindly proposed me for membership in the early 80s; his younger brother, Jamie, I had met in Johannesburg in the 60s. Jamie's wife Carole was first married to the aforementioned Charles Benson. The Guise family home was a very large pile at Elmore, near Gloucester, which had been owned by the family since the 10th century, and still is. The continuity, in

John's words, chiefly achieved by successfully sitting on every fence known to man.

For all the period since I gave up training racehorses and went to live in Barbados, John Guise always invited me to come over and stay with him at Elmore for the Festival meeting at Cheltenham in March. Now, back in England in March, we organised our own house party for Cheltenham. Naturally Pamela had friends who I did not know, among them Michael and Anne Heseltine who she had known for many years from when they were young and struggling; Michael (now Lord) Heseltine made a huge success first in the property boom in the late 1950s and then in the publishing world when he formed Haymarket Press. He wheedled his way legally out of nearly all his National Service, claiming that it interfered too much with his business. After two unsuccessful attempts he entered Parliament as Conservative Member for Tavistock in 1966. I am not going to dwell on the impact he made during many political appointments, rising to be Deputy Prime Minister. He and Anne were married in 1962, and because of their long-standing friendship Pamela was, from time to time, invited to his house, Thenford, near Banbury, for weekends. I, as her husband, was included.

It was somewhat surprising that the assembled house parties carried a strong left-wing element, among the most prominent being Anthony Howard who always seemed to be there. A paradoxical figure, Howard was the son of a Conservative Church of England parson, educated at Westminster, highly intelligent, a member of the Labour Party for sixty years, editor of the *New Statesman* and the BBC magazine, the *Listener,* and held many top line journalistic posts. He and Michael were very long-standing friends. I had nothing in common with Michael, did not take to him as a person and although he was perfectly polite, that was about it. At Thenford he has developed a magnificent garden and arboretum after his spat with Margaret Thatcher and resignation from the Cabinet over the Westland affair. Always a Europhile, he campaigned strongly for us to give up the pound in favour of the euro and now I find it intensely irritating that the Left-leaning and anti-Brexit BBC continually ask him to propound his dogmatic views. It is more than time that he retired to his garden instead of making divisive comments against Brexit, a decision voted for by the country, which the party he served for a long time is charged with implementing.

In Barbados life continued as normal with a number of corporate events and weddings; one special one, in 1991, being Pamela's eldest son who had become engaged to an American girl who he had met at his tennis club in Houston, Texas where he was then living. They wanted to be married in Barbados and it was quite a grand affair that we put on for them. The Governor General, Dame Nita Barrow, came both to the afternoon church wedding service and the reception and big dinner in the evening at Maddox. A number of his friends came out from England including his father and stepmother as well as the bride's family and friends from the USA. Maddox was bursting at the seams for over a week; some friends kindly offered to have guests to stay and I rented another house for the young overflow guests belonging to my good friends Bill and Philippa Tyrwhitt-Drake, who most kindly and generously let me have it at a very nominal rental.

Another special party was for Roddy Brinckman's 60th birthday. He and Sheira invited a number of friends to come to the island for the party, quite a number of whom I knew anyway so we had a houseful of party guests staying for several days. For the actual birthday we arranged a very festive dinner for close on fifty guests and had The Merrymen band to play. Roddy (actual name Theodore) was the son of (Sir) Napoleon (Naps) and Romie Brinckman, great friends of my parents who had a lovely house in Barbados appropriately named St Helena; Sheira was the daughter of Robert Ferris MP, who changed his name to Grant-Ferris in 1942 and became Lord Harvington in 1974. I first met Sheira in Barbados when she was in the process of divorcing her second husband, Chris Murray, who had sugar plantations in Barbados, in favour of Roddy whom she subsequently married; their home in England being another very special house and farm called Hazelton, near Cirencester which Sheira had inherited from her father. The twist to this little tale was that in 2001 Roddy and Sheira – I was and still am very fond of both – divorced and Roddy married my former wife Magsie. For a while Sheira teamed up with David Stapleton who she never married and then a rather younger man called Michael Benson – no relation to Charles.

By the time of the mid-90s, it became clear that the three-month here and there system wasn't really working. I was blissfully happy in Barbados but Pamela was tending to chip away the odd week here and there in favour of more time in England. And one had to face realities: both Maddox and The Old Hundred were expensive houses to maintain and I found myself spending a great deal on the latter as well maintaining the former. I also had to consider that property prices in prime locations in Barbados had escalated hugely in recent years and Maddox was in pole position. Another factor was that the children were all grown up, and although they still loved coming, it wouldn't be too long before they would want more to go their own ways. A heartrending decision but I made my head rule my heart and decided to sell Maddox. In hindsight I should never have done so – certainly not at that time. Finances were tight but I should have bought or rented a small house inland where I could continue to spend some time in Barbados and manage Maddox for holiday rentals for much of the year which brought in a good income. There was opposition to such a plan and I persuaded myself not to be selfish.

The whole process took the best part of a year, culminating in a month-long party for friends, home (Barbados) and abroad. The house was full to the rafters with as many friends and family from England and elsewhere that could be packed in for the whole month of March 1995. The day after the last ones left, the packers moved in and when the fateful day of final departure came, it was at that time, save the death of my parents, the saddest and most emotional of my entire life.

18

All Change

Having made the decision to return to England and a new life, it was important to get on with it without any regrets. The first project was to refurbish and improve The Old Hundred which was badly in need of attention. The house consisted of the main section plus three self-contained flats with their own entrances from the stable yard with three loose boxes, a tack room and garage block. The flats were let out; Pamela sometimes also let out the main section for short periods to make ends meet, moving into one of the flats if one was available or staying with her parents who lived only about ten miles away. Although the main house had nine bedrooms, there was no dining room and a shortage of bathrooms; the top floor had dry rot into main beams which meant that the two bedrooms and antiquated bathroom up there were pretty hazardous, with the beams having to be treated and shored up with steel bars. The plumbing, electric wiring, heating and boiler were all way beyond their sell-by date, on their last legs and probably dangerous. The house and out-buildings were Grade II listed but we engaged a local architect who was also a friend and set about a battle with the planners to create a dining room, conservatory, new kitchen with a double bedroom and bathroom over it with access areas. All this took well over a year to negotiate but eventually we were successful by submitting plans for 33 per cent more than we needed thus achieving what we wanted. I had promised Pamela £100,000 if I sold Maddox which I provided three times over and more in the construction of the above, plus an Astroturf tennis court which fitted perfectly in the old walled garden. We also had a huge party in the early summer of 1997 to celebrate the opening of the 'new' house. Pamela didn't have to let her house any more.

Next on the list was an occupation or project. In the summer of 1998 we had been invited to stay with Johnny Vestey and Judy Bathurst at Johnny's lovely house near Porto Ercole in Italy. They had never married but had been together for twenty-odd years, she having been previously married to Henry (Earl) Bathurst of Cirencester Park. We had a lot of fun playing tennis and going for day cruises in Johnny's very smart Sunseeker motor boat but for me what really got into my head was that one evening Johnny said he had heard that a car rally from London to Sydney was being organised to take place in millennium year 2000. The first such event had been in 1968 when my very dear and late lamented friend, Innes Ireland, had taken part and was in striking distance of winning when he broke down terminally in the Nullarbor Desert. I knew there and then that I had to do it. As soon as we were back in England I started making enquiries. Yes, it was on schedule for a start in early June 2000 to be run in two classes, the pros in cars first registered prior to 1980, to be crewed by professional works or private teams, and the second, called rather inappropriately the Touring Challenge, open to anybody and carrying no vehicle specification. The actual set course was the same for both classes but the special stages and times were tougher for the pro class. Also they had to carry all their own spares and were responsible for their own repairs and maintenance en route, whereas the Tourers could have service pit stops. Later in the summer we had a dinner party at The Old Hundred; among the guests were my old friend from army days, Peter Hornby, and his wife Prue. Peter, it may be remembered, was in the 17th/21st Lancers ski team with me in 1957 when I broke my leg. Late on in the evening and when he was well refreshed I told Peter about the proposed rally. 'I'm on,' he said. A couple of days later I rang him: 'I've been dreading your call,' he said, hoping that I had forgotten. It was the start of an enormous adventure which was about a year and a half in the planning. First, it was very expensive: our sizeable entry fee covered all accommodation en route – thirty-two days but not much else. The organisers were a company called Trans World Events headed by an Australian-based Englishman with a Lithuanian background called Nic Brittan. The event attracted a lot of publicity but minimal rewards except the excitement of taking part and, with any luck, finishing. It was not promoted as a charitable event but Peter and I decided that as we were going to do it anyway we wanted to make sure that our efforts would be of benefit to a charity and luckily we were at one as to which direction our thoughts lay: spinal injuries. My father had broken his neck in a racing fall and was paralysed or semi-paralysed for the rest of his life; both Peter and I knew many others similarly affected and our joint very good friend Bill Shand Kydd was a tetraplegic following a fall in a cross-country team 'chase after many years as an amateur jockey, Cresta and bob rider – in fact anything dangerous. So we called ourselves The Shand Kydd Team, made Bill our non-travelling Captain and went to see the International Spinal Injuries Research Trust. At first they were very suspicious of us, thinking that we were asking them for something. However, when they eventually woke up to the fact that all we wanted to do was to enlarge their coffers for research into cures for spinal injuries they quickly changed their tune. Peter and I got out not only our address books but any form of business or private connections that either of us had ever had, designed a letter with as much compressed detail that could be taken in without committing it to the waste paper basket and posted it.

Choosing and obtaining a suitable car was the all-important part of the enterprise. We would dearly have loved to have had an outrageous vintage car such as a 1930s Bentley but (a) we wanted to complete the rally and arrive in Sydney and (b) neither of us were anything other than very rudimentary mechanics so decided to go for a tough, reliable modern car with not too many miles on the clock. Here we were enormously helped by an old army friend of Hornby's, Gavin Thompson, who had himself competed and finished the 1968 run in a two-wheel-drive Land Rover. He found us a Subaru Outback four-wheel drive, manual transmission estate car with 16,000 miles on the clock. Perfect. Even better was that a rich City friend and colleague of Peter Hornby – or Horn as we usually called him – to whom he was telling of our proposed adventure, had a farm somewhere in New South Wales and said that he could do with a tough estate car on the farm so he sponsored us to the tune of the car if we would kindly drive it out there for him! Wow, what a stroke of luck, followed by another one: son Sam had a girlfriend who worked for the Australian airline Qantas. She got to work on her boss who agreed that if we displayed Qantas decals and large stickers on our car, which would have the large London–Sydney Marathon logo firmly fastened on the front end, Qantas would give us business class tickets for the homeward flight at the end of the rally. On the other side of the coin, I had been tipped off that Kellogg's were very generous in sponsoring worthy charitable causes so I sought out who to approach and arranged a meeting, which I thought went rather well until I received an enormous and heavy delivery of Kellogg's Nutrigrain with their compliments and instructions for us to distribute the bars of Nutrigrain to hungry passers-by en route to Australia. There wouldn't have been room for anything else in the car. We were also given a set of six tyres – we carried two spare wheels – by Michelin which, they said, were the tyres that they recommended for a distance rally of this nature but which turned out to be a mixed blessing. There were endless admin details to be completed, visas for some countries, a carnet – complicated forms to be presented on arrival and departure from all countries to prove that we had both brought in and taken out the car – health and car insurance and all sorts of other trivia but eventually all was sorted. The fund-raising for the charity had gone unbelievably and incredibly well; we had received and/or were promised amounts and covenants amounting to £250,000. Edward Gillespie, then Clerk of the Course at Cheltenham, had very kindly offered us a position for the car bedecked with all advertising in the paddock area of the racecourse for us to stand waving collection boxes, which raised a sizeable sum and a lot of flak from friends.

Quite early on in the planning, Horn's wife, Prue, had said that the rally was not for her and that we would have thrown her out of the car before we got to Dover; she might well have been right about this. Rather to my surprise, however, Pamela said that she did want to come and she certainly played her part as a member of the team. Nearer D(eparture) day, Subaru gave us a morning's mechanical course on the car given by the service manager at their depot in Cirencester and a free drive with instruction at their cross-country and obstacle course in the midlands. They also introduced us to a company called Prodrive, near Banbury, owned by a splendid man named Francis Tuthill who was competing in the professional class of the rally with Michelle Mouton, probably the greatest ever female rally driver, the winner of many major events and runner-up in the World Championship in 1982. Francis gave us the benefit not only of his own knowledge and experience but also recommended various important modifications for the car, for instance a titanium-steel plate fitted underneath to protect the oil sump, petrol tank and big end, modified carburettors and a special rally-designed Brantz remote trip recorder. He was preparing nine Porsche 911s for the rally including his own, some of them stripped right down to the bare shell of the car; he said that to prepare a professional rally car from scratch for an event such as this could cost up to £100,000. He gave us an introduction to a professional rally navigator, Pauline Gullick, a charming lady who gave us a series of lessons on how to read the Road Book on the route, about which a little more later, how to read the trip recorder, how to calculate average speeds using logarithms and all sorts of other tips which were invaluable. She advised us to be very strict about the amount of extra weight we had in the car: already we had two spare wheels, two more spare tyres, small five-litre portable fuel tanks (the maximum permitted), a good jack and other tools, first aid kits, water bottles etc. We restricted ourselves to one small suitcase no larger than an airline cabin bag and a small briefcase-type holdall each.

***

On Saturday, 29th April 2000 I was at The Old Hundred with some great friends who were staying for the weekend. In the late afternoon I received a telephone call from my former brother-in-law, David Stern, in Cheshire telling me that my daughter, Jemima, had been killed at an Event in Cheshire in which she was competing that afternoon. It was a terrible blow for me, for Zandra, her mother, and for all who knew and loved her. Her horse had fallen at a fence, she was crushed on impact and died instantly. Only two weeks beforehand she had announced her engagement and had brought Tom, her young man and husband-to-be, to meet me. The only consolation was that Jemima died doing what she loved most, suffered no pain and had no knowledge of what had happened. That afternoon I had been for a walk in the fields and had picked up a fledgling bird, a greenfinch I think, that had probably fallen out of its nest. It was alive so I brought it in, wrapped it in some cotton wool and it sipped at a little water. For some reason I had looked at my watch at the time I had picked it up. Later, after the news of Jemima's death, I had gone to look at my bird; it had disappeared. The time I had picked it up was 4.30, exactly the time of Jemima's fatal accident. The private family funeral and later

Thanksgiving Service for Jemima's life took place near the home of her mother and stepfather in Northamptonshire on 9th May. Over 500 of her friends, young and old, attended. I was hugely comforted and proud to have received hundreds of letters, all of which I answered. I was equally hugely proud of all Jemima's success and achievements during her lifetime. The unexpected sudden departure from life of someone so dear, so young and of one's own flesh and blood is overwhelming.

19

To Australia by Car – In a Hurry

On 2nd June 2000 all competitors in both classes assembled at one of those soulless hotels in the surroundings of London's Heathrow airport for a final vehicle inspection, briefing and departure dinner, the latter a very boring affair, made less so by a speech by the former chief executive of the Ford Motor Company. He alluded to the friction between Motor Rallying events and Formula 1 and related a story about a Formula 1 business meeting at the end of which the diminutive figure of Bernie Ecclestone emerged to a horde of fans waving autograph books, one of which accidentally struck Ecclestone's head, this being the first recorded incident of the fan hitting the shit.

Our alarm was set at 4.30 the next morning, 3rd June, for a photo call and interview with Annabel Heseltine who was writing a piece for the *Daily Mail* on us, the Shand Kydd Team, and Bill's notional participation, with emphasis on the funds that we were raising for spinal injuries research. By 7 a.m. we were lined up in the queue waiting our turn to drive up the ramp to the starting dais to be flagged off by Andrew Cowan, the winner of the inaugural event in 1968. A small crowd of well-wishers had gallantly turned up at that early hour including representatives of the ISRT, friends David and Jane Dollar, Nick and Vanessa Courtney, son Sam and Horn's wife and daughter.

The route took us through thirteen countries – England, France, Germany, Czech Republic, Austria, Hungary, Romania, Bulgaria, Greece, Turkey, Thailand, Malaysia and Australia.

Originally the route was to include Syria and Iran as far as Tehran, but at the last minute this section had to be cancelled due to political problems with the Iranians, with extended sections in Turkey substituted. The two air hops from Ankara to Chaing Mai and from Johor Bahru (Singapore) to Darwin were accomplished by two giant Antonov Russian freight planes. The planned route, which had to be followed by all competitors, was meticulously laid out in the Road Book, a sample page of which is shown overleaf and it was absolutely essential that it was followed totally accurately. In each diagram the black dot is the start of a manoeuvre and the arrow head the completion of same; in the left hand column is the distance in kilometres to the next black dot. The navigator held the remote trip setter in his hands and a click at each black dot immediately zeroed the trip on the driver's dashboard with the navigator calling the exact distance to be covered to the next manoeuvre and a description of it, i.e. turn right/left, bridge, hill crest, river crossing (!!) etc. The scratchings out in the illustration were done by me as I called out the instructions to the driver.

The rally was not a race but was highly competitive. The day's results, accumulative scores and positions were posted each evening together with the next day's individual starting times, usually between 6 and 7 a.m. Each day consisted of the total distance to be covered as stated in the Road Book, together with two special stages for which the rules were very different. Generally the time allowed for the day's journey was comfortably achievable unless anything went wrong such as a mechanical breakdown. Failure to reach the finish in time or to register having done so each day resulted in an automatic 100 penalty points. For the special stages, at the start it was 5,4,3,2,1 GO when a piece of paper with an average speed to be maintained throughout the stage was handed through the window of the car. The trouble was that the end of the stage was not known until one of the redshirted marshals was seen waving a flag

	Reg 32	Partacoona	Day	29	Page 11
	Reg 33	Kalabity	Recommended Time		4h 00m
Regularity 32	Partacoona		Touring	Distance	271.38 km
				Average	68 km/h

| Distance | | Direction | Information | Reverse Distance |
Total	Part			
3.23	0.58	(direction diagram) 7	!! CAUTION CREST THEN 60M TL	268.15
3.37	0.14	(direction diagram) 8	!!! CAUTION CREEK CROSSING	268.01
3.75	0.38	(direction diagram) 9	! CAUTION DIP THEN !! CAUTION ROUGH FOR 600M	267.63
4.35	0.60	(direction diagram) 10	!!! CAUTION DANGER CREST THEN DOWNHILL INTO RIVER CROSSING (D)	267.03
5.10	0.75	(direction diagram) 11	! CAUTION ROCKY FOR 1.5KM	266.28
7.04	1.94	(direction diagram) 12		264.34

on the road or track to signify the end. A stage could be 5 or up to 50 kilometres. This was where the combination of the trip recorder, speedometer and logarithmic tables came in. Horn, being a Wykehamist and therefore considered to be intelligent, was the automatic choice for this role with me as the navigator and Pamela the driver. At the end of the stage the scoring was one penalty point for every second either under or over the fixed average speed time. During the course of the stage Horn, deep in calculations with his slide rule, log tables and two stopwatches would call out whether we were running too fast or too slow. Taking into consideration the enormous variety of terrain on which the stages were run during the course of the entire rally this was a real and formidable challenge.

The first few days were relatively easy as we sped across Europe, apart from one huge blunder caused by our combined lack of experience and knowledge. During a pre-rally meeting we had determined that no personal blame was to be laid at any door for matters that would undoubtedly go wrong; it was going to be bad enough anyway for three self-willed people to be cooped up in a tin can for a month trying to keep our cool without shovelling blame around. There were bound to be times of extreme tension and possibly danger as well as, we hoped, a few lighter moments to make us laugh. And so it turned out. The first of the latter occurred about two hours before arriving in Ankara: knowing that we would have the best part of the day off after arrival I had contacted, before we left, the main Subaru agent there to arrange for the car to be checked over and serviced so, with Horn driving, I called the number on the telephone saying who we were and what we wanted. A man speaking English answered, saying 'I'm very busy. Please call later.' Plonk: the line went dead. Thirty minutes later I tried again. The same man answered saying, 'I am so very sorry to have cut you short before. You see, I am the Subaru agent in Ankara but I'm also a dentist and when you called I was in the middle of a difficult extraction for which I needed both hands with my patient under general anaesthetic.' Completely charming. An hour or so later, having found the garage, the car was up on a ramp with six mechanics giving it a very thorough service, taking well over an hour with our new best friend refusing to take any payment. This little story has a sequel: later that evening, having our first really good square meal since leaving England, Horn broke a tooth gnawing on a bone; so guess where he was at six a.m. the next morning? In the dentist's chair having his tooth fixed before we were on our way again. The scenery along the mountain roads and tracks in Turkey was indescribably beautiful but also presented a few hazards, such as rounding the umpteenth hairpin not far from Sparta to be faced by the absence of the road, due to the side of the mountain having fallen into the valley below. Moments like these required every second of the time allowed to arrive at the next control point without incurring penalties. It was in Turkey, too, that we experienced the first Michelin problem: proceeding at speed along a gravelled road, the car developed a sudden very severe juddering. Stopping, one of the rear tyres had sprouted a boil the size of a polo ball; we just changed the wheel and, at the time, put it down to a rough road, bad luck and went on our way.

Arrival in Chaing Mai from Ankara was at 5 a.m. to be greeted by a bevy of pretty, scantily clad young ladies who draped huge garlands of flowers round our necks to the sound of a band playing while we were ushered somewhat sleepily under an enormous arch decorated by a banner with the words in blue and gold THAILAND WELCOMES THE LONDON–SYDNEY RALLY. What also hit us was, after the lovely dry sun of Turkey, the oppressive and intense heat and humidity even at that time of the morning. It was monsoon time. We spent the rest of the day giving the car some much needed TLC and a wash and brush up. Early the next morning we were off again, the first stop being a place called Phetchabun, pronounced Fetch Your Bum.

For several days we drove due south through Thailand taking

in the infamous River Kwai bridge – very different from the one portrayed in the movie *Bridge over the River Kwai*, as is the factual story for that matter. Then, along the narrow, rather boring stretch which divides Thailand and Burma, into Malaysia, up into the Cameron Highlands before eventually arriving at Johor Bahru, just north of Singapore. Reading the Road Book correctly and accurately became even more vital. Most of the time we were on minor roads or tracks with no sign posts – not that we could have understood them if there had been any. During one special stage on jungle tracks there was a severe verbal altercation between navigator (me) and driver (Pamela) which went something like this:

Me: 'At fork in front go left.'

Pamela: 'All vehicle tracks go right. Left track unused.'

Me (screaming): 'Go LEFT!'

Horn, head down on his slide rule: 'You're three seconds slow.'

Pamela: 'Doesn't fucking matter; we're going the wrong way.'

Me: 'In point eight of a kilometre you'll come to a right bend and a narrow bridge over a stream.'

Spot on the point eight we did. We discovered later that several of the others fell into the trap and had turned right, so at least we scored on that one.

The most dangerous and indeed near-fatal incident on this leg of the rally happened to two crews in the pro class. Their rules for the special stages were different from ours in that they were based on pure speed, although the actual course was the same. It happened on a special stage through a palm oil plantation in Malaysia; the brothers Rex and Gary Leeson in their Ford Falcon had gone off the track after taking a corner and somersaulted into a deep monsoon culvert, ending upside down and submerged in water. They managed to extricate themselves and were standing on the bank bemoaning their fate when they saw, to their horror, another car also upside down underneath their own car and with the crew trapped inside. It was the Porsche of Stanley Illman and

Frans Strangl. They stopped the next car coming, the occupants of which raised the alarm on their telephone. Heavy lifting gear was rushed to the scene and both cars lifted out of the water. Illman and Strangl had seen bubbles rising from their pedal area – upside down remember – so discovered an air pocket which had just kept them alive until rescue came but they would certainly have died had not the Leeson car made the same mistake as they did. I saw both cars later with remarkably little damage. As it was right at the end of the SE Asia leg they had the whole of the next day to dry out the Falcon before it was put on the Antanov for the flight to Darwin so they continued in the rally. The Porsche of Illman and Strangl was not so lucky.

During the course of the rally so far we formed very agreeable friendships with many of the other crews, a high level of camaraderie having developed between us all. We helped and were helped when in distress. Johnny Vestey of course we knew; he had his attractive and great fun daughter, Torna, with him, his new wife Christl, an Austrian lady plus an old Australian friend, Henry Crouch. Several times we met up for dinner at the end of a hard day's driving. On one occasion, somewhere in southern Thailand and at a most inferior restaurant (but the best available) poor Christl had loaded a lump of food onto her fork and was in the act of transferring it to her mouth when the largest cockroach I have ever seen alighted on it. Her scream was enough to disturb the cockroach which fled in the direction of the kitchen from whence it came. Another team which we had got to know well and liked very much were four Australians, all old friends of each other, calling themselves the Seriously Driven Men. They had the same attitude to the rally as we had: to be as competitive as possible but to have as much fun as possible as well. One of them, Tim Cecil, was, believe it or not, a distant cousin of Henry Cecil's. We saw a lot of them.

The arrival in Darwin was very different to that in Chaing Mai. This time at 1 o'clock in the morning to some very grumpy

Australian immigration officials clearly not pleased about having been kept up late by a charter plane. Johnny Vestey had a half-hour argument with one of them who insisted that there was no record of him having left Australia after his last visit, thirty years beforehand. All the cars were impounded for a cleanliness and health inspection even though we had spent the whole of the previous day cleaning them with high pressure hoses while mounted on ramps, had stripped the interior down to the extent of removing all carpets, seat cushions, in fact everything that could possibly be removed to be cleaned and disinfected having been warned that the Australians would be difficult. We were put in buses, ours driven at no more than 20 mph all the way into Darwin by a man intent on giving us the entire history of the town since the arrival of Captain Cook – a history which could have been told in 2½ minutes it was so boring – while all we wanted to do was go to sleep in as comfortable a bed as Darwin could provide which, correctly, we did not over-estimate. Leaving the other two to a bit more sleep, at 9 a.m. I was back at the airport to collect the car having had the misfortune of taking the same bus with the crawling amateur historian so was forced to listen to the Darwin story all over again. At the airport, the cars were all lined up and as I approached the Subaru a youth who had been lurking nearby came up to me and without even a G'Day said: 'Is this your car?'

'Yes,' I replied.

'This is the dirtiest car I have ever seen, mate.'

I refrained from telling him that, should I wish to choose a mate, it was unlikely to be him but said, 'Well, we have come rather a long way and did spend all yesterday very thoroughly cleaning it.'

'I don't care where you've come from and your idea of cleaning is very different from mine. Go inside, get it cleaned or it stays here,' he said, slapping a sticker saying FAILED on the wind-screen. Welcome to Australia and have a nice day; it reminded me of Sgt Gubbins and Cpl Perryman at Catterick in my National Service days. 'Inside' was a corrugated shed with a few chairs and a fellow behind a desk who relieved me of the equivalent of £25 telling me to come back in two hours. When I did so the car looked exactly the same except that the FAILED sticker had been removed.

That evening we were given an official reception by the Government of the Northern Territory hosted by the Minister for Sport and Recreation in Parliament House, for which the dress on the invitation was 'Territory Rig'. On enquiry all men had to do was find a tie from somewhere; ladies: Day Dress, After Five. Simple. I had a conversation with Jenny Brittan, wife of the rally organiser Nic Brittan. She was lying in third place in the pro section as co-driver to Rick Bates, a well-known and successful driver. About her husband, she said they had been married for thirty-three years and expected to remain so as long as she didn't have to go anywhere with him in a motor car.

Before dawn the next morning we were on our way into Australia proper, the land of the outback and wide open spaces, for the longest single day's distance so far of 725 miles, including the normal two special stages. The recently finished rainy season had been one of the worst on record and had left untold damage, particularly to minor roads and river banks. In the whole Australian leg we were to cover 1,500 miles of dirt and/ or gravel roads and tracks. In addition and indeed for much of this day we were on the main highway with sustained periods of high speed, the main dangers being the famous road trains and the kangaroos. The drivers of the road trains take no prisoners; they are up to 120 feet long, incredibly powerful and travel very fast, there being no speed limits in the Northern Territory. It is only a two-lane highway so one has to be pretty sure of one's ground when overtaking these monsters of the road. At that time there was no railway connection from southern Australia north of Alice Springs (the completion of the line from Adelaide to

Darwin was in 2004). Michelin had told us that our tyres were suitable for sustained speeds of up to 110 mph, which speed we very rarely exceeded, but ran into serious trouble with three more bursts or near bursts similar to the one in Turkey, so by the time we eventually arrived at Tennant Creek, not much more than an agricultural depot and staging post for machinery, we had no more spare wheels or tyres. Directed to a garage, the owner stayed open waiting for our arrival at about 8 p.m. and fitted a complete set of five Dunlop heavy-duty tyres, ditching the remains of the Michelins. Although we had three more punctures during the rest of the rally and some very serious stuff to come, at least they were only punctures, which could be repaired. The other hazard, kangaroos, were a menace and dangerous at that, particularly in the dark. They seemed to lurk in the bush close to the road, frequently in pairs, wait until you were close and then dart across the road. Hitting a large kangaroo at speed can be curtains not just for the 'roo but for the car as well. We had one very narrow squeak when, with Horn driving, a huge beast leapt out in front of us; how he managed to miss it was miraculous.

Our routine, when driving for long distances in between the special stages, was two hours driving, two hours navigating and two hours resting, which was how we proceeded on the Stuart Highway to Alice Springs, just south of the Tropic of Capricorn and probably the most important town in central Australia, with traces of indigenous Aboriginal inhabitants going back more than 30,000 years. In fact until the Second World War hardly any white families lived there. It still has a high percentage of Aboriginals and a bad crime record, again mainly inter-Abo drink-related conflicts. During the Second World War, Alice became an important army base and major air fuel storage area. When Darwin was bombed by the Japanese, Alice became the de facto capital of the Northern Territory with army personnel and military equipment relocating there.

We had been warned that the going would get tougher in

Australia and so it turned out with two gruelling specials close to Alice Springs. The first was bad enough, but before the second we were informed that there had been so much grief in the pro ranks at this stage that it had been decided to make it voluntary with no penalty points deducted for those who ducked out. Bill Shand Kydd never ducked out of anything and neither did we; it was speed only at this stage so no average speed tables needed. I was appointed driver with Horn navigating. Twenty-two kilometres of really tough stuff lay ahead of us over crests on the track that left us with daylight under all four wheels, up and down rocky inclines which made the shocks work like never before, across a dozen river beds, most of them dry with sand so deep that we planed across using our titanium-steel plate as a surf board. At one point we seemed completely submerged in sand but our momentum just carried us through until the wheels could grip enough to carry us up the bank on the other side. Full marks to the Subaru; we overtook the two cars that had started at minute intervals in front of us and finished in a very fast time which moved us up a few places on the leader board, emerging with nothing worse than a cracked front bumper and a few bruises both in and out of the car!

Now, we had a quandary: here we were, slap in the middle of Australia and, by Australian standards, pretty close to Ayers Rock, 263 miles from Alice Springs, one of the 'must see' sites in Australia. But it was not on the rally route so what to do? The actual detour route we would have to take to get back on the route proper was about 350 miles. The rally road marshals and officials were very efficient, good natured and we got on well with them all; but they had a job to do and the rally was a competition with winners and losers. We formed up to one of them that we liked particularly and explained our problem, that we wanted to go to Ayers Rock, never having done so and probably would never have the chance again. After a lot of whee-dling and cajoling he said 'Right, as long as I have your rally passport in my hands by the scheduled time of arrival so that I can stamp it, I won't look at who is giving it to me.' Our new friends, The Seriously Driven Men, were the automatic choice to be entrusted with our rally passport and they kindly agreed to do this for us; they were, after all, Australian with Ayers Rock being the equivalent to Stonehenge to them.

Ayers Rock or, to give it the original Aborigine name, Uluru, is a gigantic sandstone monolith standing 1,140 feet high in semi-desert surroundings with a circumference of just under six miles. Like an iceberg, two thirds of the rock lies under the earth's surface. There is nothing similar in the area, so there it is like a whale beached on a vast expanse of shoreline. Geologists have found traces of human habitation here dating back well over 10,000 years; even now the area is the spiritual centre of the Aboriginal people who regard the Rock as sacred. Climbing on the Rock, although not illegal, is very frowned upon and only very recently the National Park board has announced that climbing on the Rock will be banned from October 2019. The area has extremes of climate from in excess of 100 degrees Fahrenheit in the summer to below freezing in winter; vegetation is sparse on the sandy soil with low bush and spindly trees; the wood from two species, the mulga and centralian bloodwood, is used for making boomerangs, a good source of income for the Abos. To call this huge pimple on the earth's surface dramatic is a gross understatement; during the day it goes through various changes of colour depending on the angle of the sun, the deep but vivid red at dawn and sunset being the most spectacular, so we were lucky as the sun was going down out of a clear unbroken blue sky as we approached, having driven from Alice Springs. What a sight it was; we completed a slow lap all the way round before heading off in a south easterly direction to join up with the rally route and to our next overnight stop at Coober Pedy, arriving late at night. We covered 856 miles that day, the longest of the rally. The SDMs had done their job so we suffered no penalty points for being late; here again we were lucky but in a different way. Coober Pedy, a drab, uninteresting town with summer temperatures reaching 117 degrees F, is important for one reason: opal. Opal was first found in Coober Pedy in 1915 and it has now the largest opal field in the world. Lucky? Yes, all the shops were closed when we arrived and not open by our start time of 06.40 the next morning.

Having covered about forty miles out of Coober Pedy, with Horn driving along a gravelled road, I was flicking in advance through the Road Book: 'Horn, how are we off for fuel?' I asked.

Horn: 'Oh, we're fine; just under a quarter of a tank.'

Me: 'The next fuel station is 190 miles ahead.'

'Shit,' said Horn.

'Shit,' said Pamela.

Eruptions; we knew two things: to turn back would incur 100 penalty points and there was no way we could drive 190 miles on quarter of a tank. A big row resulted in a vote on what to do. Two (Horn and I) said continue, one said go back. 'You're both fucking mad and I wish I'd never come,' said the third member. We went on very slowly with streams of other rally cars overtaking us. Then I noticed something else in the Road Book. In about eighty-five miles we would come to what seemed no more than a track crossing with a pub, called William Creek; but there was a strange warning sign in the book which said 'Beware of aeroplanes parked in the road.' Aeroplanes need fuel. Could it be that the pub had a petrol pump? For the last twenty miles to William Creek the fuel needle was firm on empty but at last there was the pub and two parked planes, the road having doubled up as a runway. To our almighty relief a hand-operated fuel pump with a hose was fixed to the pub wall. It is worth saying that the pub was the first building we had seen since leaving Coober Pedy 115 miles earlier. In our euphoria of the previous day and having written our website report we were very tired and had forgotten to do our homework for the next day

– like checking the fuel gauge. Two stages in the afternoon in the Flinders mountain range were more notable for the beautiful rocky scenery, passing through Brachina Gorge lined with enormous eucalyptus trees, rather than degrees of difficulty. On our way now to Port Augusta, our stopping place that night. At 31 degrees south and on 1st July it was decidedly cold; since leaving Darwin four days earlier we had driven 2,366 miles, plus our Ayers Rock detour of 350 miles and through 20 degrees of latitude. Now it was left turn to Sydney but still three days and another 1,433 miles to go. Two special stages between Port Augusta and our next stop, Broken Hill, included the toughest of the lot. Arriving at the start point in good time, I wandered off to a clump of trees for a pee and couldn't believe what I saw beyond the trees and over the brow of a hill: a raging river. No more dried-up river beds down there. Going back to the others I warned that we had trouble ahead. Five, four, three, two, one, GO at 48 kph average speed. Round a corner, down a bank and we were in the river. 'Keep the revs up' I yelled. We bounced, the water was in the car through the door seals but we were through and up the bank the other side.

'Point 3, sharp right followed by ridge and deep drop on right.'

'Seven seconds slow,' from Horn, head down in speed tables.

'Loose rock and steep downhill.'

Through two more rivers then 'over crest, steep decline right and river.'

'Bloody hell' from all in unison. The decline was near vertical, the river was fast running and the deepest yet. We were thrown right and left, water splashing everywhere, spares and kit all over the place, the car taking an almighty hammering but suddenly we were out. From the corner of my eye I saw what looked like a Ford half submerged being carried away downstream. 'The trip meter's buggered' from Horn; 'No speedometer or rev counter,' from Pamela. All electrics failed so navigating was pure guesswork, trying to follow the Road Book and estimating the distances. No more rivers but fiendish blind hairpins, deep holes and boulders to be avoided, sheer drops on one side or the other. Ten minutes later, a shout from Horn: 'Trips back on'; 'So is rev counter and speedo.' I picked up a landmark: 'We're OK.' We saw other crews standing by broken-down cars. Then, at last, the finishing flag, with the holder springing out of nowhere, after 55 minutes and 1 second. And it was still only a quarter past nine in the morning. There was grief with crews all round examining the damage to their cars: our front bumper was completely shattered and we had a flat tyre that we hadn't even noticed, but it must have happened close to the finish. However, we were lucky compared to some of the others. The Ford that I had seen floating away was that of the former world rally champion Hannu Mikkola. Miraculously it was retrieved and limped the last two days of the rally but well down the field. The adrenalin flowed as never since my riding days.

There was no time for commiseration or sympathy for others. A quick wheel change before a 170-mile dash to the next stage over rough country, with a time limit of four hours, and then another four hours to Broken Hill, the night's stop, and not high on the return visit list. Isolated in the far west of the New South Wales outback, it is the oldest mining town in Australia with huge deposits of silver, lead and zinc which have been mined since 1844. Enough said. Wagga Wagga was next, a mere 533 miles away including the statutory two special stages, crossing One Tree Plain; actually we saw three trees in ninety-five miles. Nothing else and certainly no human beings. Nearing Wagga Wagga, suddenly it all changed; gone was the desert and in its place cultivated farmland, green and lush with gently flowing rivers and lakes, with cattle grazing in the fields, small agricultural-based towns and, in Wagga Wagga itself, sympathetic architecture, well-laid-out parks and flower beds, tree-lined avenues and a welcoming, friendly atmosphere. I had always wanted to come here and see the racecourse where my dear friend and brilliant

Australian jockey, Scobie Breasley, learnt his trade; he told me that it made Chester racecourse seem like a gentle, wide-open track. Sadly there was no time for this; we were only two days from Sydney and a lot of admin, trip resetting and calibrating to be done on our navigation instruments plus some service work on the car.

The distance between Wagga Wagga and Canberra – our last overnight stop before Sydney – is only about a hundred miles but that would have been too easy so we were directed up into the Brindabellas, a mountain range with peaks up to a little over 6,000 feet about fifty miles to the east of Canberra. It was mid-winter so after three and a half weeks of hot sunshine we were slopping and sliding round hairpin bends on a gravel surface through first rain and then serious snow as we climbed higher and higher during a very difficult stage, both from the navigational and driving points of view, ever mindful that Sydney really was, as it seemed, just round the corner. We were overjoyed not only to arrive later in Canberra but to learn that evening on the rally notice board that we had scored zero penalty points for the above stage; in other words we were spot on the exact time specified. We were, therefore, the leaders of the day.

Canberra, the capital of Australia, is a comparatively modern city, built from scratch and officially opened by the future King George VI in 1927. During our very brief stay we found it rather dull and soulless but we had a very jolly and end-of-termish dinner with our friends the SDMs in a restaurant known to them. Day 32 of the rally dawned grey and drizzly as we set off for one more stage in the Brindabellas before the last straightforward 190-mile dash to Sydney for our last control point and assembling area at Homebush Park, the site of the 2000 Olympic Games due to take place a couple of months later. There was an overwhelming sense of joy, happiness, relief and achievement with everybody going around hugging, congratulating, swapping stories and commiserating. The pro section was won by the former World

Champion Stig Blomqvist and Ben Rainsford, with our friend Francis Tuthill and Michelle Mouton second and Rick Bates with Nic Brittan's wife Jenny finishing third. Seventy-seven out of ninety starters completed. In our amateur section, the winners were a father and son combination of Stefan and Dirk Schneider from Germany, who had led from start to finish and were very experienced rally competitors; of the twenty-four out of twenty-nine starters to finish we came 11th with 362 penalty points. Considering that one point equals one second, we were only 6.03 minutes wrong over a total rally distance of approximately 10,500 miles. If we hadn't made a catastrophic mistake on Day 2, which cost us 96 penalty points, we would have finished in the first half dozen. There were many hard luck stories but one of the most unlucky concerned a Mexican lawyer named Hector Calatayud who we had got to know quite well and who had brought his car all the way from Mexico. All was going fine for him until the border crossing from Romania to Bulgaria, by means of a very grimy ferry across the river Danube. On arriving on the Bulgarian side poor Hector was told that his visa issued in Mexico City was not in order; he was not allowed in and told to go back to Romania on the return ferry. Arriving back on the other side he was told, 'Sorry chum, you can't come in to Romania because your visa was for single entry only and you've already been here so … back to Bulgaria you go.' The poor chap could see the rest of his life panning out going backwards and forwards on this filthy ferry. Eventually it was half sorted by a telephone call to an influential contact in Mexico, but he still wasn't allowed into Bulgaria and by a very roundabout route managed to get to Istanbul and caught up with us several days later. Officially he was placed last with 2,581 penalty points.

The rally competition might have been over but there was still the official finish at Sydney Opera House. For this all the cars, in order of finishing, were given a police escort and a 'green corridor' from Homebush Park to the Opera House. It was a complete shambles; the police escort, if there ever was one, disappeared, the Road Book finished at Homebush Park so we had no directions to follow and it was a mad rush ignoring red traffic lights and any other obstructions to keep tabs on the line of rally cars in front of us. We hadn't come halfway round the world to get lost in the final furlong. Approaching the Opera House the crowds on the streets got larger and larger, shouting and waving Union Jacks and flags of other nationalities; the entrance to the Opera House was jammed solid with people, leaving only a narrow corridor for the cars to proceed. Suddenly a young man dashed out of the crowd towards us waving a bottle of champagne: it was Horn's son Will who was living and working in Hong Kong but had flown down specially, and without his father's knowledge, to greet him. All very moving. As we passed the actual finishing dais each car and crew member was announced over the tannoy and presentation mementos were handed to each of them. Then it was off to the Westin Hotel where we climbed out of the Subaru for the last time. It seems soppy and sentimental but I think we all shed a tear to say goodbye to this hunk of machinery that had performed so brilliantly and brought us all the way across the world through innumerable adventures safely. I hope she had a honourable retirement trundling round the farm of her owner in New South Wales, who had so generously sponsored us, so helping to raise such a sizeable sum for research into spinal injuries.

That evening there was a farewell dinner and prize-giving at the Westin Hotel with speeches from all and sundry. Frankly it was a bit of an anti-climax after all the excitement of not only that day but also the previous thirty-one. Rather more fun was a cruise the next day starting from the Opera House, round the harbour, under the famous bridge and as far as the Anzac bridge with champagne, wine and lunch provided by the Australian Radio station 2UE. So that was finally that; it was to take a while to come down off an immense high with so many memories.

Now, nearly nineteen years later, it seems like yesterday. As soon as I returned to England I set about writing a short book about the whole experience based on the notes and statistics I had scribbled down as we were going along. I called it *East into the Sun,* as we always seemed to have the sun in our eyes on our early morning starts going east.

I had known Peter Hornby since I was nineteen; he had been a friend ever since but the rally and all that went with it provided a tremendous bond and made us very close friends for the rest of his life. He and his wife Prue were fairly near neighbours in Gloucestershire and we had some lovely holidays together in the South of France where he had a house and a very smart ocean-going speedboat. However, the dreaded cancer got him in the end and he died in 2012. A true friend who I miss very much.

2 0

From Here To There

Nearly all of the twelve months leading up to the rally departure date of 3rd June had been taken up with the massive
amount of preparation work and fund-raising, plus the family
tragedy of Jemima's death. But now, in mid-July, it was all over
and time to re-group and look ahead. It was millennium year,
never mind the mathematicians and computer plutocrats who
insisted that the new millennium didn't start until 1st January
2001. Astonishingly the dreaded euro only came into being that
year when twelve out of the then fifteen members of the EU
voted to adopt the euro as their universal currency; apart from
ourselves the other two counties deciding to keep their existing
currencies were Sweden and Denmark. Partly fuelled by the
excitement and experience gained in the rally, I looked to travel
planning and organising as a natural next step as a business.

Wearing different hats I had been lucky to travel extensively
in my industrial, racehorse training and Caribbean days, so hit
on the idea that people might be interested in going to some of
the countries and places that I had been fortunate enough to
visit but who would need advice, help and detailed planning to
make the best of their visits. While I was still living in Barbados,
and subsequently in the late 90s, I had arranged holidays with
friends to other Caribbean islands, Argentina, Chile, Peru,
Central America, South East Asia and Southern Africa. In doing
so I had acquired quite a lot of detailed knowledge and had met
on-the-spot ground agents as we went along. Why not make this

pleasurable occupation a business?

I had been introduced by my good friends Nicholas and Vanessa Courtney to Robin Hanbury-Tenison, the well-known travel writer and explorer. Nick himself is the author of many books, mainly biographical, including of members of the Royal Family, and on subjects as diverse as *The Queen's Stamps* and *Gale Force 10,* the life of Admiral Beaufort, inventor of the Beaufort Scale. As a young man he was Colin Tennant's (later Lord Glenconner) first manager on the island of Mustique where Princess Margaret was a regular guest; Nick later wrote Glenconner's biography *Lord of the Isle.* His wife Vanessa worked for a long time for the BBC and was the principal researcher for Michael Palin's television travel programmes. They live in a lovely house in Kempson Road, Fulham, known as 'The Kempson', due to the number of friends, myself included, who often cadge a bed when staying in London. They also have a holiday house in Trebetherick, Cornwall given to Vanessa by her father, hence them knowing Robin Hanbury-Tenison and his wife Louella who live on Bodmin Moor. Robin was the first Chairman of the Countryside Alliance. He told me that he was planning a small expedition to Niger, more specifically to the Air Mountain range in the Tenere section of the Sahara Desert, and asked if I would like to come.

Niger was the largest in a group of North African countries, including Algeria, Tunisia, Morocco, Chad and Mali, that by a series of treaties came under direct or indirect French rule from around 1830 until the break-up started soon after the Second World War, Niger becoming finally independent in 1960. However, many left-over French traditions remain, with French being the official language, although tribes have their own language with many different dialects. I learnt a great deal. For much of the time our small team were on our own, riding camels with a guide, Mohammed Ixa, plus a cook and two helpers, carrying our own food and water in the desert, passing over 500-foot dunes which constantly move with the wind and therefore cannot be guaranteed as landmarks, interspersed with the occasional oasis, the range of high mountains standing stark and black against the sky, all vestiges of sand, earth or plant life having long ago been blown away by the wind. And no other people; except one day a lone figure came from being a spot on the summit of a dune to materialising into a Tuareg riding a camel. He and Mohammed greeted each other enthusiastically and had a long chat before he went on his way. 'Où va il?' I asked, where's he going? 'D'ici là,' Mohammed replied, with a shrug, 'From Here To There.' I was looking for a name for my proposed travel business and there it was. Perfect.

Robin knew I was planning to start a small travel business of my own and kindly said that I would not be treading on his toes if I brought clients to Niger, so some months later I did just that with a party of eight, which included Peter and Prue Hornby. The policy of the business, which I have adhered to throughout, is that no party shall number more than ten participants and that they should be friends or friends of friends. In this way the numbers are manageable and participants are kindred spirits; therefore friction is unlikely.

Niger is the largest country in West Africa but, by nature of the terrain, sparsely populated. It is difficult to take in that 10,000 years ago what is now the Sahara Desert was a huge agricultural plain dotted with mountain ranges. Niamey, the capital of Niger, lies to the very south of the country on the river Niger. From there a day's drive took us to Agadez from where we launched into the desert proper before saying goodbye to all mechanised transport and linking up with our camels. We had the same Tuareg guide, Mohammed and camp crew; as before we started at sunrise and kept going, with a few breaks during the day, until about 4.30 in the afternoon. Where we stopped we slept by unrolling a mattress and bedding down on it. No tents were needed; usually, if the crew managed to find enough brushwood, a fire was lit for cooking. The vastness of the desert, the majesty of the immense dunes, the black starkness of the mountains and the unbelievable stillness only broken, while on the move, by the swishing noise made by the camels as they walked through the sand, were the dominating features of the journey. We seemed to be moving so slowly until, looking down from a camel, anybody walking was struggling to keep up.

The Tuaregs are a nomadic Muslim Berber tribe, very proud and dominating over others, so tended to be the ruling tribe of the Sahara, where most countries were under French control until 1958. There followed in Niger a succession of revolts and uprisings from which the nomadic Tuaregs suffered severe loss of power. Our camel trail ended at the small desert town of Iferouane, really not much more than a collection of single-storey mud houses, a store and guest house. Here, our transport back to Niamey was waiting. Civilisation, as we knew it, was a world away.

***

That was the start. Since the beginning of the century, under the From Here to There banner, we have taken trips to thirty-five individual countries and to areas as wide apart as Eastern Siberia and the southern tip of South America, and in all continents of the world. It is difficult to single out any of them but I'll mention a couple, as a bit of an adventurer and very amateur historian. One was following as far as possible the journey and physical deprivations and hardships experienced by the group of Russian aristocratic noblemen who plotted to overthrow Czar Nicholas I in 1825, in what is known as the Decembrist Uprising. On Boxing Day 1825 the rebels were defeated in St Peter's Square, St Petersburg; after a summary trial the five main ringleaders were executed by hanging a week later, but 120 others were exiled to Siberia for life and were declared 'non persons'. Enter a romantic twist: one of the foremost of the 120, a high ranking aristocratic army officer, Prince Sergei Volkonsky, had been married for less than a year to the daughter, Maria, of one of the Czar's senior generals, Nikolai Raevski. She formed up to the Czar and insisted that she would follow her husband into exile. At first the Czar refused permission but one year later she set out on an incredible journey of 4,000 miles taking many months, virtually alone. Her story is beautifully told in a book, *The Princess of Siberia* by Christine Sutherland. We, however, took a small party by air from St Petersburg to Irkutsk and then overland for several days the rest of the way, nearly as far as the border with China to where the Decembrists had been incarcerated. This included crossing the frozen Lake Baikal on a horse-drawn sleigh with the sun shining out of a cloudless sky at a temperature of minus 20 degrees centigrade, a distance of twenty-six miles taking exactly the same route as Maria Volkonsky had taken 188 years previously.

The other historically themed trip was much more modern. Again a small party, this time overland from Mandalay, Burma north-westerly to Tamu, the border of Burma and the Indian state of Manipur, on to Imphal and then on the road to Kohima in Nagaland. The siege of Imphal and the battle of Kohima – known as the battle of the tennis court for reasons which follow – were two hugely important military engagements that had a direct influence on the outcome of the Second World War. The Japanese had driven the Allies out of Burma in 1942 but the Allies' counter-attack by the 14th Army under the command of General William (Bill) Slim in 1944 was one of the major turning points in the war. Slim realised that the Japanese believed that penetration into India via the Burmese eastern border into the Indian states of Manipur and Nagaland would leave the whole of India ready for the taking so he directed his troops to hold that area at all costs. The siege of Imphal and battle of Kohima, fought in appalling mountainous and tropical monsoon conditions against a force numerically far superior, was one act of heroism after another. At Kohima the main battle lasted from 4th April to 22nd June, with hand-to-hand fighting for two solid weeks taking place on and around the tennis court of the then Deputy High Commissioner, Charles Pawsey. Japanese casualties during the campaign amounted to 55,000 men, with the Allies losing 17,000. It is here, next to the tennis court and by the side of the military cemetery with individual crosses with the name, rank and regiment of all who died, that a Memorial is erected with the inscription: WHEN YOU GO HOME, TELL THEM OF US AND SAY FOR YOUR TOMORROW WE GAVE OUR TODAY.

The South American continent has been a very happy hunting ground for us and, by all accounts, those who have come with us. The temptation here is to try to take in too much in one trip; the distances are so vast. Brazil, for instance, covers a larger area than the whole of the United States with enormous differences in scenery, culture, ways of life and climate. Peru, a great favourite, again with great variety; from the Loreto region in the north with its capital Iquitos, the centre of the Amazon Basin covering a vast area of jungle, fantastic bird and aquatic life, the source of the Amazon, very sparsely populated with remote villages in the depth of the jungle only approachable via tiny tributaries of the great river, some of which lead into hundred-acre-plus lagoons teeming with pink dolphins. Further south and high in the Andes, vivid reminders of the Inca civilisation, Machu Picchu and the rest, the Colca Canyon, deepest and most dramatic in the world with condors nesting in the walls of the canyon, Lake Titicaca, the highest navigable lake in the world, more an inland sea than a lake, with so much more. Really a must for any would-be traveller. Chile, long and thin from the amazing Atacama Desert in the north to Chilean Patagonia in the south with a beautiful and dramatic Lake District halfway between the two. Patagonia, not a country but a huge area partly in Argentina and partly in Chile, at the southern end of the Andes mountain chain which, under different names, stretches from Cape Horn northwards into Canada where it is known as the Rockies. The only 'break' is the man-made Panama Canal. Argentinian Patagonia is fabulous, eerie and beautiful; wide open spaces, fantastic mountains, a micro climate in the far south with lovely trees and vegetation at 55 degrees south, 20 degrees further south than Cape Town, the phenomenal Perito Moreno Glacier, a mile wide with ice cliffs 250 feet high moving slowly forward before huge blocks of ice crash with a noise to be heard five miles away into Lago Argentino, emerging a minute later as icebergs floating downriver and emptying into the Atlantic Ocean near Rio Gallegos some 300 miles away.

In the mid-1860s a small group of Welsh settlers arrived in mid-Patagonia as an escape from what they saw as deteriorating situations in Wales. To begin with it was by no means plain sailing, but twenty-five years or so later they were awarded citizenship by the Argentinian government and have been there ever since, even sending over choirs to Eisteddfods 'back home'. Buenos Aires is one of my favourite cities in the world, perhaps indeed at the pinnacle. It has everything: a lovely atmosphere, beautiful architecture and buildings, a most hospitable climate, great culture and music with wide streets and boulevards interspersed with lovely little squares with gardens and statues of heroes. From some way south and well to the north of Buenos Aires you are in horse and cattle country – a lot of it stretching over many horizons where farming and ranching is the order of the day. To the very north Iguacu Falls, shared with Brazil, is a wonder of the world rivalling anything anywhere. Leave it out or die. In all the many times I have been to Argentina I have never had one word spoken to me antagonistically regarding the Falklands. The Central American countries, too, have tremendous cultural, historical and scenic value. The ones I know best are Mexico, Guatemala and Belize, and the latter two can be combined into one fabulous trip.

This is not meant to be a travelogue but I cannot leave the

subject without giving a quick rundown on some of the wonderful and exciting times we have had in the South East Asian countries of Thailand, Burma, Vietnam, Laos, Malaysia and Cambodia; all different in their own ways and all with points of interest guaranteed to warrant a visit on their own. In incredible India, a sub-continent on its own, there are many areas that we have not touched but Delhi, Rajasthan, the Madhya Pradesh, Nagaland, Kerala and the Calcutta area of West Bengal leave lasting memories crying out for return, as do exploits into Bhutan and Nepal. I have referred previously to the African continent but in addition to those countries mentioned, Namibia, Botswana and areas of RSA such as KwaZulu-Natal and the Cape are special and should never be left out. I do have an underlying sadness about the whole of South Africa; here is a gigantic part of the world's surface that has everything that anybody needs – excepting, you might say, oil – but has always been an area of conflict. Having always been deeply interested in the history for several different reasons – my first ocean voyage was a three-week one from Southampton to Cape Town – I firmly believe that we did a better job in attempting to govern and develop South Africa than any other nationality would have done and yet are regarded as the whipping boys. Too often in the modern world of today judgement is passed on events of long ago based on knowledge acquired since by improvements in technology and communication not previously available. Perhaps those passing judgement should ask themselves 'What would I have done THEN?'

Closer to home we have taken a number of trips into countries in Eastern Europe such as Poland, Georgia, Romania and Ukraine, including Crimea. Poland is now a only a third the size it was at the time of the abdication of the last King of Poland, Stanislaw Poniatowski, in 1795. He was, incidentally, one of the first lovers of the lady destined to become Catherine the Great of Russia. The trouble with the Poles, a splendid race of people, is that they developed a nasty habit of what we used to call in racing 'seconditis'. Krakow and Warsaw, two totally contrasting cities, lovely country areas, immense primeval forests – one of them, Bialowieza, close to the border with Belarus, the home of a third of the world's bison population – magnificent castles and huge country mansions. Georgia, a country small in size but big in heart and spirit, fiercely independent and anti-Russian even though Stalin was Georgian, sandwiched between Russia to the north and Turkey, Armenia and Azerbaijan to the south. Plenty of very well worthwhile places to visit, including fabulous mountain areas. Romania, where Prince Charles has an active interest, very beautiful in the northern Transylvania area with fortified medieval villages with painted monasteries depicting the history of Christianity, very lovely rolling farming countryside in the centre dotted with pretty, welcoming villages, having one wide street along which livestock is driven to grazing pastures in the early morning, returning in the evening. Ukraine's capital Kiev, built on hills both sides of the River Dnieper, a somewhat forbidding but magnificently sad city, having been raped and pillaged throughout the ages; the gateway to the Crimea, now annexed by Russia from where, it has to be said, it came by way of a gift from Nikita Khrushchev. From our point of view Crimea is of strong interest owing to the Crimean War of 1853–56. The famous battlefields are little changed today and a visit to see them is a very memorable experience, as are the nearby castles and summer retreats of the Czars of Russia, kept and maintained in excellent condition. Sadly, today is not the best time to go to Ukraine or Crimea, but in a year or two the signs are that all will be well again and they will need the visitors. It will be well worth it. The same message applies to Eastern Turkey along the borders with Iraq, Iran and Syria. They must be going through very hard times now. The memories of crossing the Tigris and Euphrates rivers and walking the last half mile to the summit of Nemrut Dagi are very poignant.

I suppose both Georgia and Turkey are not, strictly speaking, in Europe but I hope I am forgiven for a bit of licence. To finalise this little review, the magical island of Sicily cannot be omitted. Historical with a capital H it is. Siracusa, for instance, is probably the oldest commercial port in the world, dating back to 750 BC, and was visited by both Plato and Archimedes. Sicily has been occupied and ruled by every strong power in the history of the Mediterranean: Arabs, Greeks, Normans, Romans, Spanish, each of whom has left many marks. Great to visit, easy to get around, wonderful places to stay. And the home of the Mafia who are still there, make no mistake and always will be. Nevertheless, from a visitor's point of view, couldn't recommend it highly enough.

The Last Lap – Nearly

I had settled down in Gloucestershire but somehow it never felt like 'home'. I missed Maddox and life in Barbados but I made the decision and that was that. Life was changing there too; building and tourism was taking over too many of the rural areas. I left many Barbadian friends – Nick and Sheila Parravicino, Pat and Grainne Kearns, Margot Walsh, Simon Foster, Jack and Margaret Leacock and many more. Of the above only Margaret Leacock and Grainne Kearns are still alive in Barbados; Margot, though, is very much alive, aged ninety-one but living in Texas.

My eldest son Richard married a very nice girl, I thought, called Sarah Cairns. They lived first in London; she had a high-powered job in one of the top hotels in London but was transferred to Hong Kong where Richard joined her, having got a job there himself. Pamela and I flew out to see them and also made forays into China and Macao. Sadly Richard and Sarah's marriage did not last: the hours and constant hospitality work that she was required to do many nights per week was not conducive to a young married couple's lifestyle. Luckily there were no children. He married his second wife, Sophie, and they now live in Cheshire; they have two children, Ben(edict), born in 2001 and Georgina a couple of years later. The next to marry was my middle son, Simon, having played the field, one of whom was a German lady called Tatania whom we labelled The Titanic. He actually met his future wife, Marietta, the daughter of friends in Gloucestershire, at Richard's second wedding. Marietta's sister is the wife of Richard's wife's brother. Work that one out. They have two super children, both boys: Oliver, always called Ollie but prefers Oliver, and Archie, born within two years of each other but totally different in character. Archie looks like a ready-made second-row forward and Ollie … doesn't. They live outside an attractive village in Hertfordshire. Simon runs his own recruitment business specialising in private banking, rather worryingly having various high-powered Russian clients. Marietta also works part-time but at a high level for an American merchant bank of renown. My youngest, Sam, was the last to marry in 2004, after a succession of nubile and seemingly eligible girlfriends, to Camilla who comes from a Jewish family so the wedding was a little different. In fact Sam broke the impending news to me by saying: 'Dad, we're getting married: it's not going to be in a church but not in a synagogue either.' In fact it was in an elaborately decorated ballroom at the Four Seasons Hotel in Park Lane. A string band played the overture to *Fiddler on the Roof* as the wedding guests assembled and took their places but, at the entrance of the bride on the arm of her father, struck up 'If I were a Rich Man'. They now have two lovely children, Charlie and Ella, both of whom seem extraordinarily bright, goodness knows from whence seeing that not only was Sam's scholastic career undistinguished but also brought short by having been caught driving his car, forbidden at school, at speed round the parade ground at Pangbourne (the only school that would accept him), scattering gravel in all directions and nearly running over the headmaster's wife's dog. Neither Sam nor his brother Simon, nor for that matter their father, ever attended university. Sam now has a top job in the City, probably earns millions and I hope will soon provide a carer for his father.

After eighteen years together Pamela and I separated and were divorced a year or so later, sadly rather acrimoniously in the end. Our differences had become too great and were irreconcilable.

It is pointless and provocative to go into the various chinks that penetrated the armour but, in most people's eyes, I was the villain of the piece. In 2005, having lived for ten years at The Old Hundred, all our children were married except for Pamela's second son who seemed destined to remain a bachelor and still is, now in his mid-to-late 50s. I began to think that, setting aside all the expense of maintaining a large house such as The Old Hundred that I had been bearing, we shouldn't be rattling around for practically all the time in a nine-bedroom house. The market at that time was particularly strong for country house properties; we should look to downsize into something more manageable but with enough room to accommodate much of the family at any one time. I put this to Pamela but was met with a complete rebuff: 'This is my children's inheritance and I shall leave this house in a box.' The fact that she could create a Trust Fund to cater for their needs from much of the proceeds of the sale did not seem to occur to her. Naturally I also considered my own investment in the property and the fact that I lived there too but that, evidently, was not part of the 'deal'. When we lived at Maddox her family were made welcome at all times and, that was where her eldest son was married. This same son, after an undistinguished record at school and a stint at Cirencester Agricultural College, launched himself into a series of financial disasters. In order to help him and at the request of his mother, I lent him a considerable sum of money which remains unpaid. There's nowt so queer as folk.

I left The Old Hundred for the last time in the summer of 2009. Three or four years later Pamela sold the house and land for about a million pounds less than the separate valuations I had obtained previously from two of the leading estate agents in the UK.

Sometime before then I had been asked to organise and take a From Here To There trip to Vietnam and Laos for an artist friend, Clare Inskip, taking a party of her artist students. The party numbered fourteen, rather more than I usually like to take but I knew some of them, and the others being friends of Clare's I agreed. I mention this because among the party was a lady, Cilla Perry, accompanied by a male friend of hers. I took them to be an item and thought no more about it. The trip went pretty well but I was kept very busy; being artists they were, correctly, quite fussy about the different locations, where and what they wanted to paint as well as with the normal paraphernalia of moving people from place to place in, to them, strange countries. At the end of the trip Cilla Perry, her friend and one other wanted to go on by themselves for a few days to Cambodia so I was also very busy planning this for them; it was only then that I discovered that Cilla and her companion, although old friends, were definitely not an item, his interests lying elsewhere. Still, that was their business and I thought no more about it. It was several months later that Cilla telephoned me to ask if I could help plan part of a gap year for her daughter in Argentina. We arranged to meet to discuss this plan which led to another meeting ... and another one. The following year I took an FHTT trip to Rajasthan, India. Clare Inskip, who knows India very well so did not require any help from me, was also taking a party of artists at about the same time of which Cilla had signed up to be a member. However, my trip started a few days before Clare's so Cilla spent a few days with me and my team before leaving to join Clare.

The upshot of all this was that after leaving The Old Hundred, I rented a cottage near Cattistock in Dorset where, not long afterwards, Cilla joined me and has not left – so far. It seems such a pity not to have been able to bring Cilla into this story until so comparatively late but that's life, I suppose. I can say, though, that for ten years now she has been not just a loving companion but an adoring, greatest friend and soulmate and I know how lucky I am to have her. We now live in a small old farmhouse tucked away at the end of a private lane with no neighbours and fabulous views of the West Dorset countryside stretching as far as a distant sight of the sea on a clear day with scarcely a building in sight. Real Thomas Hardy stuff. It was my old and very dear friend, David Marchwood and his wife Sylva, who suggested Dorset having moved there themselves quite a few years previously; they live only about twenty minutes away from us. Never have I received better advice: Dorset is really lovely and we have been very happy here ever since and are extremely lucky to have met a superb bunch of new friends living comparatively locally.

Early on we were introduced to a lovely family who lived only a few hundred yards from the little cottage that we rented when we arrived in Dorset. Nigel and Bumble Hadden-Paton, great kindred spirits. Nigel, ex-Blues and Royals, entrepreneur, traveller, shoots a disgraceful number of days each year and, above all, a great family man with Bumble, his beautiful wife, always looking as though she has stepped out of *Vogue*, whether in jeans or a ball gown; both of them huge fun and terrific to be with. They have one son and three fabulous-looking daughters. Their son, Harry, is a coming-to-be-well-known actor, having had leading parts in *Downton Abbey, The Crown* and *Versailles* and now playing Professor Higgins in the revival on Broadway of *My Fair Lady*. Subsequently there have been so many – far too many to mention – that have become very close friends with whom we have a lot of fun at home and, sometimes, abroad. There is a coterie of geriatric tennis players of which I am by far the oldest and therefore among the worst, organised by the splendid Tony Thompson; we play, for a hangover cure, on Sunday mornings either on his court or on that of another member of the coterie, prior to drinking quantities of vin rosé, the house rules being a minimum of a bottle per set played.

One doesn't expect, late in life, to find all this. Cilla and I have not married – yet. We have thought and talked about it from time to time and may well get around to it but maybe there is the feeling in the back of our minds that marriage has not been very lucky for us in the past and we certainly wouldn't want to rock any boat.

It is nearly twenty years since I started From Here To There. During many of these years I ran four, occasionally five, trips per year. Recently this has come down to two or three. Being not a heavy sleeper I have often found myself planning where to go next while lying awake during the night but not long ago I sat up with a start asking myself if, as a forty-, fifty- or even a sixty-year-old, would I like to go travelling to a distant foreign country organised and run by an octogenarian? The answer was probably not. I have therefore decided to act more in an advisory and management capacity than as an active participant. In other words, I will organise and arrange trips for family or friends to places that I know well and have confidence in my ground agents in the countries and areas concerned but not, unless particularly requested, go myself. It's been huge fun and I've loved (nearly) every second!

**

So that's about it, really. But I can't stop without having a crack at our inane governmental, nanny-state behaviour and instruction, for want of a better word, known as political correctness. What a load of codswallop: words ending in 'ism' or 'ist' which mustn't be thought, let alone spoken. It all started with the ghastly Blair, a champagne socialist if ever there was one. A man without principle except for what he could gain for himself, left his public school with the words of his headmaster ringing in his trumpet-like ears, 'Blair you leave this school without any distinction except having played Hamlet – rather badly.' Equipped with a power complex, he saw an opening in politics to exert this sense of power – but how to use it to his advantage? It seems as though, looking at both political parties, he realised that his chances of reaching the top were far better from the Labour benches than the Conservatives. In this he was aided and abetted by the equally appalling Mrs Blair who, having received an invitation as wife of the Prime Minister for a weekend at Balmoral as a guest of the Queen, signed her name in the visitors' book as Cherie Booth QC. A lady so obviously bored to tears while attending the local Highland Games, being caught by a press photographer having opened her cavernous grouper-like mouth in a yawn but without the good manners of shielding it with her hand. I met her once at a small reception at 10 Downing Street for a charity for which I had been, jointly with Peter Hornby, instrumental in raising a large sum of money. The reception, incidentally, had been instigated by Mrs Blair's predecessor Norma Major whose husband was no longer in office by the time the reception was held. Mrs Blair arrived late and invited the selected guests to come closer to her with the words, 'I won't bite, you know.'

I've always been keen on Gilbert & Sullivan, and couldn't resist a new take on the 'The First Lord's Song' from *Pinafore* to mark the occasion when Comrade Corbyn became leader of the Labour Party. So here, with profound apologies to W. S. Gilbert, it is:

THE HONOURABLE MEMBER

When I was a lad I did insist
On becoming an active Trade Unionist
I boiled the kettle and made the tea
And ensured there was paper in the lavatory

I boiled that kettle so brilliantly
That now I am the leader of the Labour Partee

In the Union's affairs I made such a hit
That I soon became a proper good shit
When a strike was called by the worker's shout

ANTONY JOHNSON

I got on my bike to get them all out

I called that strike so successfully
That now I am the leader of the Labour Partee

Unlike the first Duke of Wellington
I ride my bike from Islington
I always act like a sly old fox
As I cast each vote in the ballot box

I ride my bike so expertly
They made me leader of the Labour Partee.

In Parliament I knew how to behave
And never, never, ever did wash or shave
The clothes I wore had been worn before me
And I always looked so very untidy

To look untidy so suited me
That now I am the leader of the Labour Partee

Now Lefties all wherever you may be
If you want to become a prat like me
If you think you can all of us fool
Please be guided by this golden rule

Try to be as bad as me
And you all could be leaders of the Labour Partee.

We are a multicultural society ruled by bureaucracy: commissions for this, regulators for that, councils for the other, change-your-knickers-on-a-Monday, only-drink-half-a-glass-of-wine-a-week-or-you'll-get-breast-cancer. The Care Quality Commission has 2,147 employees in full-time work. Its report is full of failing to meet targets, certificates being lost and a leaked report on one establishment saying that hundreds of people had died due to poor health standards only a month after care was certified as 'good'. Why is a native Barbadian, for instance, referred to as an 'Afro-Caribbean'? Am I a 'Caucasian Anglo-Saxon'? Why can't we be plain Black, White or even Yellow? In Mexico City recently I asked a taxi driver if there were many Chinese in Mexico? He replied that they had a severe epidemic of Yellow Fever. As for the sexes – well I never knew there were so many alternatives: evidently, apart from being either male or female, one can be lesbian, gay, bisexual, transgender or queer and what's more, after taking advice from one or more of the fifteen regulatory medical bodies, one can change from one to another. What makes it all the more confusing is that if one happens to touch a member of one of the other above listed sexes in what is described as an 'inappropriate' manner one can be had up for rape or attempted rape, thereby becoming a rapist. Sooner rather than later, please will our Government shrug off the Blair image of a 'nanny state'. How is one to encourage strong-minded, intelligent, public-spirited men and women to enter politics if they are forever being watched by busybody, interfering, praying mantis, sharp-eyed, snivelling knockers in case they 'touch somebody else's knee'? It is difficult enough to govern the country both internally and in the face of increasing worldwide competition in commerce, trade and hostility without having to bother with the likes of the above. Let those who do wrong be brought to task by our long-standing, thoroughly excellent judicial system.

The late Peter Walwyn, whose funeral I attended, along with 600–700 others, in December 2017 in Lambourn, wrote in his inimitable book *Handy All The Way* that he would like to assemble all those whom he disliked or considered had done him down, put them in a double-decker bus, lock it from the outside and programme for it to be driven over Beachy Head. I wouldn't need a double-decker, a single one would do but as nearly all (but not quite all!) of the culprits are dead, I'll save on the expense of the bus and wait for the Devil to do his stuff on them. I do, however, have another bus – a double- or even triple-decker – that I would fill with so many marvellous people with whom I have ridden the roads, sailed the seas, flown the skies now rising higher and higher to the racecourses, theatres, mountains and plains of whatever lies beyond the ever-extending horizon.

Acknowledgements

This book could not have been written without the encouragement, help and support of family and friends in all areas of production. To all I am extremely grateful.

I am firstly deeply indebted to my guide, mentor and editor, Sam Carter. He has, metaphorically, held my hand since I sent him the first completed draft a year ago. I 'found' him via the airwaves of Radio H-P, my first and only venture into what I believe is called 'Social Media', invented and founded by my very dear friend Nigel Hadden-Paton who has an address list longer than that of Methuselah.

To Robin Oakley, the former BBC Chief Political Editor, who to my great pleasure and surprise has most kindly written the flattering Foreword, I am especially grateful. I've always been a big fan of his racing column in the *Spectator* since he kindly gave a plug to a short book, *East into the Sun,* in millennium year. I sent him a preliminary version of the beginning of *A Crack of the Whip* which he took the trouble to, correctly, tear to shreds. I hope the final version is an improvement.

I had a spoof run round a few friends concerning the title of the book, the winner being Will Wyn-Williams. Thank you very much, Will. Among the titles rejected was the one proposed by my sons, Simon and Sam, of *Four – Not Out*.

A very special and enormous thank-you to Della Burke who literally has held my hand over my incompetence on the computer. She has spent countless hours by my side or at her own home helping me all the while and putting up with my tantrums, finding extracts lost in cyberspace and always so encouraging and understanding.

But the big rock behind the last three years spent in researching and writing the book has been my wonderful Cilla. Writing is a selfish occupation but she has never complained, has read each draft and offered many very valuable and constructive criticisms. She has devotedly helped and supported me, and I hope I can reciprocate.

Index

Francis, Dick xi, 16-17, 97
Francis, Doug 96-7, 98, 115-18, 156
Francome, John 195
Frank, Charles 201-202
Franz Josef, Emperor 52-3

Gaggero, Marie-Lou 84
Gairy, Eric 300
Gaselee, Nick 110, 114, 194, 257
Gaskell, Dickie 221
Gerard Leigh, Col. William 224
Gibbs, Chris 271, 294
Gill, Arthur 123
Gillespie, Edward 331
Gillies, Harold 67
Gloucester, Prince William of 111-12
Gooch, Captain Richard 157
Gordon, Iain 319
Graham, Clive 65-6, 69, 217
Grant, Eddy 308
Greenall, 'Toby' 87
Greenway, Ted 86
Grey family 40
Grey, Sir Raleigh 40
Gubbins, Sgt 21-22, 342
Guinness, Oonagh 113, 214, 215, 218
Guise, Carole see Master, Carole
Guise, Jamie 302, 322
Guise, Sir John 192, 222, 322-3
Guler, Ruth 112
Gullick, Pauline 331-2

Hadden-Paton, Bumble 367
Hadden-Paton, Harry 367
Hadden-Paton, Nigel 367, 373

Hall, Jerry 235, 308
Hamilton-Renwick, Lionel 108
Hanbury, Ben 212
Hanbury, 'Chunky' 212
Hanbury-Tenison, Robin 354, 355
Hardie, Reginald 73, 122, 123
Harman, Major General Sir Jack 12
Harper, Gerald 246
Harper, Philippa 218
Harriman, Averell 280, 283
Harriman, Pamela 280-83
Harrington, Bill Earl of 200
Harrison, Noel 34, 81
Harrison, Rex 34, 81
Hatch, Andrew 321
Hatch, Sheila 321
Hawley, James 265
Hayward, Leland 281, 283
Heath, Edward 151, 207, 208, 290
Heggs, Geoffrey 153, 154
Heimann, David 295
Heinzel, Dr 32, 33, 35
Henderson, Johnny 200-201
Henderson, Nicky 200-201
Hern, Dick 146, 194, 295
Heseltine, Annabel 334
Heseltine, Anne 323
Heseltine, Michael 323-4
Hesketh-Harvey, Kit 314-15
Hide, Eddie 149, 158
Higgins, Frederick 54
Higgins, James 54
Hills, Barry 150, 184, 212, 223, 240, 242, 289
Hills, John 185
Hills, Maureen 184-5
Hills, Michael 185